IMMORTAL RAIN

VOLUME 2

BY
KAORI OZAKI

HAMBURG // LONDON // LOS ANGELES // TOKYO

Immortal Rain Vol. 2
created by Kaori Ozaki

Translation - Michael Wert
English Adaptation - Sam Stormcrow Hayes
Copy Editors - Troy Lewter and Alexis Kirsch
Retouch and Lettering - Kristi Kovack and John Lo
Production Artist - Louis Csontos
Cover Design - Anna Kernbaum

Editor - Bryce P. Coleman
Digital Imaging Manager - Chris Buford
Pre-Press Manager - Antonio DePietro
Production Managers - Jennifer Miller and Mutsumi Miyazaki
Art Director - Matt Alford
Managing Editor - Jill Freshney
VP of Production - Ron Klamert
President and C.O.O. - John Parker
Publisher and C.E.O. - Stuart Levy

A  Manga

TOKYOPOP Inc.
5900 Wilshire Blvd. Suite 2000
Los Angeles, CA 90036
E-mail: info@TOKYOPOP.com
Come visit us online at www.TOKYOPOP.com

ISBN: 978-1-59182-723-8

First TOKYOPOP printing: August 2004
10 9 8 7 6 5 4
Printed in the USA

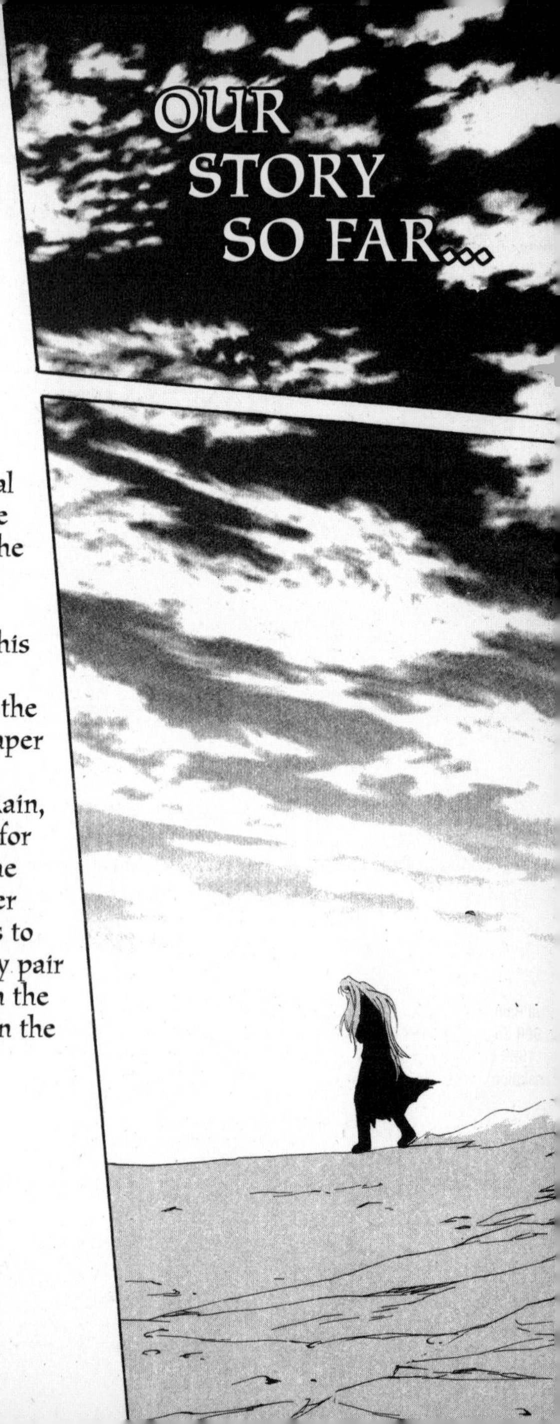
OUR STORY SO FAR...

Across an arid wasteland strides the man known as Rain, The Immortal Methuselah. Those who would know the secret of his immortality have placed a price on his head. Machika, granddaughter of the assassin Grim Reaper Zol, has sworn vengeance upon Rain, whom she blames for Zol's death. But the line between hunter and hunted begins to blur as the unlikely pair find themselves on the run and all alone in the world–together.

IMMORTAL RAIN

CONTENTS

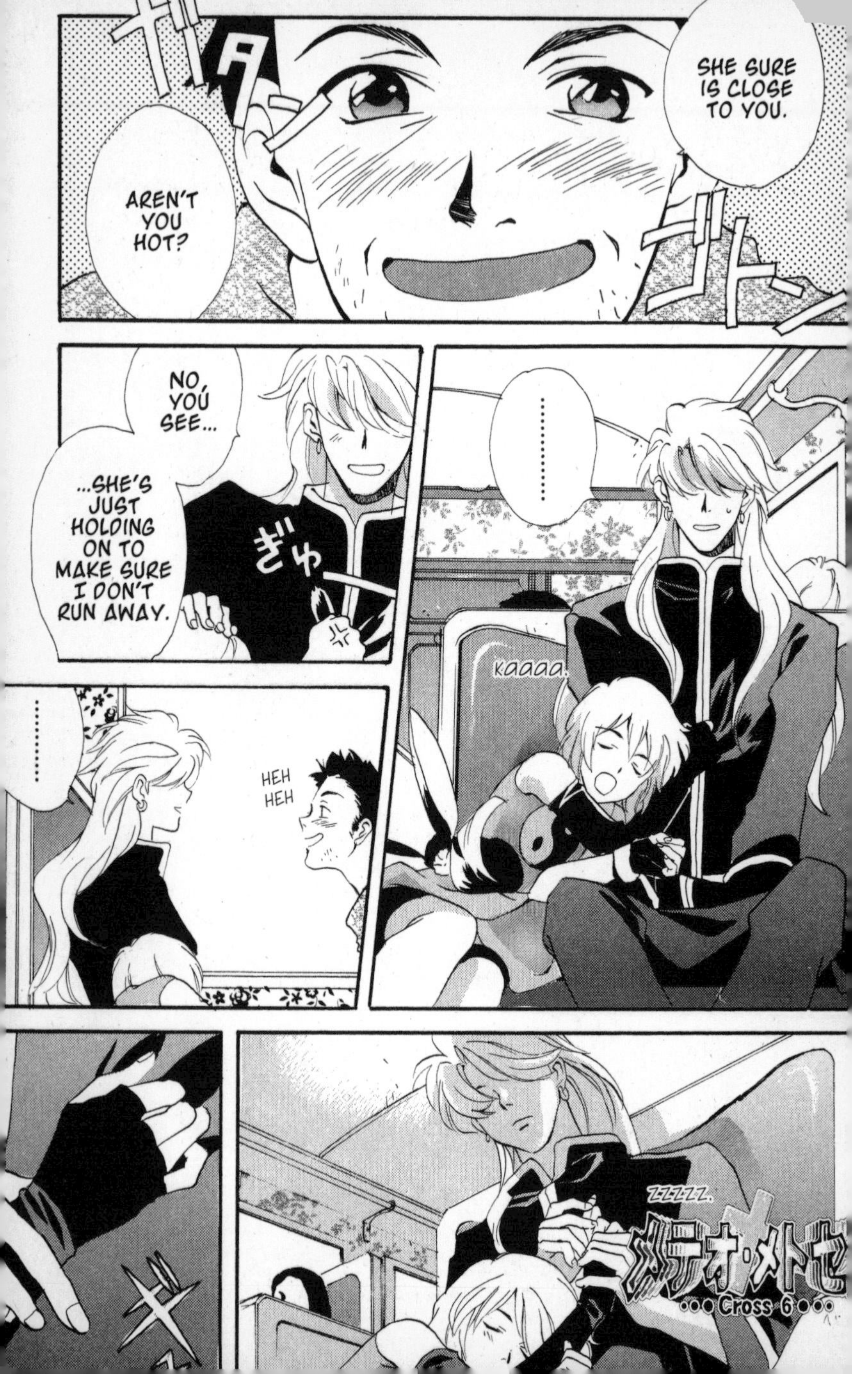
SHE SURE IS CLOSE TO YOU.
ガタ
AREN'T YOU HOT?
ゴトン
......
kaaaa.
NO, YOU SEE...
...SHE'S JUST HOLDING ON TO MAKE SURE I DON'T RUN AWAY.
ぎゅ
......
HEH HEH
zzzzz.
メテオ・メトセ
Cross 6

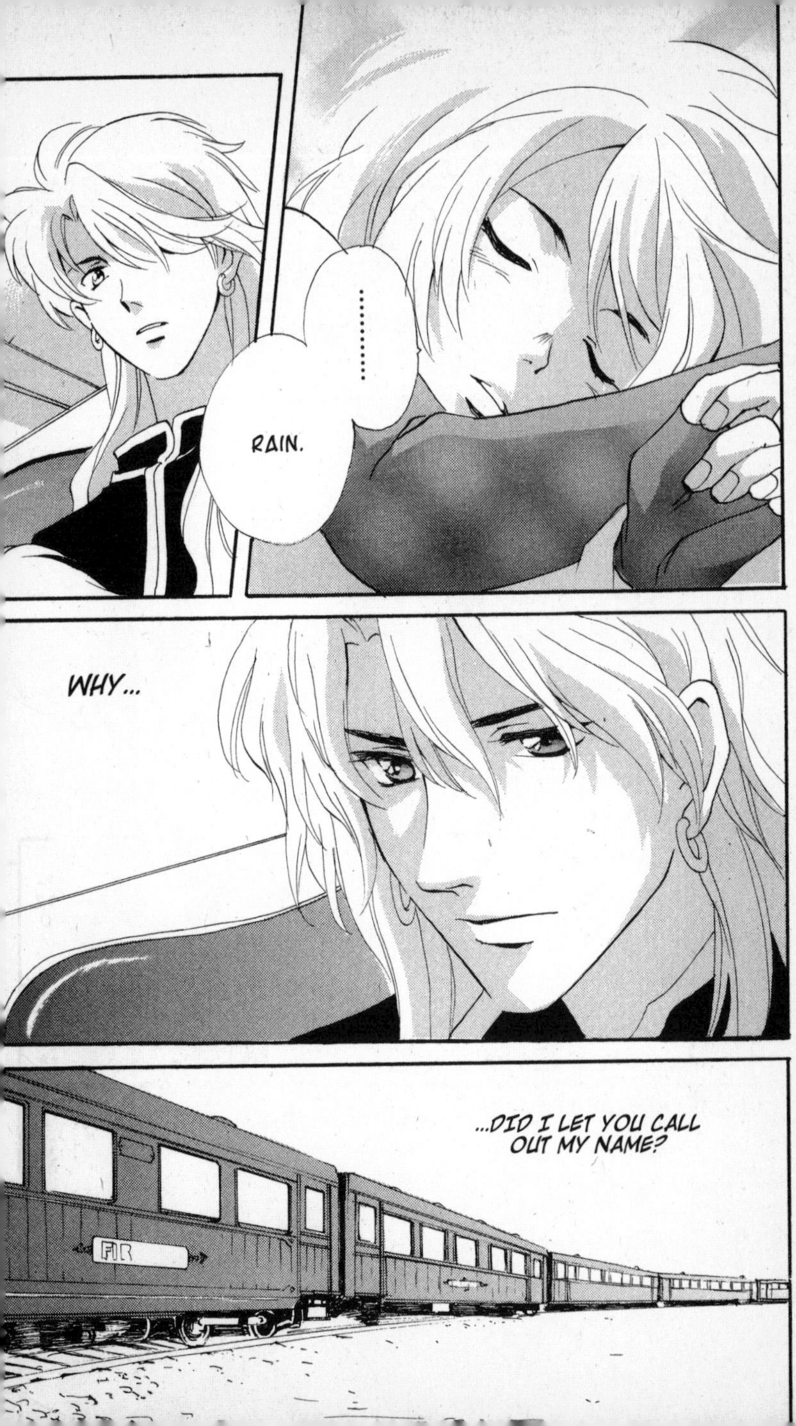
......
RAIN.
WHY...
...DID I LET YOU CALL OUT MY NAME?

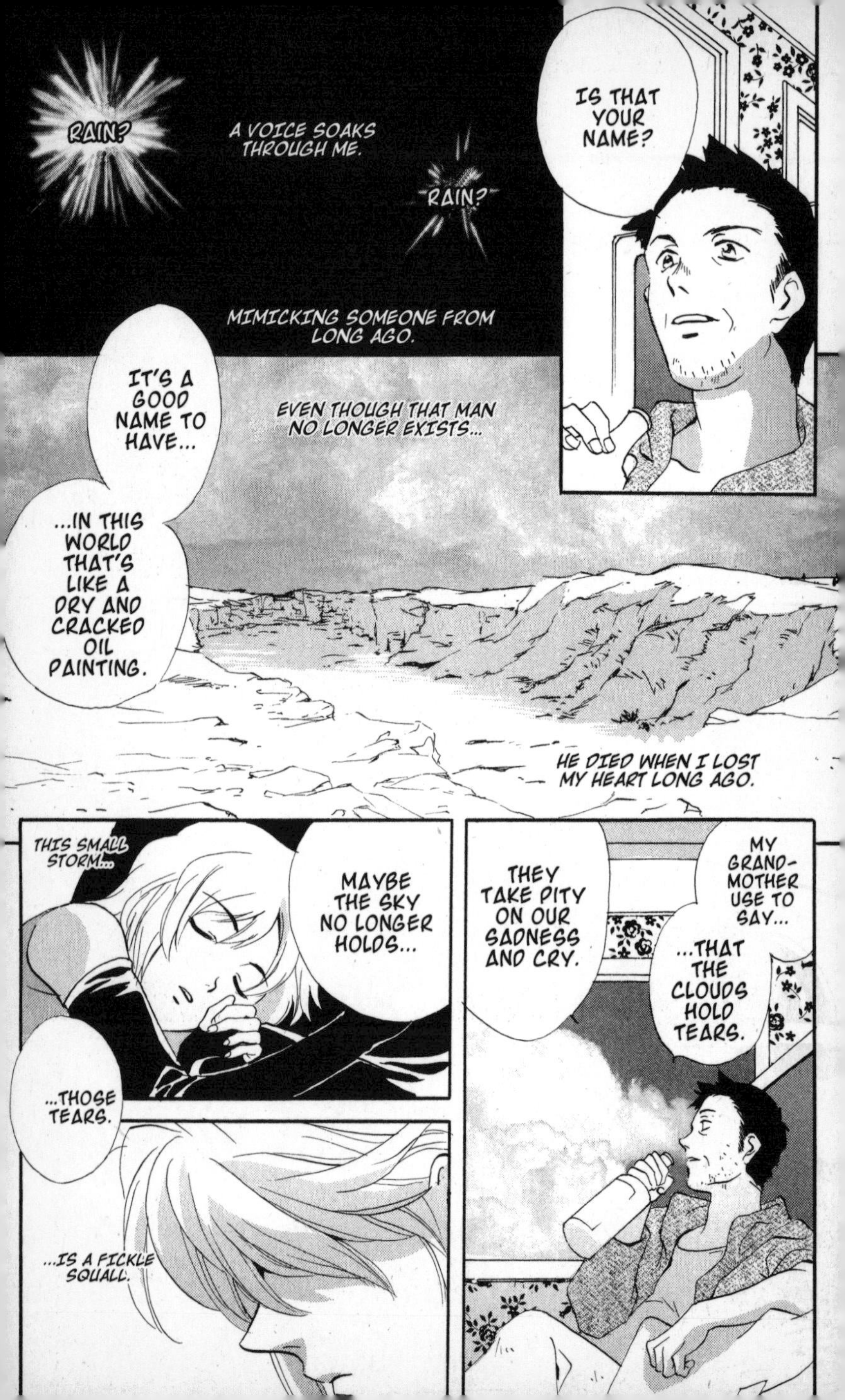

IS THAT YOUR NAME?
RAIN?
A VOICE SOAKS THROUGH ME.
RAIN?
MIMICKING SOMEONE FROM LONG AGO.
IT'S A GOOD NAME TO HAVE...
EVEN THOUGH THAT MAN NO LONGER EXISTS...
...IN THIS WORLD THAT'S LIKE A DRY AND CRACKED OIL PAINTING.
HE DIED WHEN I LOST MY HEART LONG AGO.
MY GRANDMOTHER USE TO SAY...
...THAT THE CLOUDS HOLD TEARS.
THEY TAKE PITY ON OUR SADNESS AND CRY.
MAYBE THE SKY NO LONGER HOLDS...
THIS SMALL STORM...
...THOSE TEARS.
...IS A FICKLE SQUALL.

THEY DRY UP AND DISAPPEAR WITHOUT A TRACE...
...IN THIS CHEST LIKE A DESERT.
SINCE I NO LONGER...
...HAVE A HEART.
Cross 6

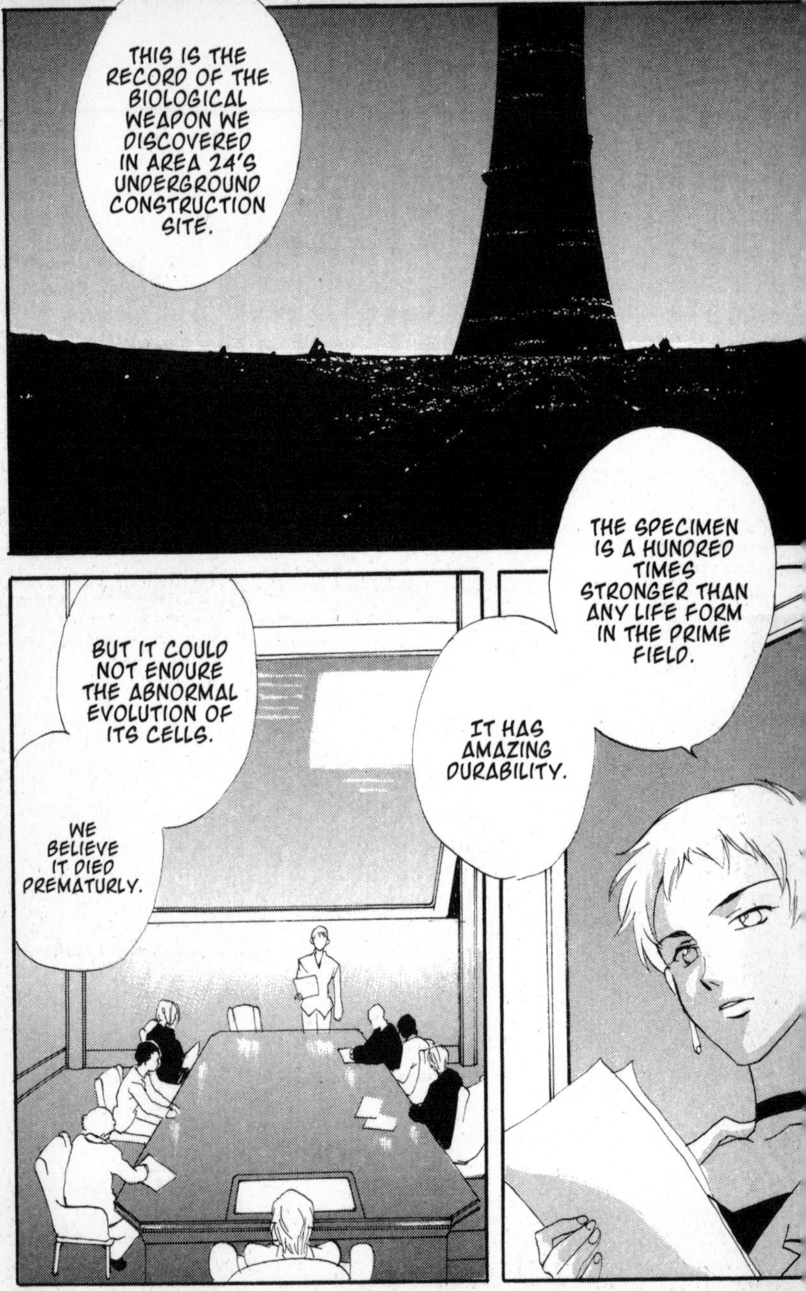
THIS IS THE RECORD OF THE BIOLOGICAL WEAPON WE DISCOVERED IN AREA 24'S UNDERGROUND CONSTRUCTION SITE.
THE SPECIMEN IS A HUNDRED TIMES STRONGER THAN ANY LIFE FORM IN THE PRIME FIELD.
IT HAS AMAZING DURABILITY.
BUT IT COULD NOT ENDURE THE ABNORMAL EVOLUTION OF ITS CELLS.
WE BELIEVE IT DIED PREMATURLY.

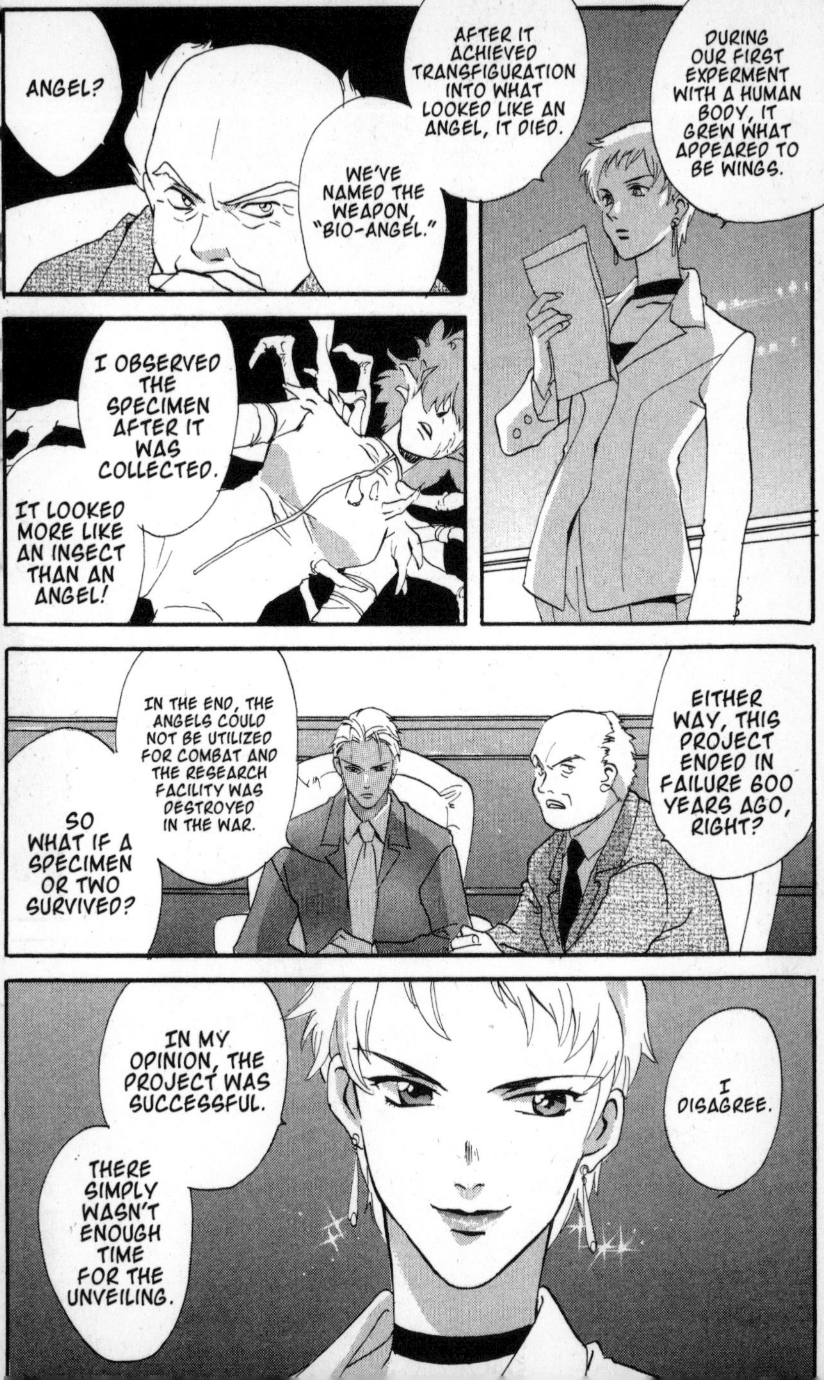
DURING OUR FIRST EXPERMENT WITH A HUMAN BODY, IT GREW WHAT APPEARED TO BE WINGS.
AFTER IT ACHIEVED TRANSFIGURATION INTO WHAT LOOKED LIKE AN ANGEL, IT DIED.
WE'VE NAMED THE WEAPON, "BIO-ANGEL."
ANGEL?
I OBSERVED THE SPECIMEN AFTER IT WAS COLLECTED.
IT LOOKED MORE LIKE AN INSECT THAN AN ANGEL!
EITHER WAY, THIS PROJECT ENDED IN FAILURE 600 YEARS AGO, RIGHT?
IN THE END, THE ANGELS COULD NOT BE UTILIZED FOR COMBAT AND THE RESEARCH FACILITY WAS DESTROYED IN THE WAR.
SO WHAT IF A SPECIMEN OR TWO SURVIVED?
I DISAGREE.
IN MY OPINION, THE PROJECT WAS SUCCESSFUL.
THERE SIMPLY WASN'T ENOUGH TIME FOR THE UNVEILING.

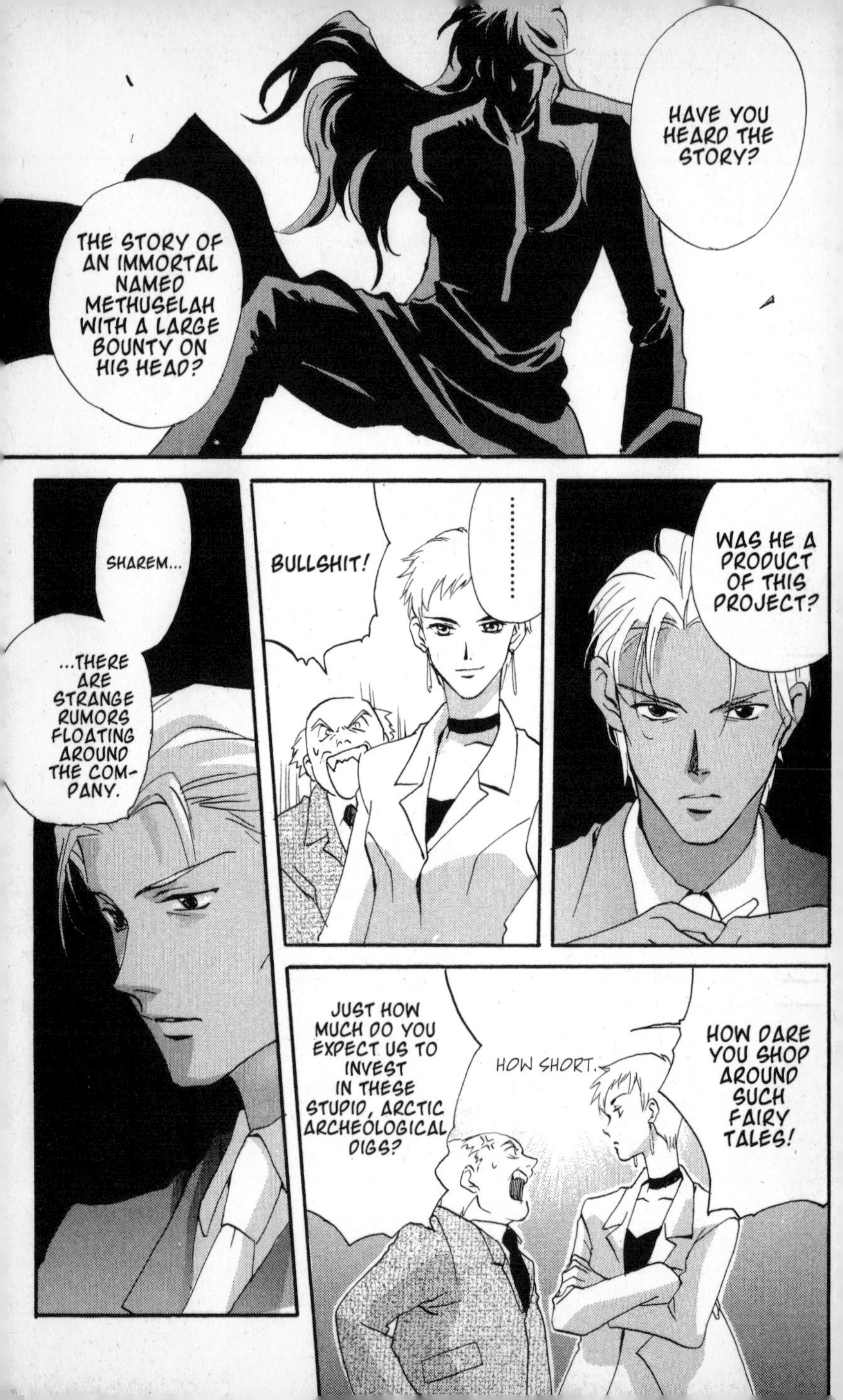
HAVE YOU HEARD THE STORY?
THE STORY OF AN IMMORTAL NAMED METHUSELAH WITH A LARGE BOUNTY ON HIS HEAD?
WAS HE A PRODUCT OF THIS PROJECT?
......
BULLSHIT!
HOW DARE YOU SHOP AROUND SUCH FAIRY TALES!
HOW SHORT.
JUST HOW MUCH DO YOU EXPECT US TO INVEST IN THESE STUPID, ARCTIC ARCHEOLOGICAL DIGS?
SHAREM...
...THERE ARE STRANGE RUMORS FLOATING AROUND THE COMPANY.

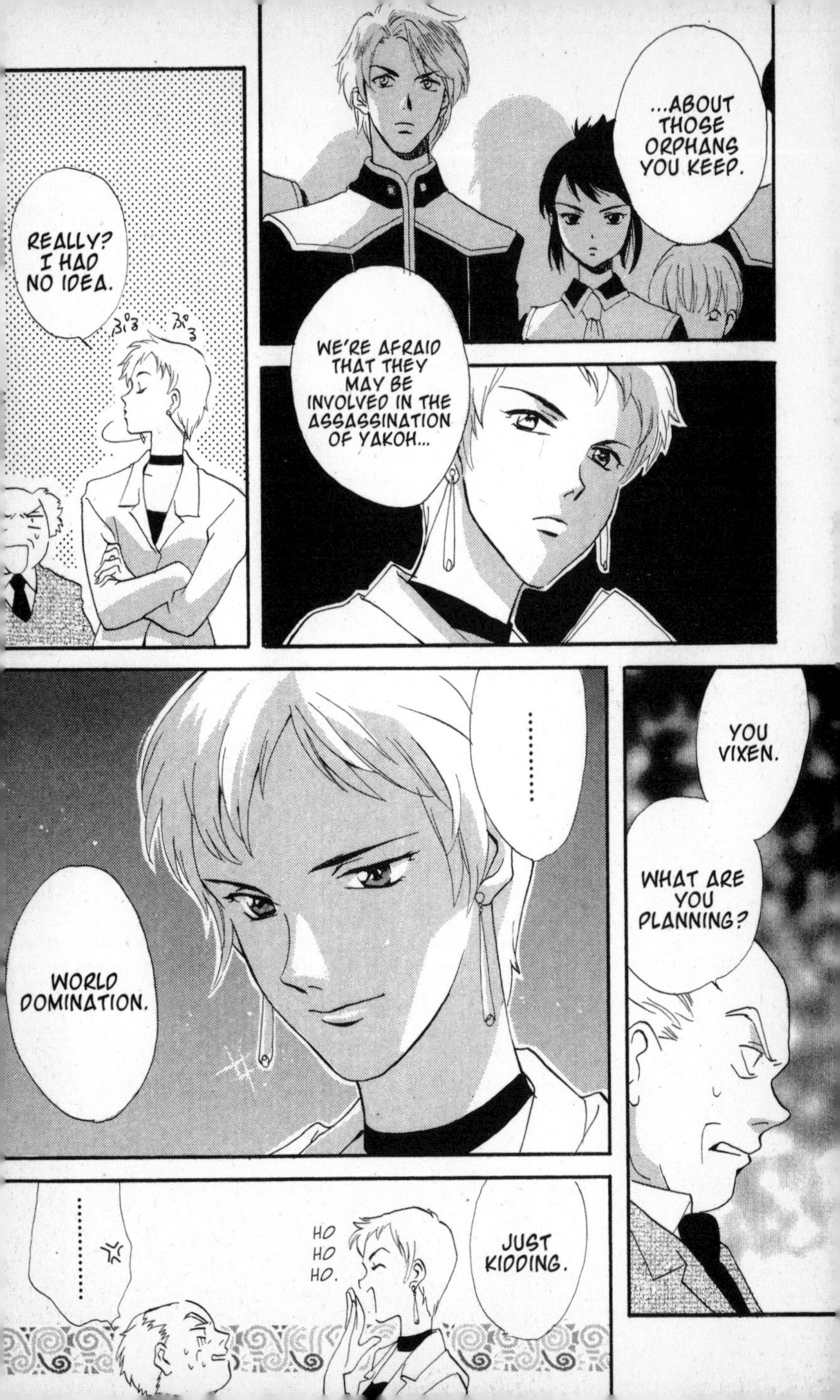
...ABOUT THOSE ORPHANS YOU KEEP.
WE'RE AFRAID THAT THEY MAY BE INVOLVED IN THE ASSASSINATION OF YAKOH...
REALLY? I HAD NO IDEA.
YOU VIXEN.
WHAT ARE YOU PLANNING?
......
WORLD DOMINATION.
JUST KIDDING.
HO HO HO.
......

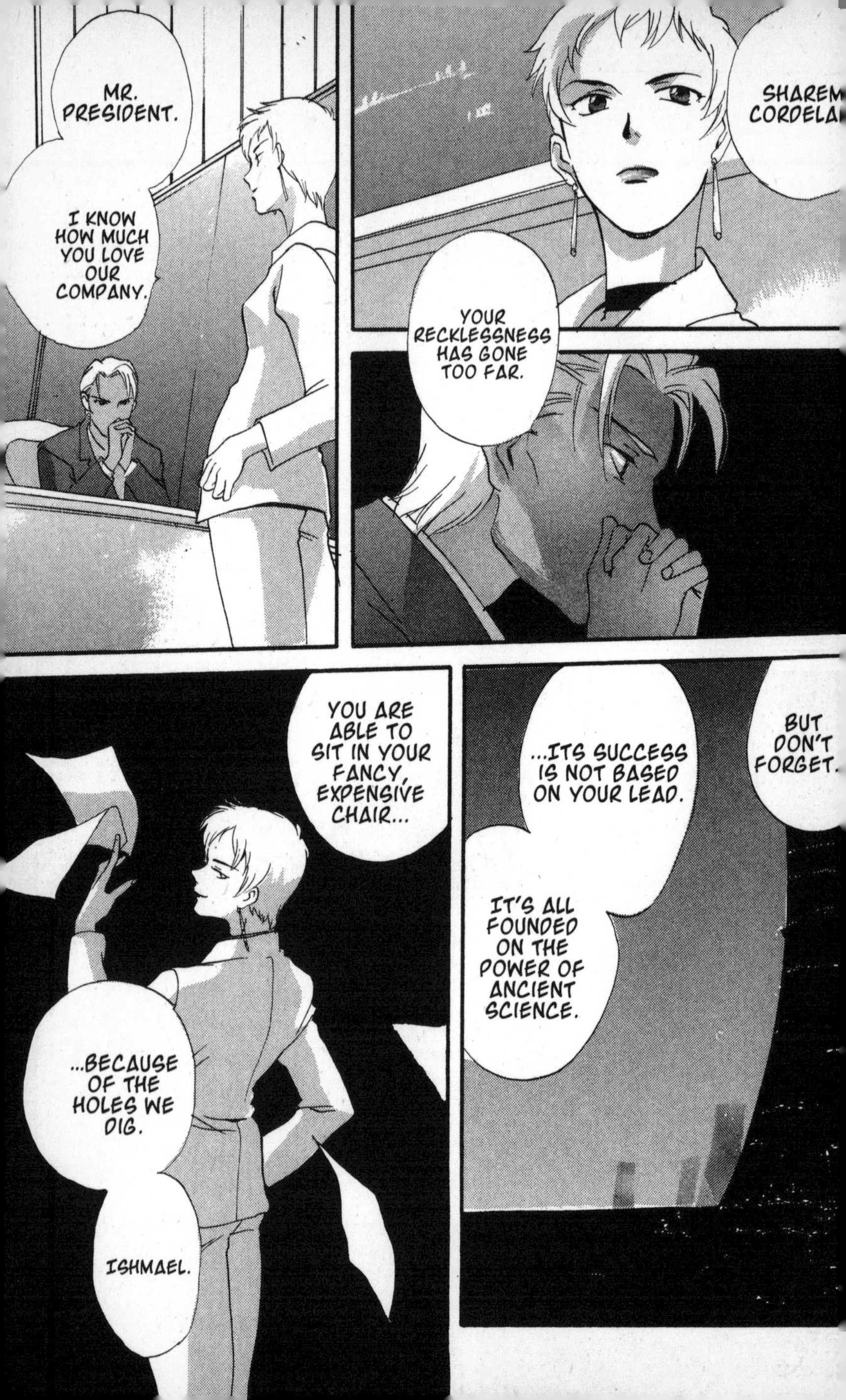
SHAREM CORDELA
YOUR RECKLESSNESS HAS GONE TOO FAR.
MR. PRESIDENT.
I KNOW HOW MUCH YOU LOVE OUR COMPANY.
BUT DON'T FORGET.
...ITS SUCCESS IS NOT BASED ON YOUR LEAD.
IT'S ALL FOUNDED ON THE POWER OF ANCIENT SCIENCE.
YOU ARE ABLE TO SIT IN YOUR FANCY, EXPENSIVE CHAIR...
...BECAUSE OF THE HOLES WE DIG.
ISHMAEL.

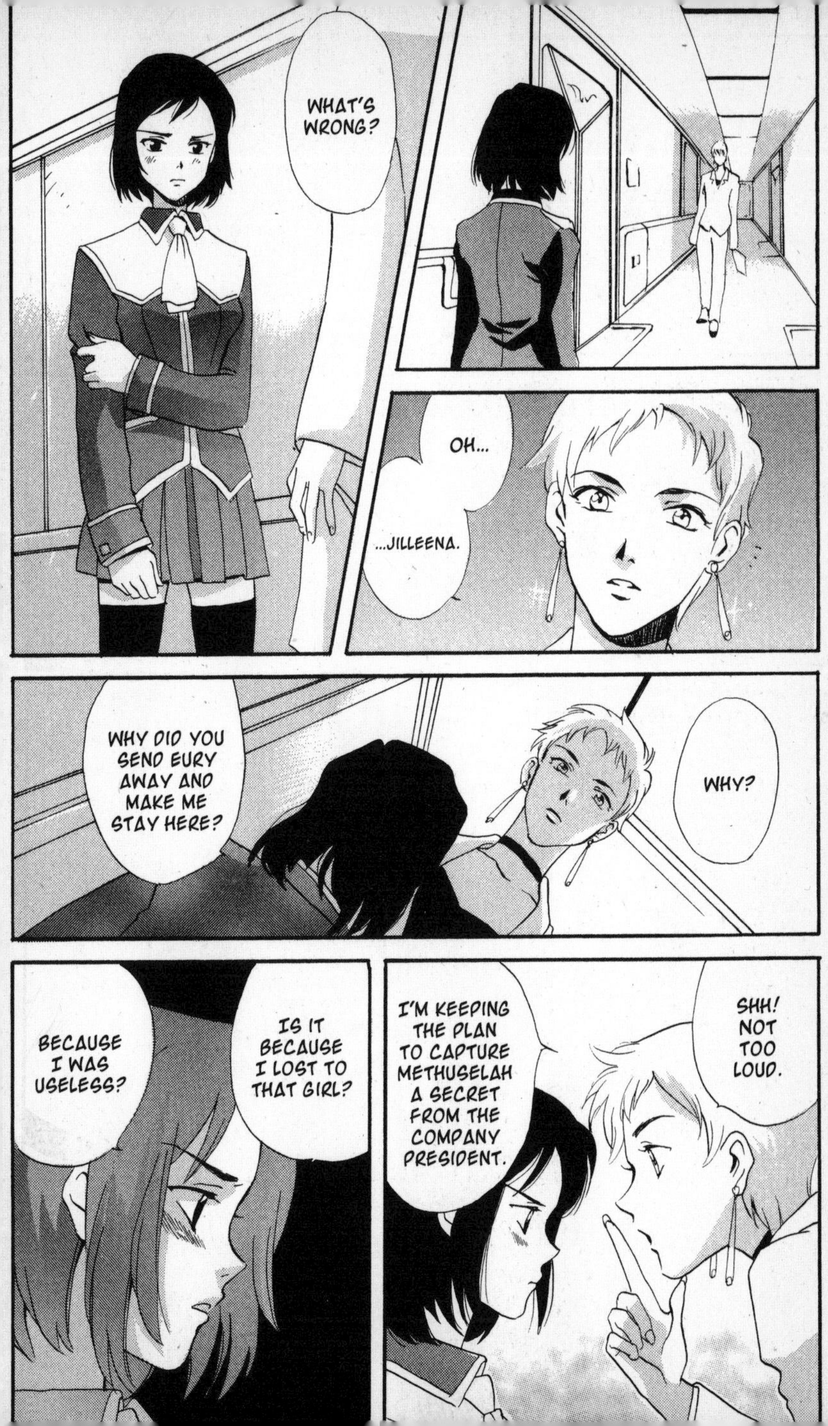
OH...
...JILLEENA.
WHAT'S WRONG?
WHY?
WHY DID YOU SEND EURY AWAY AND MAKE ME STAY HERE?
SHH! NOT TOO LOUD.
I'M KEEPING THE PLAN TO CAPTURE METHUSELAH A SECRET FROM THE COMPANY PRESIDENT.
IS IT BECAUSE I LOST TO THAT GIRL?
BECAUSE I WAS USELESS?

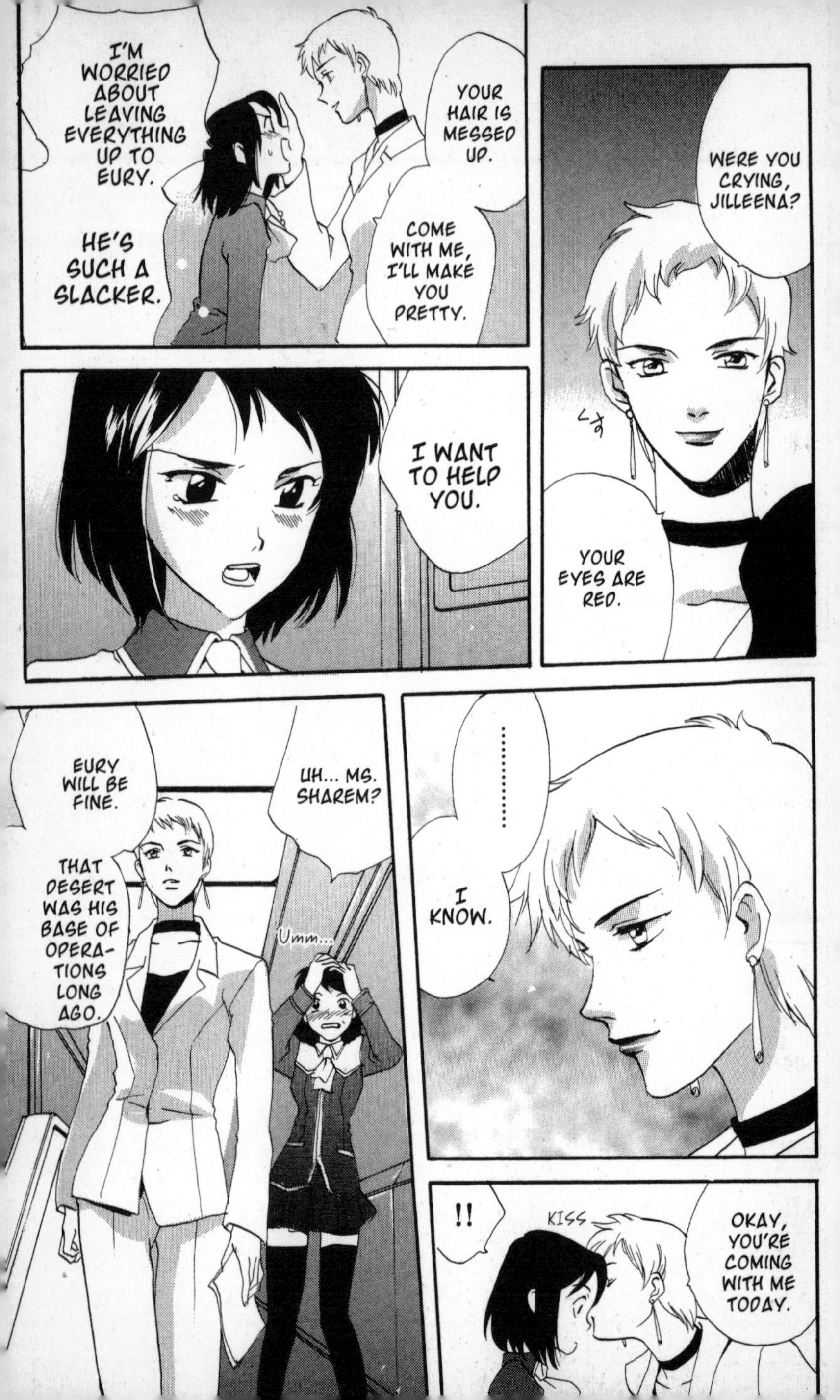
WERE YOU CRYING, JILLEENA?
くす
YOUR EYES ARE RED.
YOUR HAIR IS MESSED UP.
I'M WORRIED ABOUT LEAVING EVERYTHING UP TO EURY.
COME WITH ME, I'LL MAKE YOU PRETTY.
HE'S SUCH A SLACKER.
I WANT TO HELP YOU.
......
I KNOW.
OKAY, YOU'RE COMING WITH ME TODAY.
KISS
!!
UH... MS. SHAREM?
EURY WILL BE FINE.
THAT DESERT WAS HIS BASE OF OPERATIONS LONG AGO.
Umm...

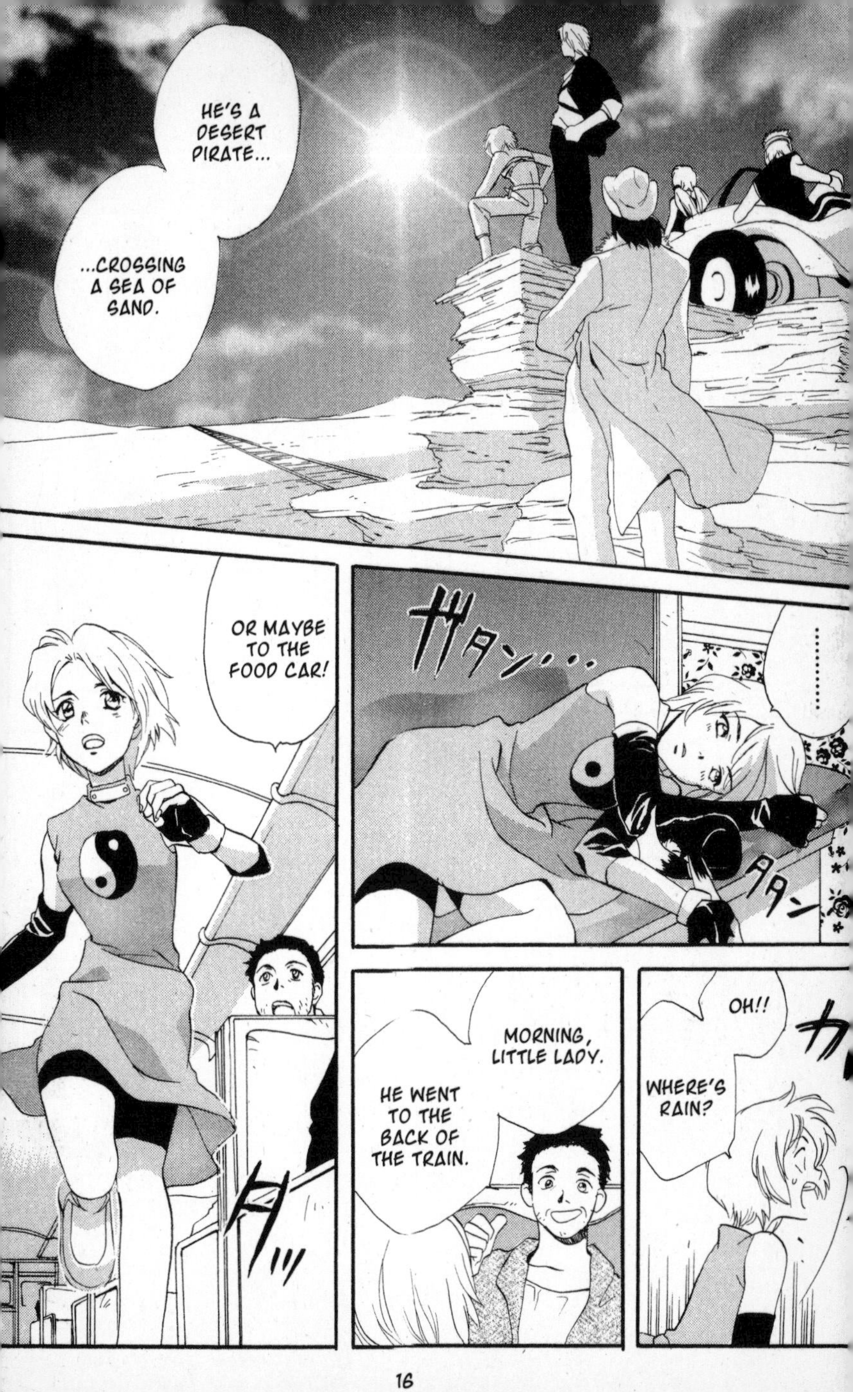
HE'S A DESERT PIRATE...
...CROSSING A SEA OF SAND.
ガタン…
……
タタン
OH!!
WHERE'S RAIN?
カ
MORNING, LITTLE LADY.
HE WENT TO THE BACK OF THE TRAIN.
OR MAYBE TO THE FOOD CAR!
タッ

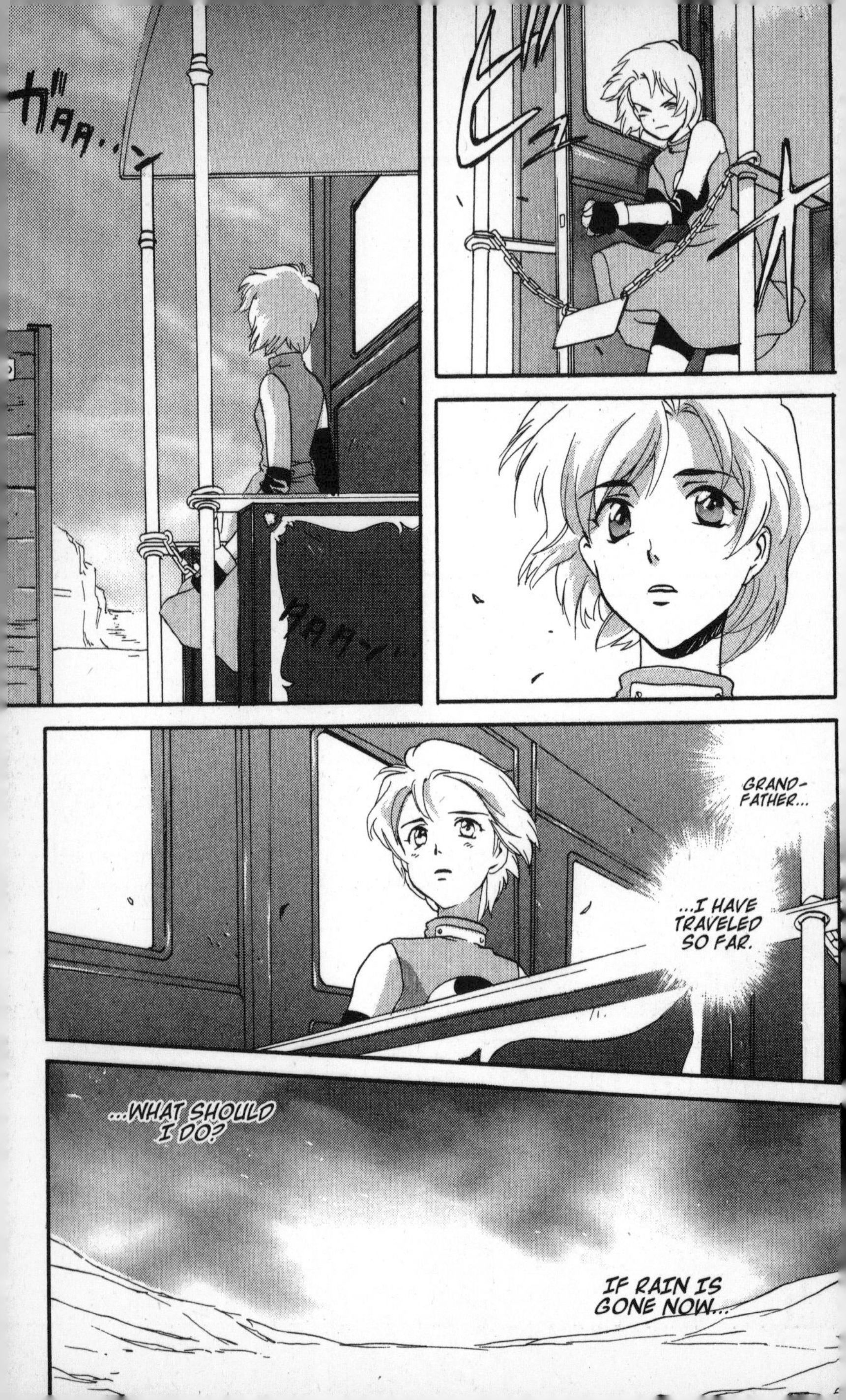
GRAND-FATHER...
...I HAVE TRAVELED SO FAR.
...WHAT SHOULD I DO?
IF RAIN IS GONE NOW...

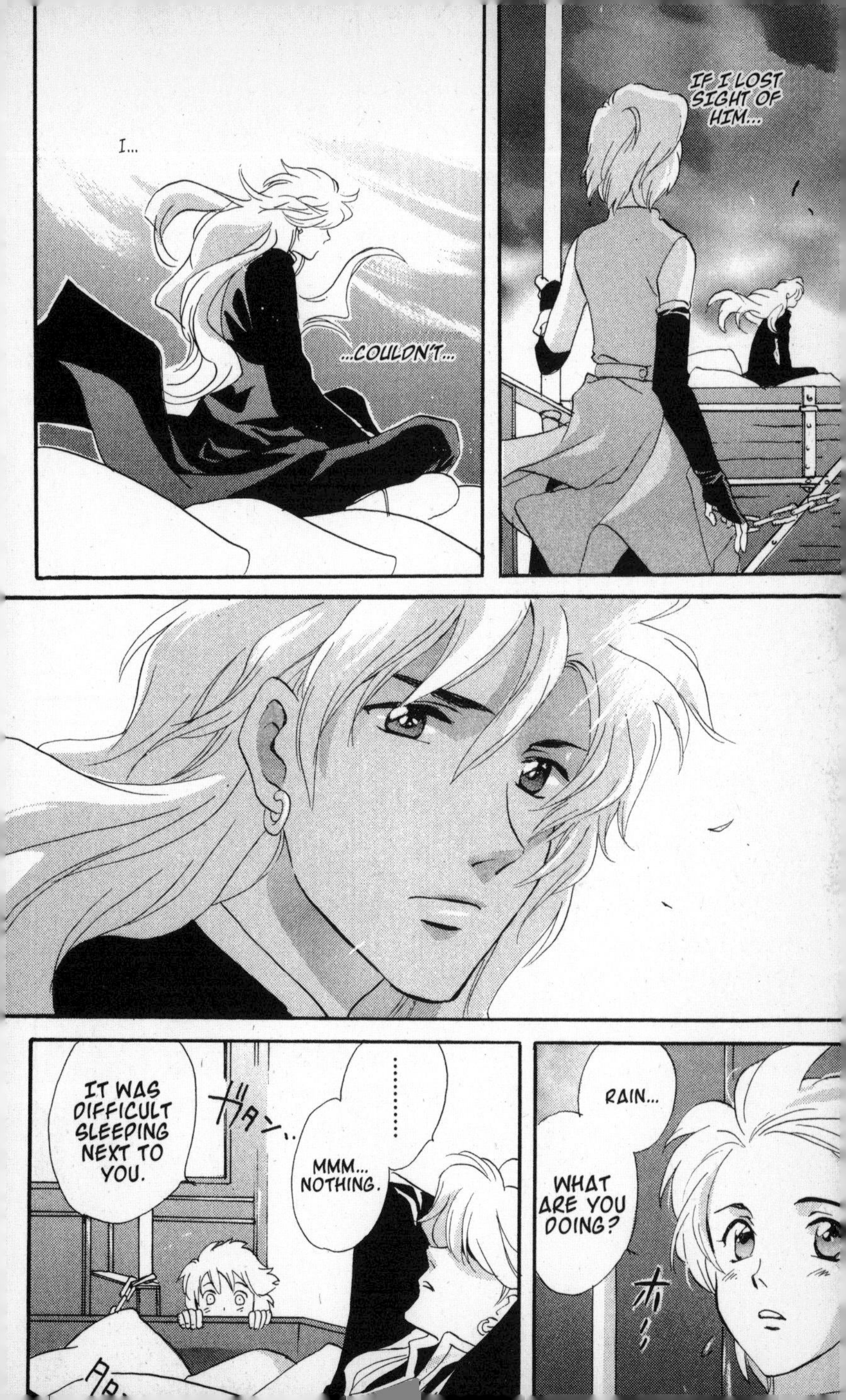
IF I LOST SIGHT OF HIM...
I...
...COULDN'T...
RAIN...
WHAT ARE YOU DOING?
......
MMM... NOTHING.
IT WAS DIFFICULT SLEEPING NEXT TO YOU.

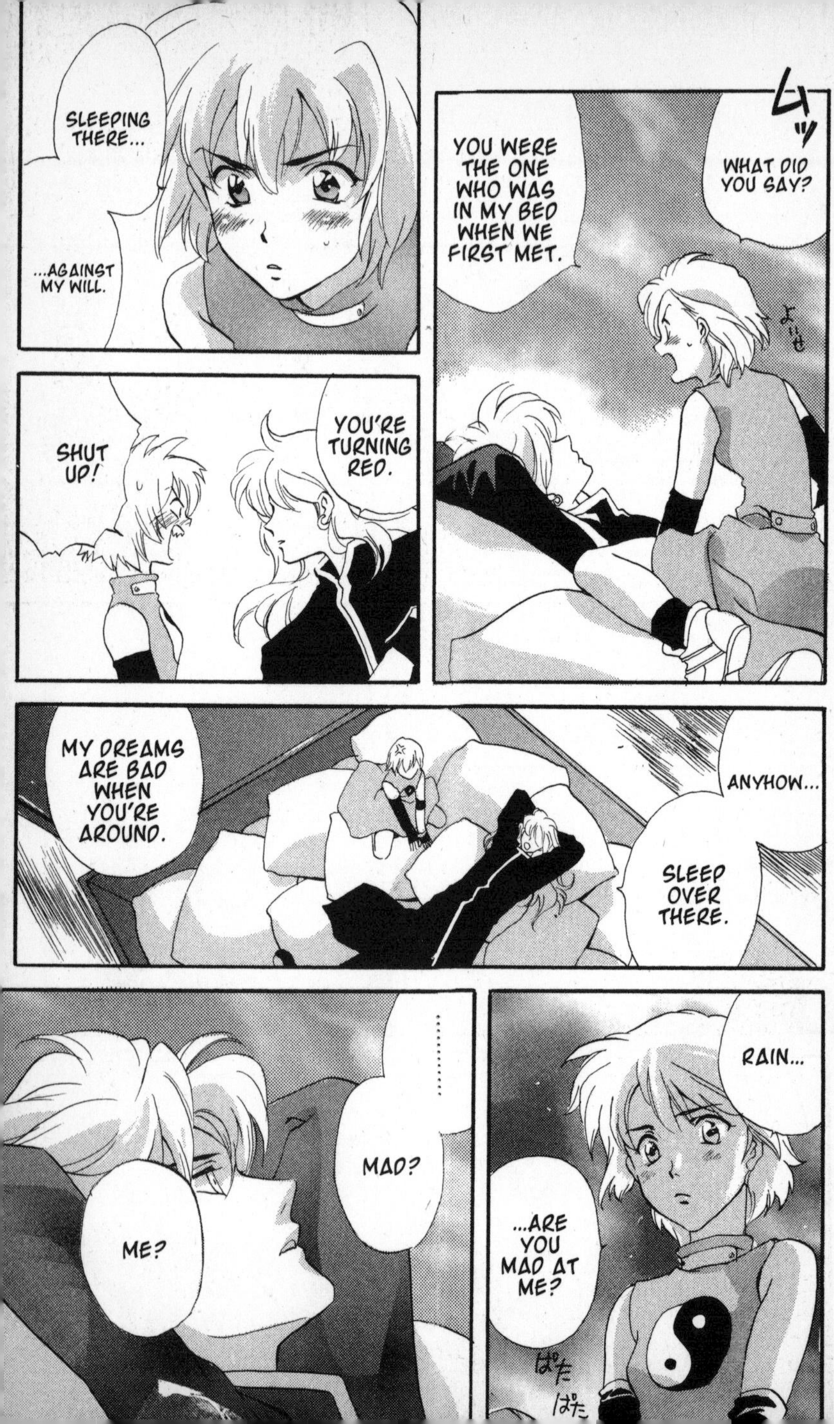
ムッ
WHAT DID YOU SAY?
YOU WERE THE ONE WHO WAS IN MY BED WHEN WE FIRST MET.
よいせ
SLEEPING THERE...
...AGAINST MY WILL.
YOU'RE TURNING RED.
SHUT UP!
ANYHOW...
SLEEP OVER THERE.
MY DREAMS ARE BAD WHEN YOU'RE AROUND.
RAIN...
...ARE YOU MAD AT ME?
ぱた ぱた
......
MAD?
ME?

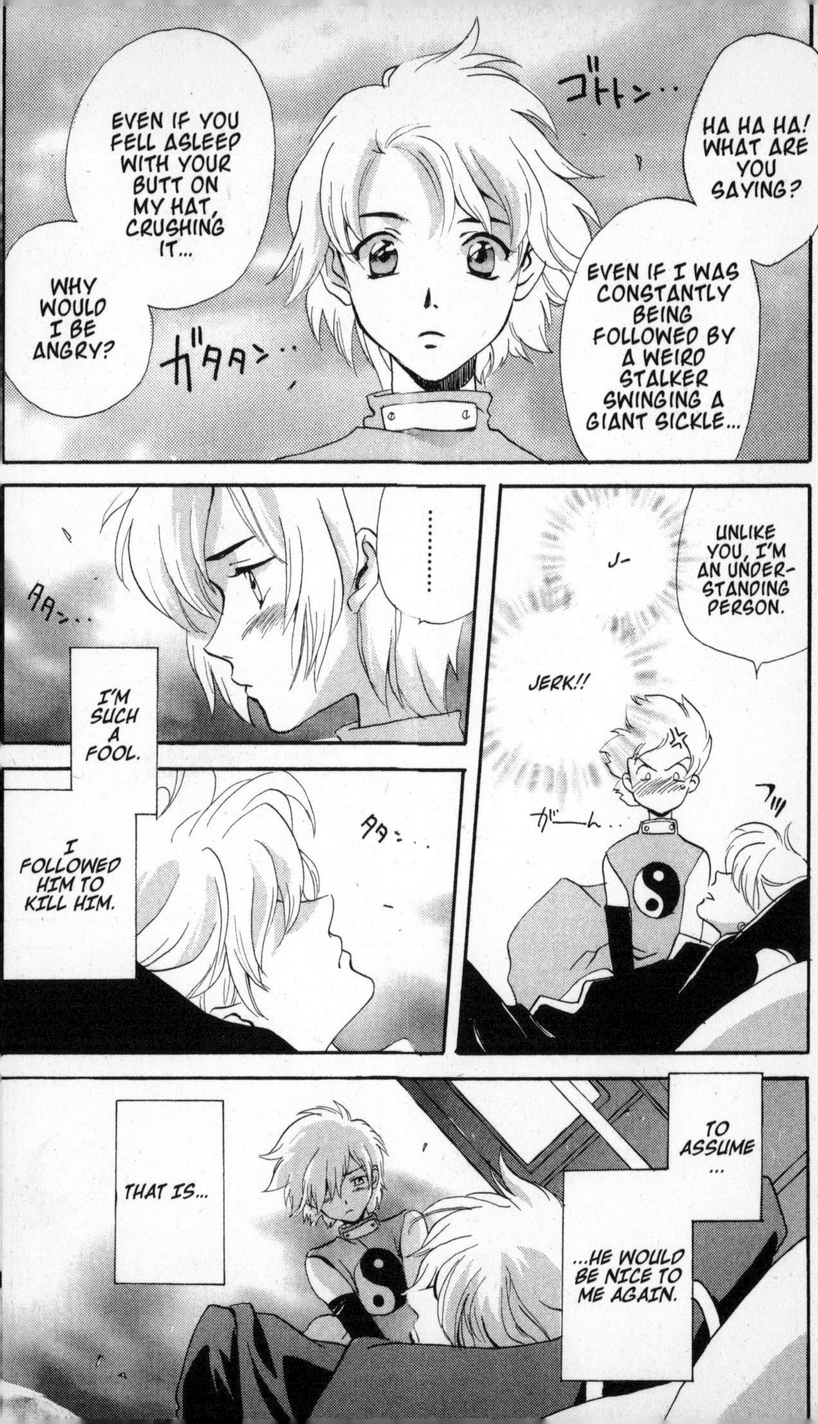
HA HA HA! WHAT ARE YOU SAYING?
EVEN IF I WAS CONSTANTLY BEING FOLLOWED BY A WEIRD STALKER SWINGING A GIANT SICKLE...
EVEN IF YOU FELL ASLEEP WITH YOUR BUTT ON MY HAT, CRUSHING IT...
WHY WOULD I BE ANGRY?
UNLIKE YOU, I'M AN UNDER-STANDING PERSON.
JERK!!
......
I'M SUCH A FOOL.
I FOLLOWED HIM TO KILL HIM.
TO ASSUME ...
...HE WOULD BE NICE TO ME AGAIN.
THAT IS...

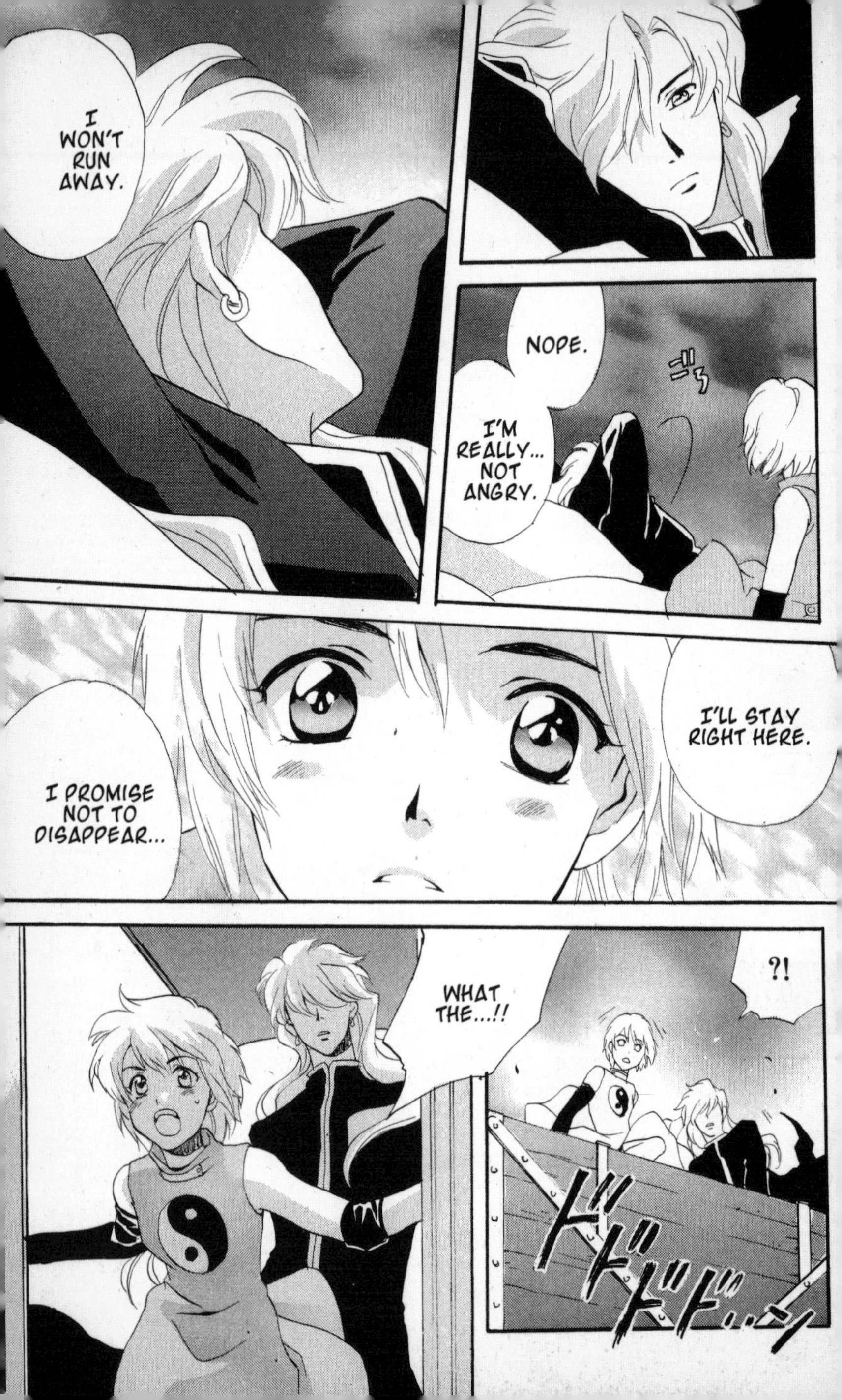
NOPE.
I'M REALLY... NOT ANGRY.
I WON'T RUN AWAY.
I'LL STAY RIGHT HERE.
I PROMISE NOT TO DISAPPEAR...
?!
ドドドド...
WHAT THE...!!

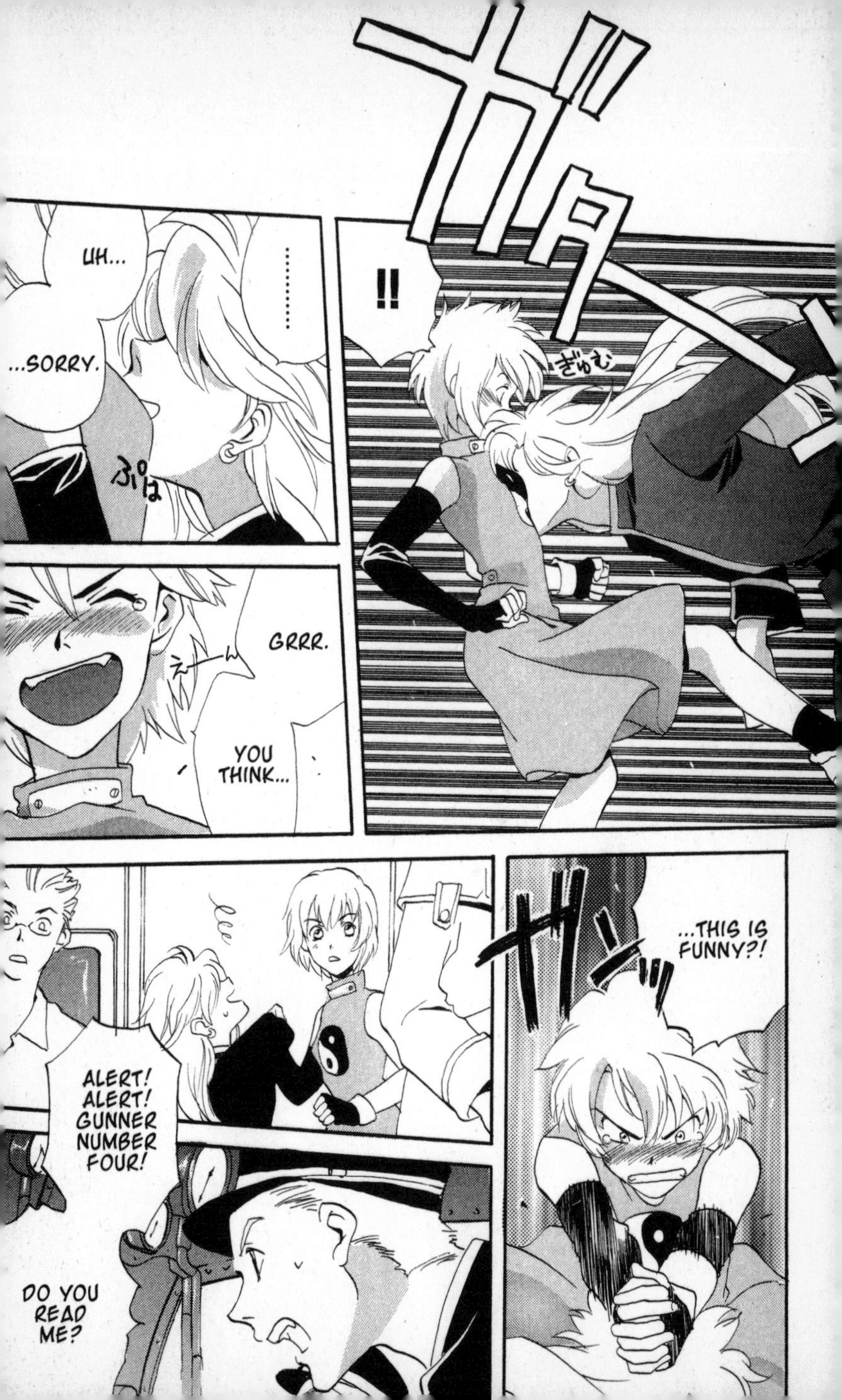
ガタ
!!
ぎゅむ
......
UH...
...SORRY.
ぷは
GRRR.
えーん
YOU THINK...
ザン
...THIS IS FUNNY?!
ALERT! ALERT! GUNNER NUMBER FOUR!
DO YOU READ ME?

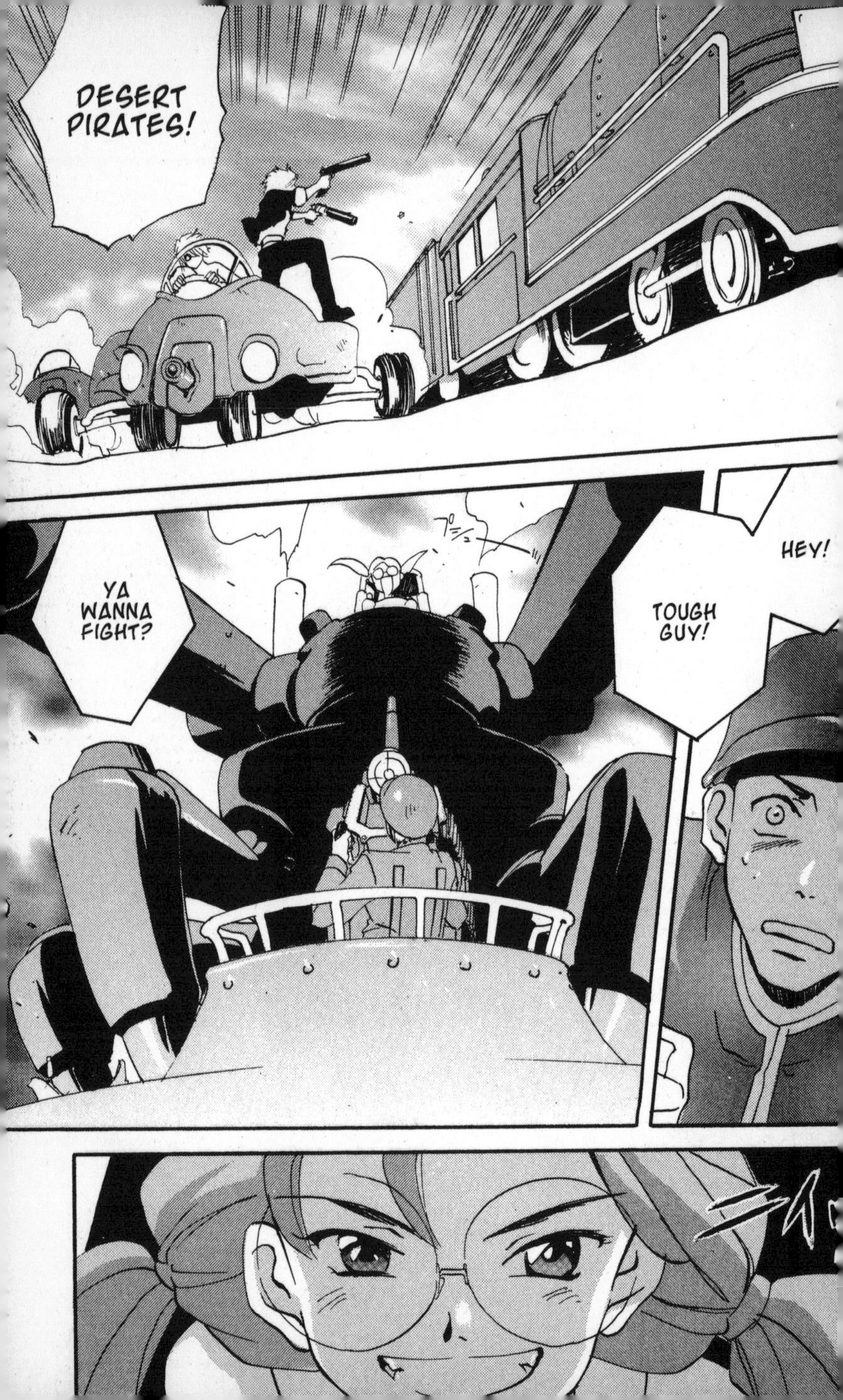
DESERT PIRATES!
HEY!
TOUGH GUY!
YA WANNA FIGHT?

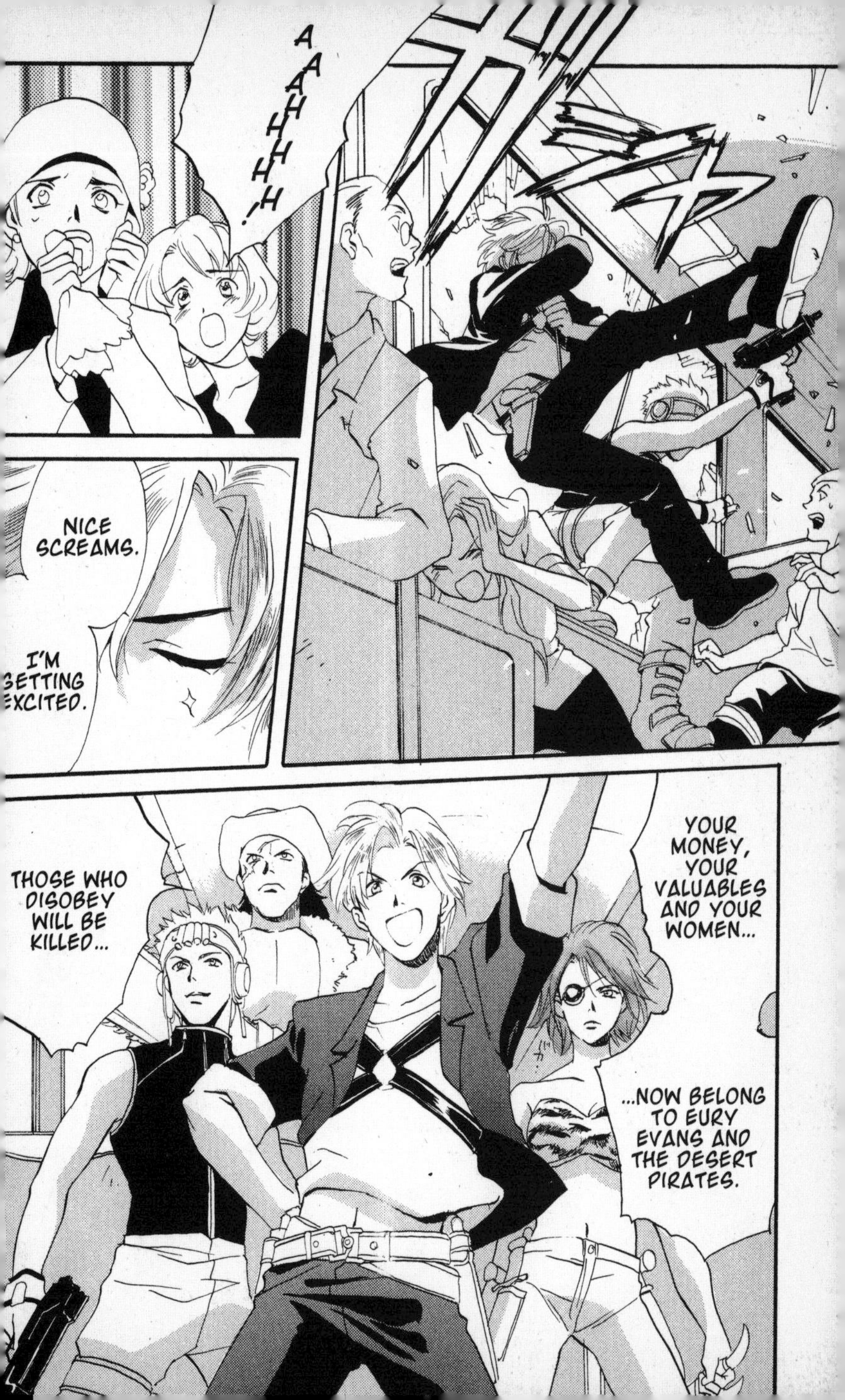
AAAHHHH!
NICE SCREAMS.
I'M GETTING EXCITED.
YOUR MONEY, YOUR VALUABLES AND YOUR WOMEN...
...NOW BELONG TO EURY EVANS AND THE DESERT PIRATES.
THOSE WHO DISOBEY WILL BE KILLED...

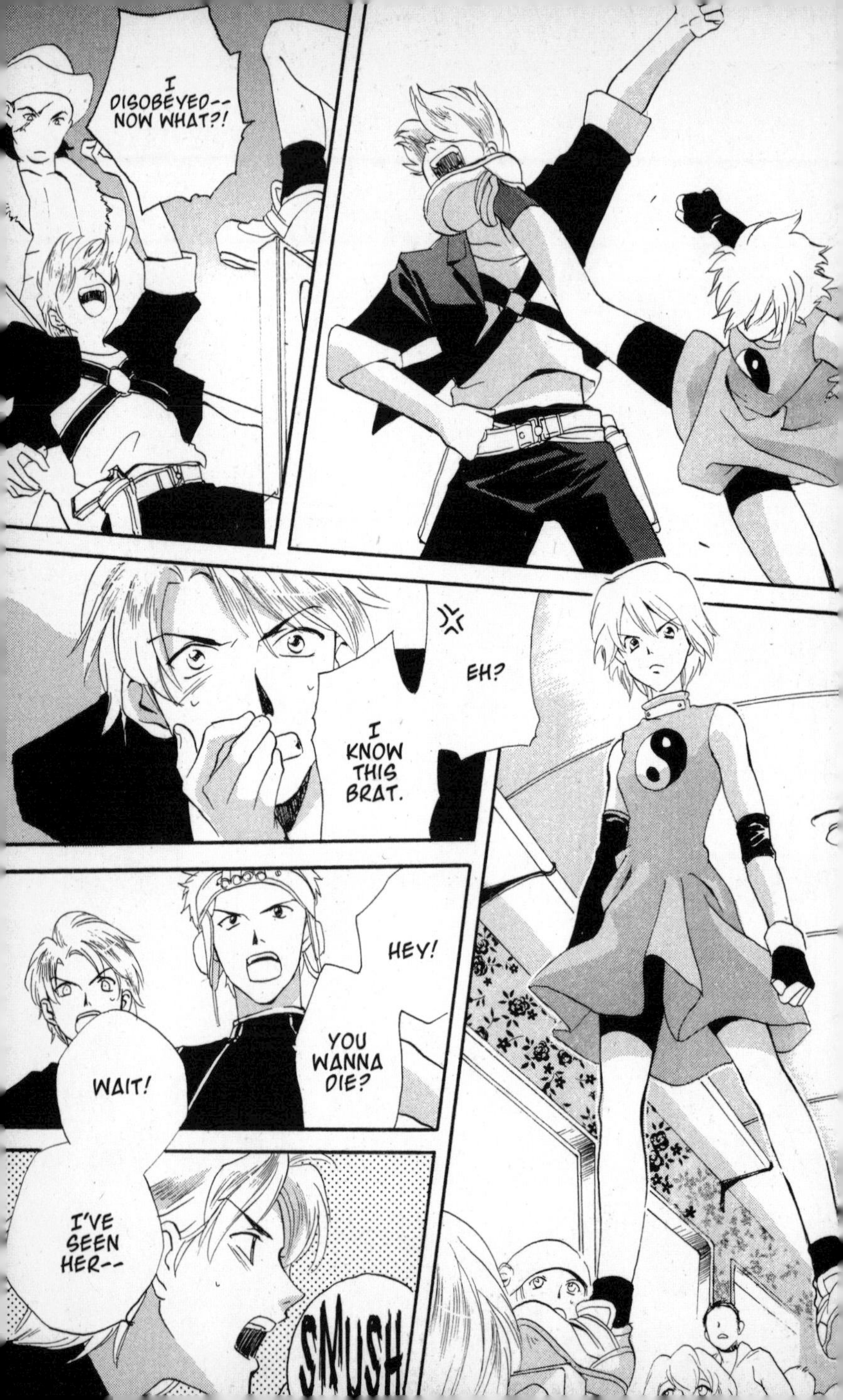
I DISOBEYED-- NOW WHAT?!
EH?
I KNOW THIS BRAT.
HEY!
YOU WANNA DIE?
WAIT!
I'VE SEEN HER--
SMUSH

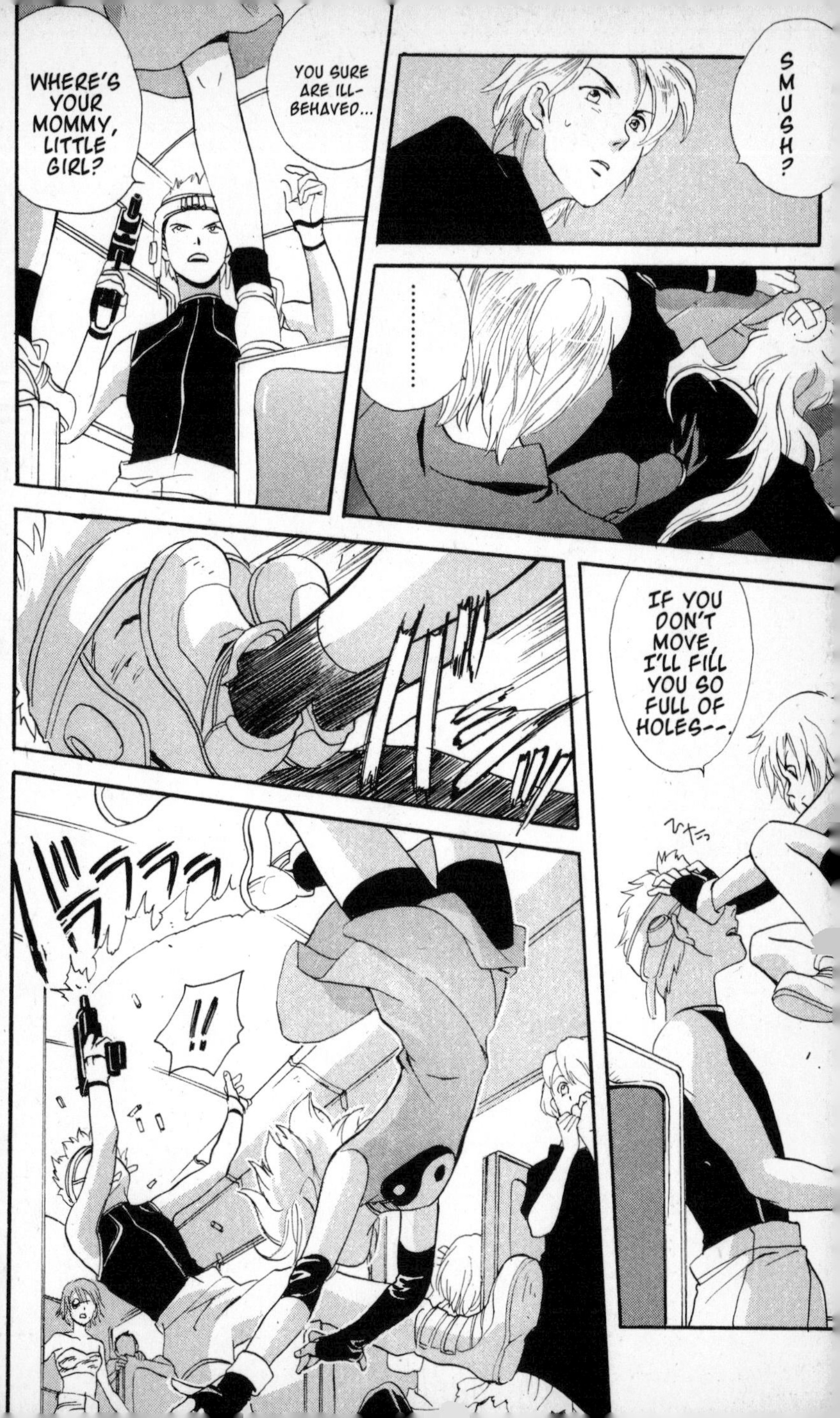
SMUSH?
......
YOU SURE ARE ILL-BEHAVED...
WHERE'S YOUR MOMMY, LITTLE GIRL?
IF YOU DON'T MOVE, I'LL FILL YOU SO FULL OF HOLES--.
ドララララ
!!

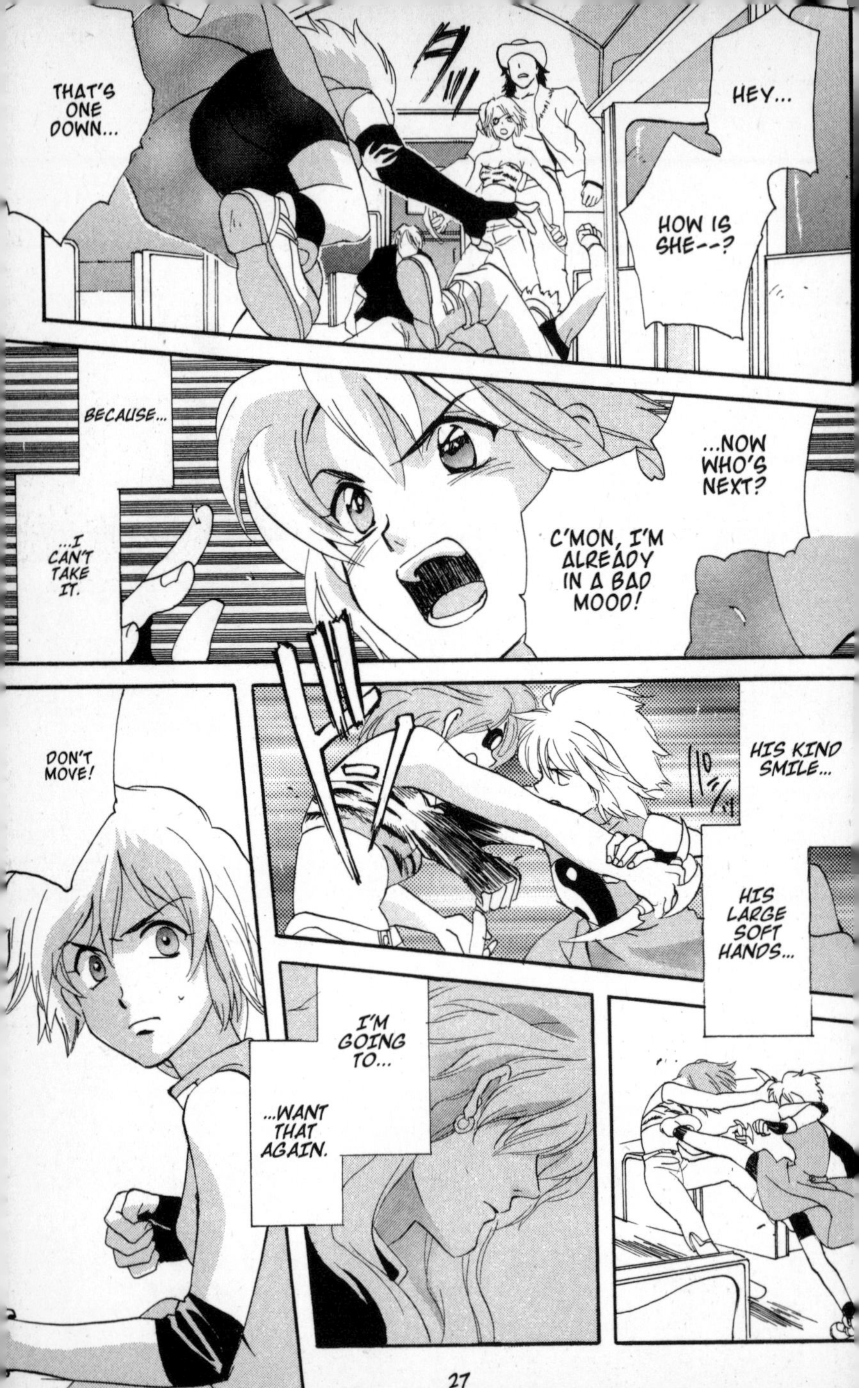
HEY...
HOW IS SHE--?
THAT'S ONE DOWN...
...NOW WHO'S NEXT?
C'MON, I'M ALREADY IN A BAD MOOD!
BECAUSE...
...I CAN'T TAKE IT.
HIS KIND SMILE...
HIS LARGE SOFT HANDS...
I'M GOING TO...
...WANT THAT AGAIN.
DON'T MOVE!

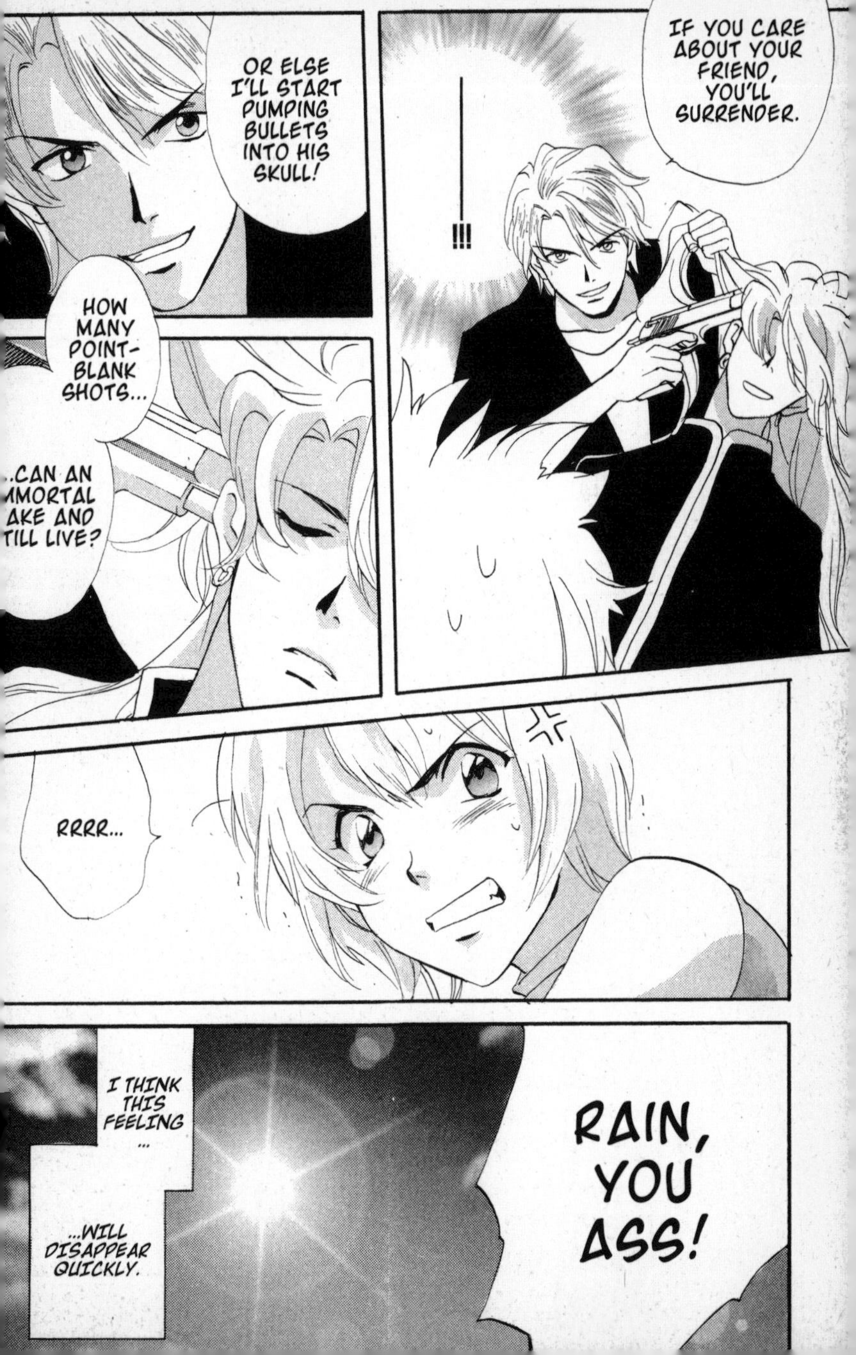
IF YOU CARE ABOUT YOUR FRIEND, YOU'LL SURRENDER.
!!!
OR ELSE I'LL START PUMPING BULLETS INTO HIS SKULL!
HOW MANY POINT-BLANK SHOTS...
..CAN AN MMORTAL AKE AND TILL LIVE?
RRRR...
RAIN, YOU ASS!
I THINK THIS FEELING ...
...WILL DISAPPEAR QUICKLY.

EURY EVANS

Age:18
Height:175cm
Blood type:B

COMMAND

FIGHT
PERSUADE
FLEE

LV : 28

HP : 547/547

OFFENSE
STRENGTH : 52

DEFENSE
STRENGTH : 48

SPEED : 43

CLEVERNESS : 48

LUCK : 79

EQUIPMENT
WEAPON: GUNS X TWO/ OFFENSE
STRENGTH + 42
ARMOR: BUSINESSMAN SUIT/
DEFENSE STRENGTH + 12
ACCESSORY: BUSINESS CARD/
BUSINESS SUCCESS + 5

DEATHBLOW TECHNIQUE
COMMAND
PICKUP MOVES ⬎Ⓟ
MEN'S ELEGY SHOOTOUT
                HIT Ⓟ REPEATEDLY
SIBLING ASSAULT ⇨Ⓟ+Ⓚ+Ⓖ

A DELINQUENT BUSINESSMAN WHO MAKES BAD LUCK
WORK AND LIVES FLIPPANTLY. EVERY TIME HE
MEETS A WOMAN, HE TRIES TO PICK HER UP.

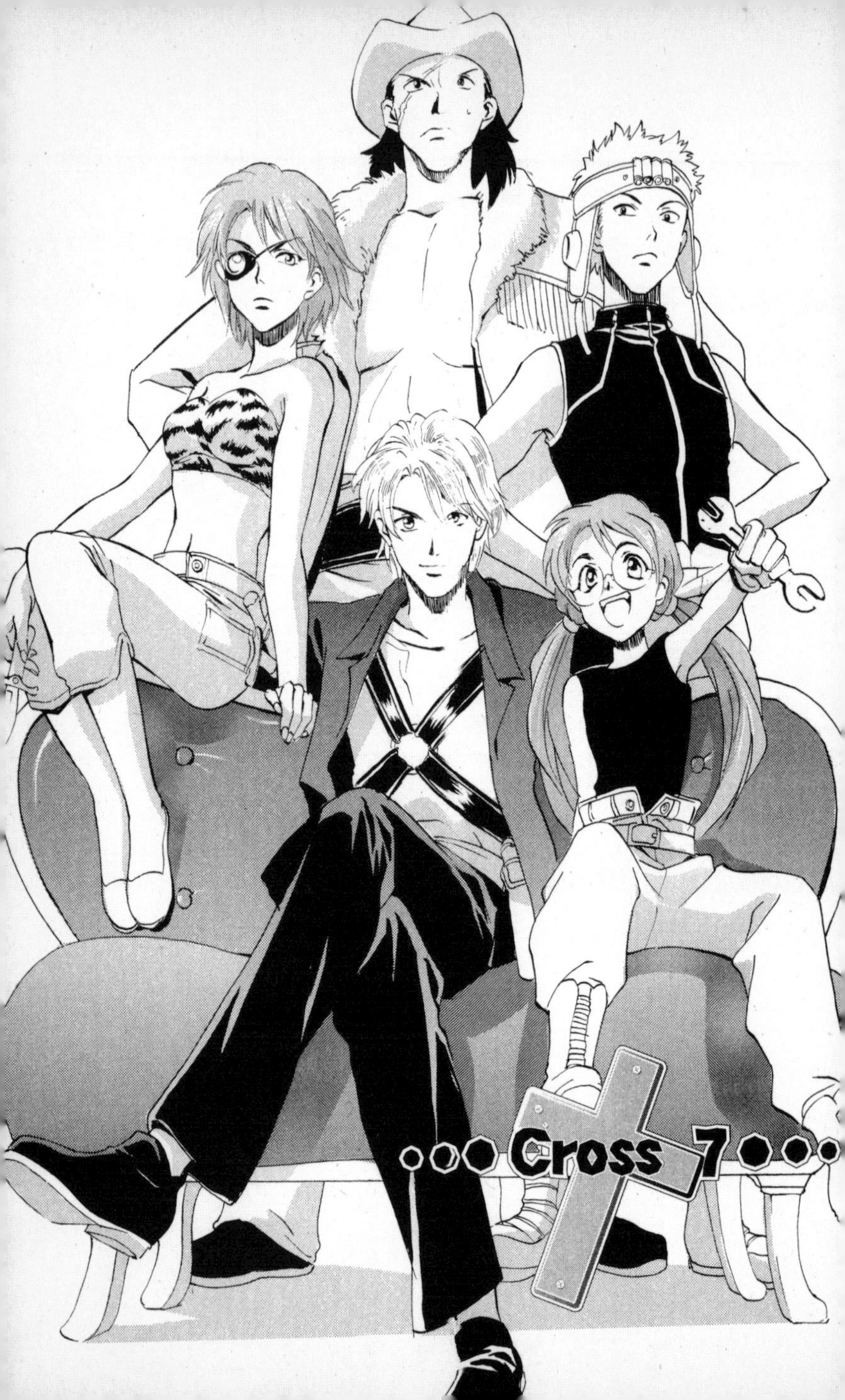
Cross 7

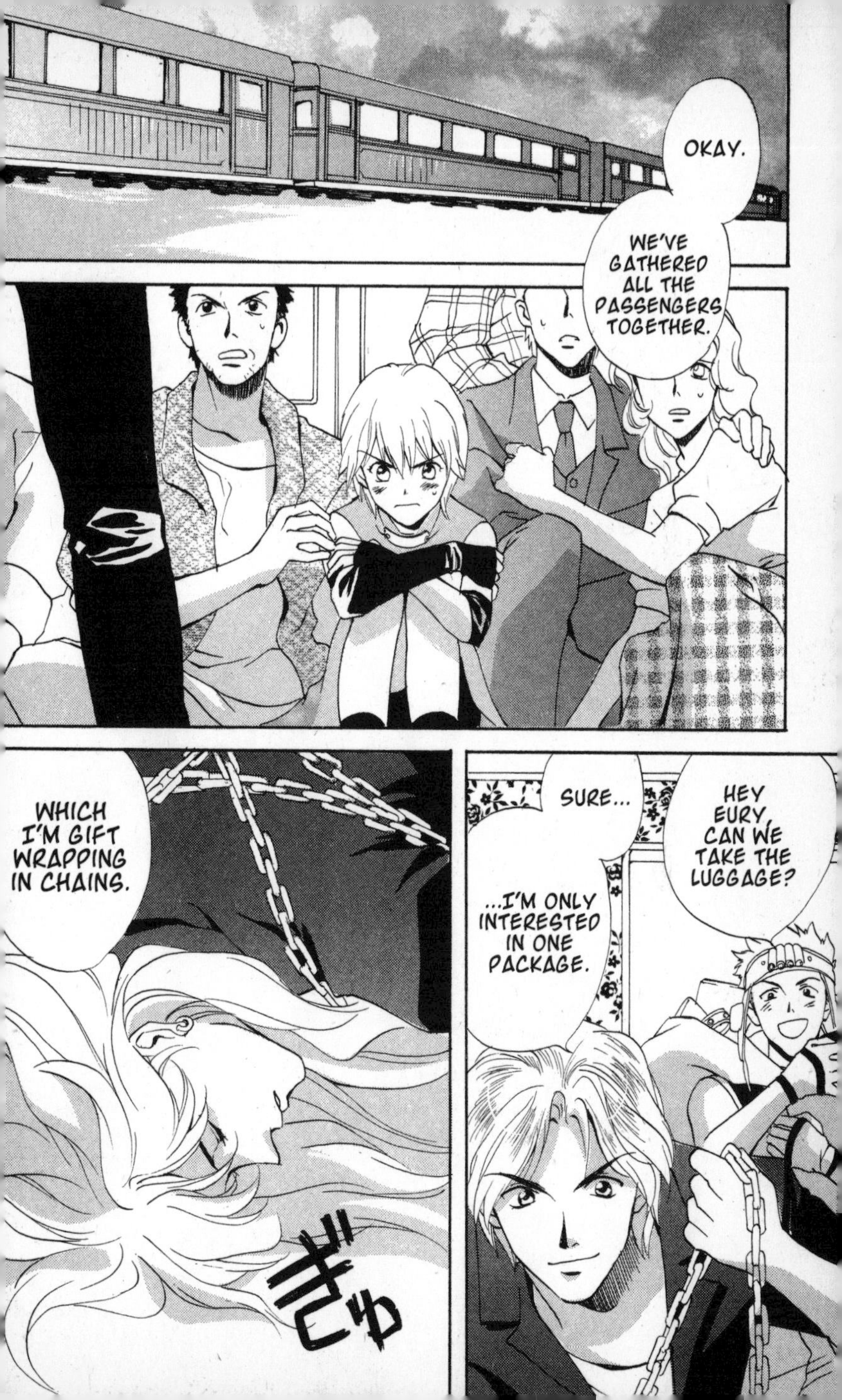
OKAY.
WE'VE GATHERED ALL THE PASSENGERS TOGETHER.
HEY EURY CAN WE TAKE THE LUGGAGE?
SURE...
...I'M ONLY INTERESTED IN ONE PACKAGE.
WHICH I'M GIFT WRAPPING IN CHAINS.
ぎゅ

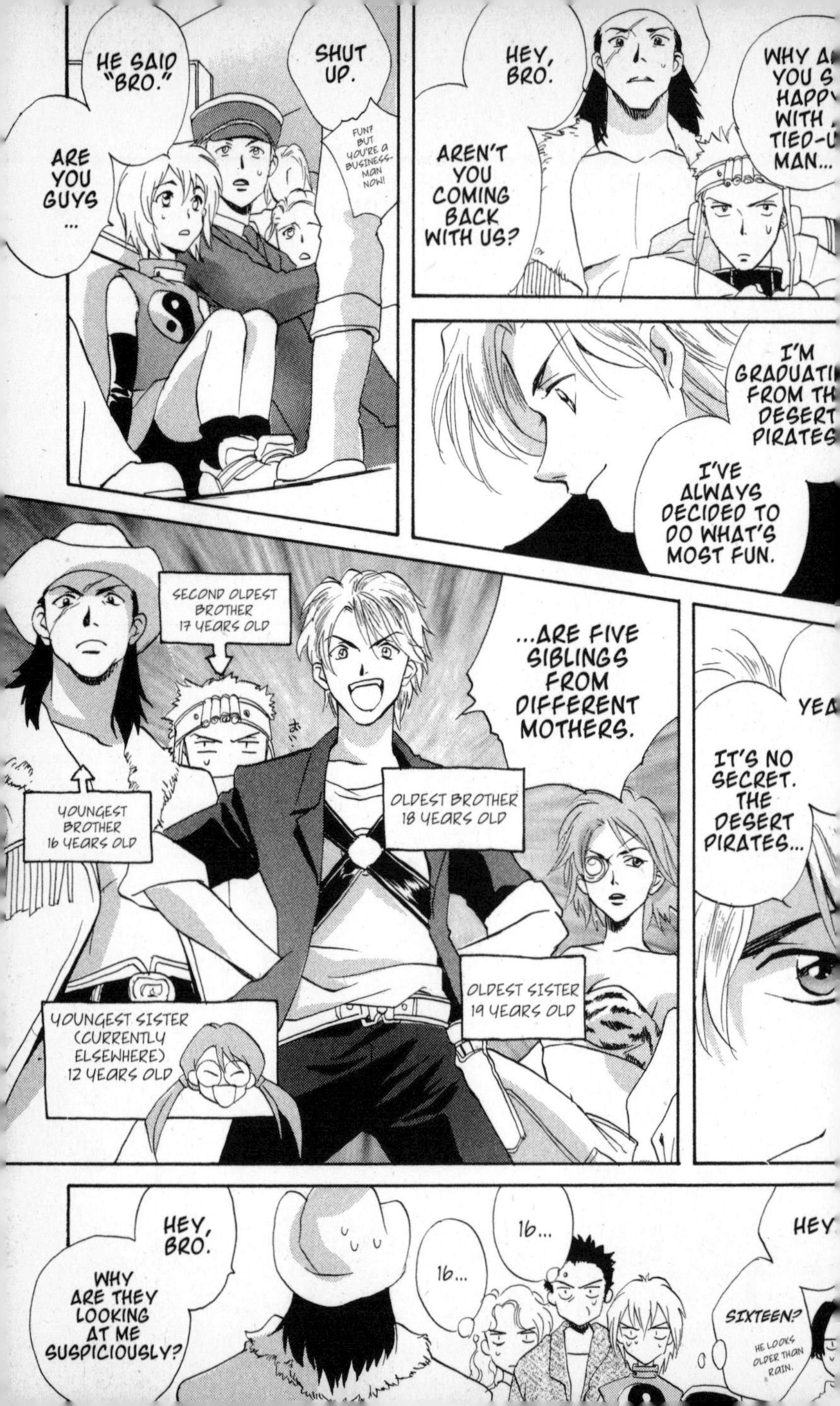
WHY A
YOU S
HAPP
WITH
TIED-U
MAN...
HEY, BRO.
AREN'T YOU COMING BACK WITH US?
I'M GRADUATI
FROM TH
DESERT
PIRATES
I'VE ALWAYS DECIDED TO DO WHAT'S MOST FUN.
HE SAID "BRO."
SHUT UP.
FUN? BUT YOU'RE A BUSINESS-MAN NOW!
ARE YOU GUYS ...
YEA
IT'S NO SECRET. THE DESERT PIRATES...
...ARE FIVE SIBLINGS FROM DIFFERENT MOTHERS.
OLDEST SISTER 19 YEARS OLD
OLDEST BROTHER 18 YEARS OLD
SECOND OLDEST BROTHER 17 YEARS OLD
YOUNGEST BROTHER 16 YEARS OLD
YOUNGEST SISTER (CURRENTLY ELSEWHERE) 12 YEARS OLD
HEY
SIXTEEN?
HE LOOKS OLDER THAN RAIN.
16...
16...
HEY, BRO.
WHY ARE THEY LOOKING AT ME SUSPICIOUSLY?

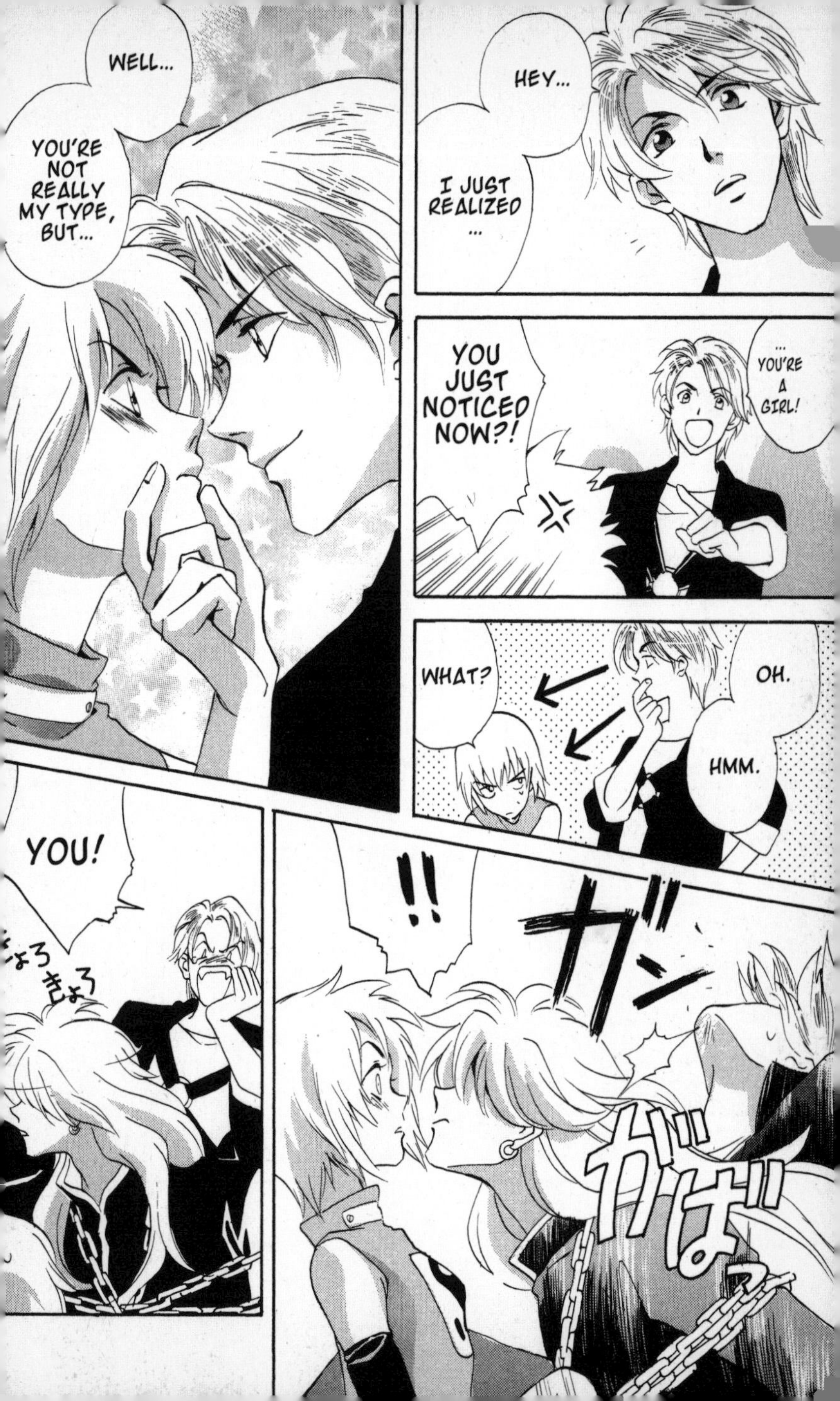
HEY...
I JUST REALIZED...
...YOU'RE A GIRL!
YOU JUST NOTICED NOW?!
OH.
HMM.
WHAT?
WELL...
YOU'RE NOT REALLY MY TYPE, BUT...
!!
ガン
がばっ
YOU!
きょろきょろ

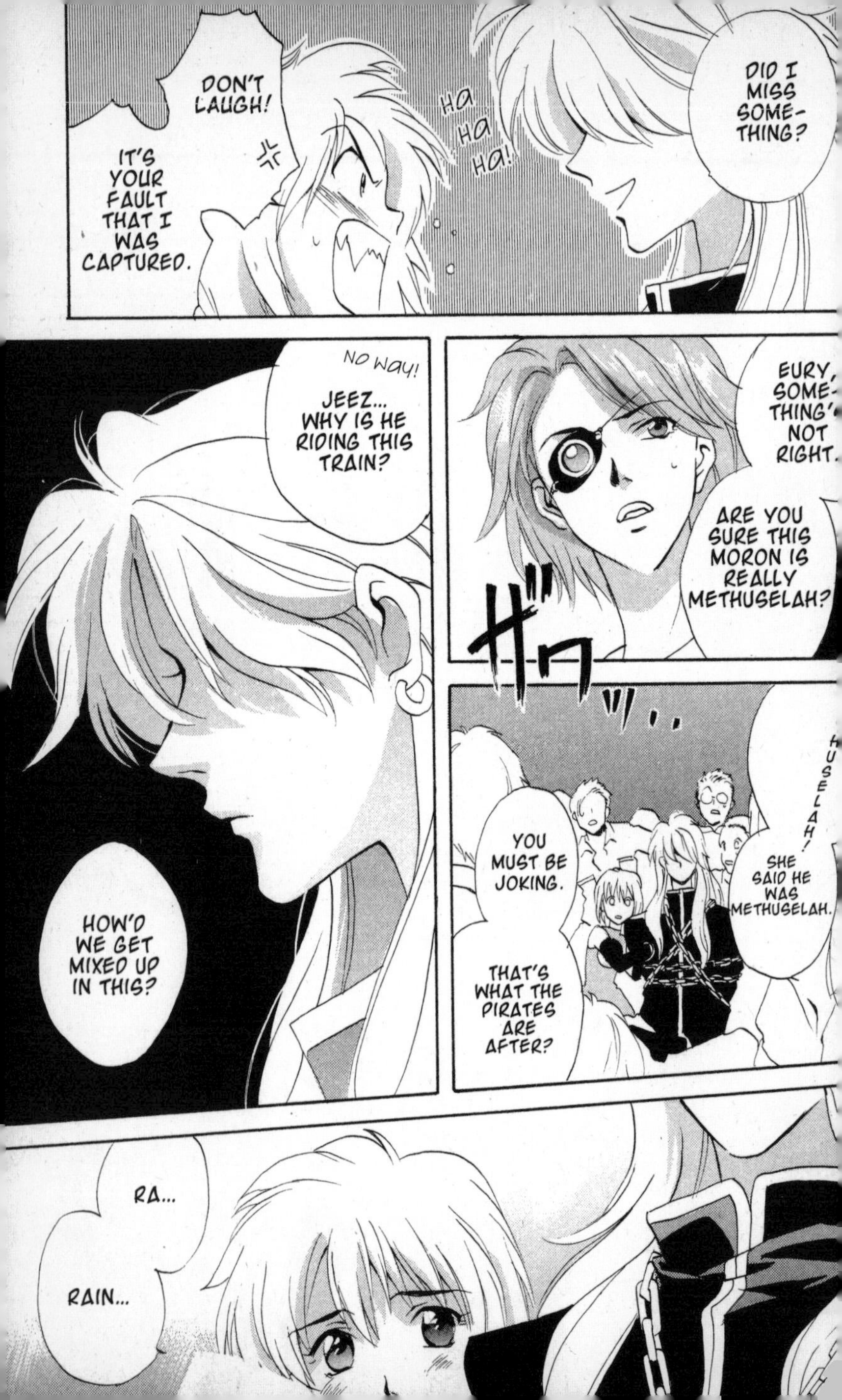
DID I MISS SOME-THING?
Ha Ha Ha!
DON'T LAUGH!
IT'S YOUR FAULT THAT I WAS CAPTURED.
EURY, SOME-THING' NOT RIGHT.
ARE YOU SURE THIS MORON IS REALLY METHUSELAH?
ザワッ..
HUSELAH!
SHE SAID HE WAS METHUSELAH.
YOU MUST BE JOKING.
THAT'S WHAT THE PIRATES ARE AFTER?
No way!
JEEZ... WHY IS HE RIDING THIS TRAIN?
HOW'D WE GET MIXED UP IN THIS?
RA...
RAIN...

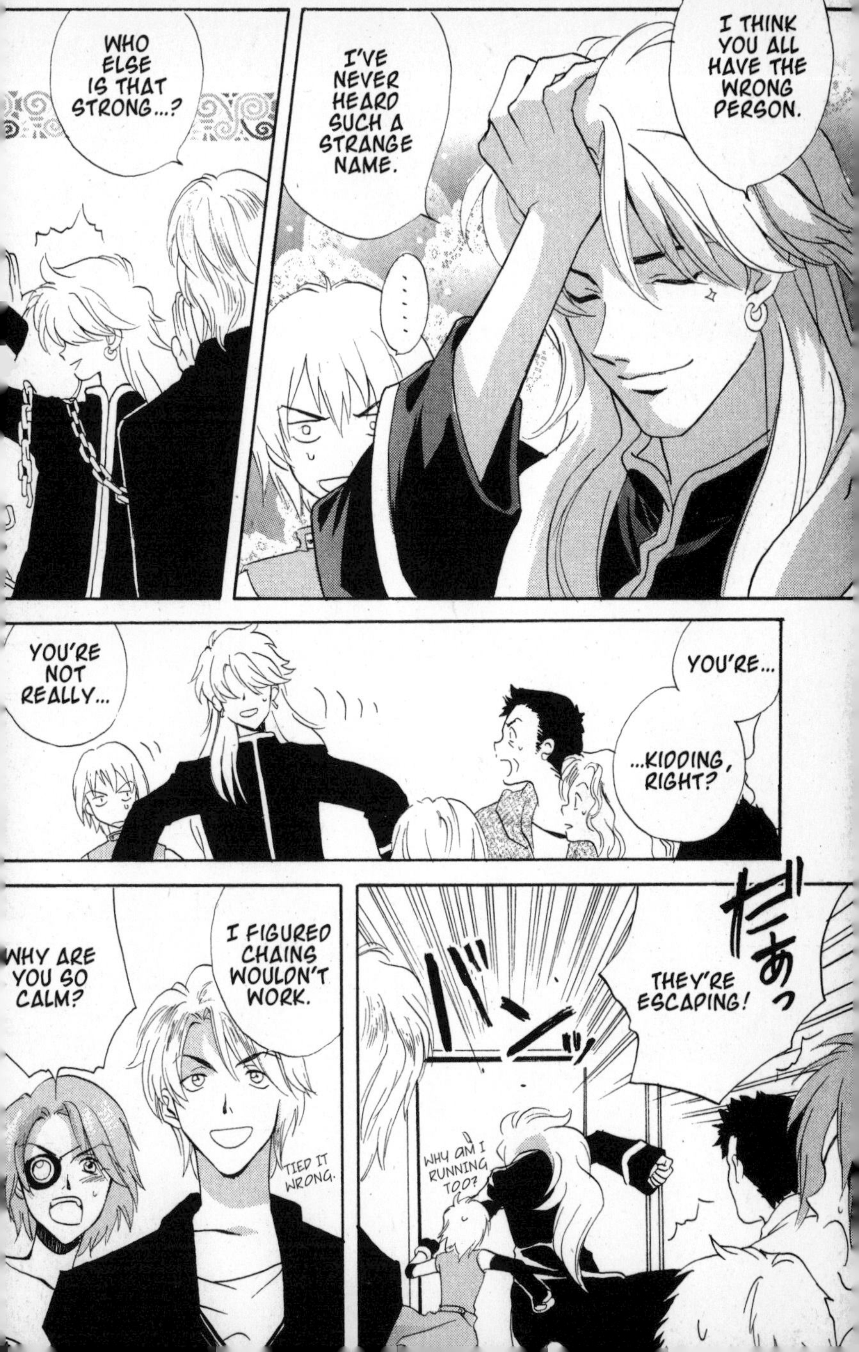
HEH.
I THINK YOU ALL HAVE THE WRONG PERSON.
I'VE NEVER HEARD SUCH A STRANGE NAME.
...
WHO ELSE IS THAT STRONG...?
YOU'RE...
...KIDDING, RIGHT?
YOU'RE NOT REALLY...
だあっ
THEY'RE ESCAPING!
バンッ
WHY AM I RUNNING TOO?
I FIGURED CHAINS WOULDN'T WORK.
WHY ARE YOU SO CALM?
TIED IT WRONG.

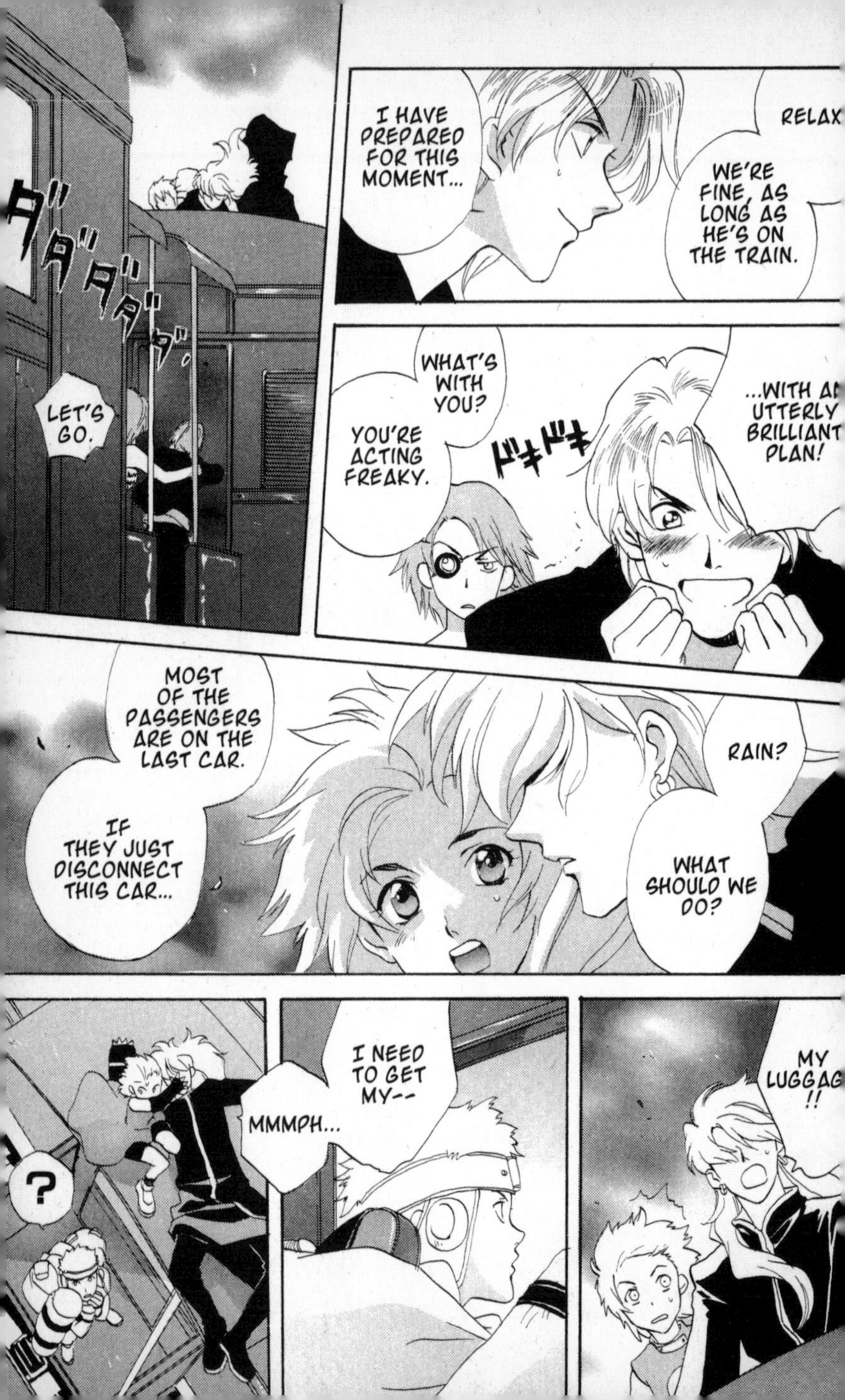

RELAX
WE'RE FINE, AS LONG AS HE'S ON THE TRAIN.
I HAVE PREPARED FOR THIS MOMENT...
...WITH A UTTERLY BRILLIANT PLAN!
ドキドキ
WHAT'S WITH YOU?
YOU'RE ACTING FREAKY.
ダダダダダダダ
LET'S GO.
RAIN?
WHAT SHOULD WE DO?
MOST OF THE PASSENGERS ARE ON THE LAST CAR.
IF THEY JUST DISCONNECT THIS CAR...
MY LUGGAG !!
I NEED TO GET MY--
MMMPH...
?

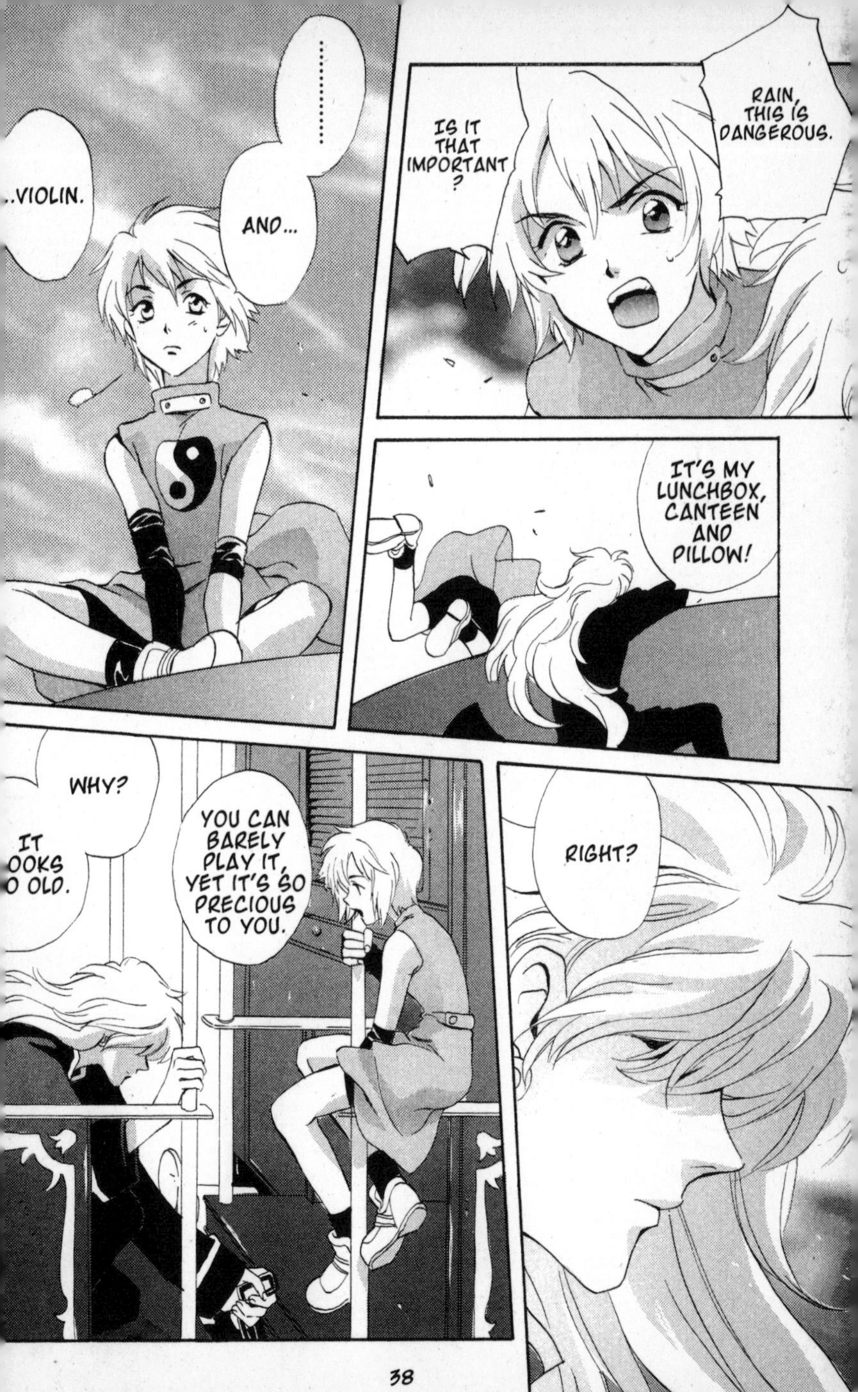
RAIN, THIS IS DANGEROUS.
IS IT THAT IMPORTANT?
IT'S MY LUNCHBOX, CANTEEN AND PILLOW!
......
AND...
..VIOLIN.
RIGHT?
YOU CAN BARELY PLAY IT, YET IT'S SO PRECIOUS TO YOU.
WHY?
IT OOKS O OLD.

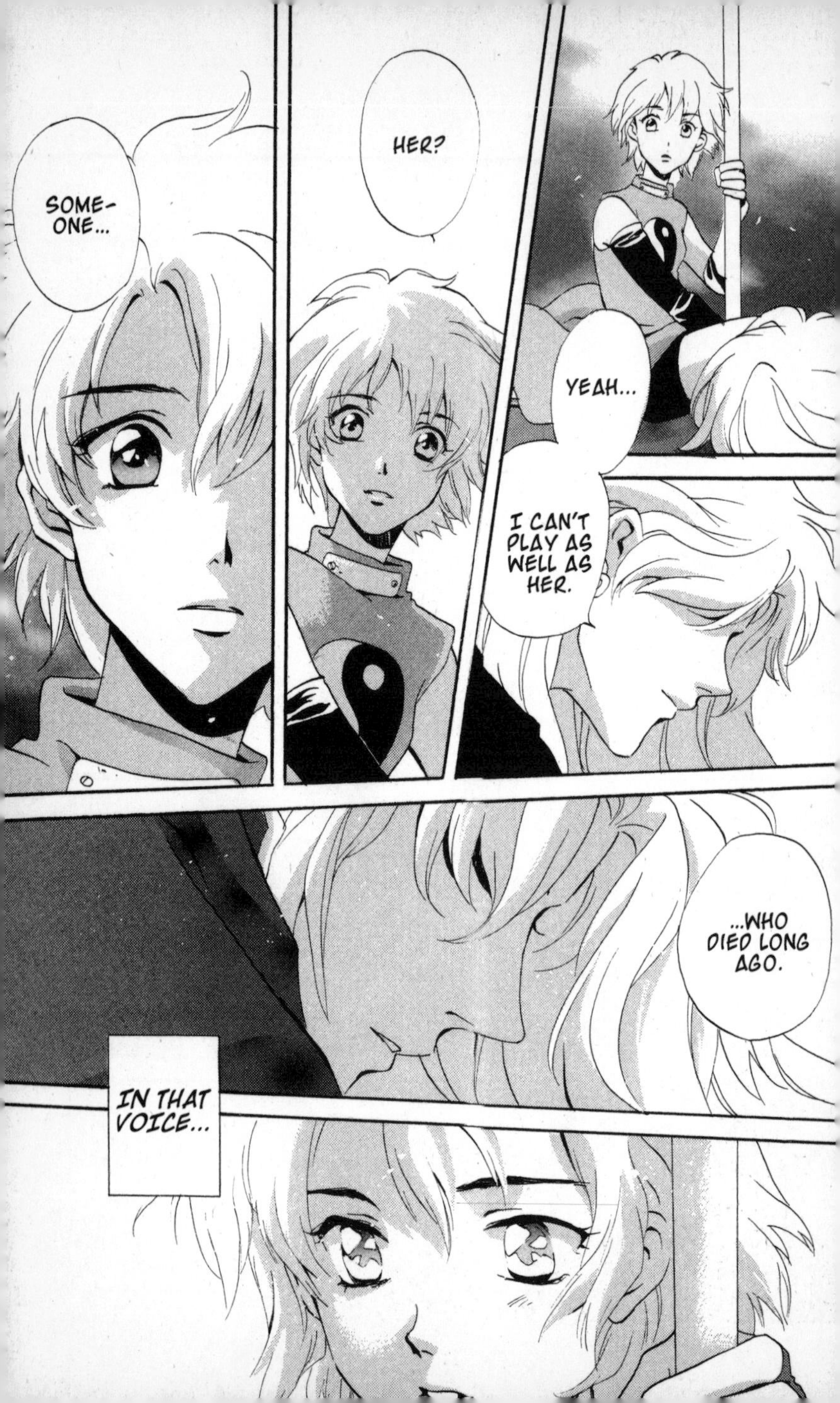
YEAH...
I CAN'T PLAY AS WELL AS HER.
HER?
SOME-ONE...
...WHO DIED LONG AGO.
IN THAT VOICE...

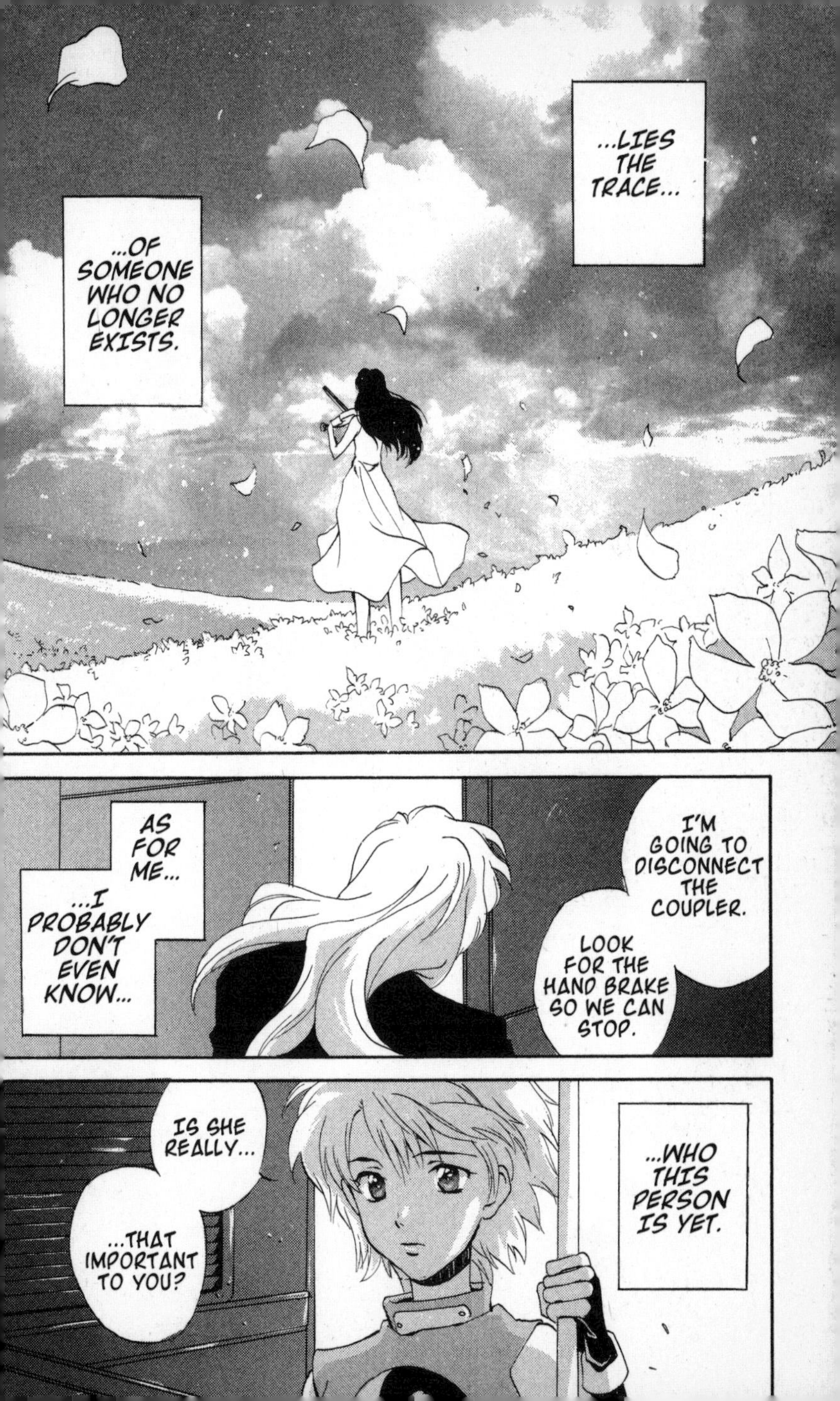
...LIES THE TRACE...
...OF SOMEONE WHO NO LONGER EXISTS.
I'M GOING TO DISCONNECT THE COUPLER.
LOOK FOR THE HAND BRAKE SO WE CAN STOP.
AS FOR ME...
...I PROBABLY DON'T EVEN KNOW...
...WHO THIS PERSON IS YET.
IS SHE REALLY...
...THAT IMPORTANT TO YOU?

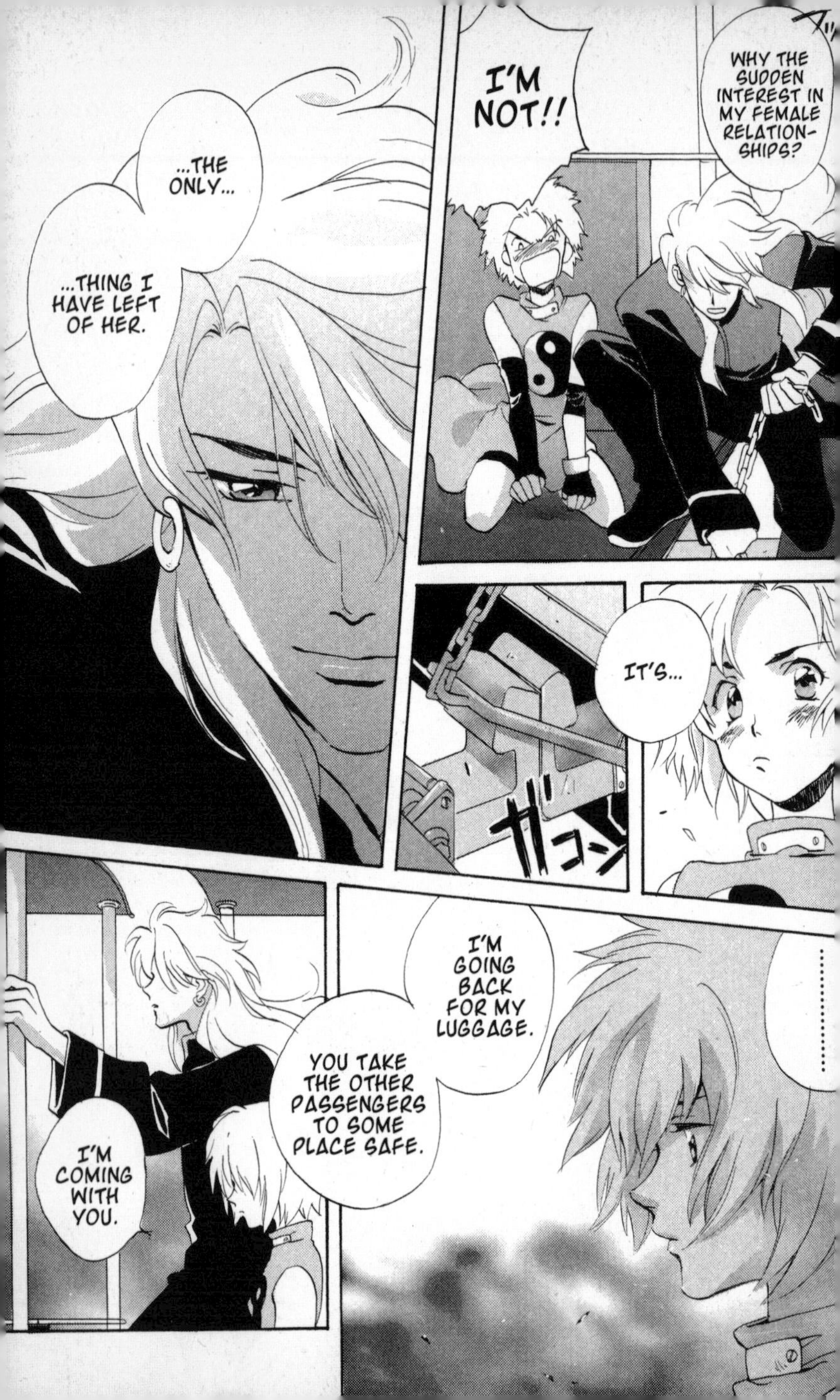
WHY THE SUDDEN INTEREST IN MY FEMALE RELATION-SHIPS?
I'M NOT!!
IT'S...
ガコーン
...THE ONLY...
...THING I HAVE LEFT OF HER.
......
I'M GOING BACK FOR MY LUGGAGE.
YOU TAKE THE OTHER PASSENGERS TO SOME PLACE SAFE.
I'M COMING WITH YOU.

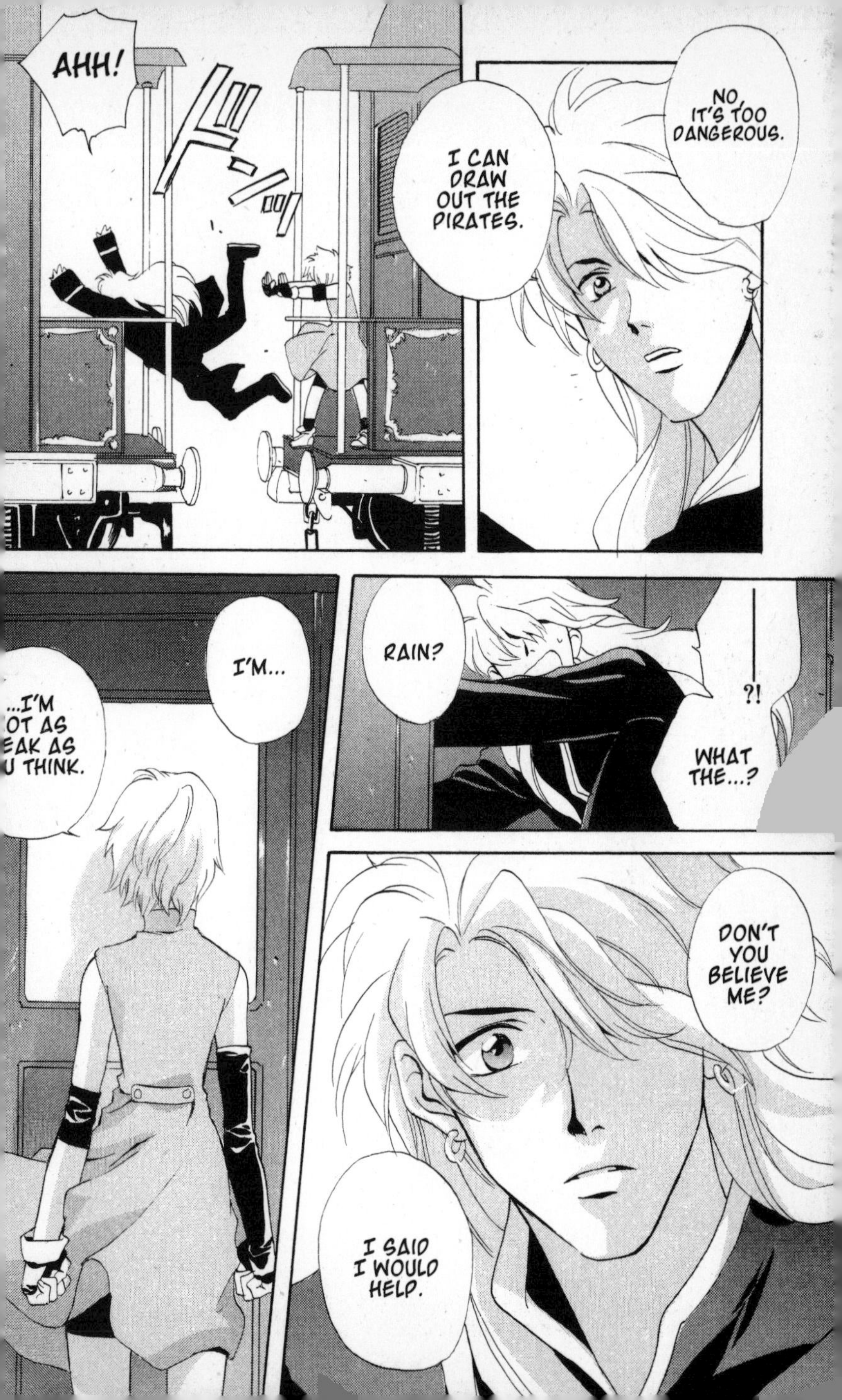
NO, IT'S TOO DANGEROUS.
I CAN DRAW OUT THE PIRATES.
AHH!
?!
WHAT THE...?
RAIN?
DON'T YOU BELIEVE ME?
I SAID I WOULD HELP.
I'M...
...I'M OT AS EAK AS U THINK.

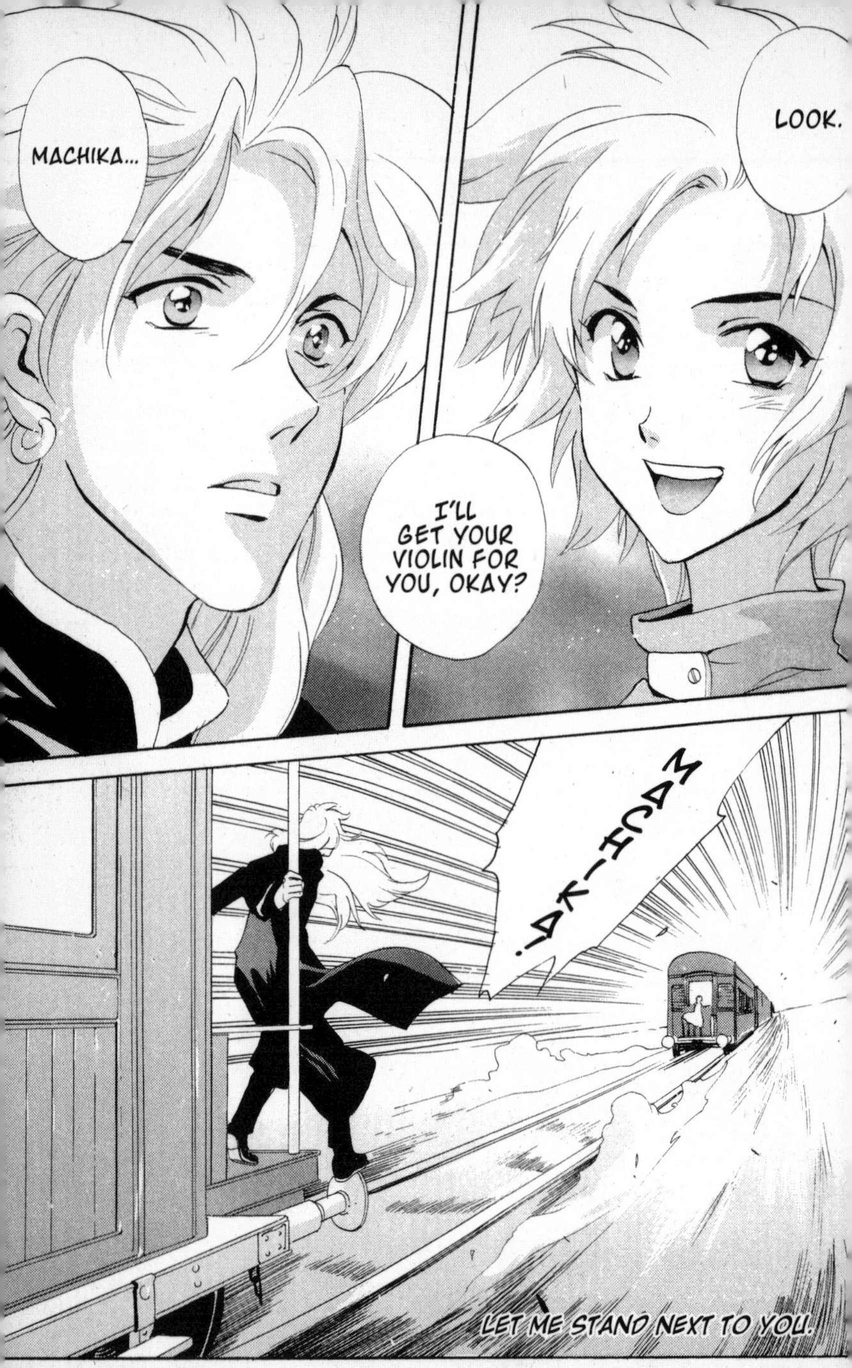
LOOK.
I'LL GET YOUR VIOLIN FOR YOU, OKAY?
MACHIKA...
MACHI-KA!
LET ME STAND NEXT TO YOU.

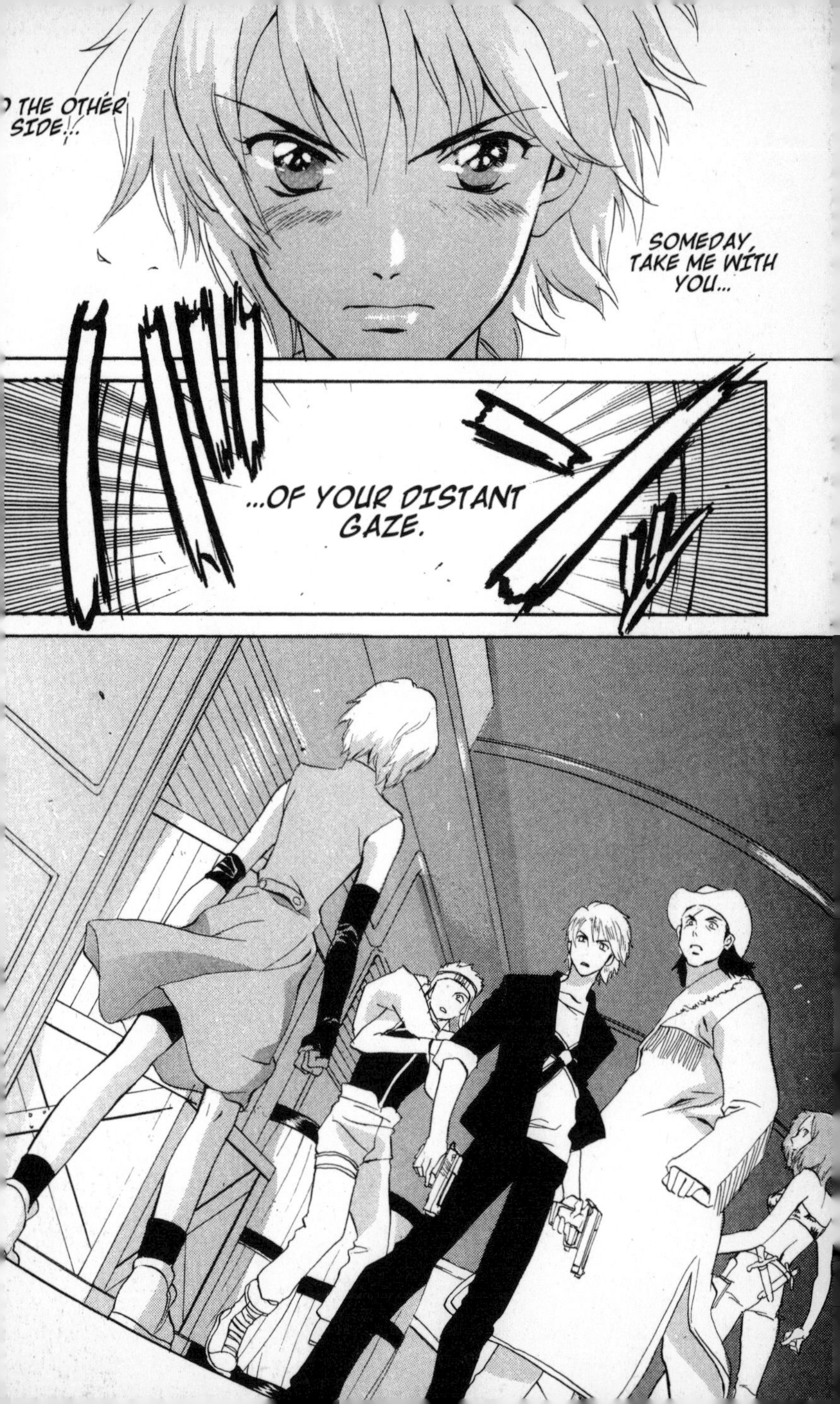
SOMEDAY, TAKE ME WITH YOU...
THE OTHER SIDE...
...OF YOUR DISTANT GAZE.

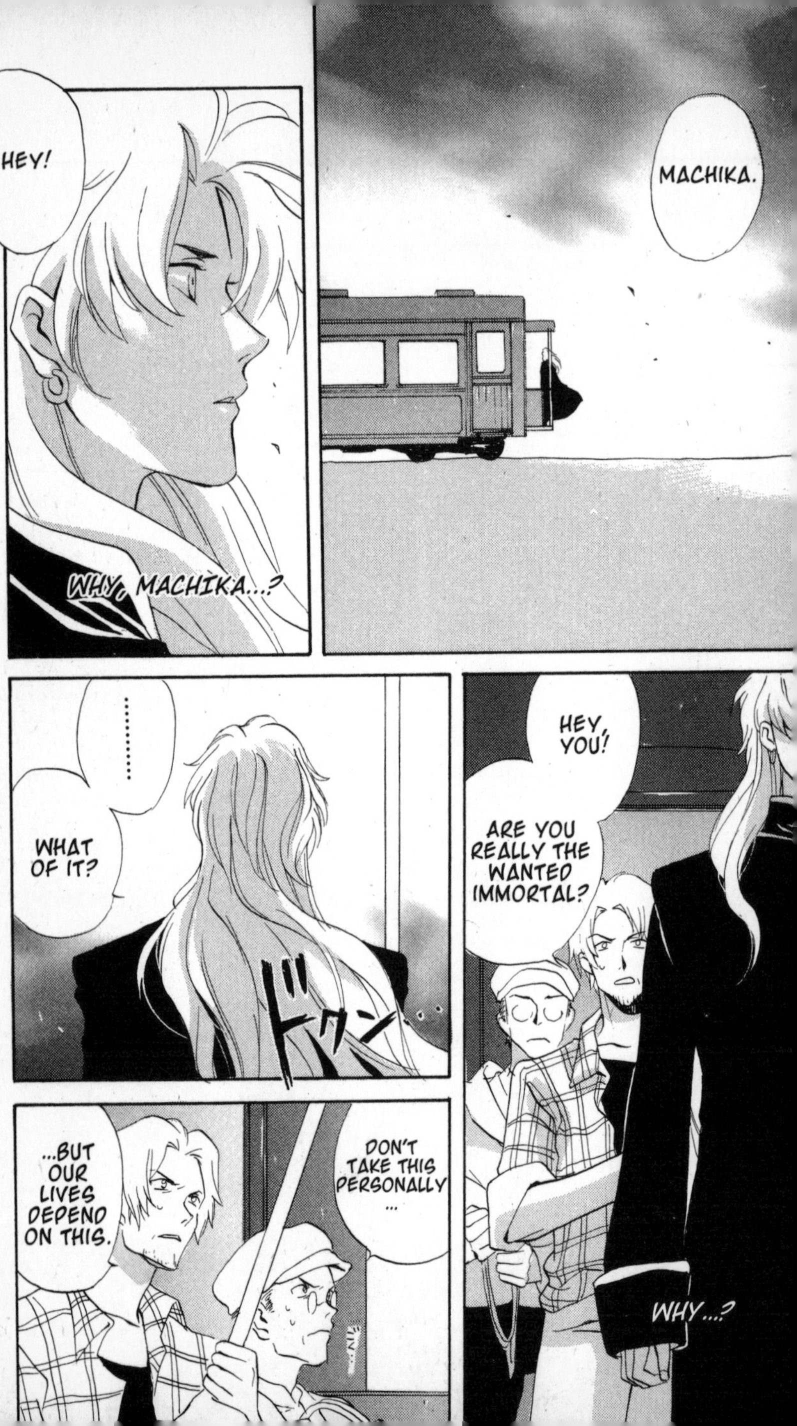
MACHIKA.
HEY!
WHY, MACHIKA...?
HEY, YOU!
ARE YOU REALLY THE WANTED IMMORTAL?
WHY...?
......
WHAT OF IT?
ドクン
DON'T TAKE THIS PERSONALLY...
...BUT OUR LIVES DEPEND ON THIS.

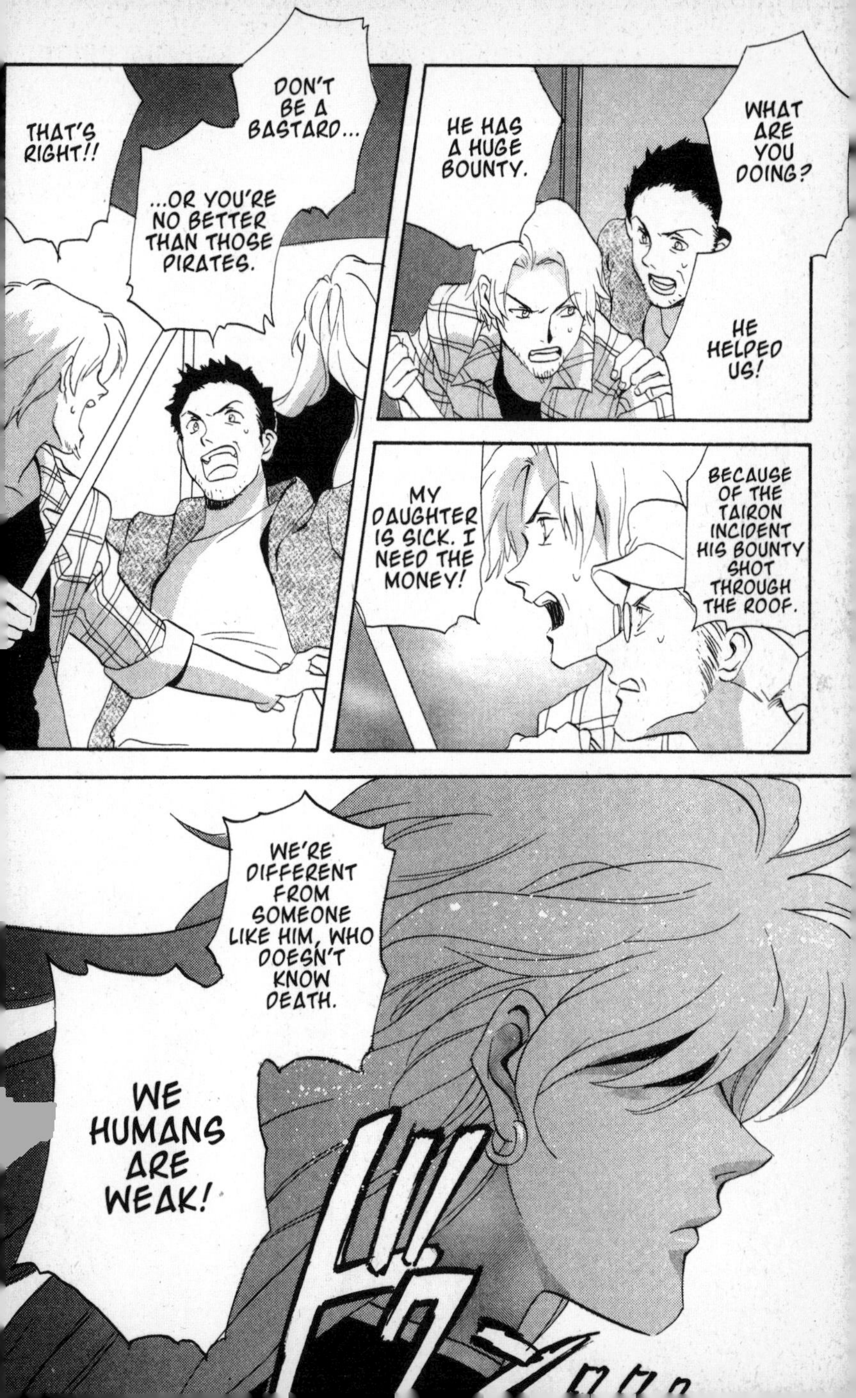
WHAT ARE YOU DOING?
HE HAS A HUGE BOUNTY.
HE HELPED US!
BECAUSE OF THE TAIRON INCIDENT HIS BOUNTY SHOT THROUGH THE ROOF.
MY DAUGHTER IS SICK. I NEED THE MONEY!
DON'T BE A BASTARD...
THAT'S RIGHT!!
...OR YOU'RE NO BETTER THAN THOSE PIRATES.
WE'RE DIFFERENT FROM SOMEONE LIKE HIM, WHO DOESN'T KNOW DEATH.
WE HUMANS ARE WEAK!

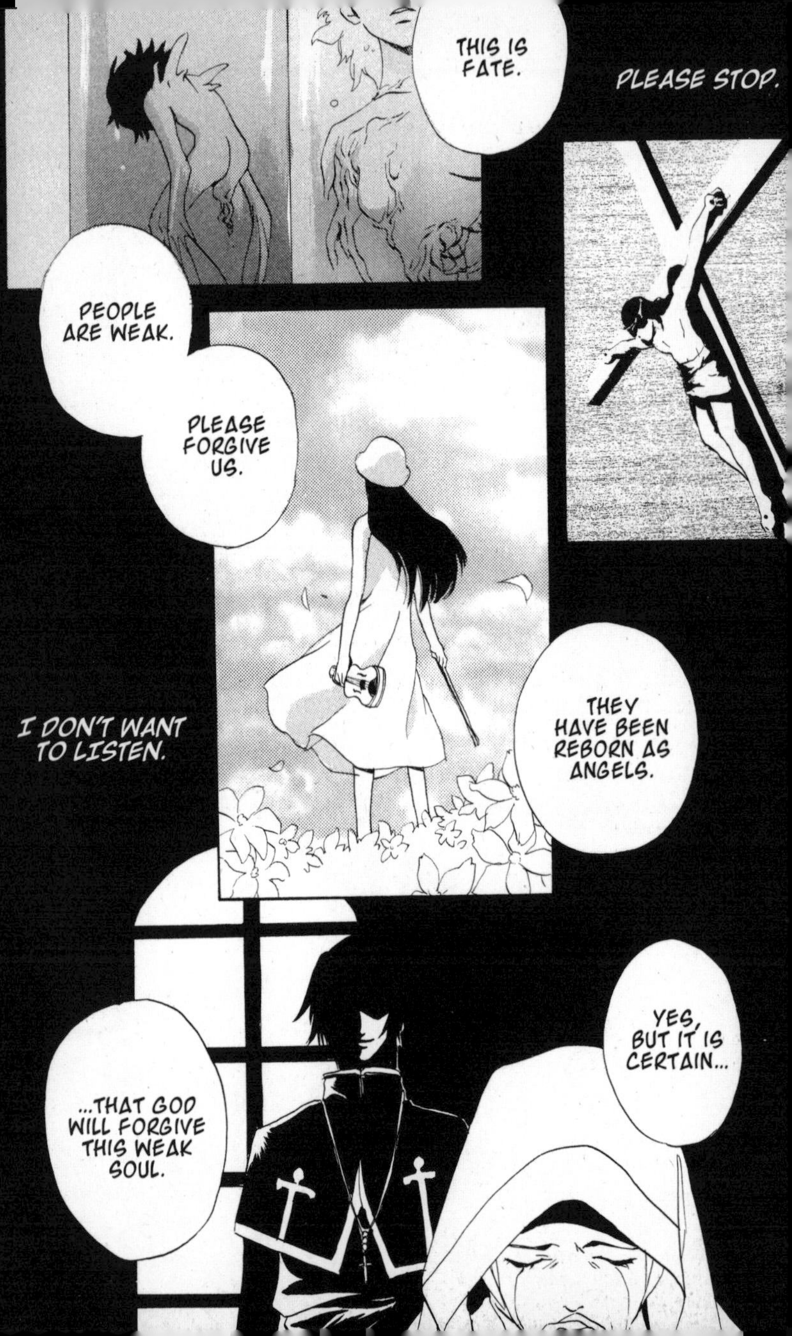
PLEASE STOP.
THIS IS FATE.
PEOPLE ARE WEAK.
PLEASE FORGIVE US.
THEY HAVE BEEN REBORN AS ANGELS.
I DON'T WANT TO LISTEN.
YES, BUT IT IS CERTAIN...
...THAT GOD WILL FORGIVE THIS WEAK SOUL.

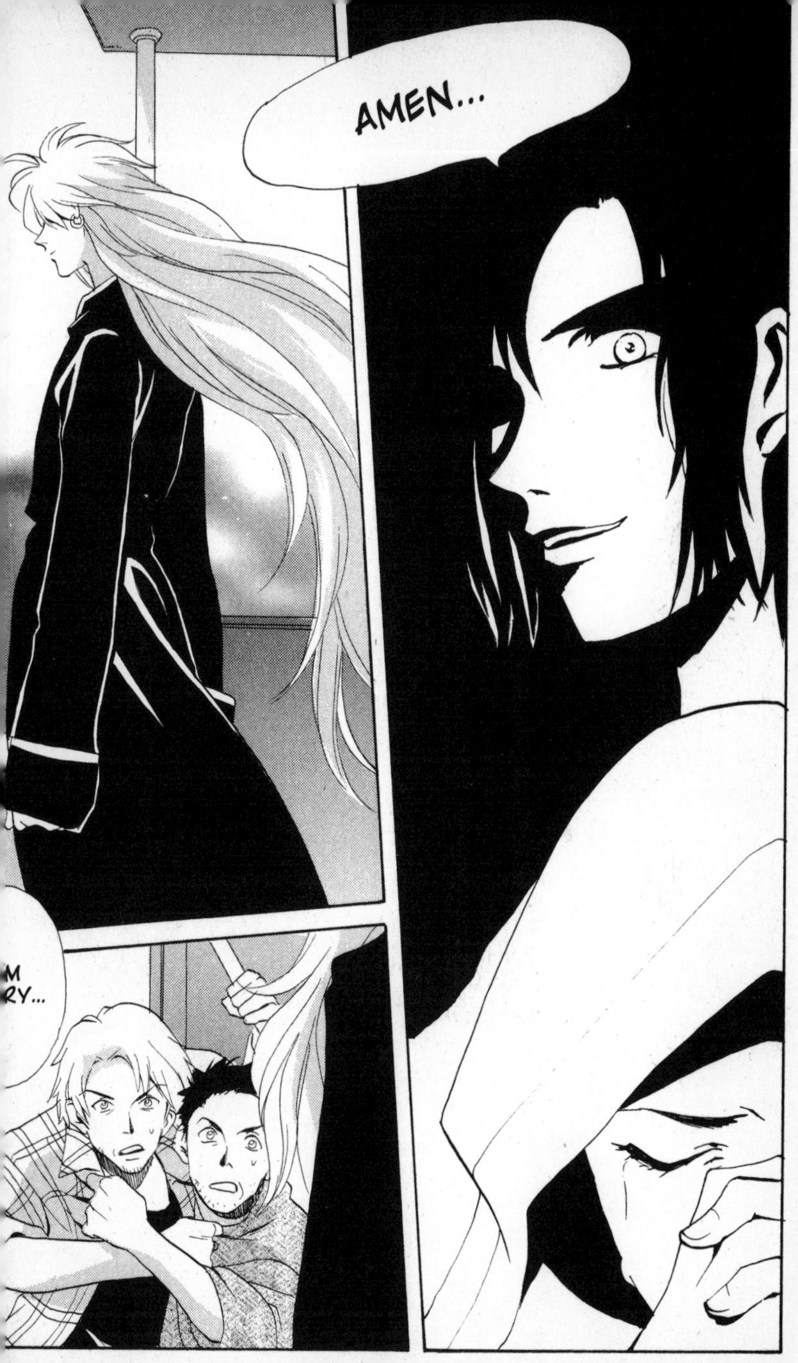
AMEN...

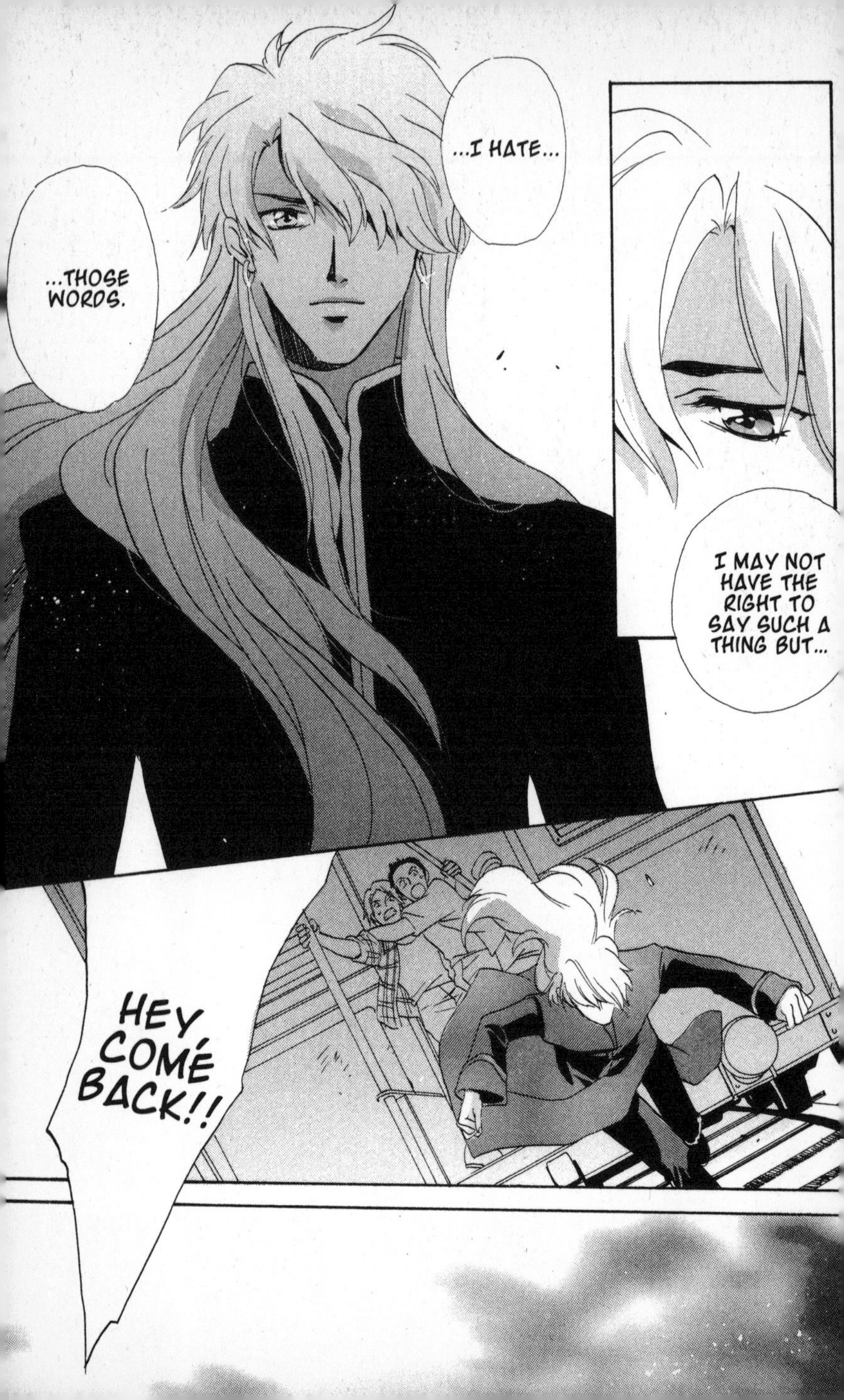
I MAY NOT HAVE THE RIGHT TO SAY SUCH A THING BUT...
...I HATE...
...THOSE WORDS.
HEY COMÉ BACK!!

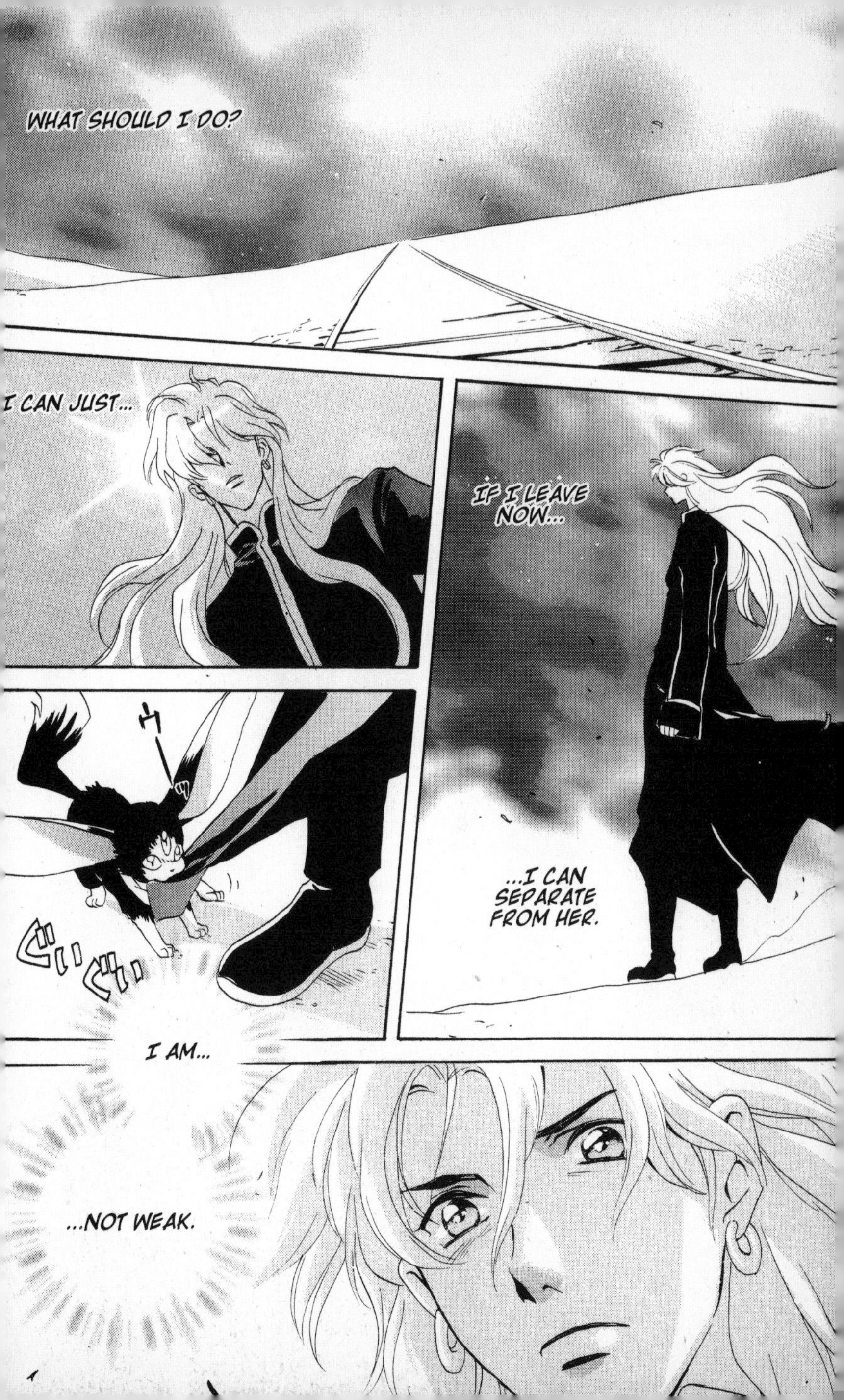
WHAT SHOULD I DO?
IF I LEAVE NOW...
...I CAN SEPARATE FROM HER.
I CAN JUST...
I AM...
...NOT WEAK.

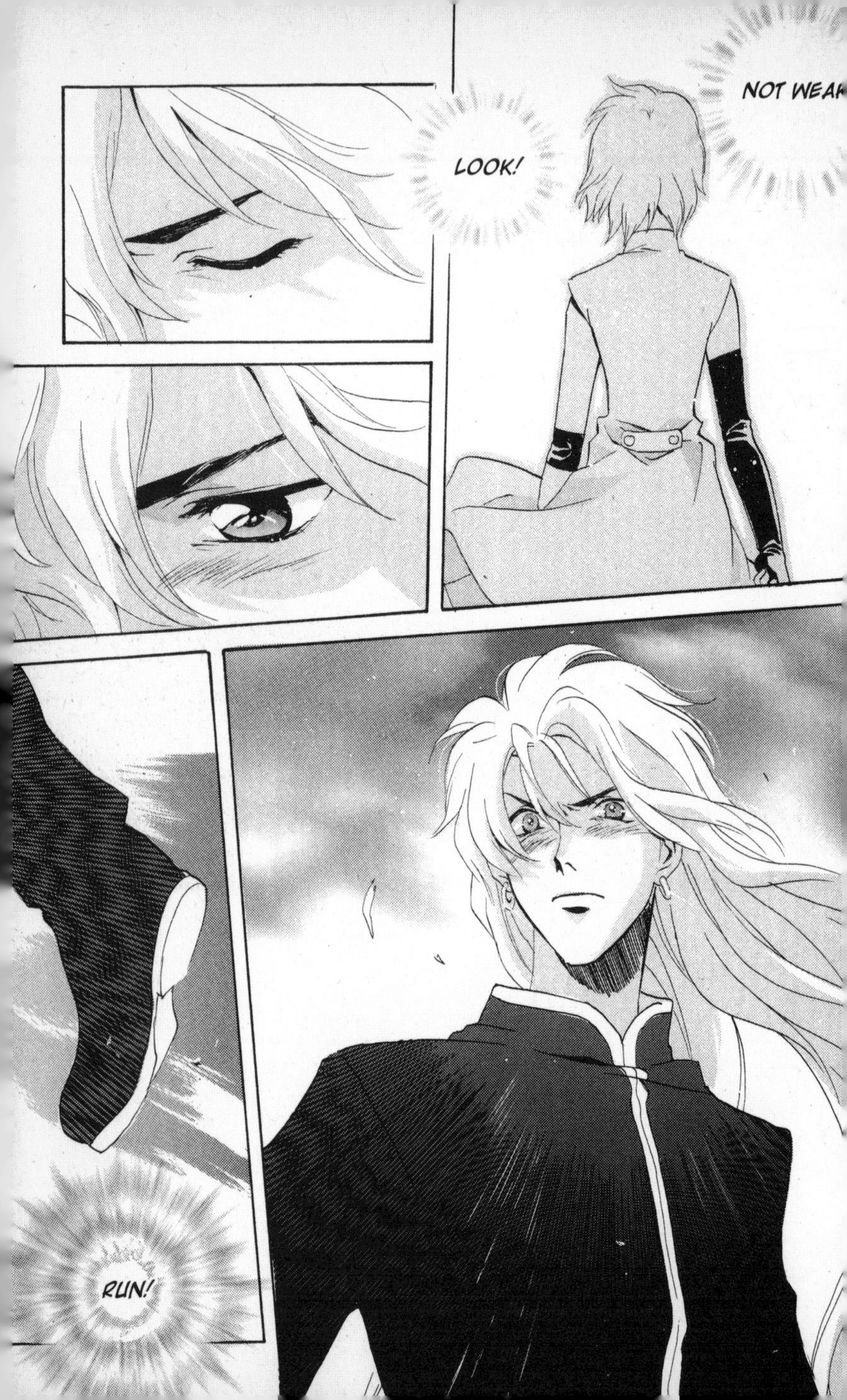
NOT WEA
LOOK!
RUN!

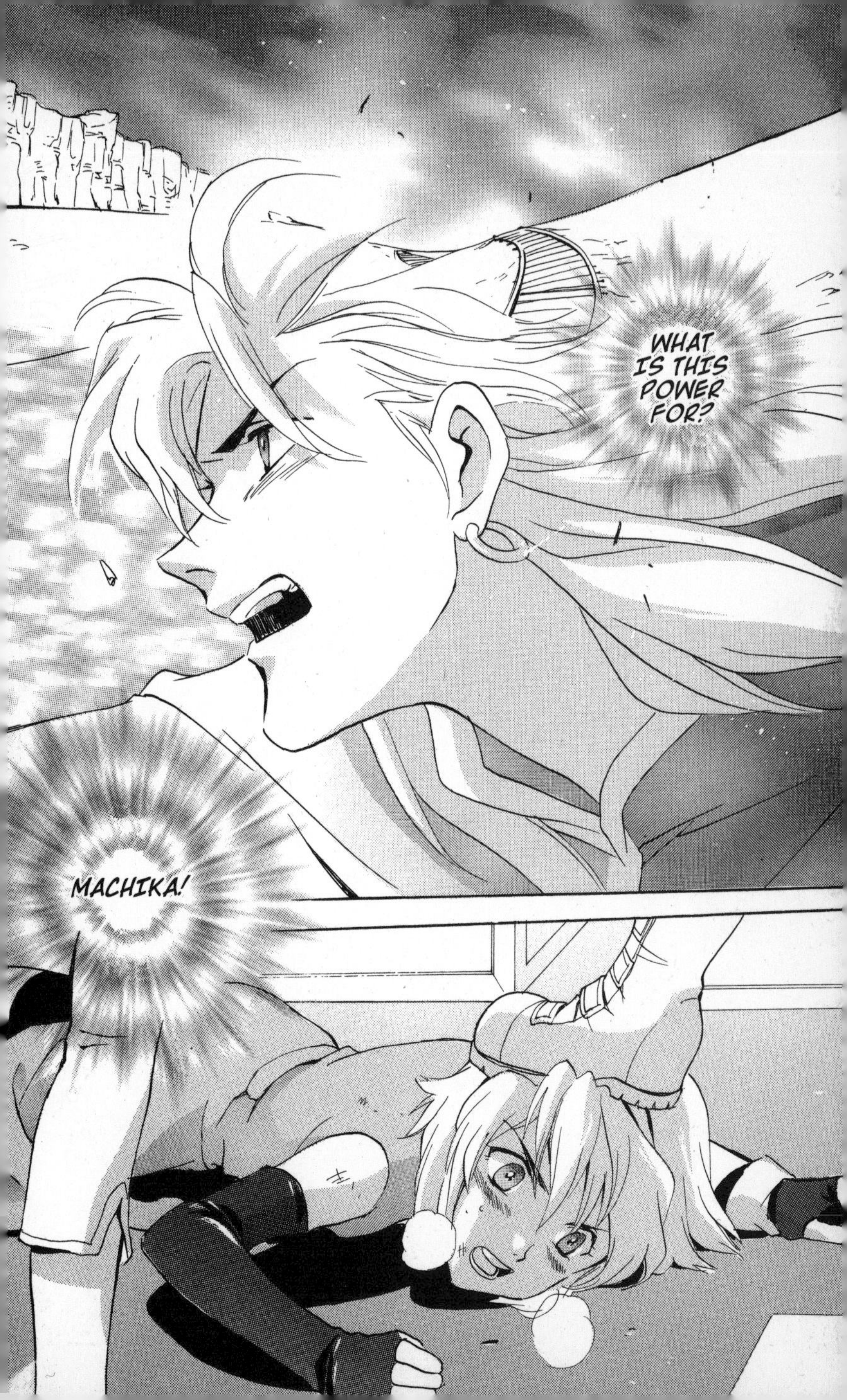
WHAT IS THIS POWER FOR?
MACHIKA!

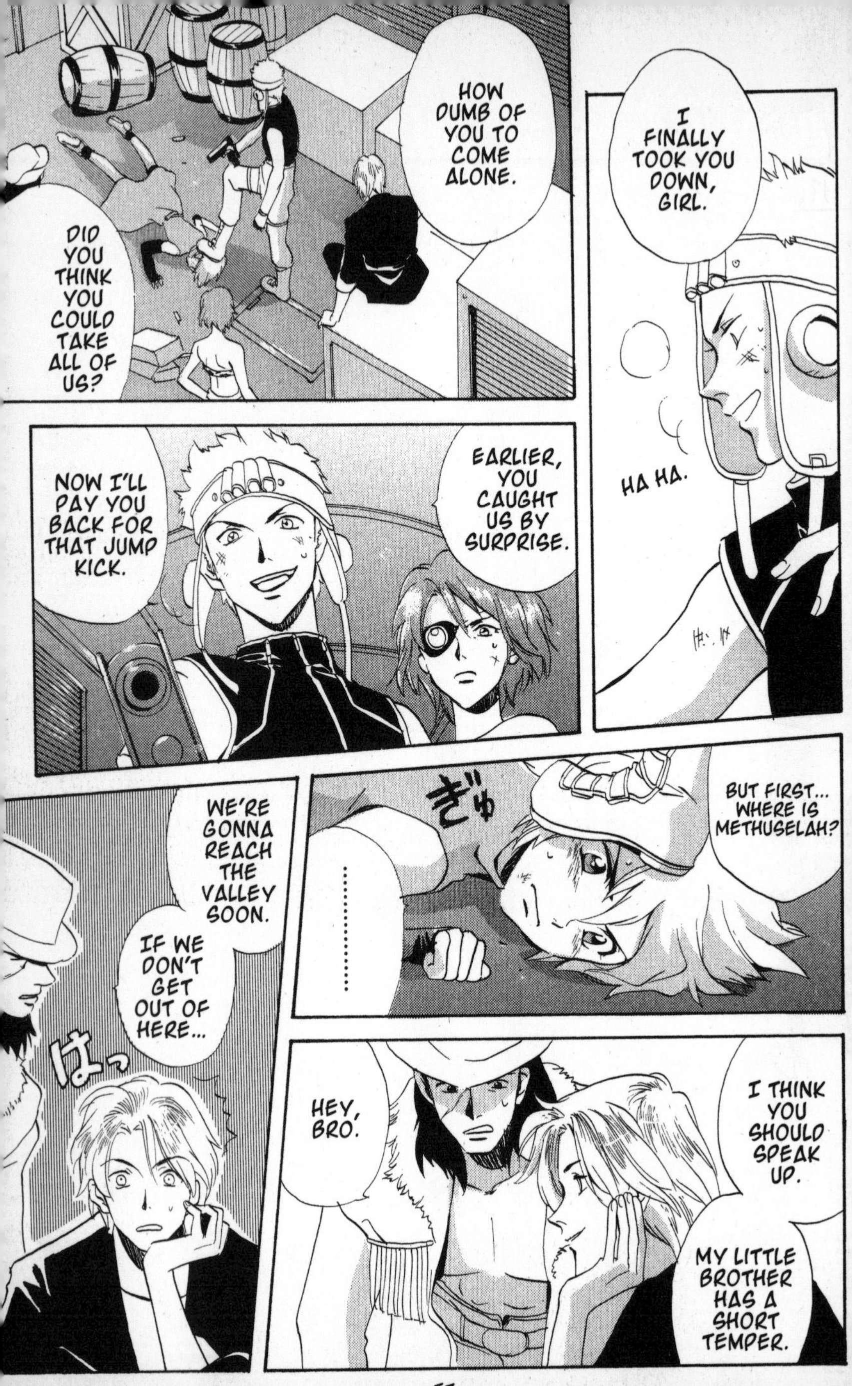
I FINALLY TOOK YOU DOWN, GIRL.
HA HA.
HOW DUMB OF YOU TO COME ALONE.
DID YOU THINK YOU COULD TAKE ALL OF US?
EARLIER, YOU CAUGHT US BY SURPRISE.
NOW I'LL PAY YOU BACK FOR THAT JUMP KICK.
BUT FIRST... WHERE IS METHUSELAH?
ぎゅ
....
I THINK YOU SHOULD SPEAK UP.
MY LITTLE BROTHER HAS A SHORT TEMPER.
HEY, BRO.
WE'RE GONNA REACH THE VALLEY SOON.
IF WE DON'T GET OUT OF HERE...
はっ

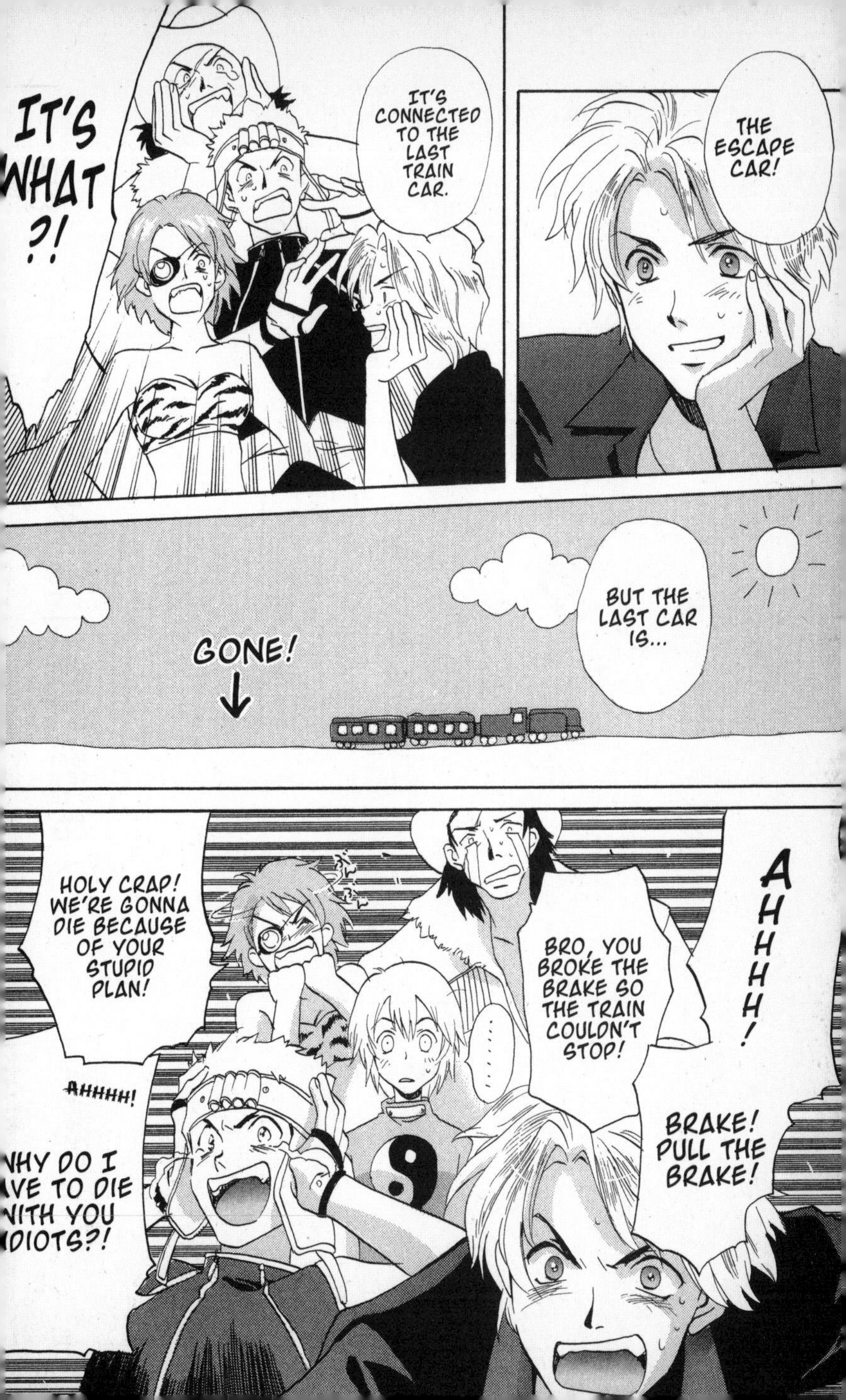

THE ESCAPE CAR!
IT'S CONNECTED TO THE LAST TRAIN CAR.
IT'S WHAT?!
BUT THE LAST CAR IS...
GONE!
AHHHH!
BRAKE! PULL THE BRAKE!
BRO, YOU BROKE THE BRAKE SO THE TRAIN COULDN'T STOP!
...
HOLY CRAP! WE'RE GONNA DIE BECAUSE OF YOUR STUPID PLAN!
AHHHH!
WHY DO I AVE TO DIE WITH YOU DIOTS?!

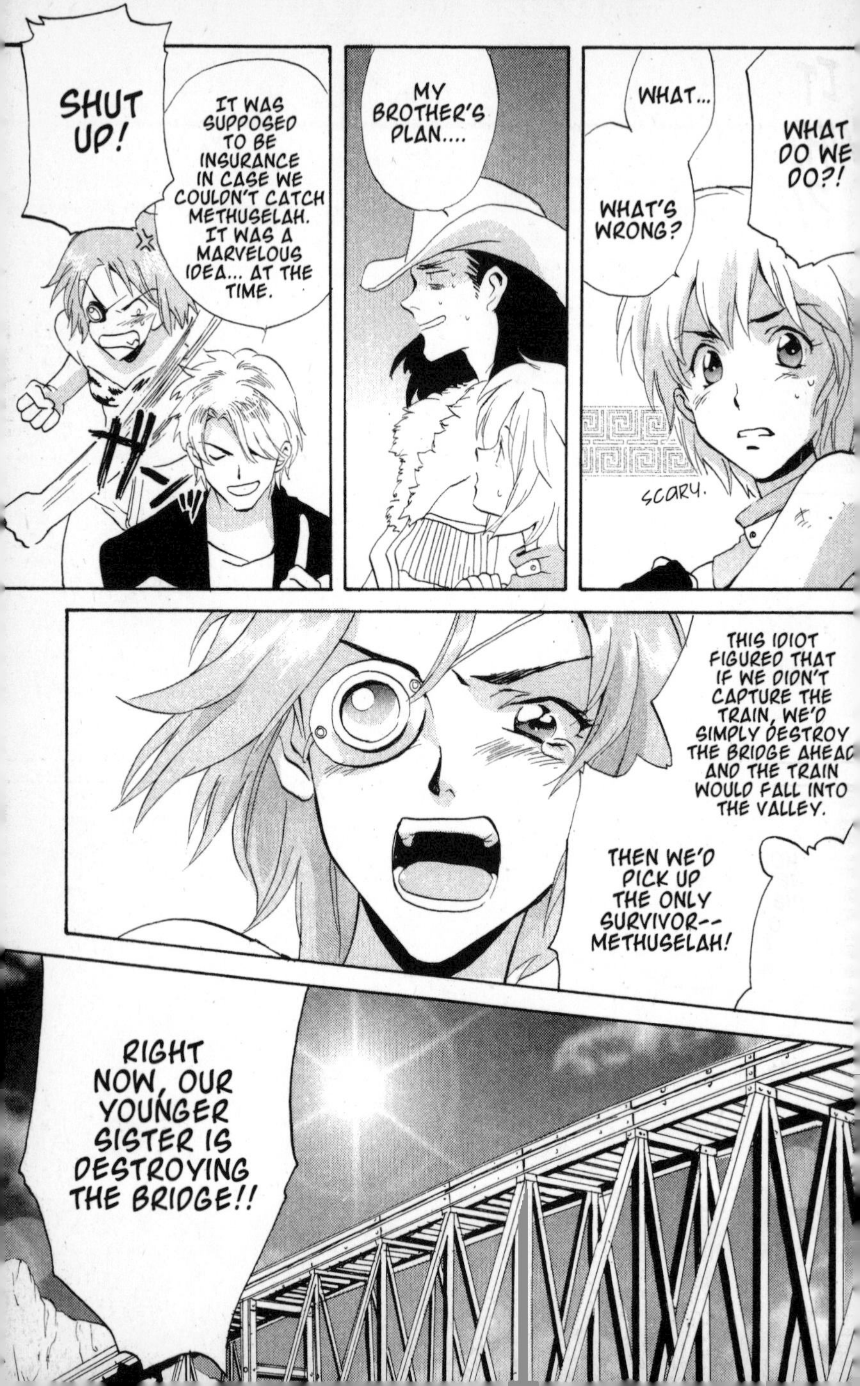
WHAT DO WE DO?!
WHAT... WHAT'S WRONG?
SCARY.
MY BROTHER'S PLAN....
IT WAS SUPPOSED TO BE INSURANCE IN CASE WE COULDN'T CATCH METHUSELAH. IT WAS A MARVELOUS IDEA... AT THE TIME.
SHUT UP!
THIS IDIOT FIGURED THAT IF WE DIDN'T CAPTURE THE TRAIN, WE'D SIMPLY DESTROY THE BRIDGE AHEAD AND THE TRAIN WOULD FALL INTO THE VALLEY.
THEN WE'D PICK UP THE ONLY SURVIVOR--METHUSELAH!
RIGHT NOW, OUR YOUNGER SISTER IS DESTROYING THE BRIDGE!!

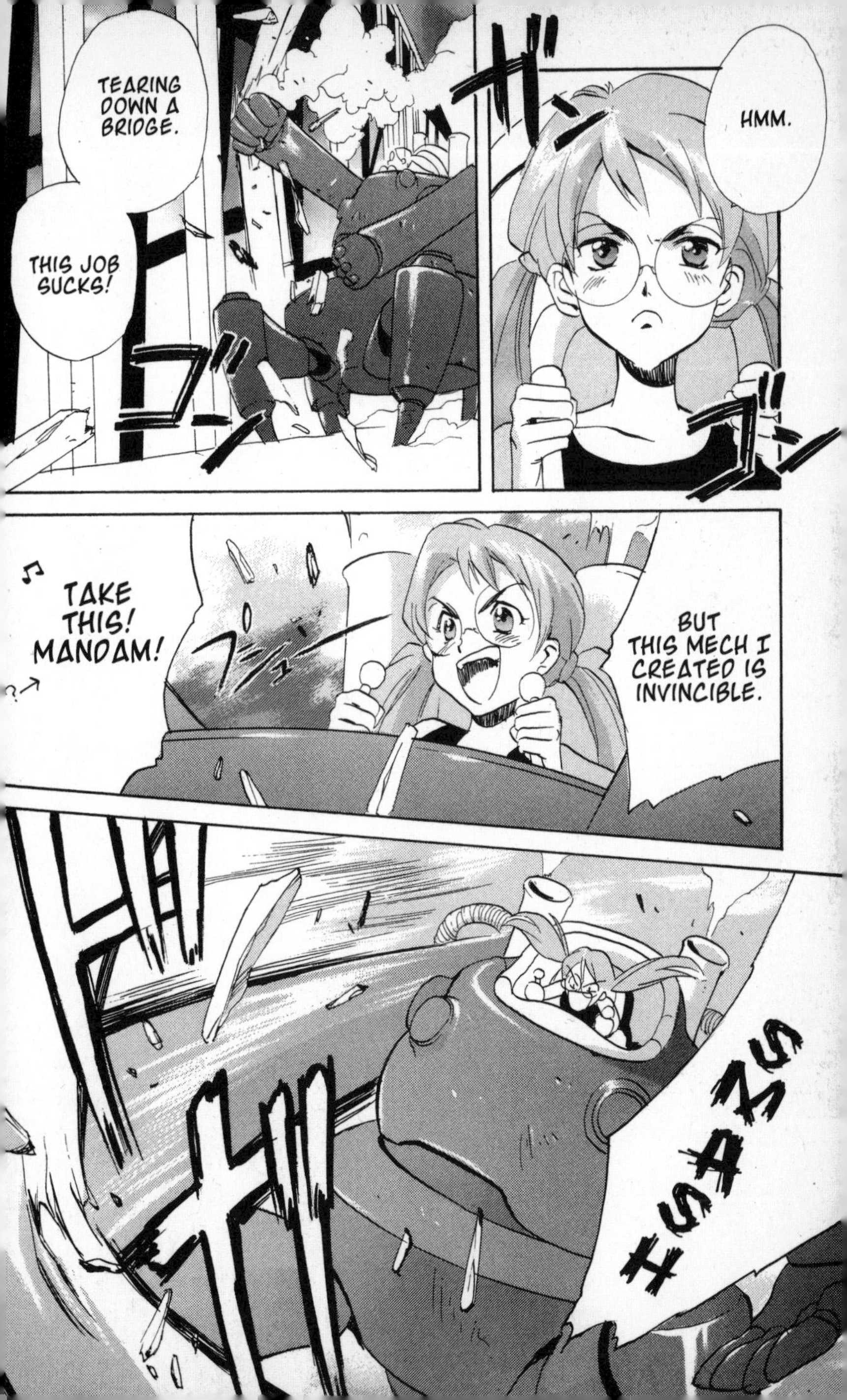
HMM.
TEARING DOWN A BRIDGE.
THIS JOB SUCKS!
BUT THIS MECH I CREATED IS INVINCIBLE.
TAKE THIS! MANDAM!

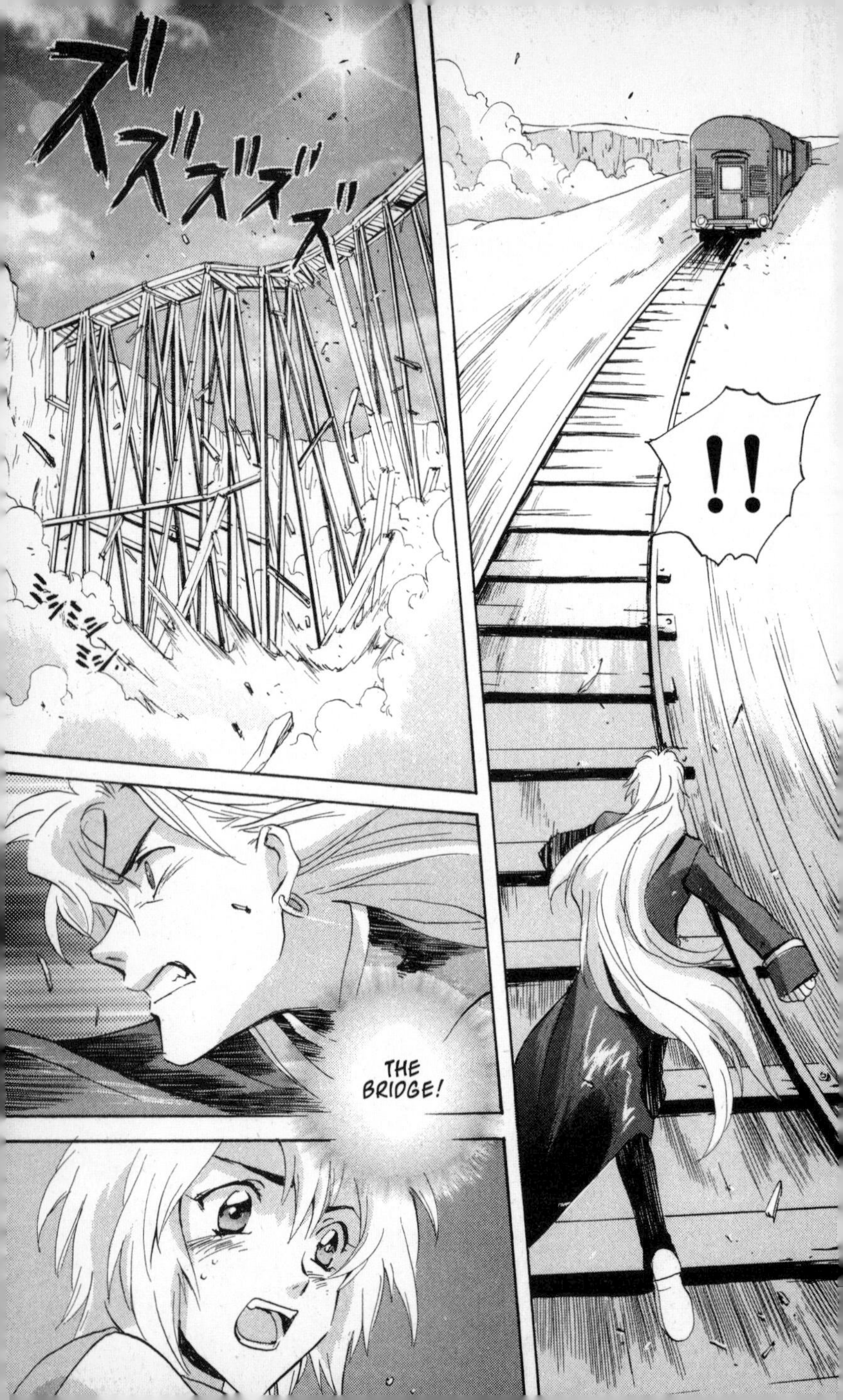
!!
ズズズズズズ
ミシミシ ミシ…
THE BRIDGE!

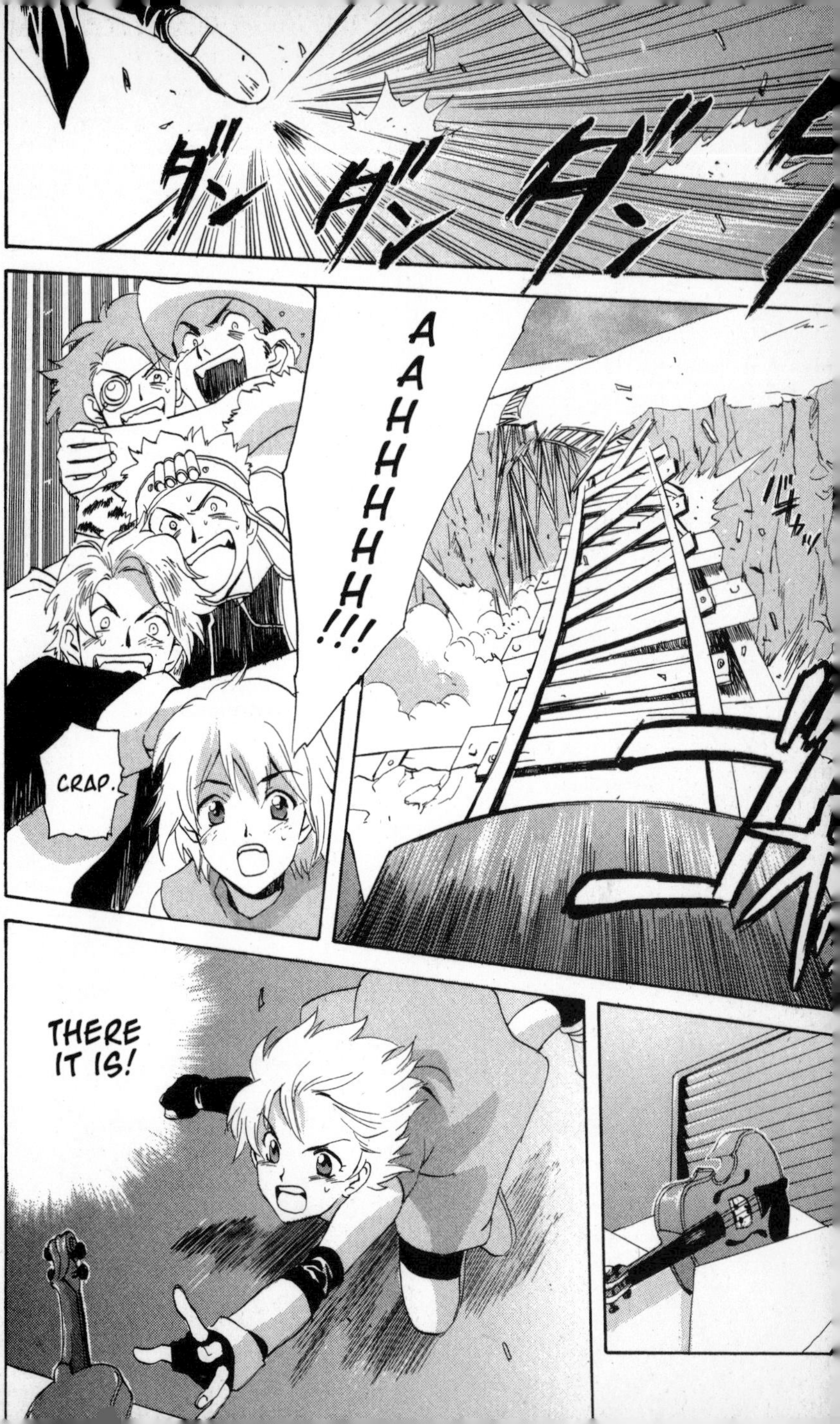
ダン ダン ダン
AAHHHHHHH!!!
CRAP.
THERE IT IS!

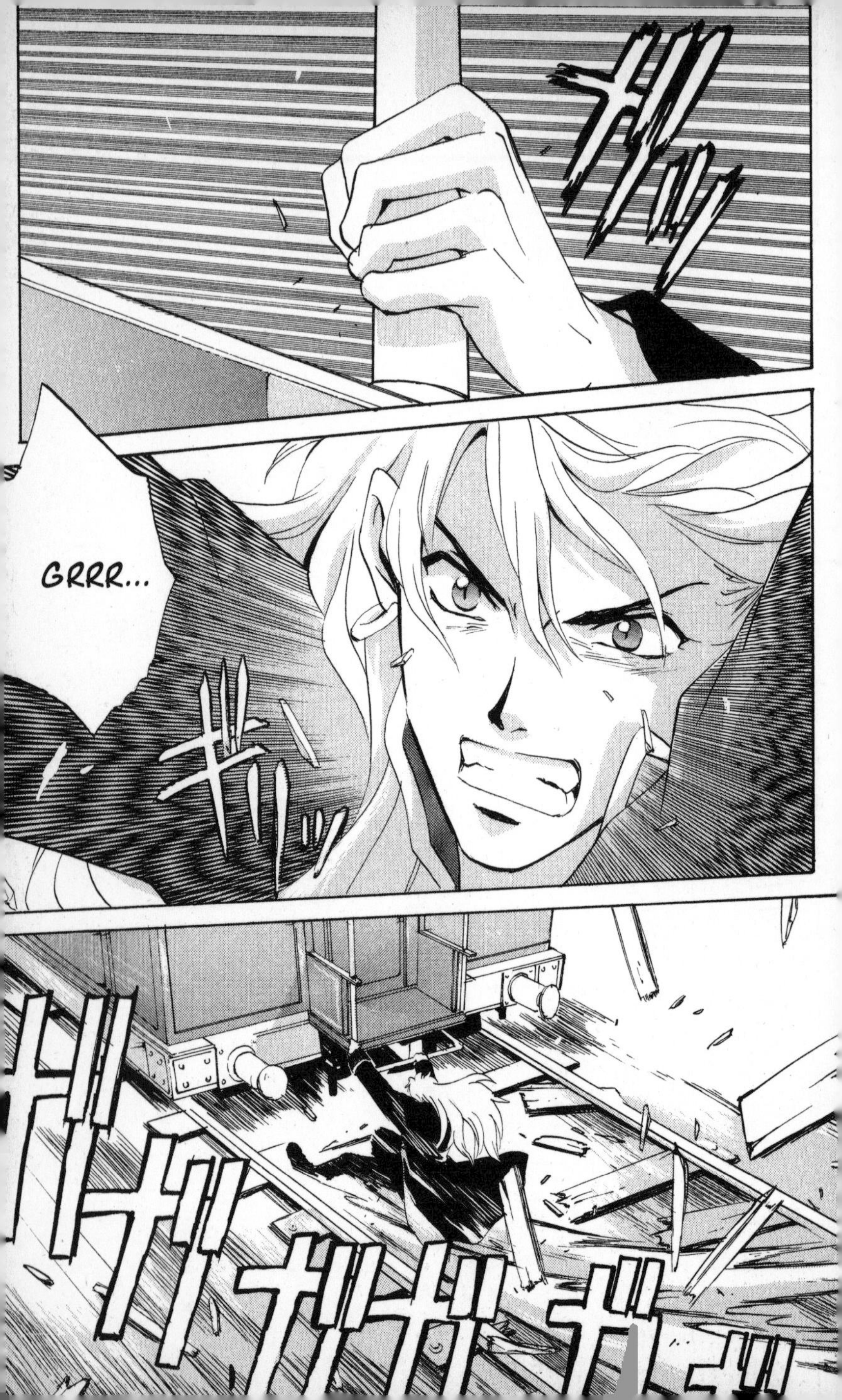
GRRR...

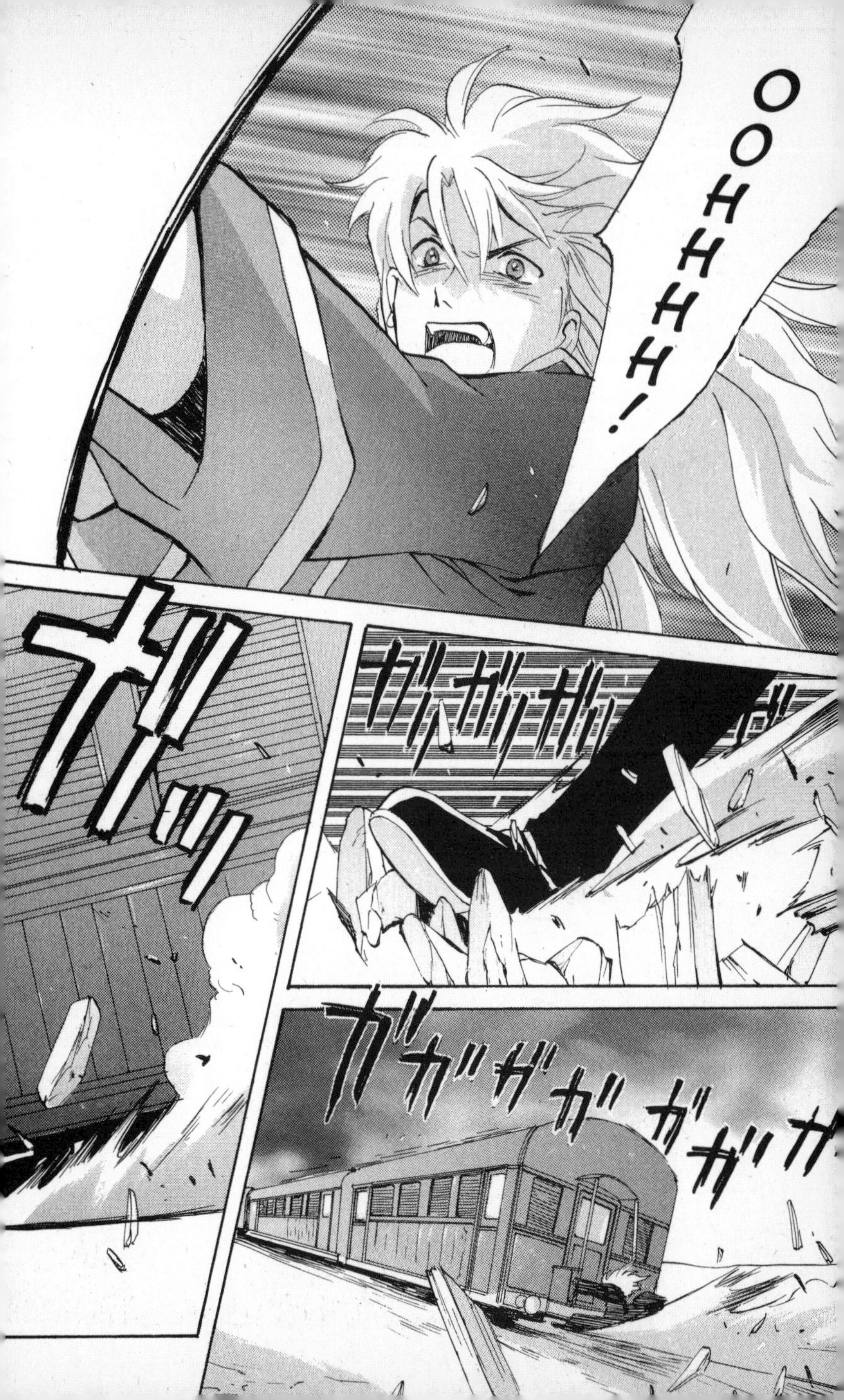
OOHHHHH!
ガリガリガリ
ガガガガガガ
ザッ

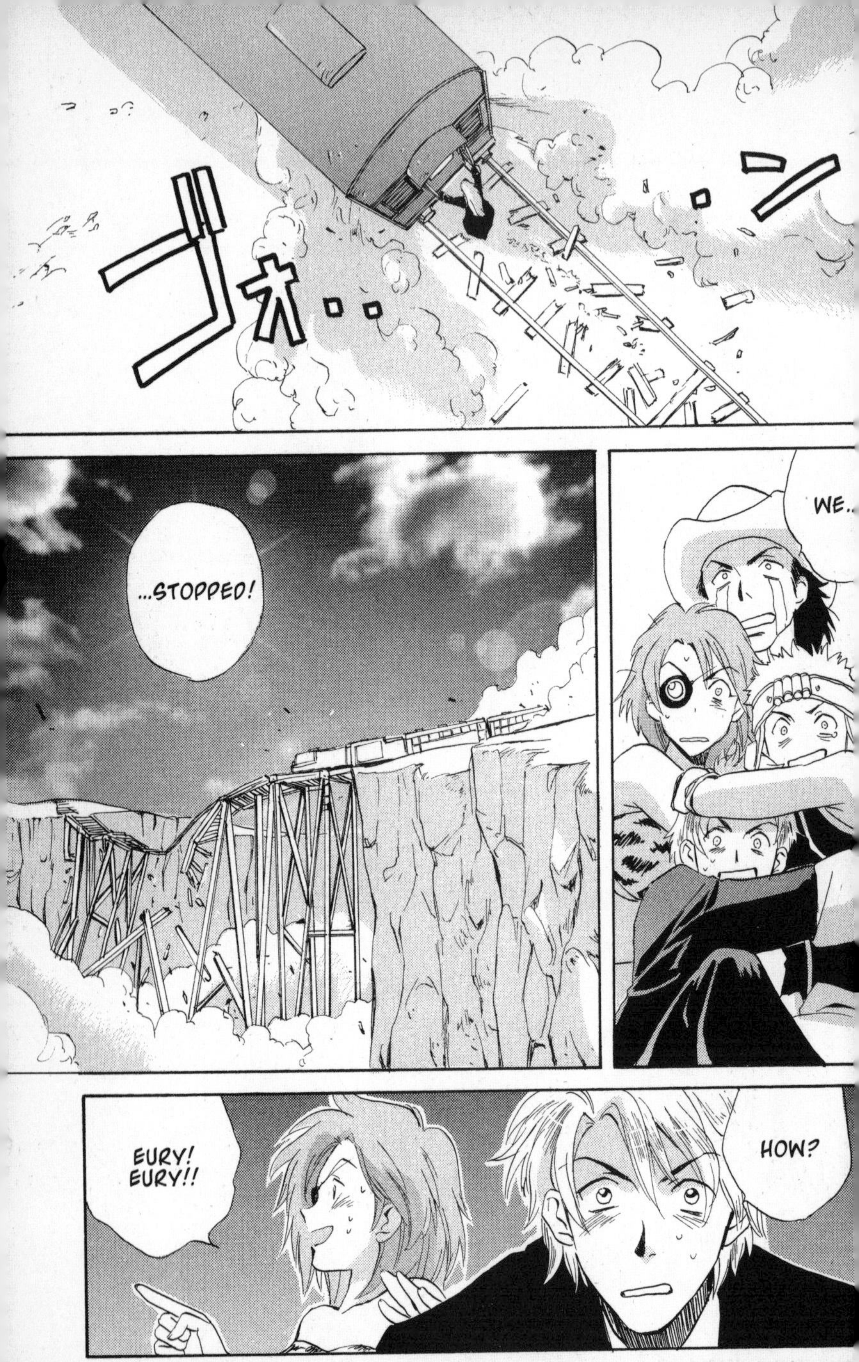
ゴォ・・・ン
WE...
...STOPPED!
HOW?
EURY!
EURY!!

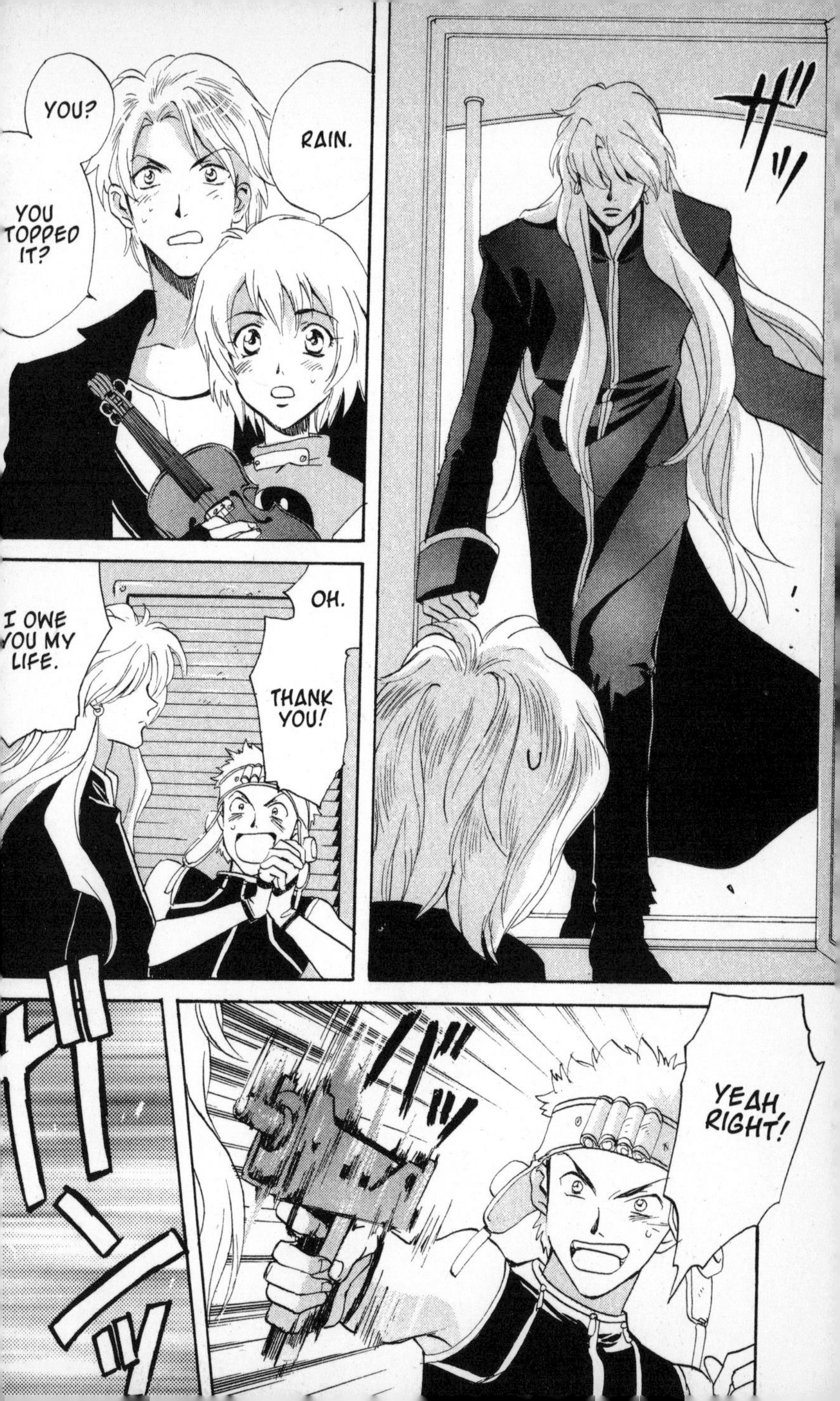
RAIN.
YOU?
YOU TOPPED IT?
OH.
THANK YOU!
I OWE YOU MY LIFE.
YEAH RIGHT!

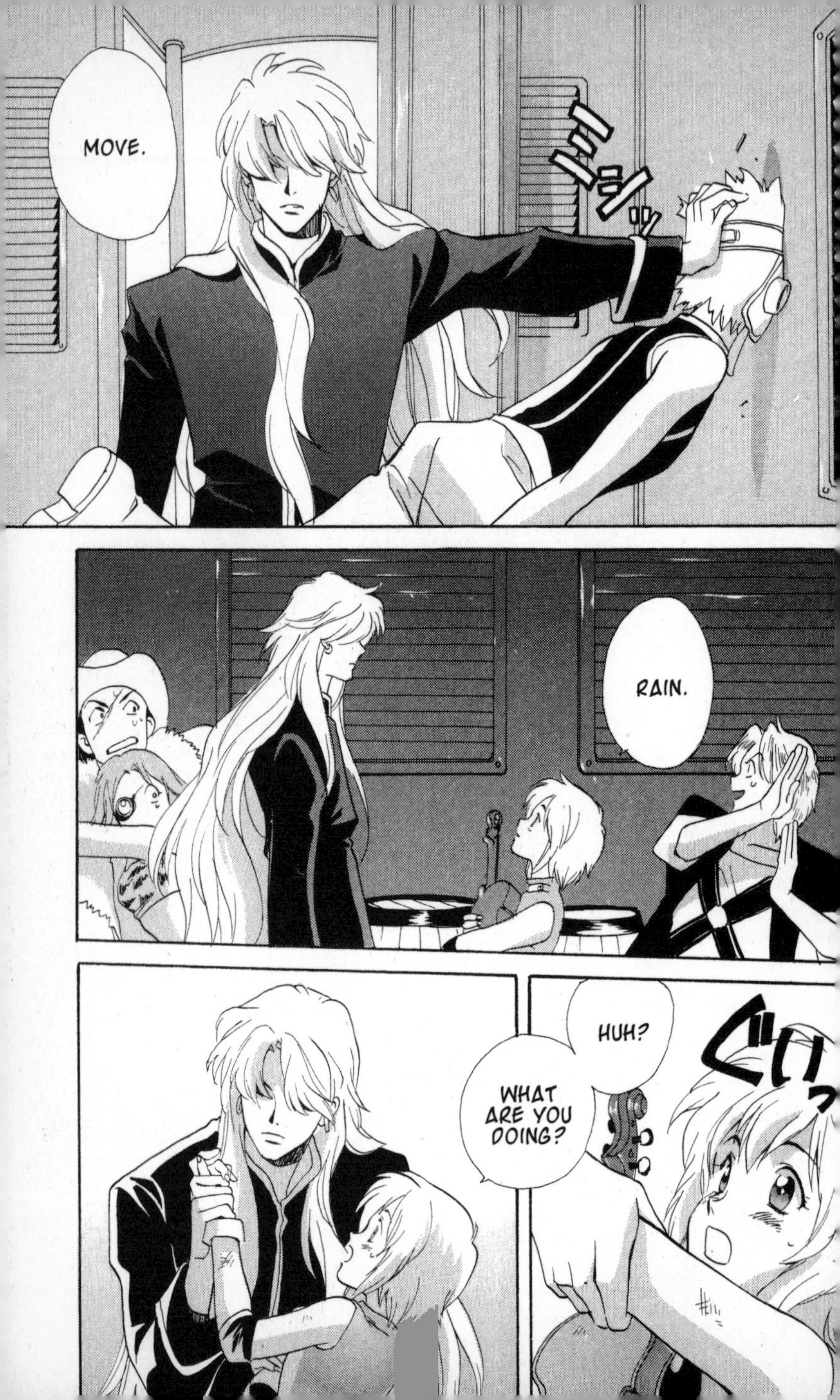
MOVE.
RAIN.
HUH?
WHAT ARE YOU DOING?

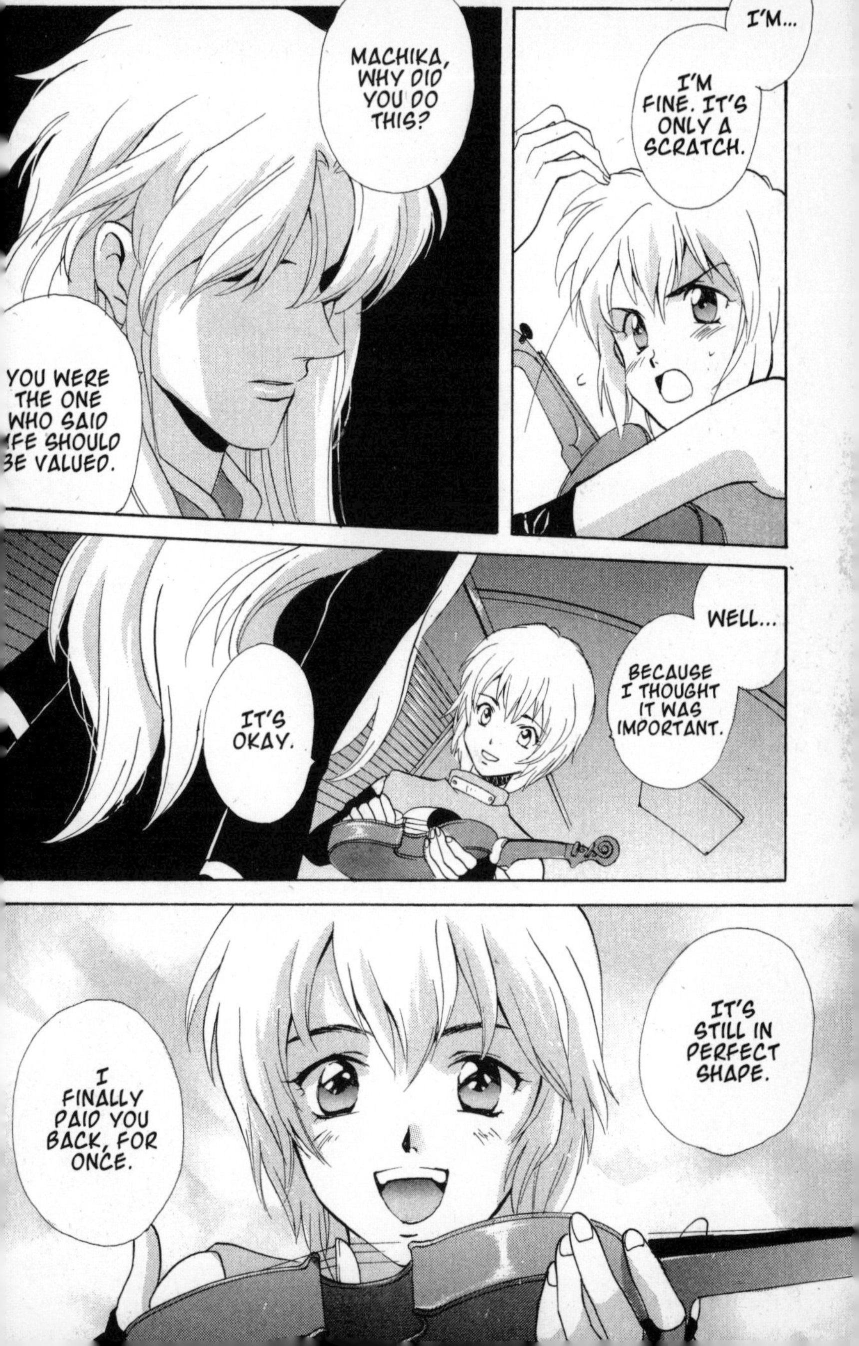
I'M...
I'M FINE. IT'S ONLY A SCRATCH.
MACHIKA, WHY DID YOU DO THIS?
YOU WERE THE ONE WHO SAID IFE SHOULD BE VALUED.
WELL...
BECAUSE I THOUGHT IT WAS IMPORTANT.
IT'S OKAY.
IT'S STILL IN PERFECT SHAPE.
I FINALLY PAID YOU BACK, FOR ONCE.

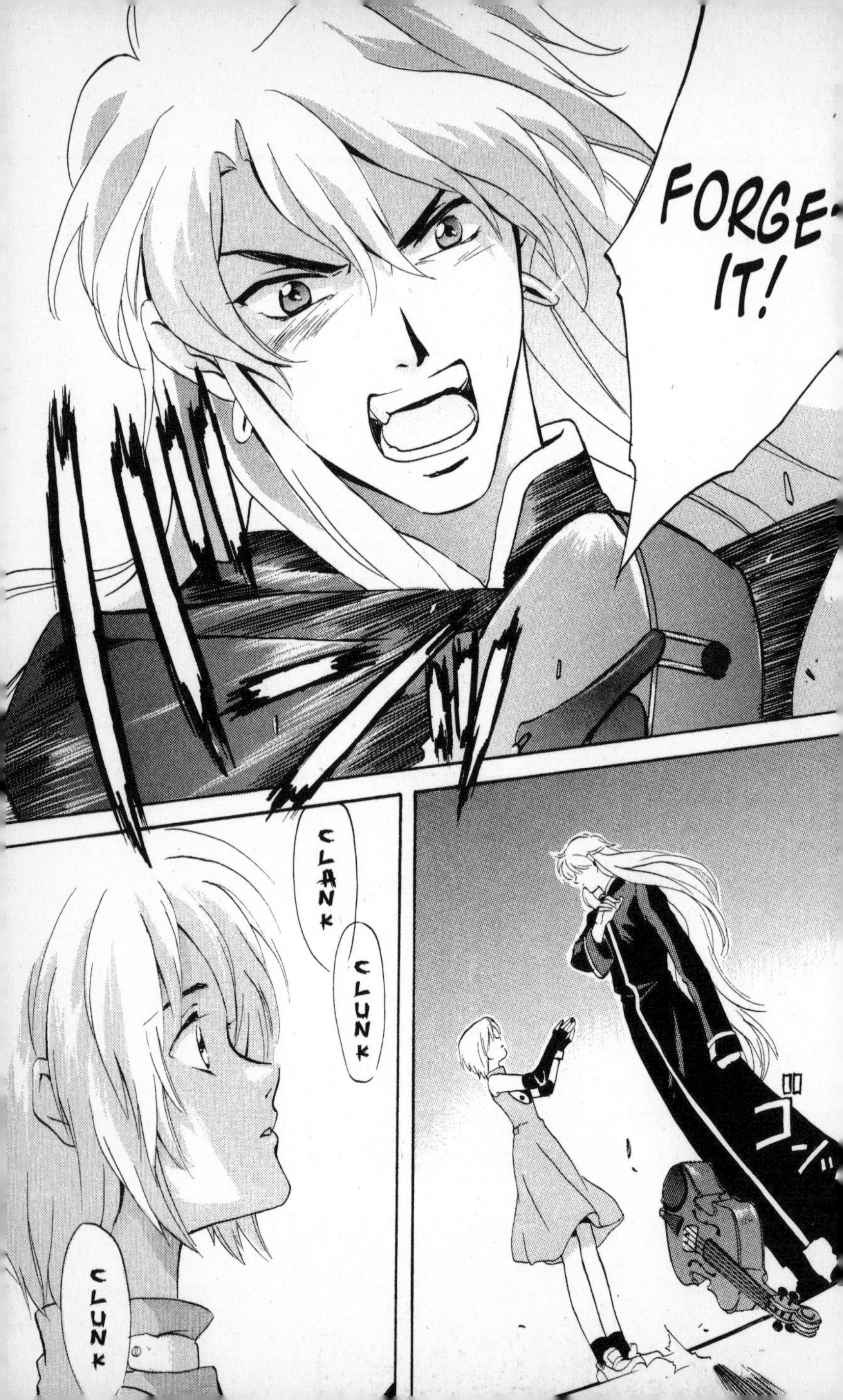
FORGE-IT!
CLANK
CLUNK
CLUNK

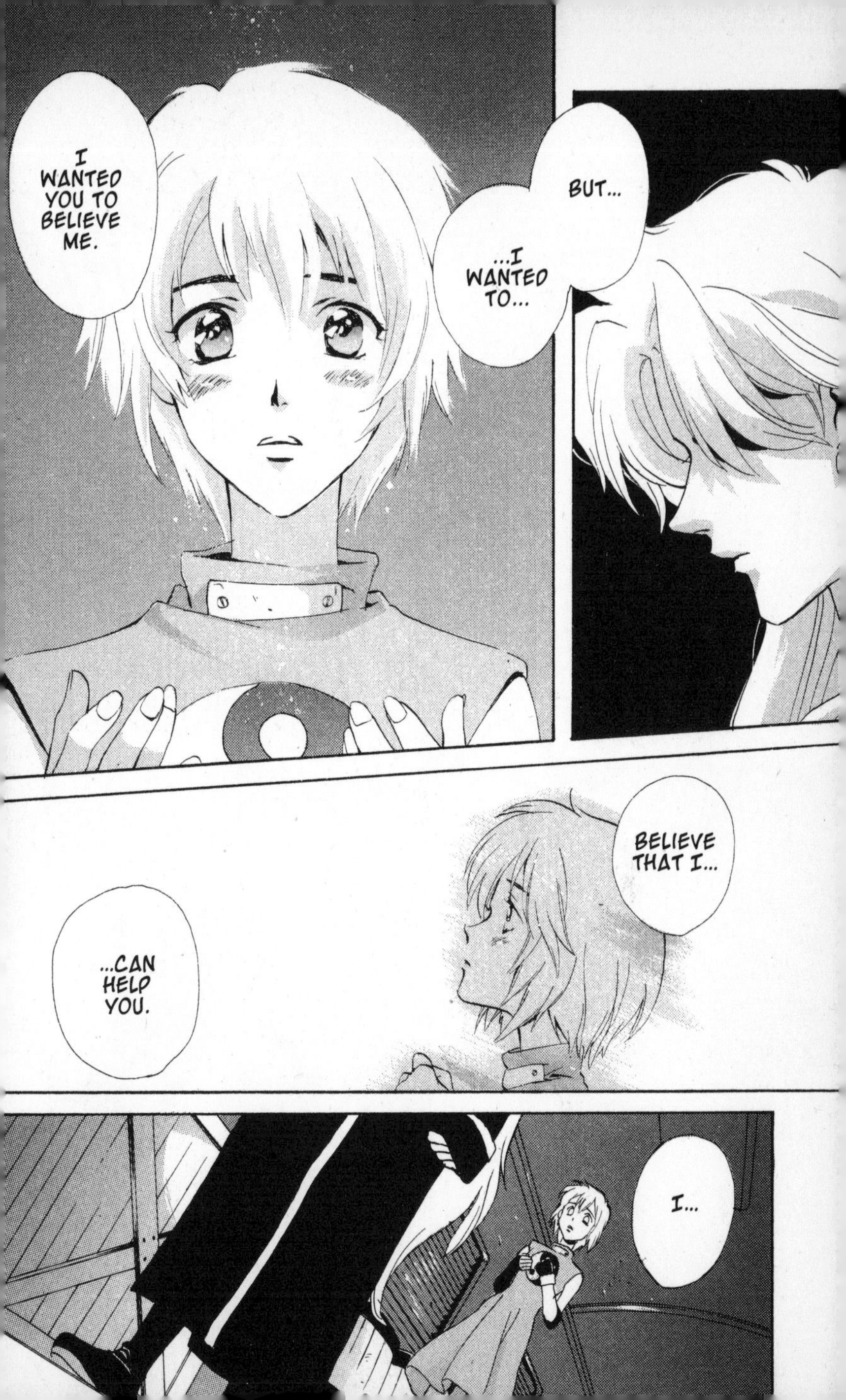
BUT...
...I WANTED TO...
I WANTED YOU TO BELIEVE ME.
BELIEVE THAT I...
...CAN HELP YOU.
I...

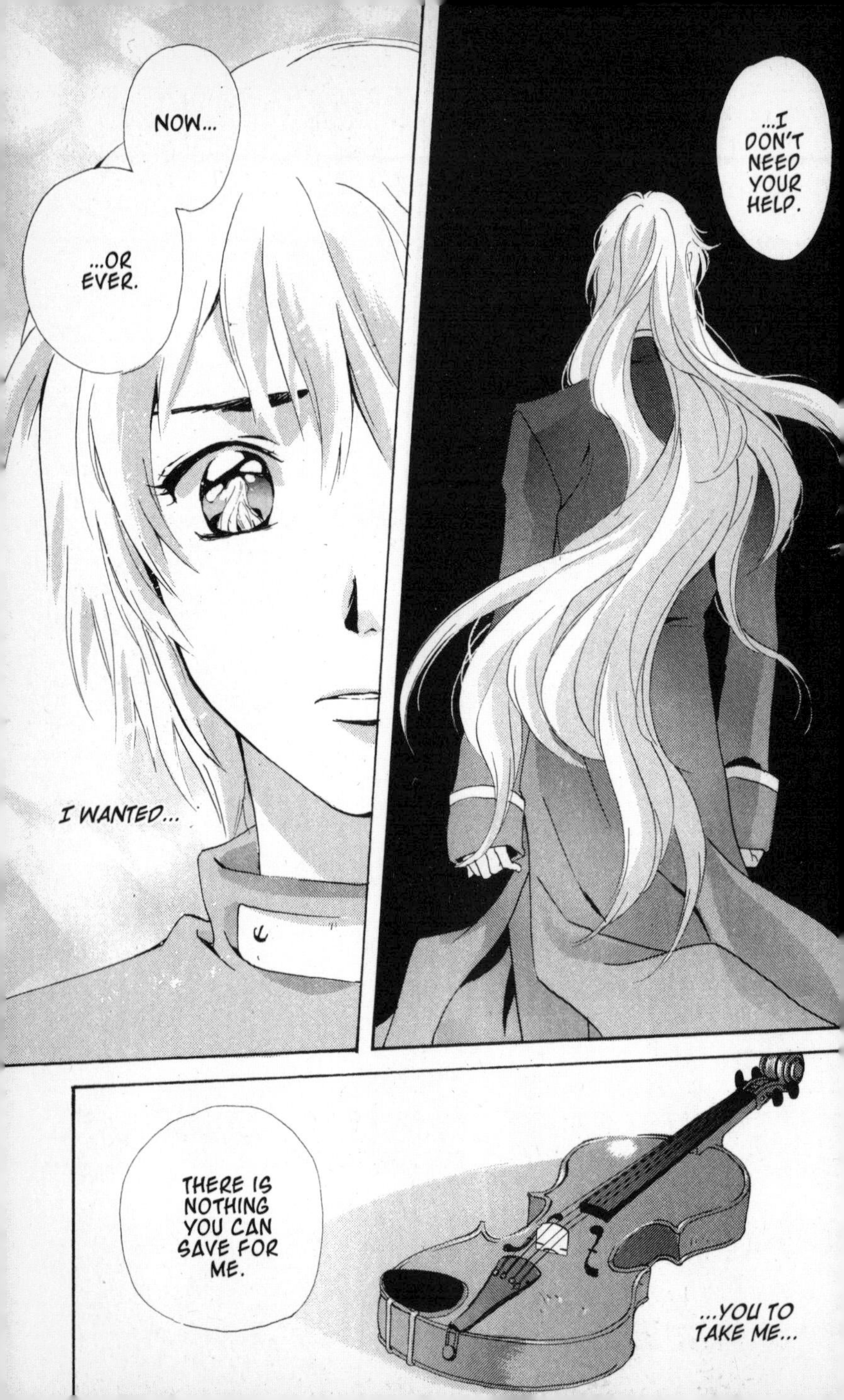
...I DON'T NEED YOUR HELP.
NOW...
...OR EVER.
I WANTED...
THERE IS NOTHING YOU CAN SAVE FOR ME.
...YOU TO TAKE ME...

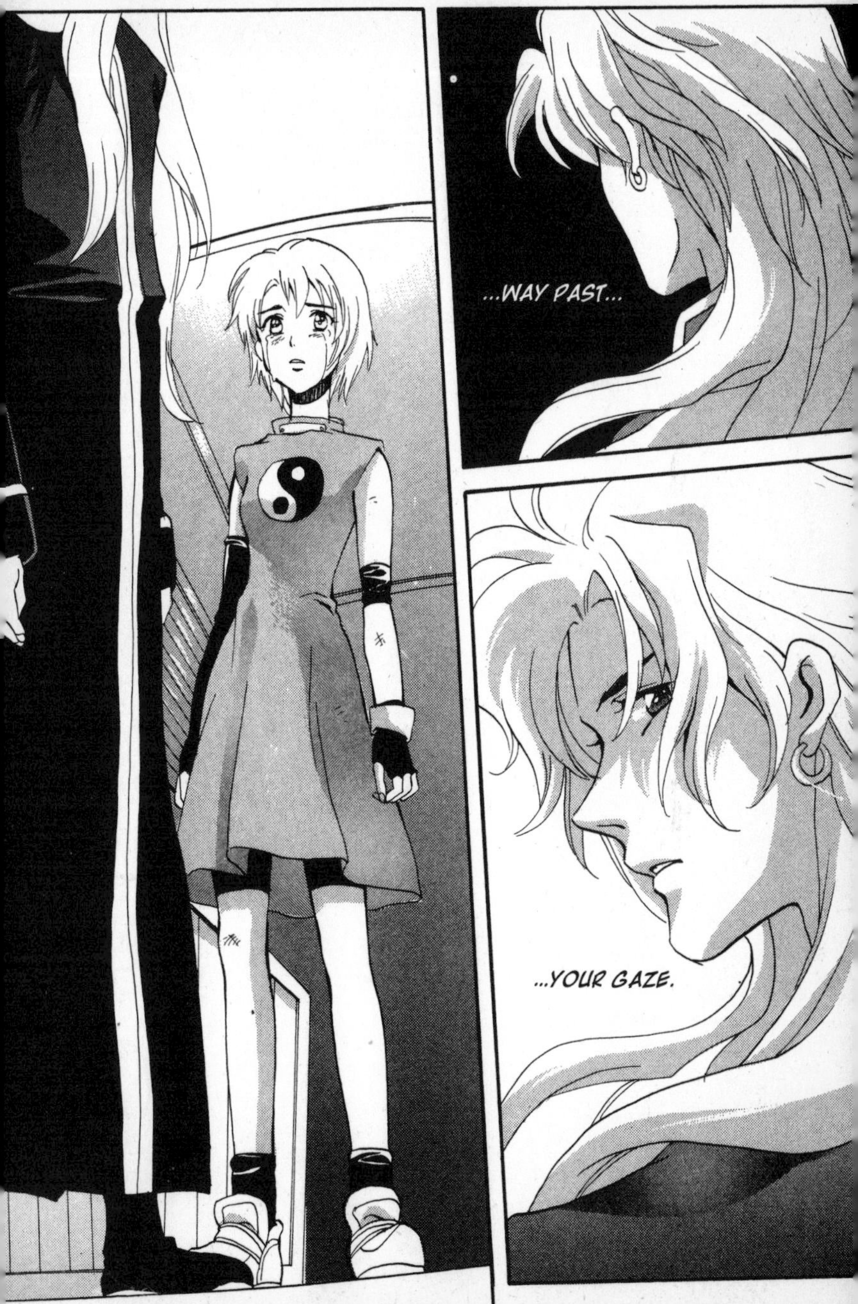
...WAY PAST...
...YOUR GAZE.

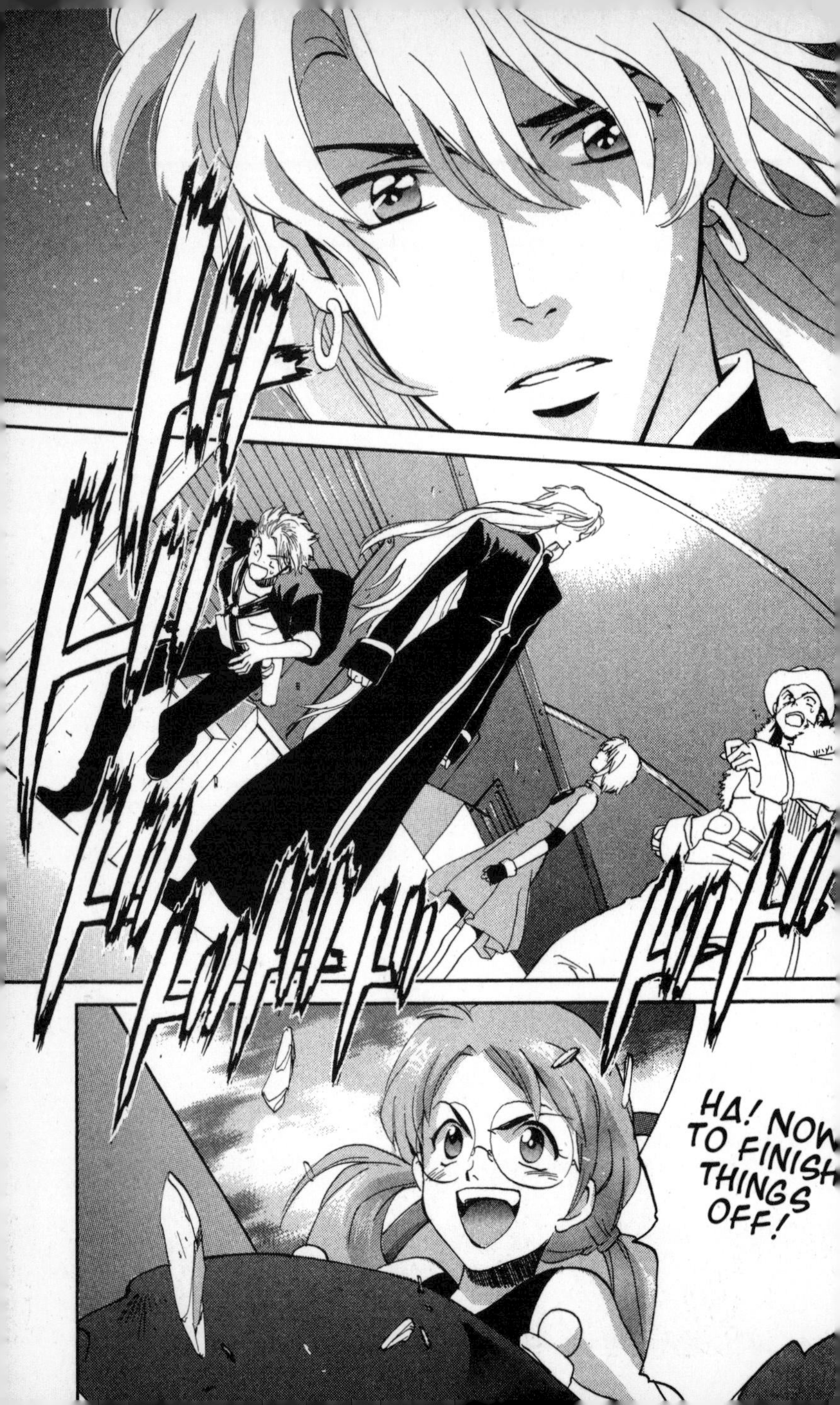
HA! NOW TO FINISH THINGS OFF!

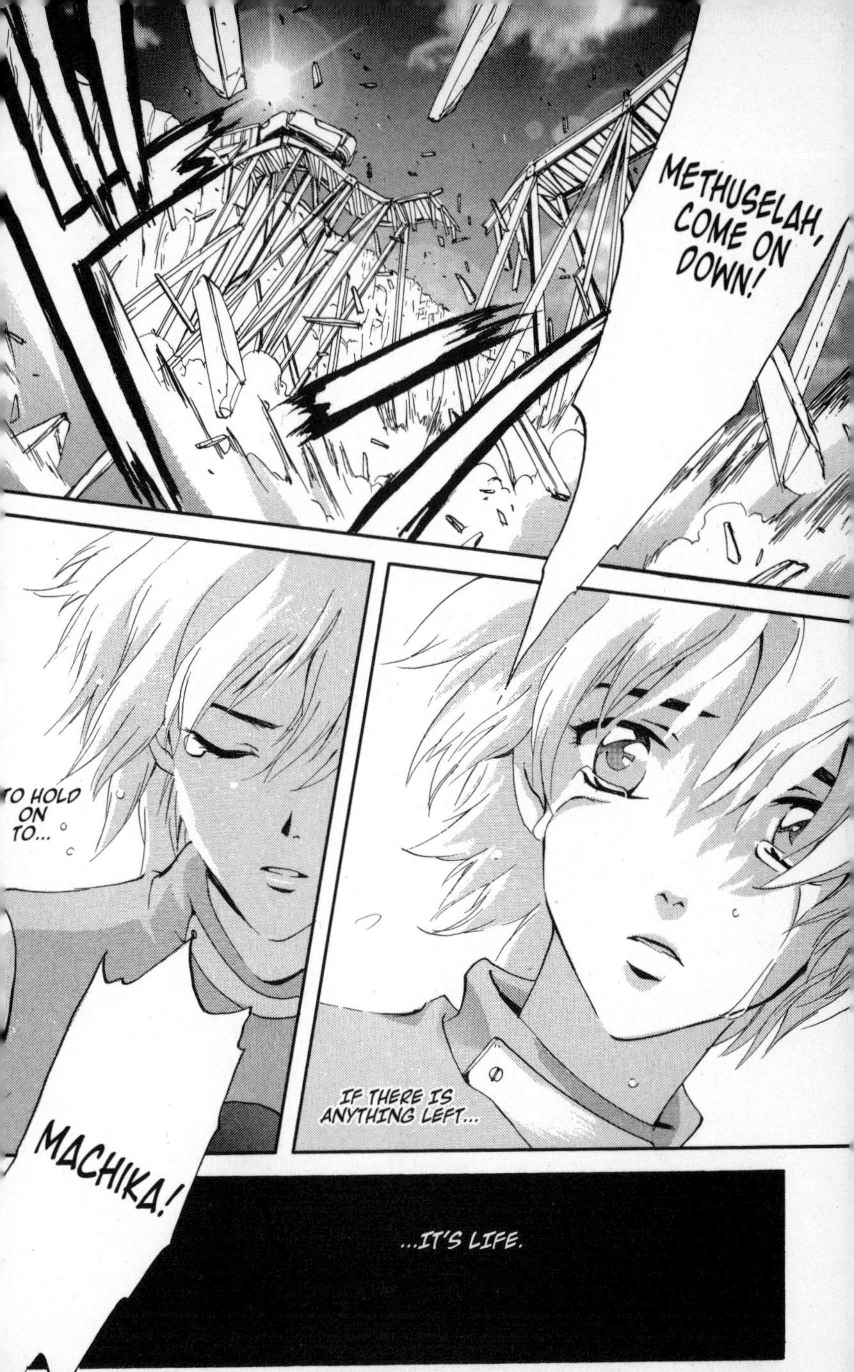
METHUSELAH, COME ON DOWN!
IF THERE IS ANYTHING LEFT...
TO HOLD ON TO...
...IT'S LIFE.
MACHIKA!

PEARL EVANS
Age:19
Height:168cm
Blood type:O

JETT EVANS
Age:17
Height:171cm
Blood type:A

THE SUCCESS OF THE SIBLINGS' ATTACK DEPENDS ON EURY'S "CLEVERNESS." HE NEEDS TO SEND LOTS OF MONEY TO RAISE MANDAM'S LEVEL.

RAY EVANS
Age:16
Height:203cm
Blood type:A

AMY EVANS
Age:12
Height:142cm
Blood type:AB

I HAVE NO NAME.
I HAVE NO FORM.
I HAVE NO HOME.

I WILL TAKE YOUR HAND WITH
THESE ETHEREAL FINGERS.

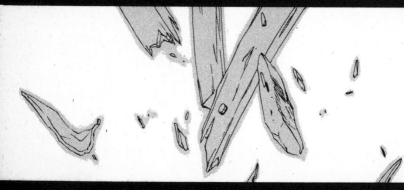

I WILL CALL YOU WITH THIS
SOUNDLESS VOICE.

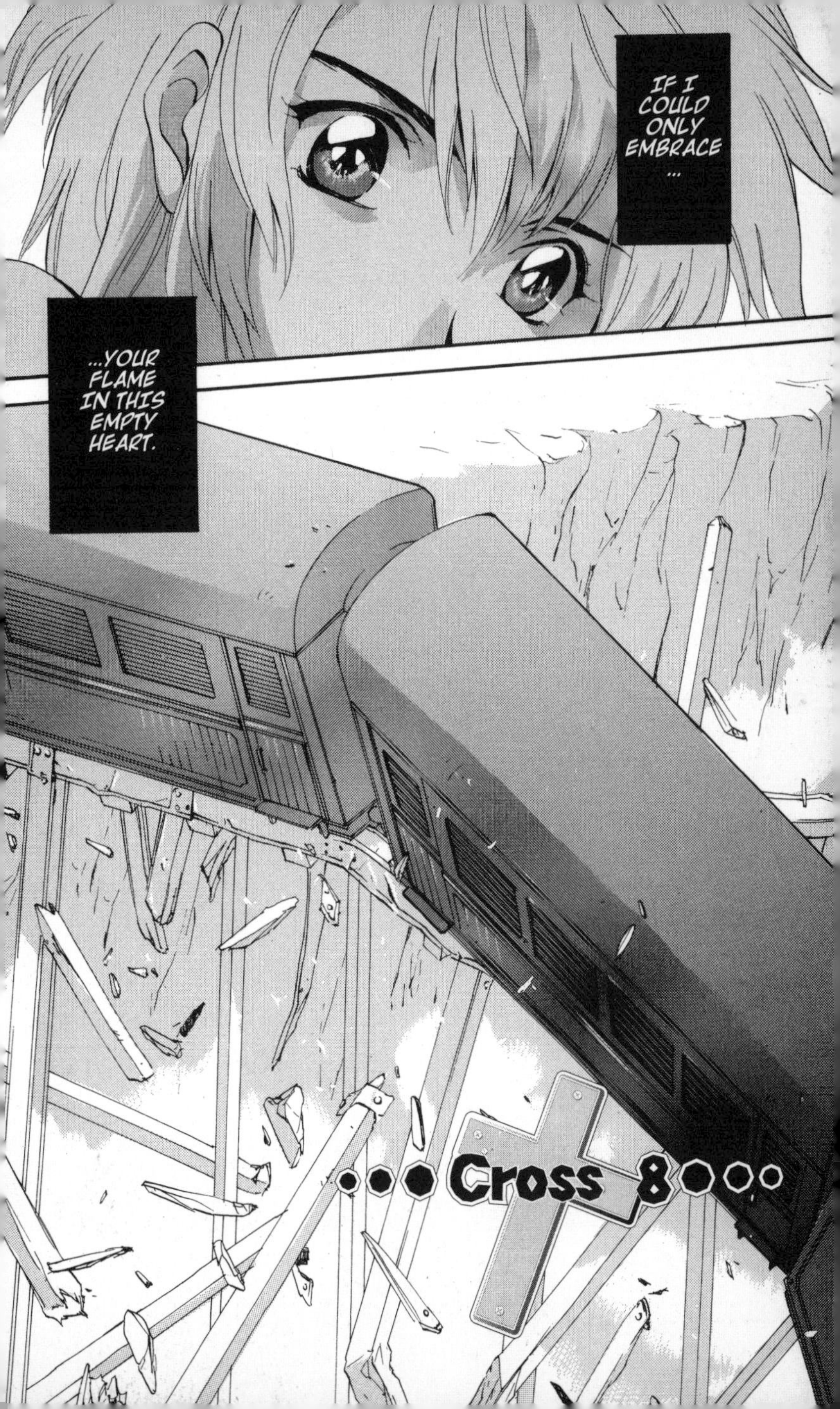
IF I COULD ONLY EMBRACE ...
...YOUR FLAME IN THIS EMPTY HEART.
Cross 8

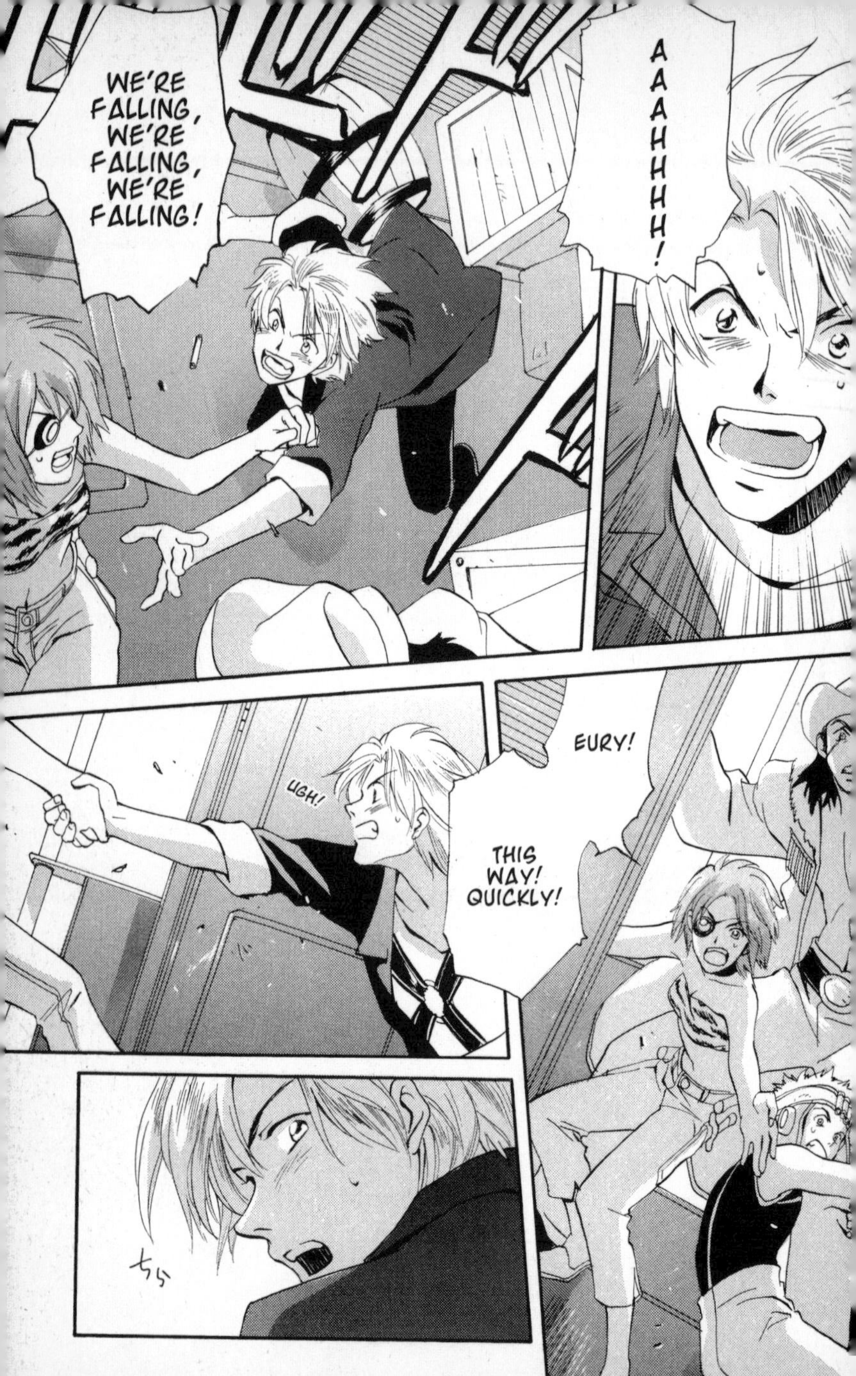
AAAAHHHHH!
WE'RE FALLING, WE'RE FALLING, WE'RE FALLING!
EURY!
THIS WAY! QUICKLY!
UGH!
ちら

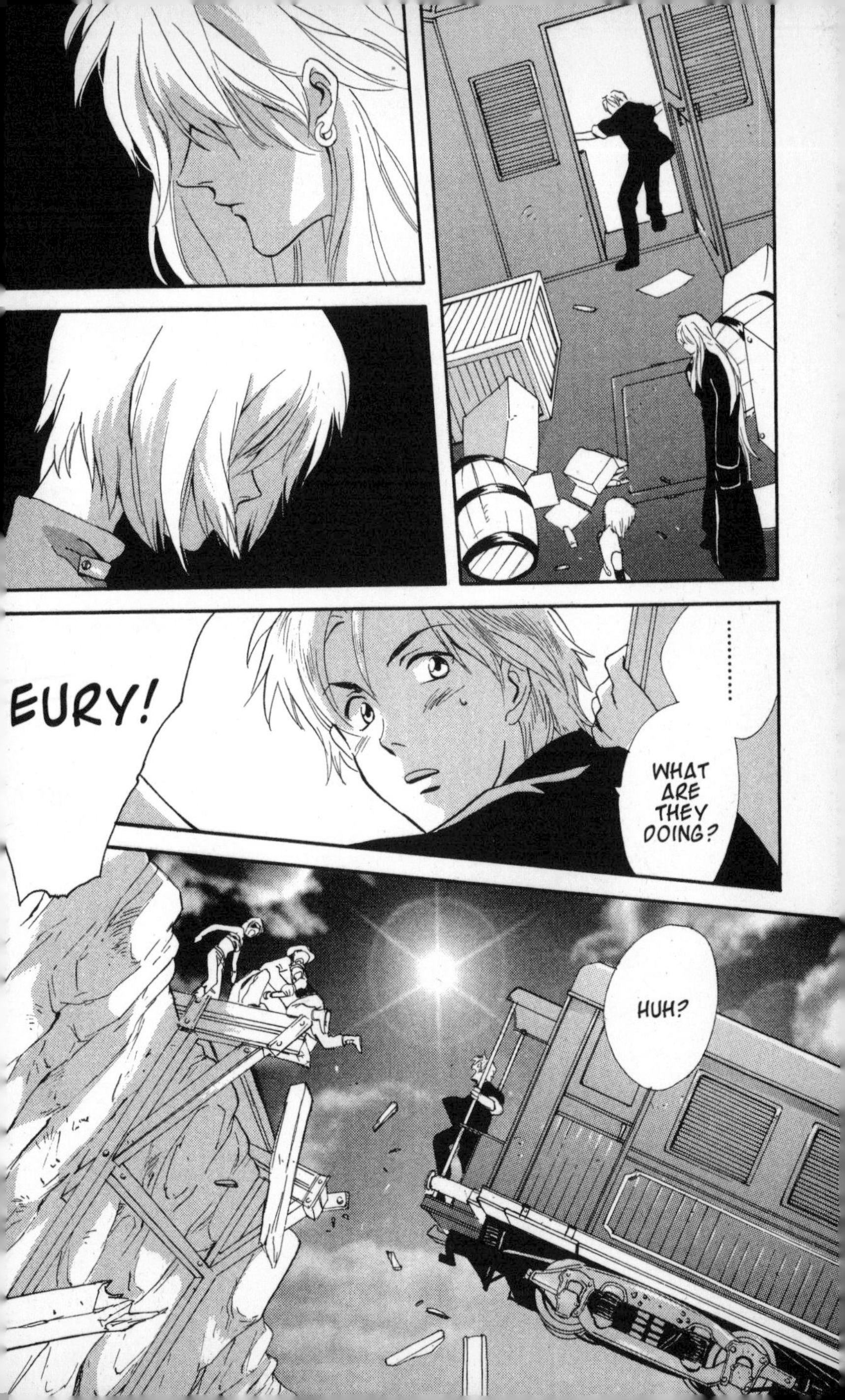
......
WHAT ARE THEY DOING?
EURY!
HUH?

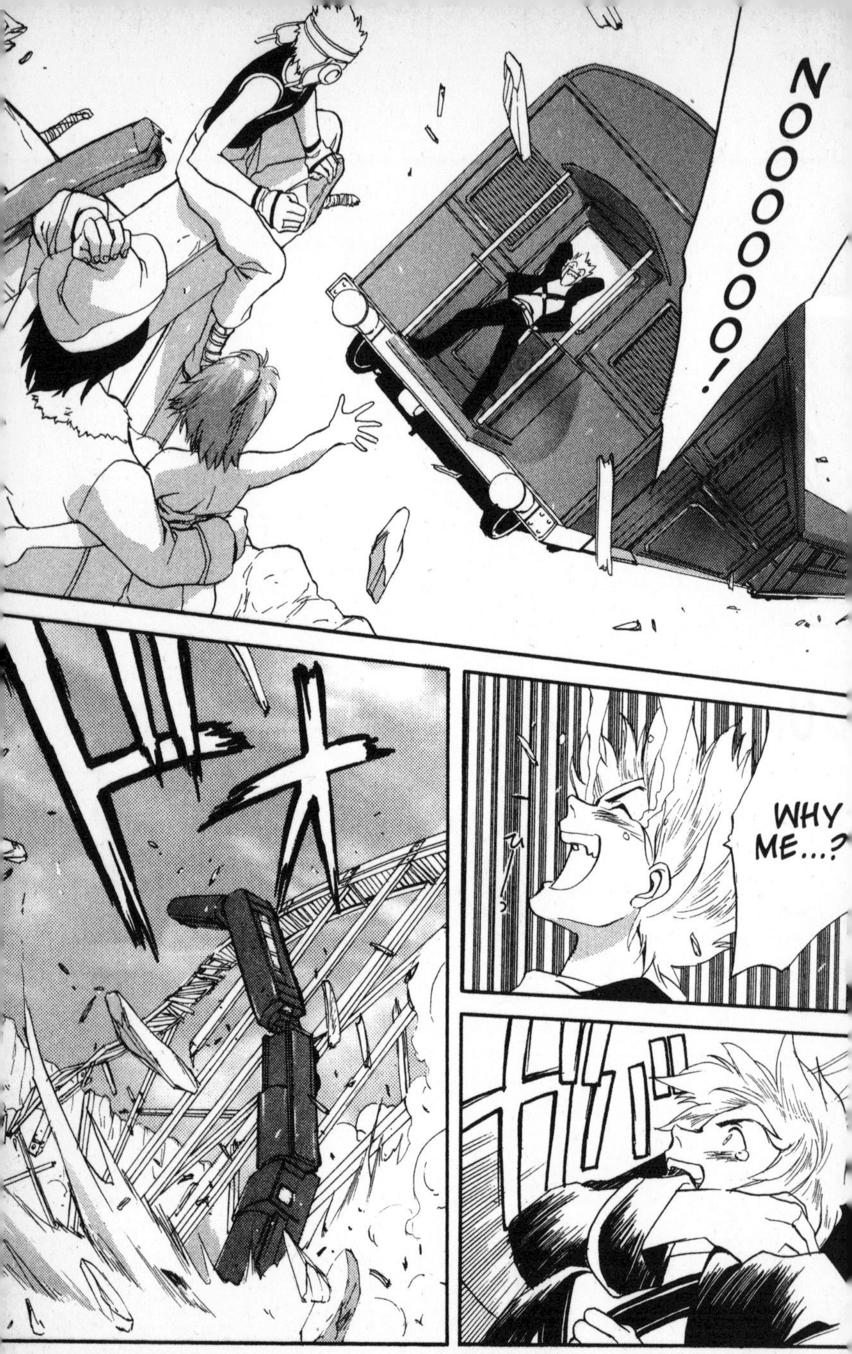
NOOOOOOOO!
WHY ME...?

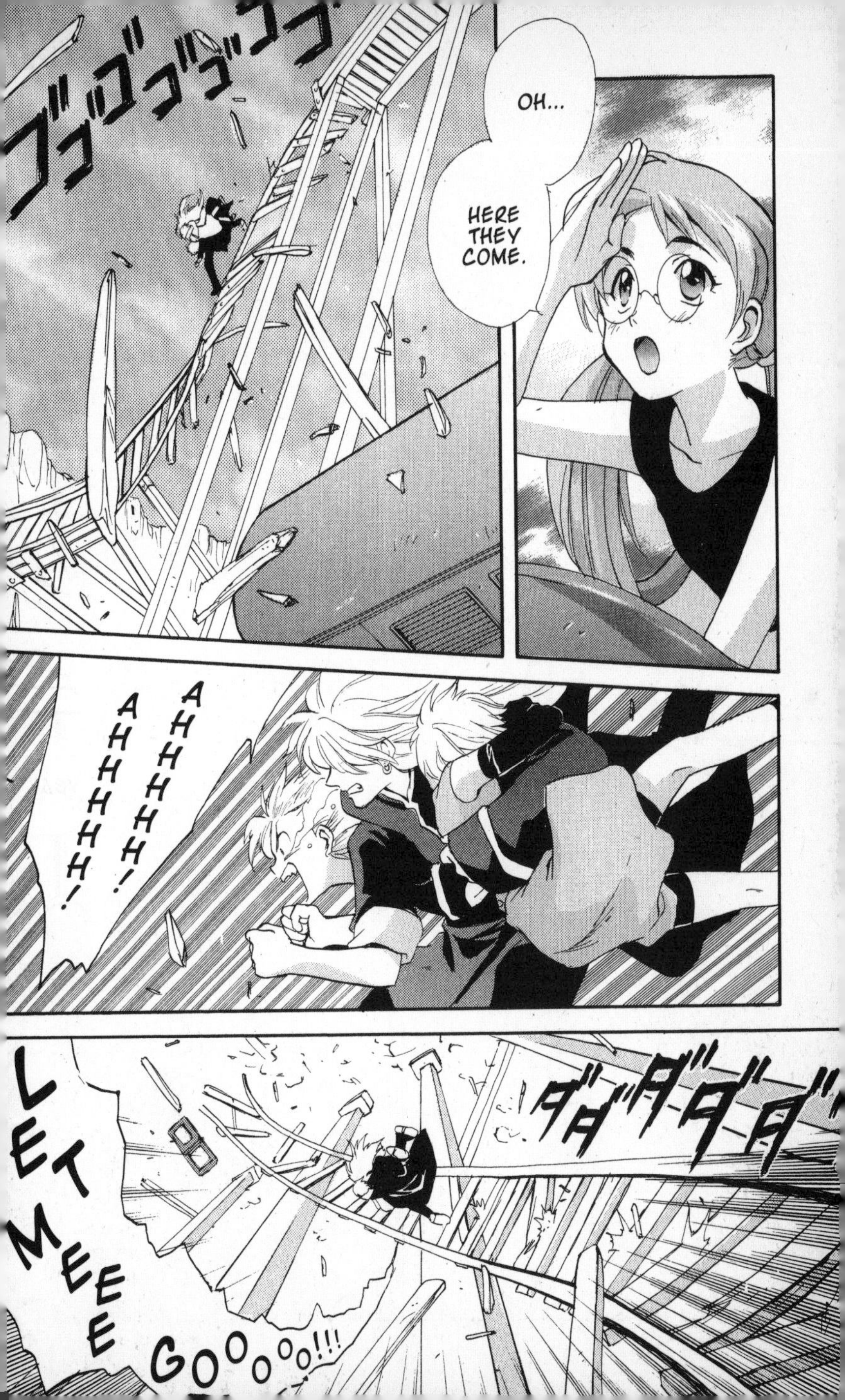
OH...
HERE THEY COME.
ゴゴゴゴゴ
AHHHHHHH!
AHHHHHHH!
ダダダダダ
LET MEEE GOOooo!!!

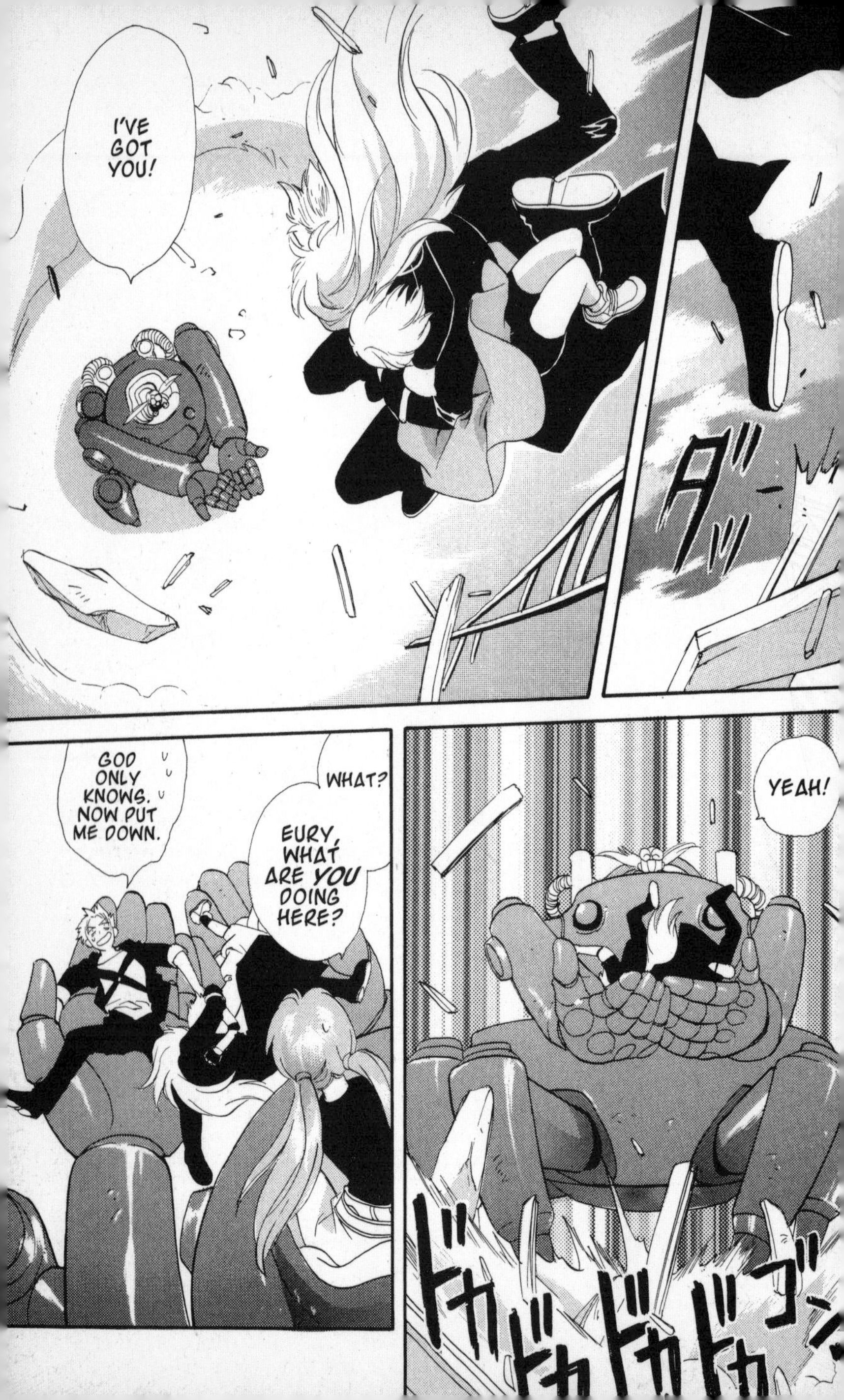
ダッ
I'VE GOT YOU!
YEAH!
ドカドカドカドカゴン
WHAT?
EURY, WHAT ARE *YOU* DOING HERE?
GOD ONLY KNOWS. NOW PUT ME DOWN.

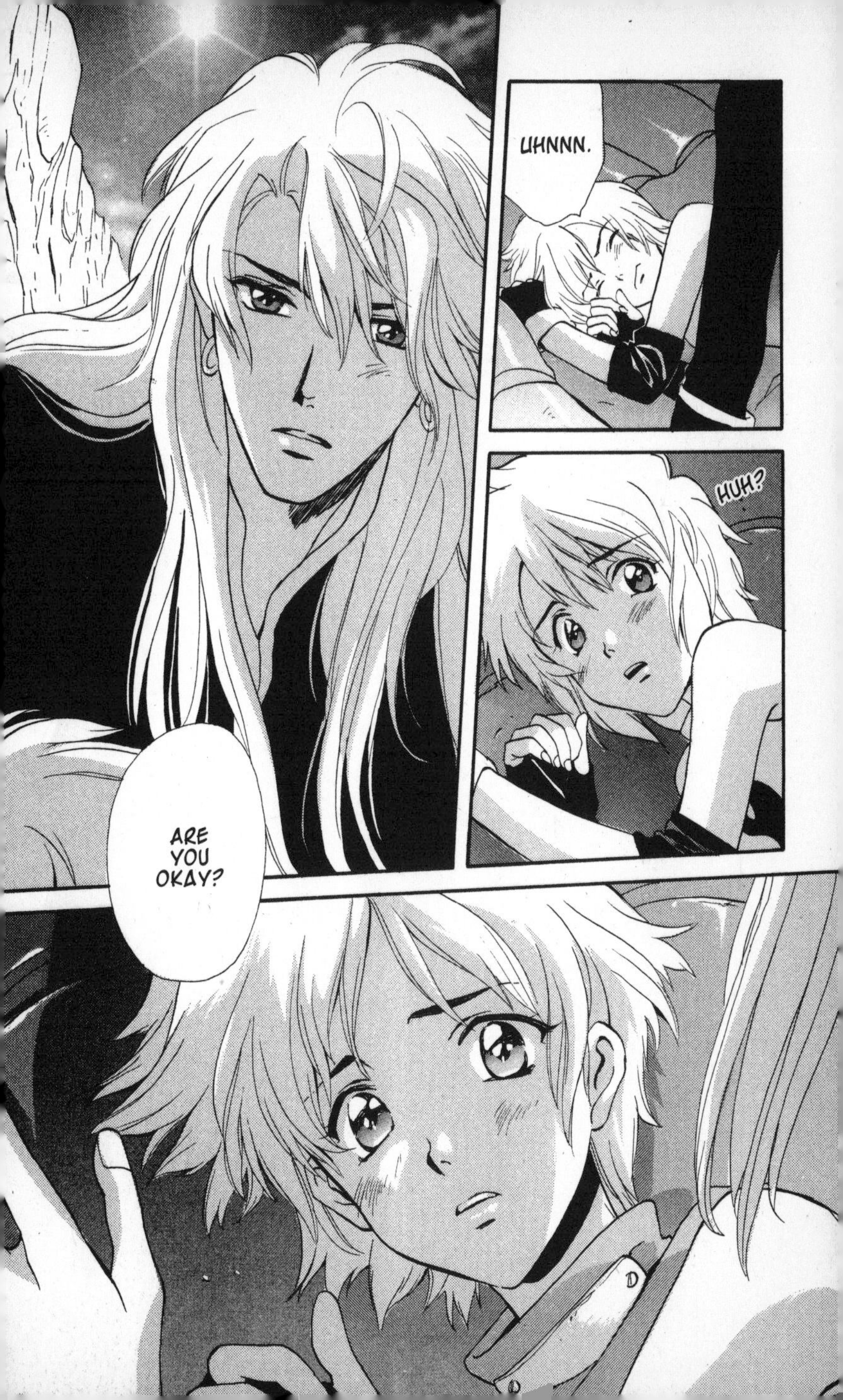
UHNNN.
HUH?
ARE YOU OKAY?

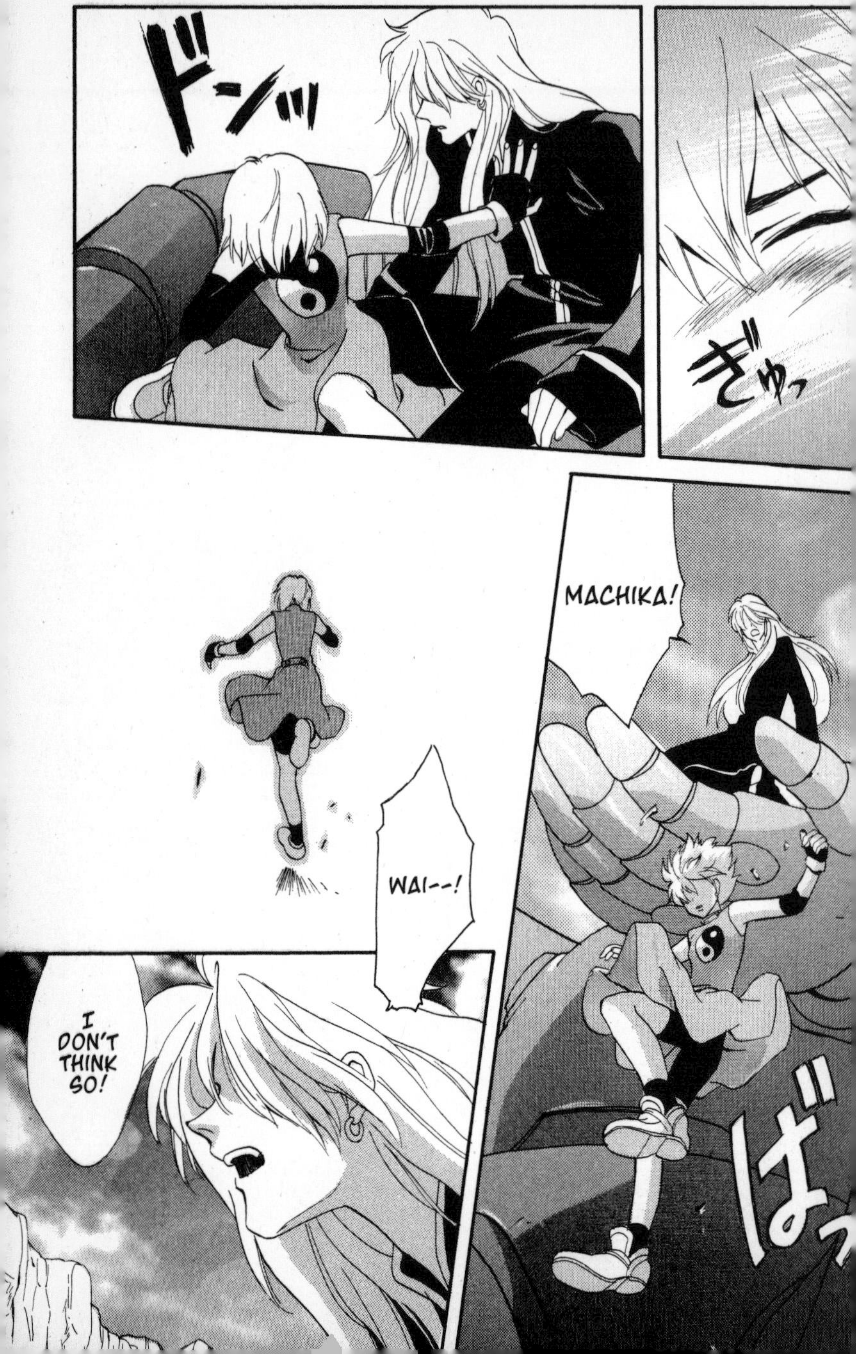
ぎゅっ
ドーンッ
MACHIKA!
ばっ
WAI--!
I DON'T THINK SO!

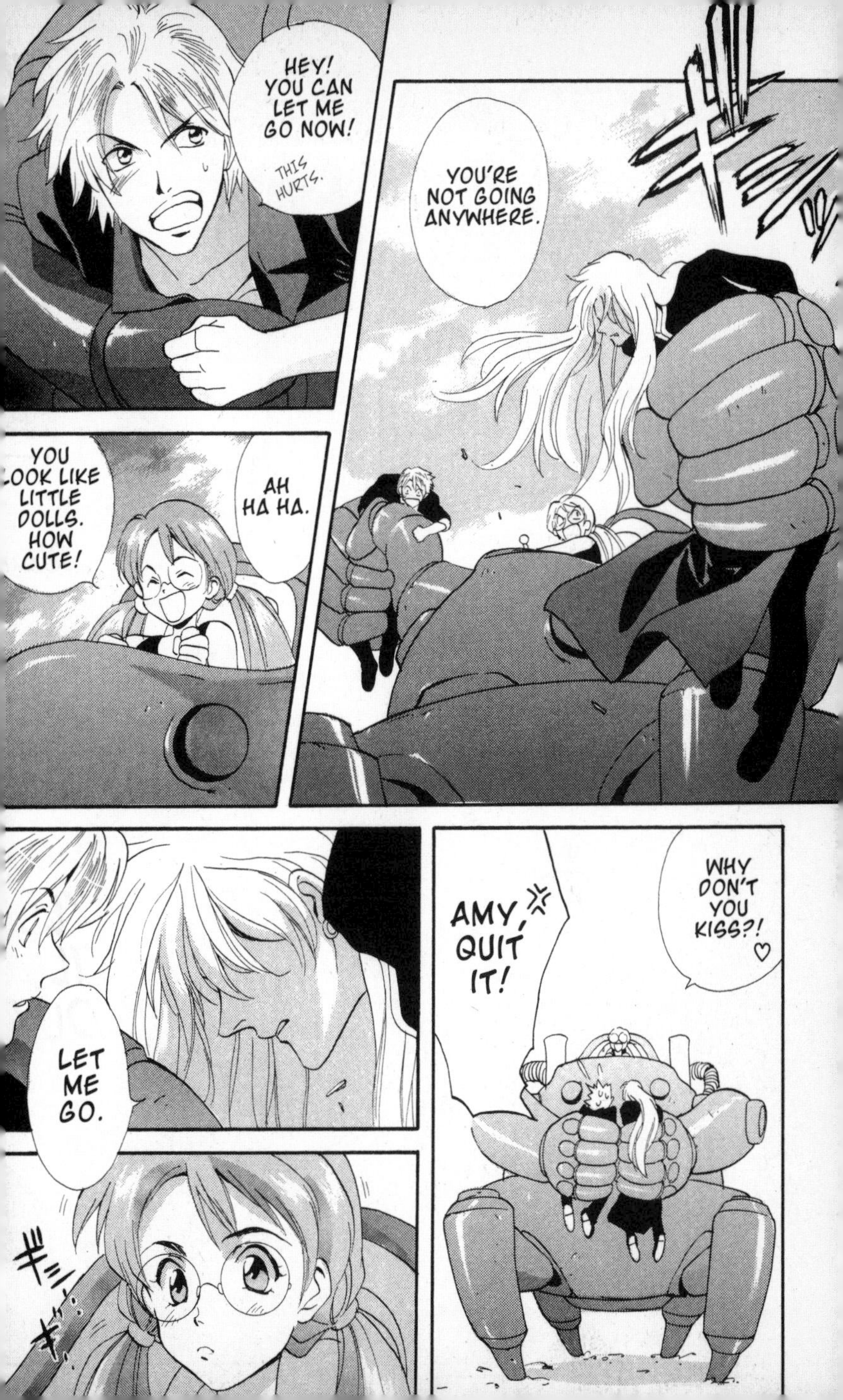
YOU'RE NOT GOING ANYWHERE.
HEY! YOU CAN LET ME GO NOW!
THIS HURTS.
AH HA HA.
YOU LOOK LIKE LITTLE DOLLS. HOW CUTE!
WHY DON'T YOU KISS?! ♡
AMY, QUIT IT!
LET ME GO.

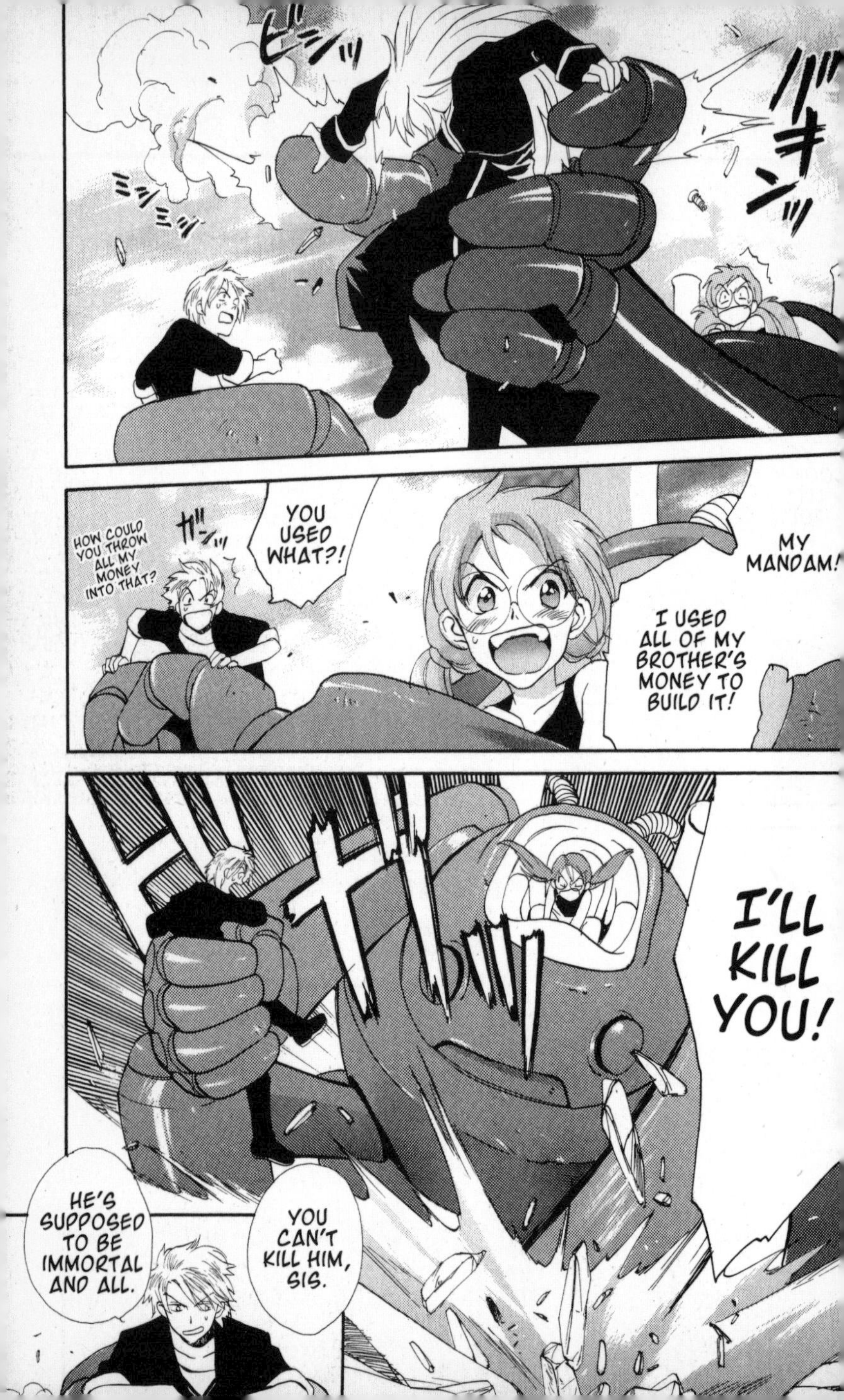
バキンッ
ビシッ
ミシミシ
MY MANDAM!
I USED ALL OF MY BROTHER'S MONEY TO BUILD IT!
YOU USED WHAT?!
HOW COULD YOU THROW ALL MY MONEY INTO THAT?
I'LL KILL YOU!
YOU CAN'T KILL HIM, SIS.
HE'S SUPPOSED TO BE IMMORTAL AND ALL.

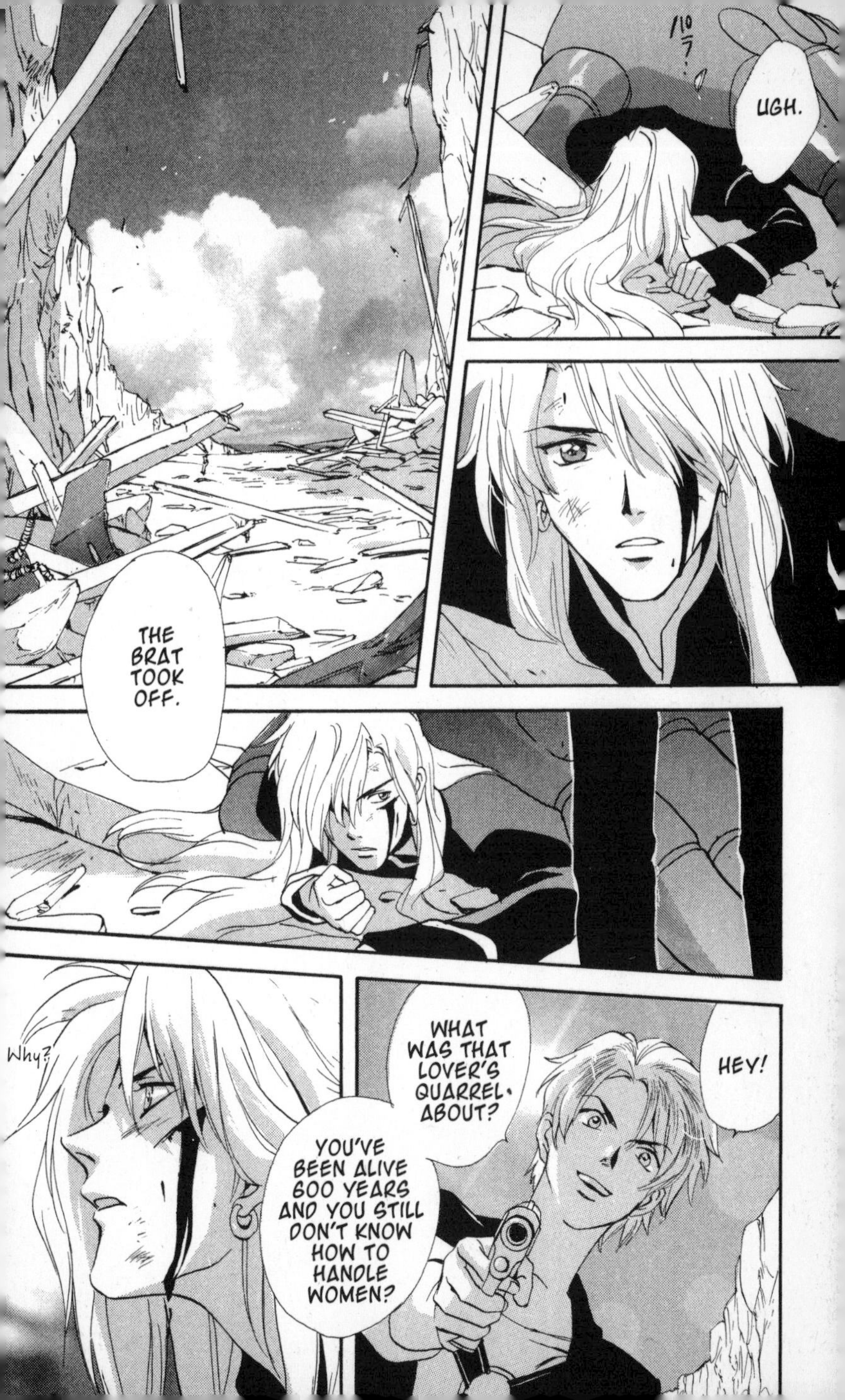
UGH.
THE BRAT TOOK OFF.
HEY!
WHAT WAS THAT LOVER'S QUARREL. ABOUT?
YOU'VE BEEN ALIVE 600 YEARS AND YOU STILL DON'T KNOW HOW TO HANDLE WOMEN?
Why?

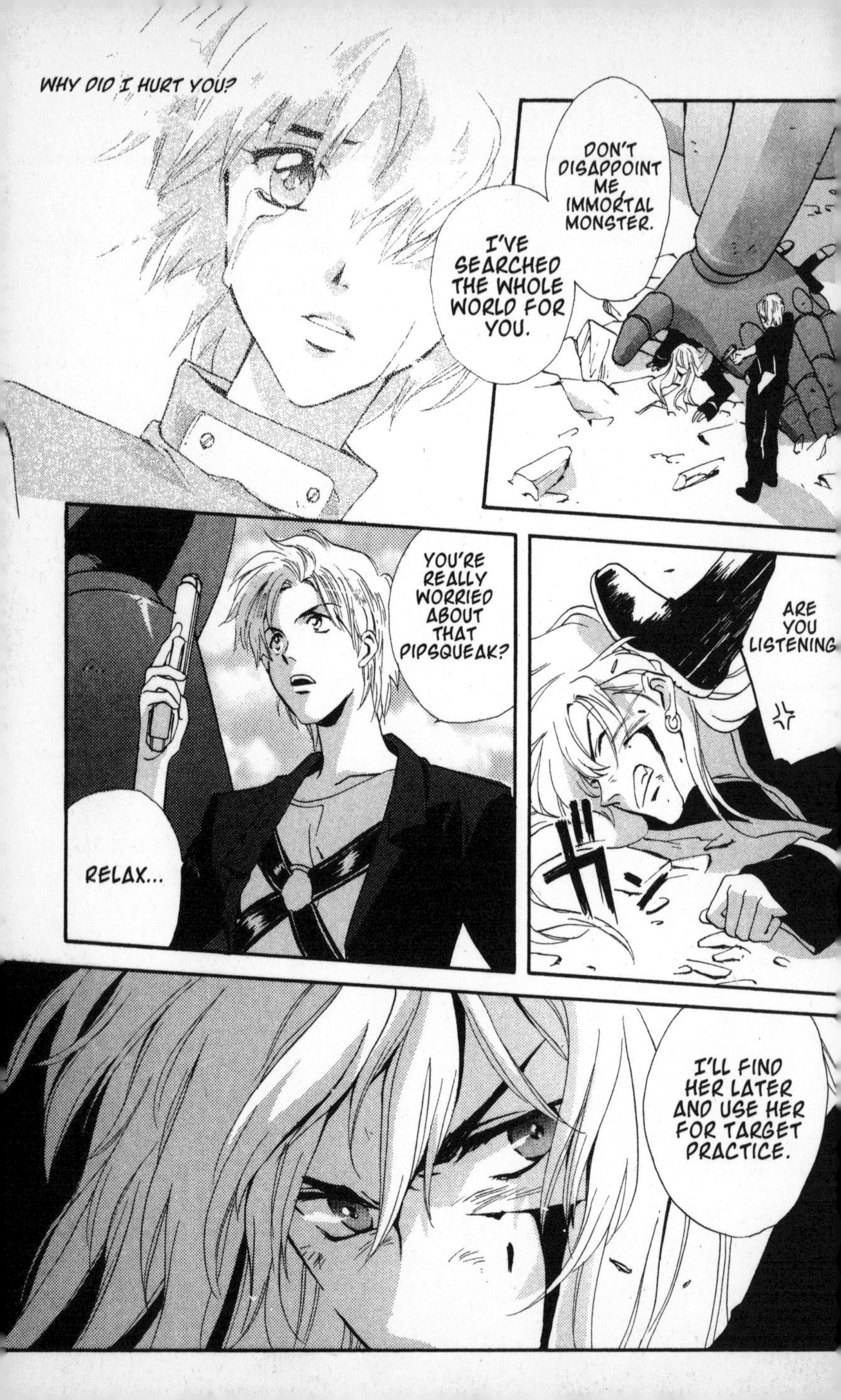
DON'T DISAPPOINT ME, IMMORTAL MONSTER.
I'VE SEARCHED THE WHOLE WORLD FOR YOU.
WHY DID I HURT YOU?
ARE YOU LISTENING
YOU'RE REALLY WORRIED ABOUT THAT PIPSQUEAK?
RELAX...
I'LL FIND HER LATER AND USE HER FOR TARGET PRACTICE.

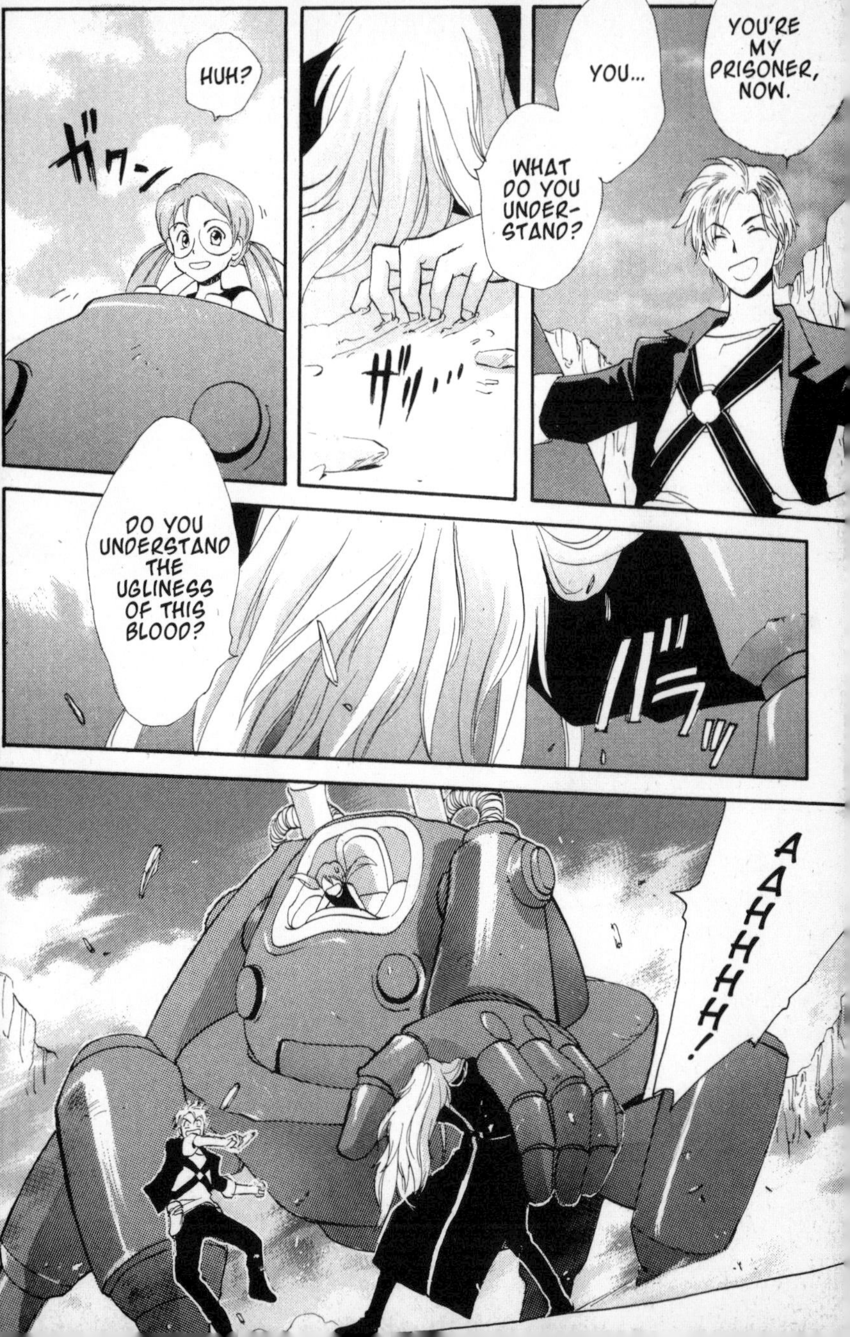
YOU'RE MY PRISONER, NOW.
YOU...
WHAT DO YOU UNDERSTAND?
ザリッ
HUH?
ガクーン
DO YOU UNDERSTAND THE UGLINESS OF THIS BLOOD?
バラッ
AAHHHHH!

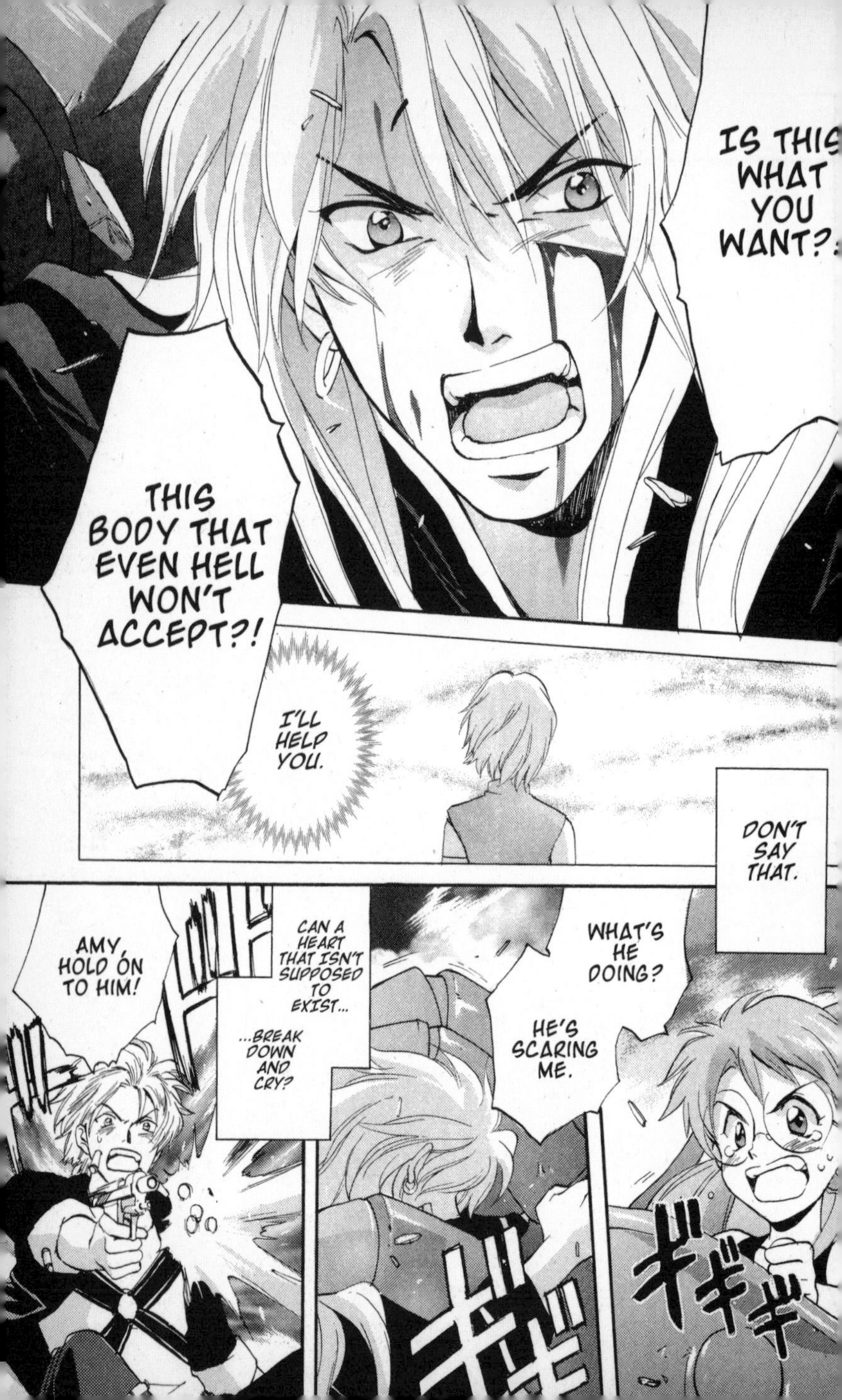
IS THIS WHAT YOU WANT?!
THIS BODY THAT EVEN HELL WON'T ACCEPT?!
DON'T SAY THAT.
I'LL HELP YOU.
WHAT'S HE DOING?
HE'S SCARING ME.
ギギギ
ギギ
CAN A HEART THAT ISN'T SUPPOSED TO EXIST...
...BREAK DOWN AND CRY?
AMY, HOLD ON TO HIM!

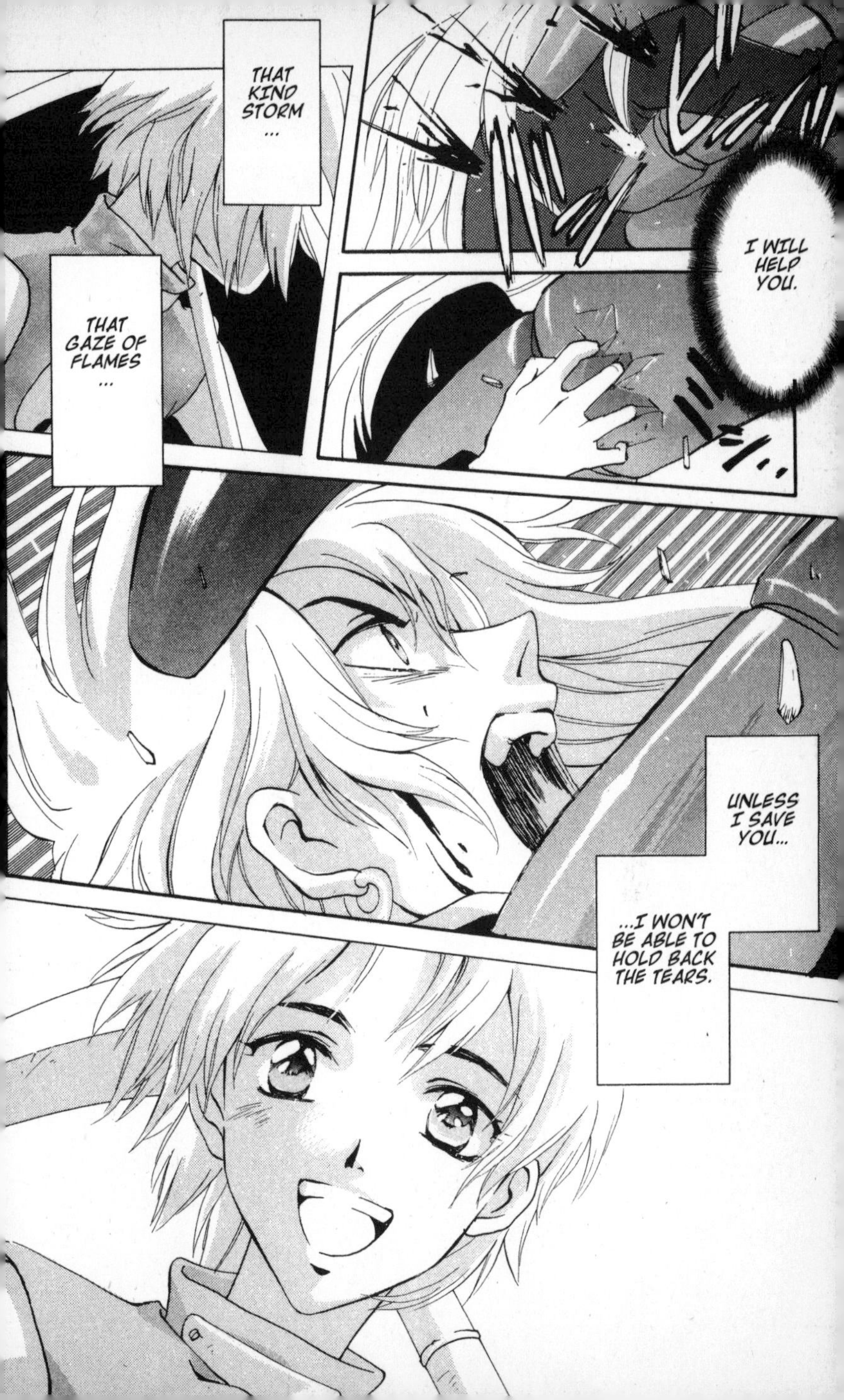
I WILL HELP YOU.
THAT KIND STORM ...
THAT GAZE OF FLAMES ...
UNLESS I SAVE YOU...
...I WON'T BE ABLE TO HOLD BACK THE TEARS.

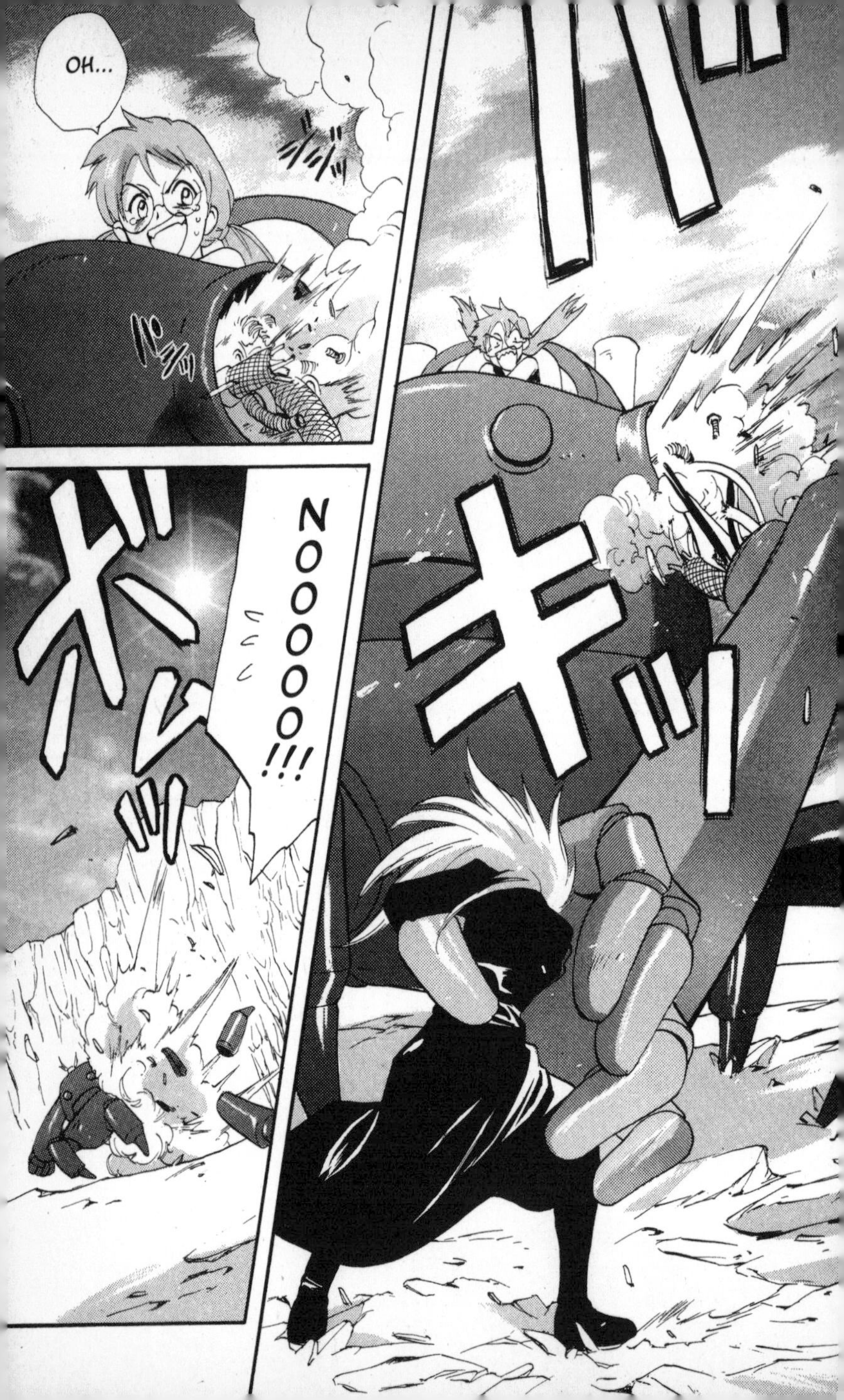
OH...
NOOOOO!!!

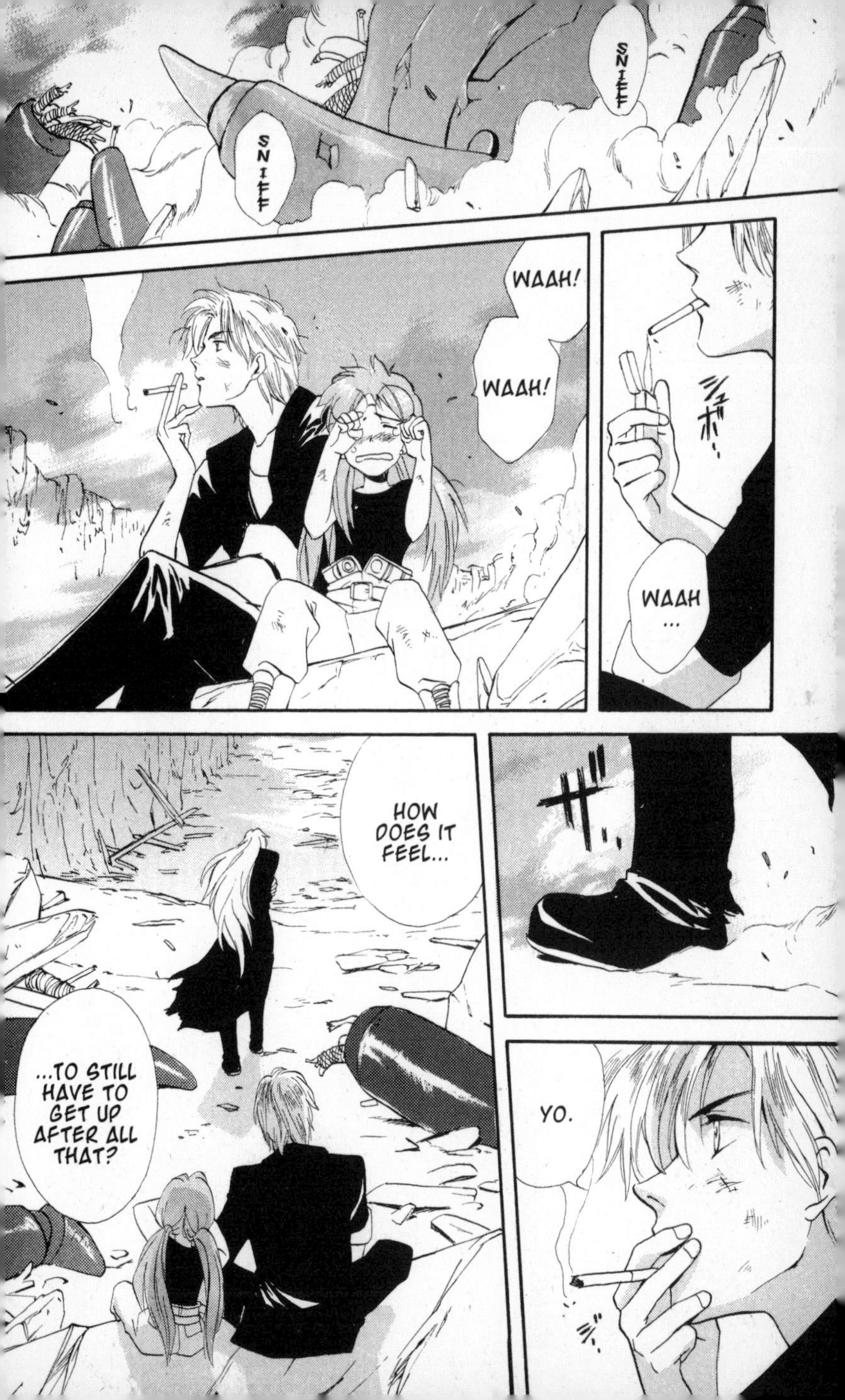
SNIFF
SNIFF
シュボ
WAAH ...
WAAH!
WAAH!
ザッ
YO.
ジ
HOW DOES IT FEEL...
...TO STILL HAVE TO GET UP AFTER ALL THAT?

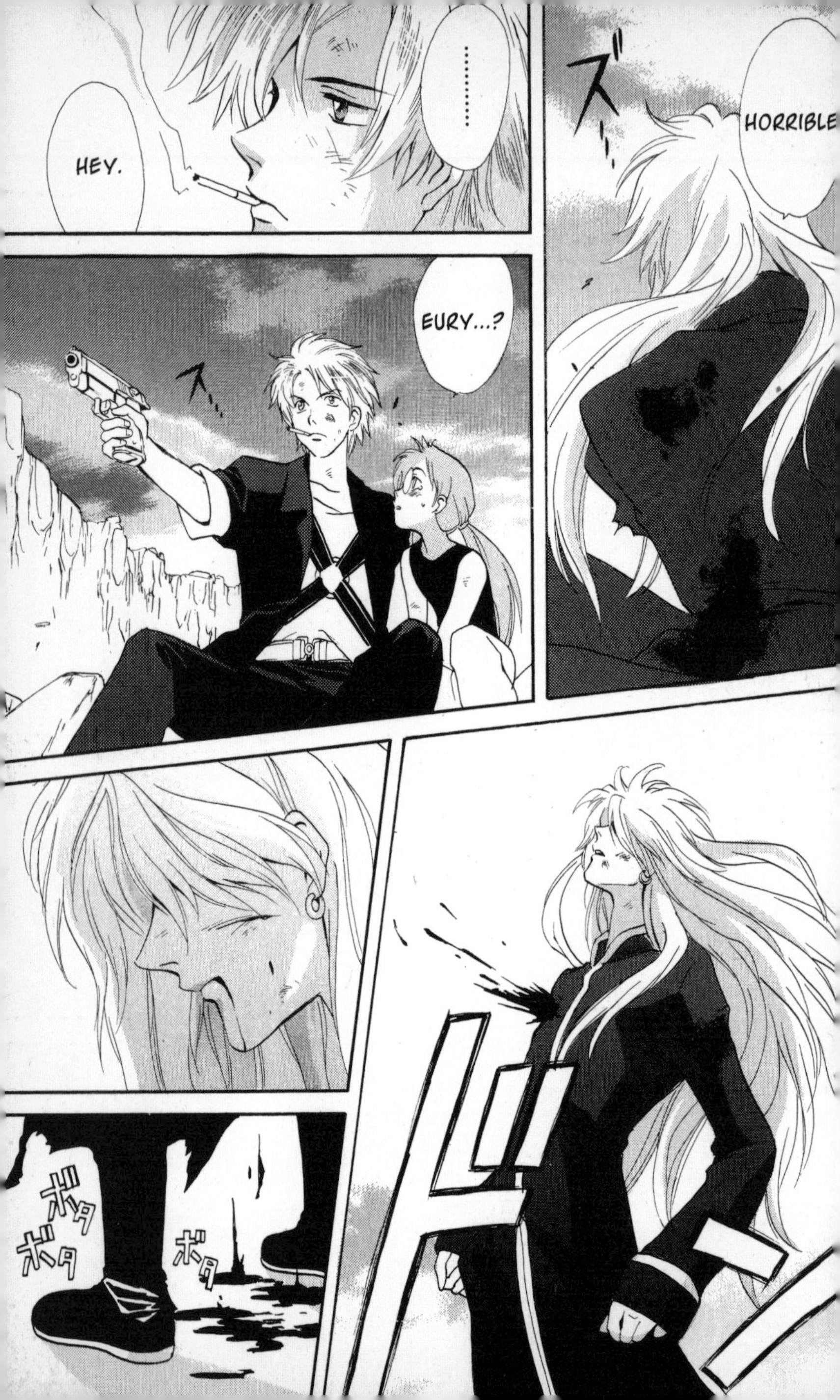
ズ
HORRIBLE
......
HEY.
EURY...?
ハ
ボタ
ボタ
ボタ

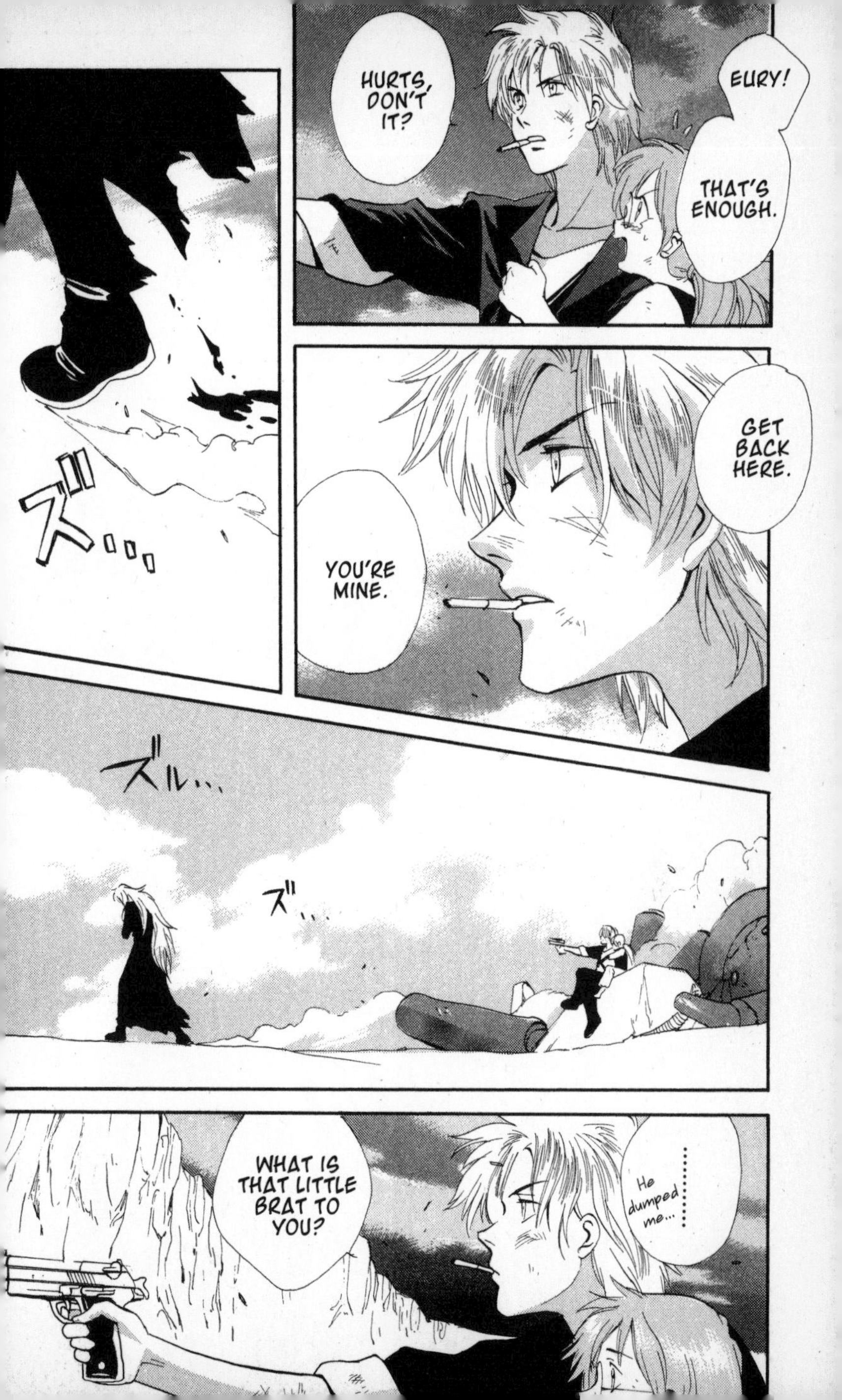
EURY!
THAT'S ENOUGH.
HURTS, DON'T IT?
GET BACK HERE.
YOU'RE MINE.
ズ…
ズル…
ズ…
He dumped me……
WHAT IS THAT LITTLE BRAT TO YOU?

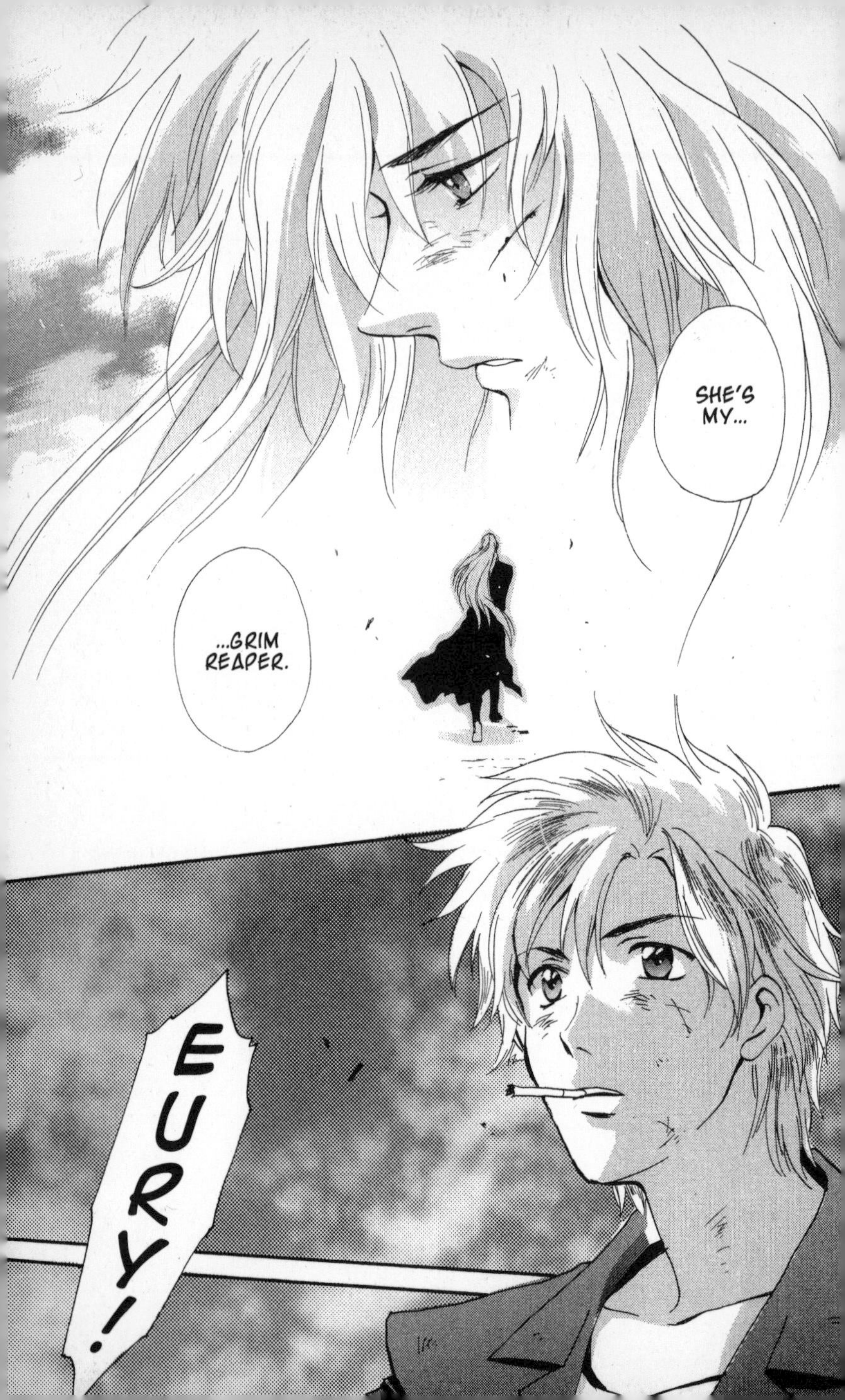
SHE'S MY...
...GRIM REAPER.
EURY!

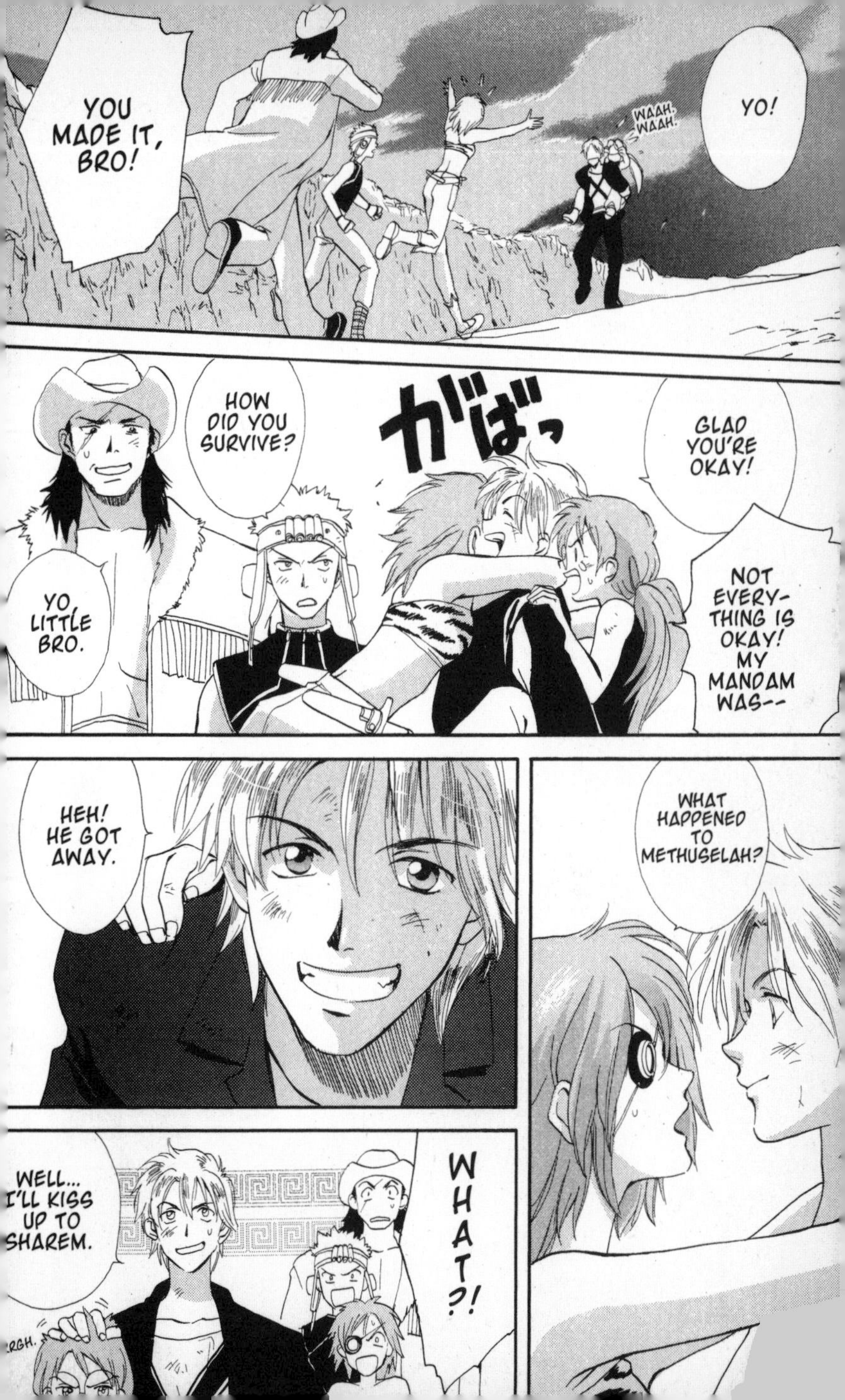
YO!
WAAH. WAAH.
YOU MADE IT, BRO!
GLAD YOU'RE OKAY!
NOT EVERY-THING IS OKAY! MY MANDAM WAS--
がばっ
HOW DID YOU SURVIVE?
YO, LITTLE BRO.
WHAT HAPPENED TO METHUSELAH?
HEH! HE GOT AWAY.
WHAT?!
WELL... I'LL KISS UP TO SHAREM.
RGH.

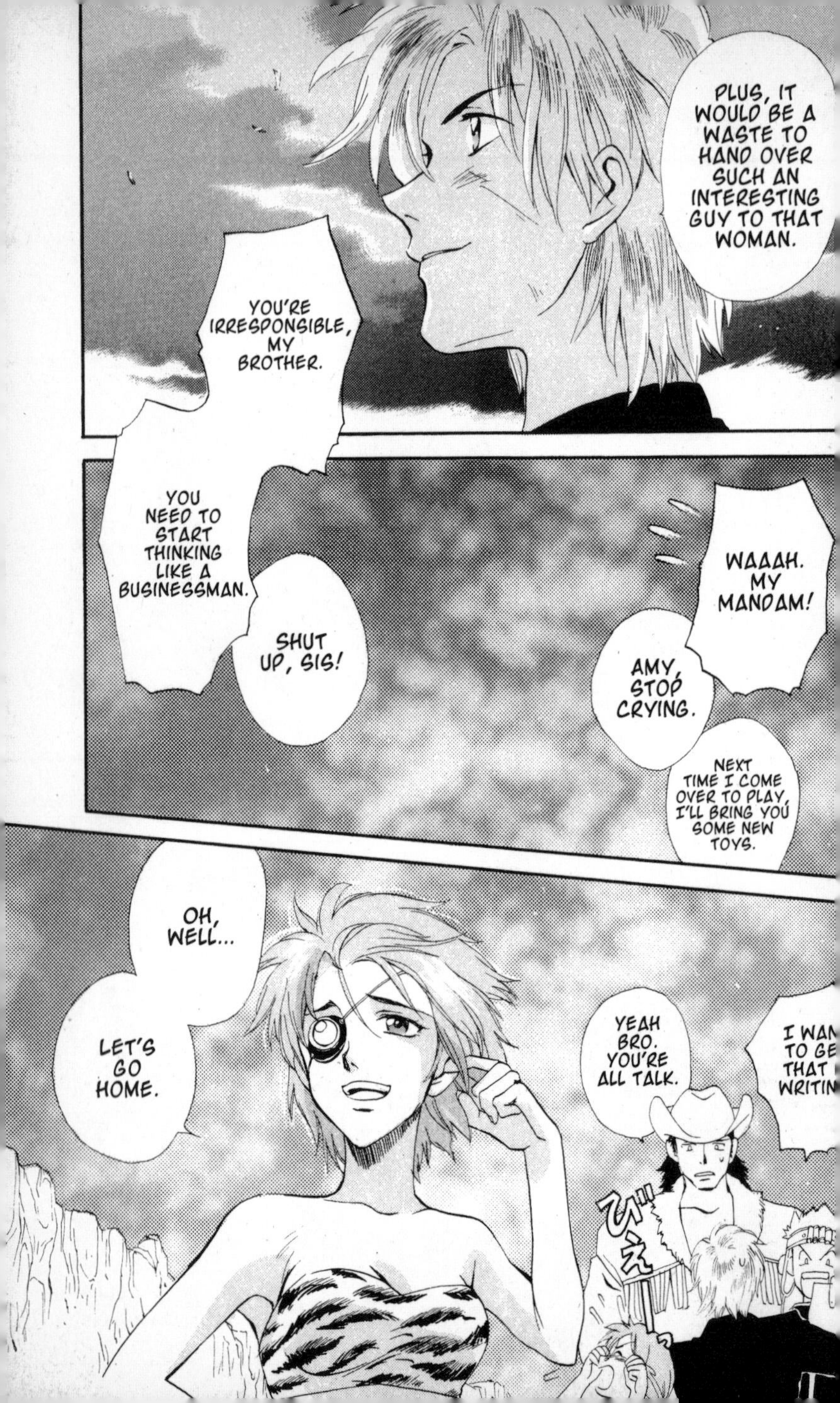
PLUS, IT WOULD BE A WASTE TO HAND OVER SUCH AN INTERESTING GUY TO THAT WOMAN.
YOU'RE IRRESPONSIBLE, MY BROTHER.
WAAAH. MY MANDAM!
AMY, STOP CRYING.
NEXT TIME I COME OVER TO PLAY, I'LL BRING YOU SOME NEW TOYS.
YOU NEED TO START THINKING LIKE A BUSINESSMAN.
SHUT UP, SIS!
I WAN TO GE THAT WRITIN
YEAH BRO. YOU'RE ALL TALK.
OH, WELL...
LET'S GO HOME.

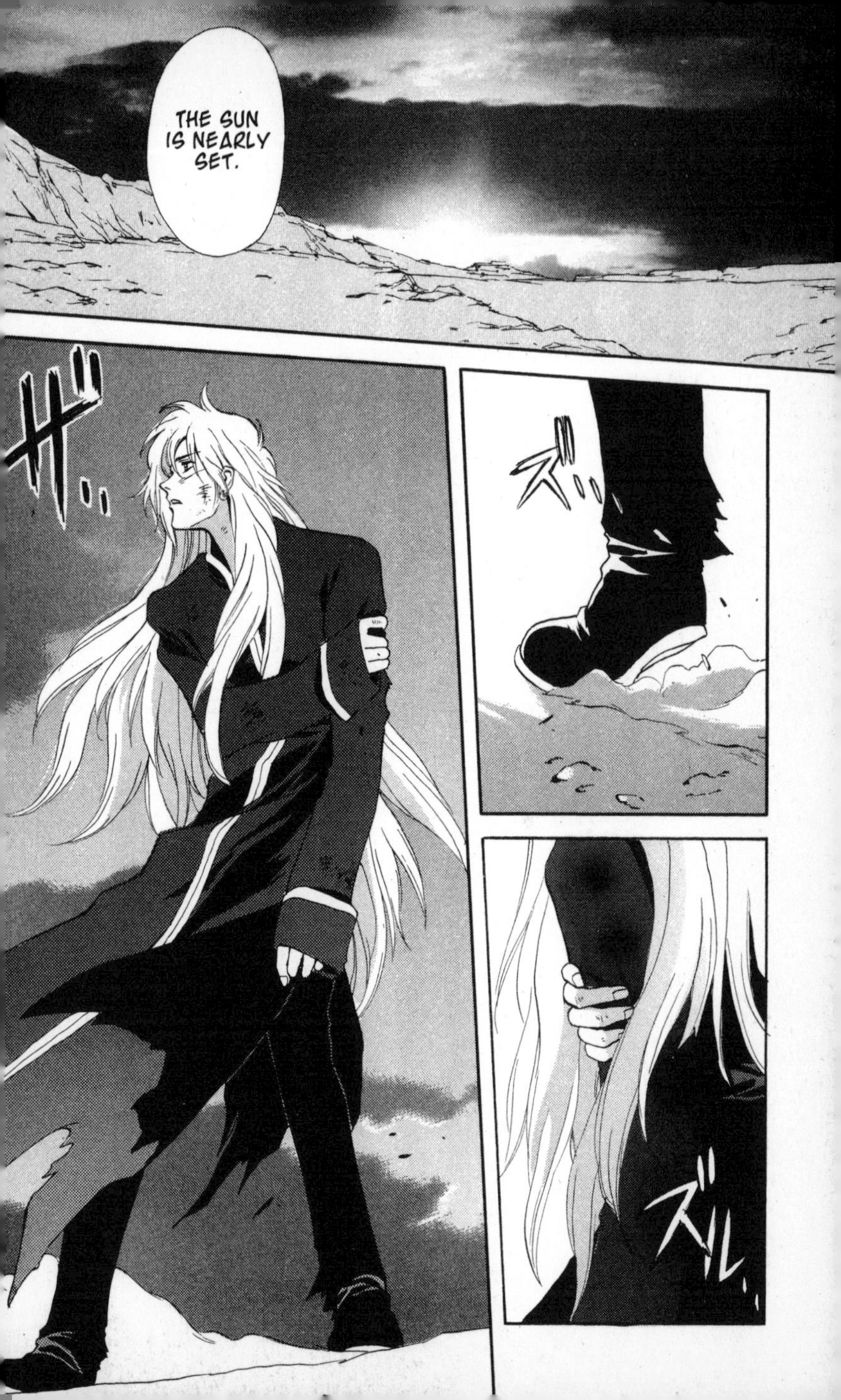
THE SUN IS NEARLY SET.
ズ..
ズル..
ザ..

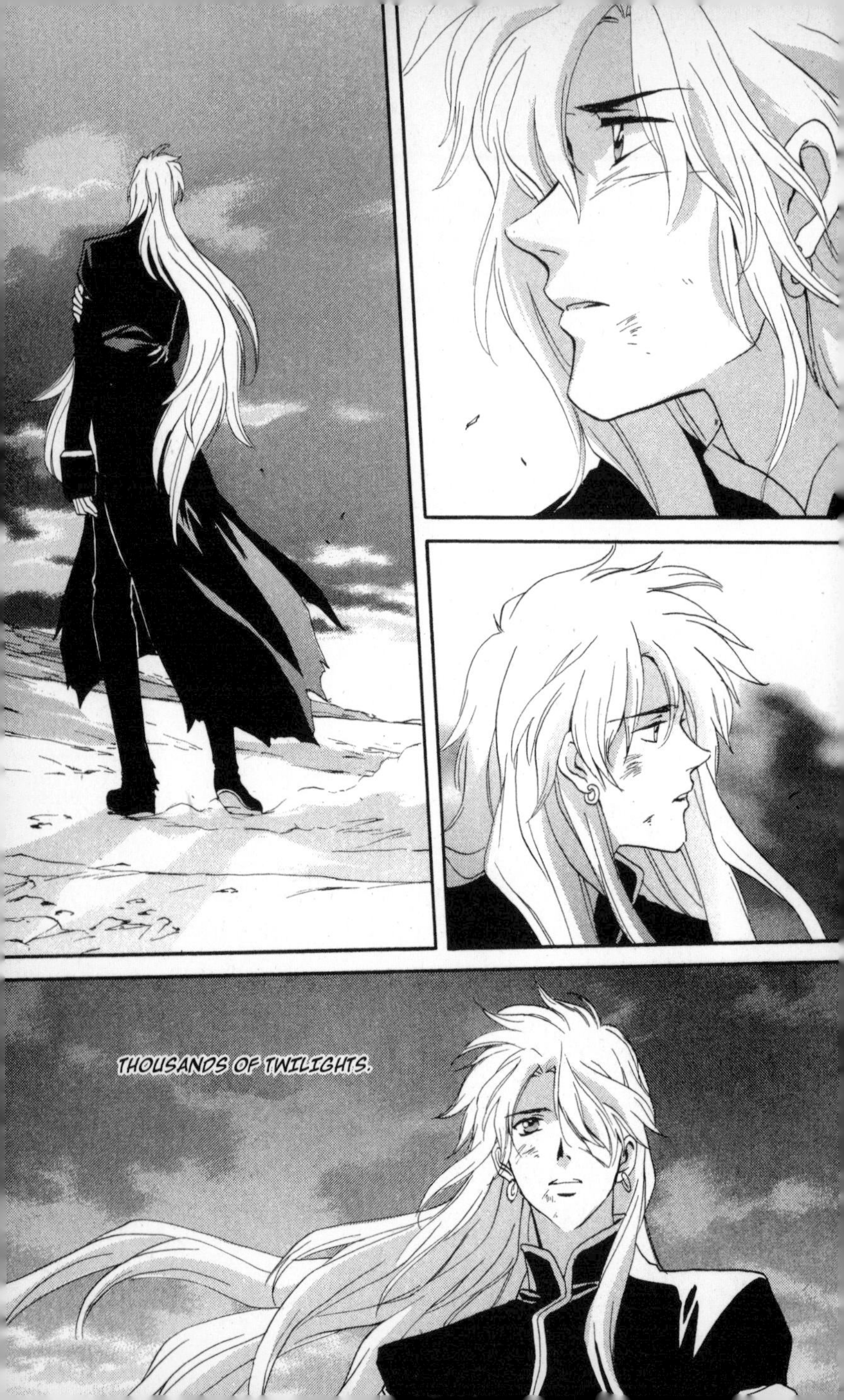
THOUSANDS OF TWILIGHTS.

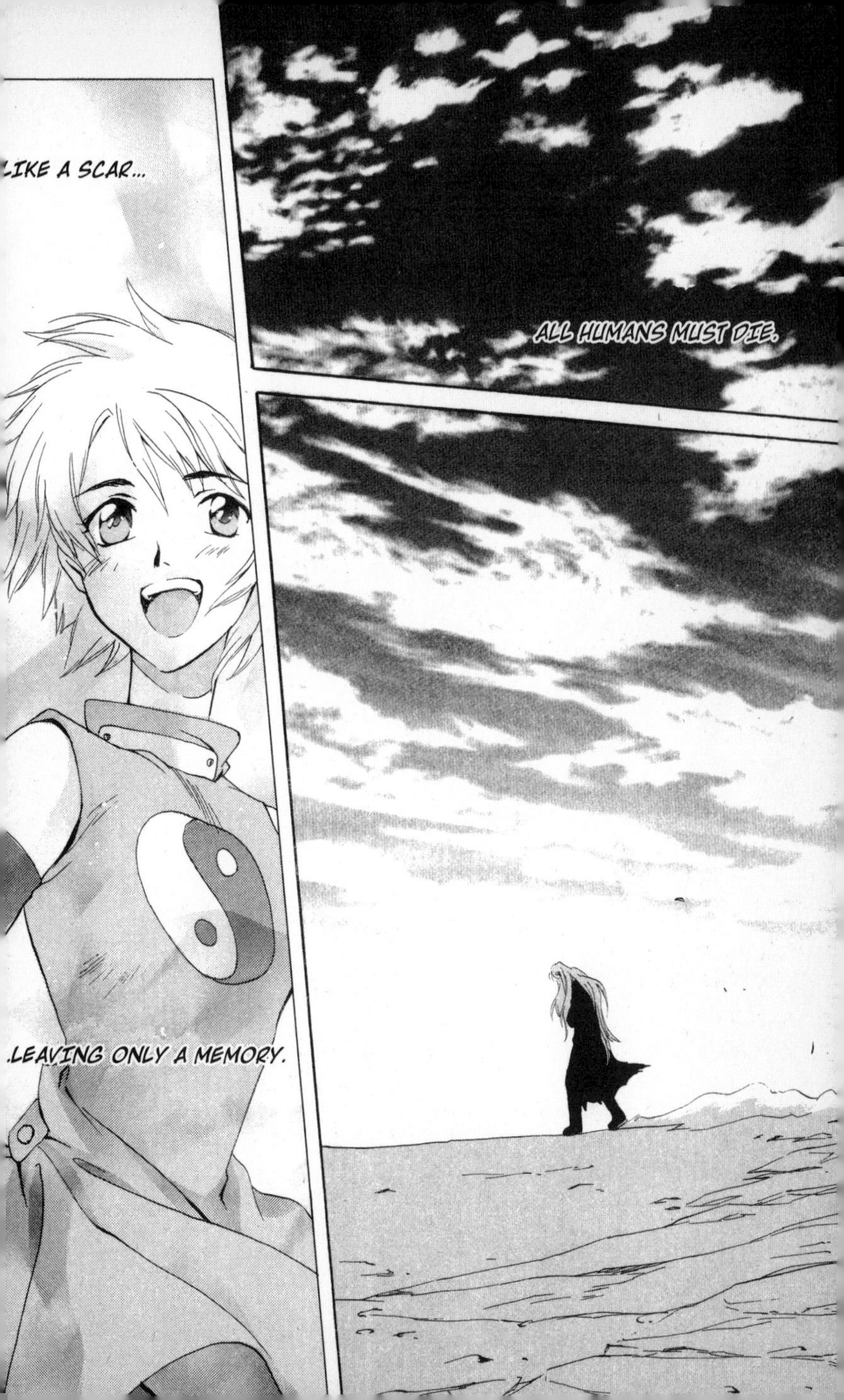
ALL HUMANS MUST DIE.
LIKE A SCAR...
LEAVING ONLY A MEMORY.

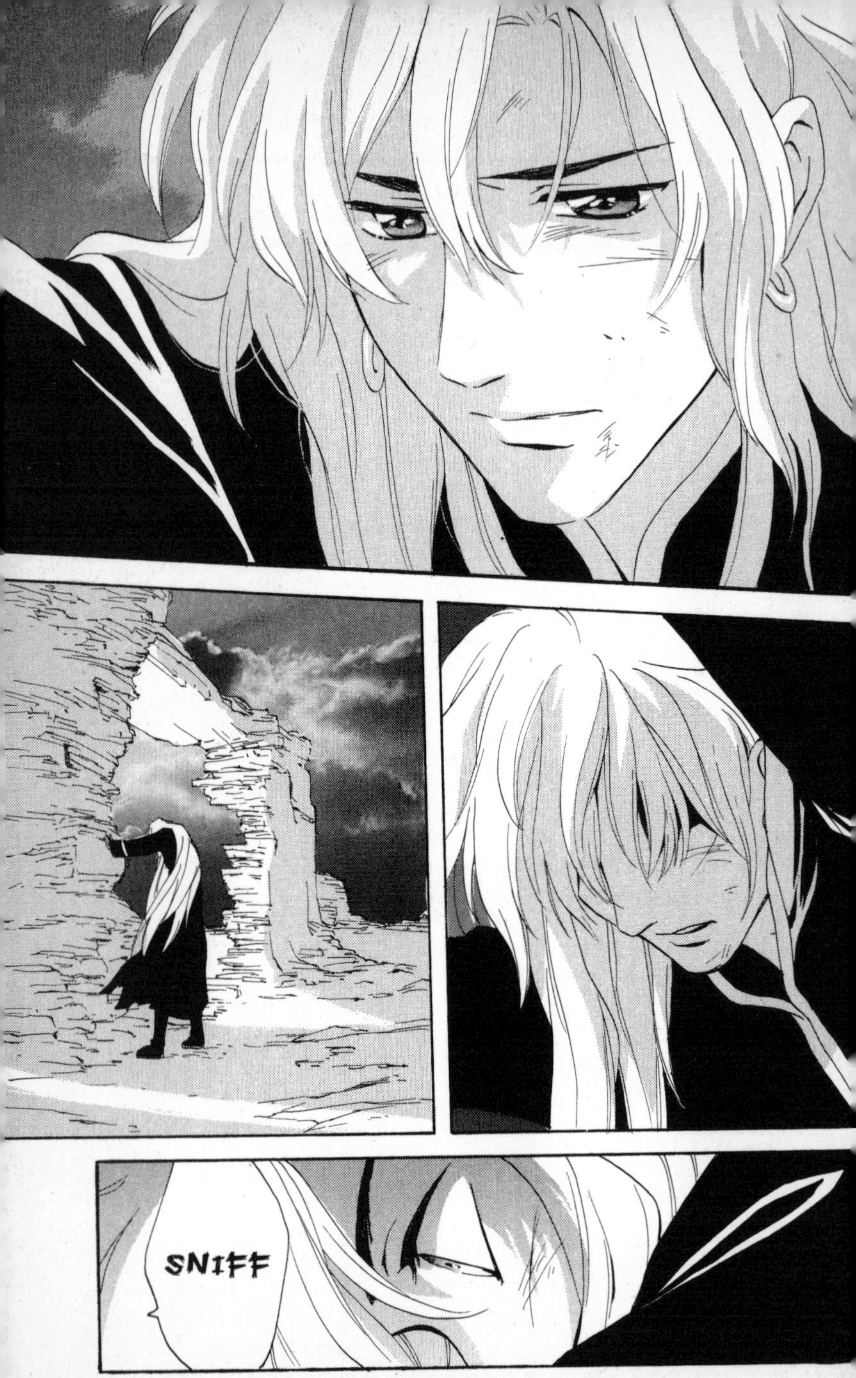
SNIFF

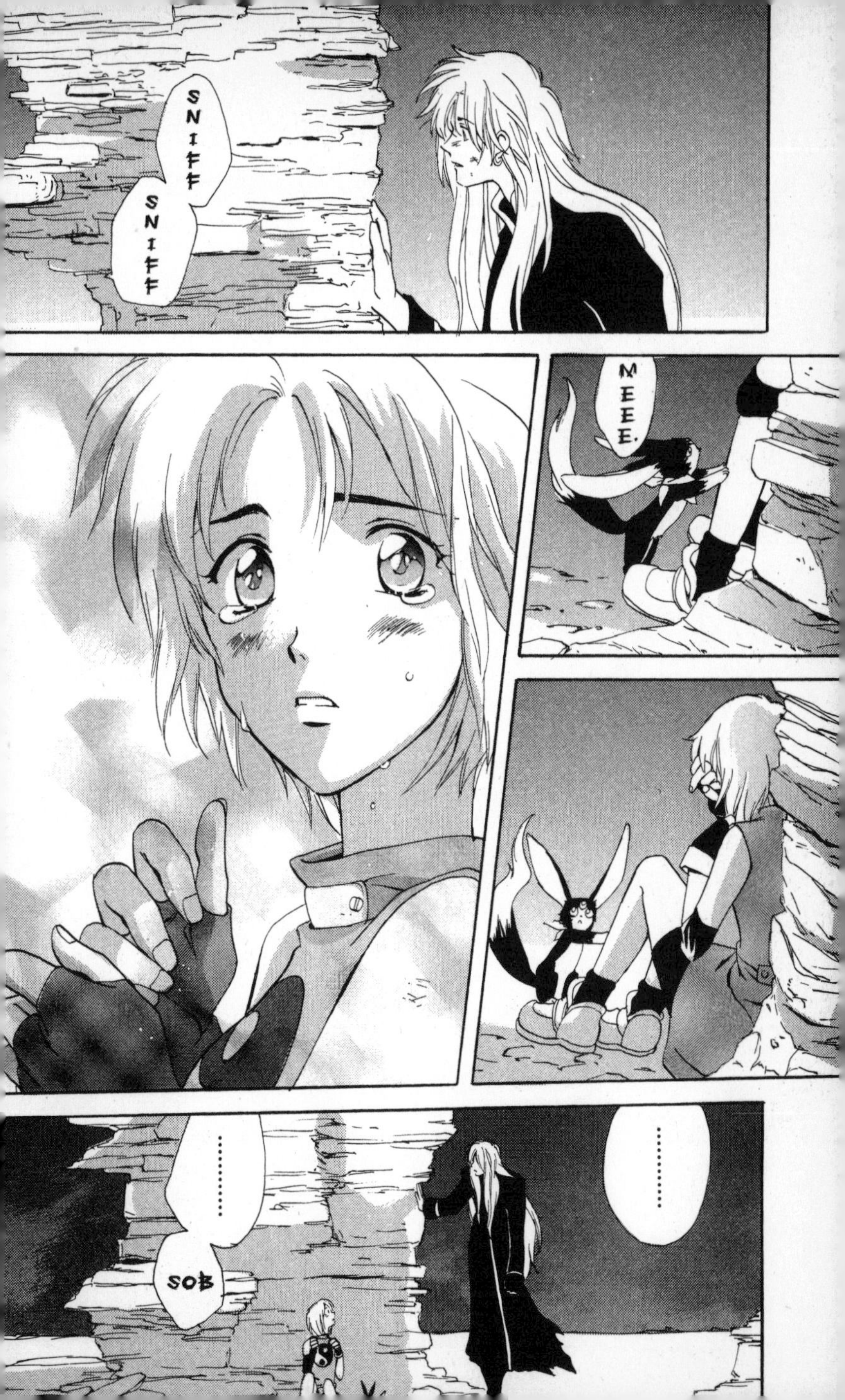
SNIFF
SNIFF
MEEE.
....
......
SOB

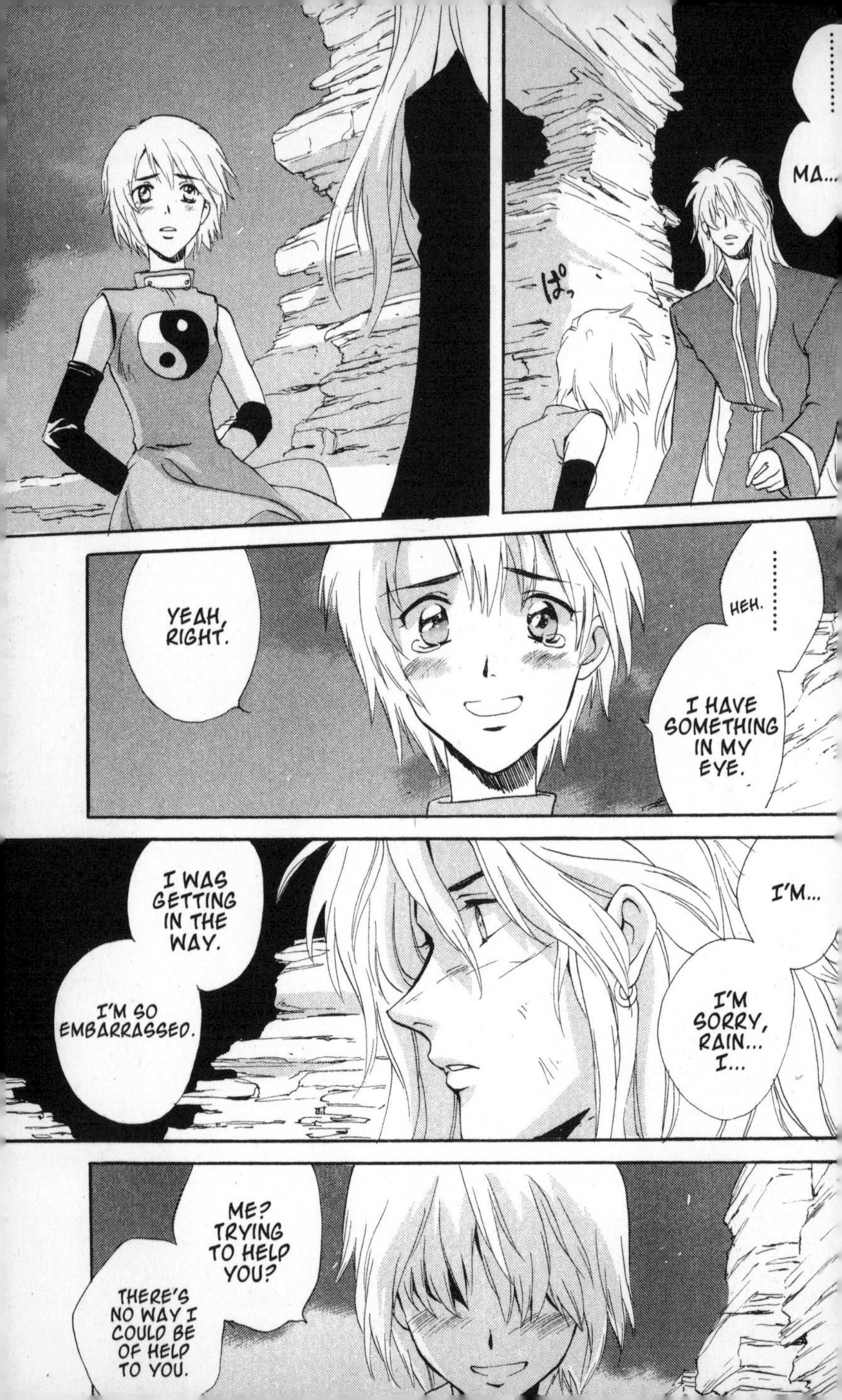
......
MA...
ぱっ
......HEH.
I HAVE SOMETHING IN MY EYE.
YEAH, RIGHT.
I'M...
I'M SORRY, RAIN... I...
I WAS GETTING IN THE WAY.
I'M SO EMBARRASSED.
ME? TRYING TO HELP YOU?
THERE'S NO WAY I COULD BE OF HELP TO YOU.

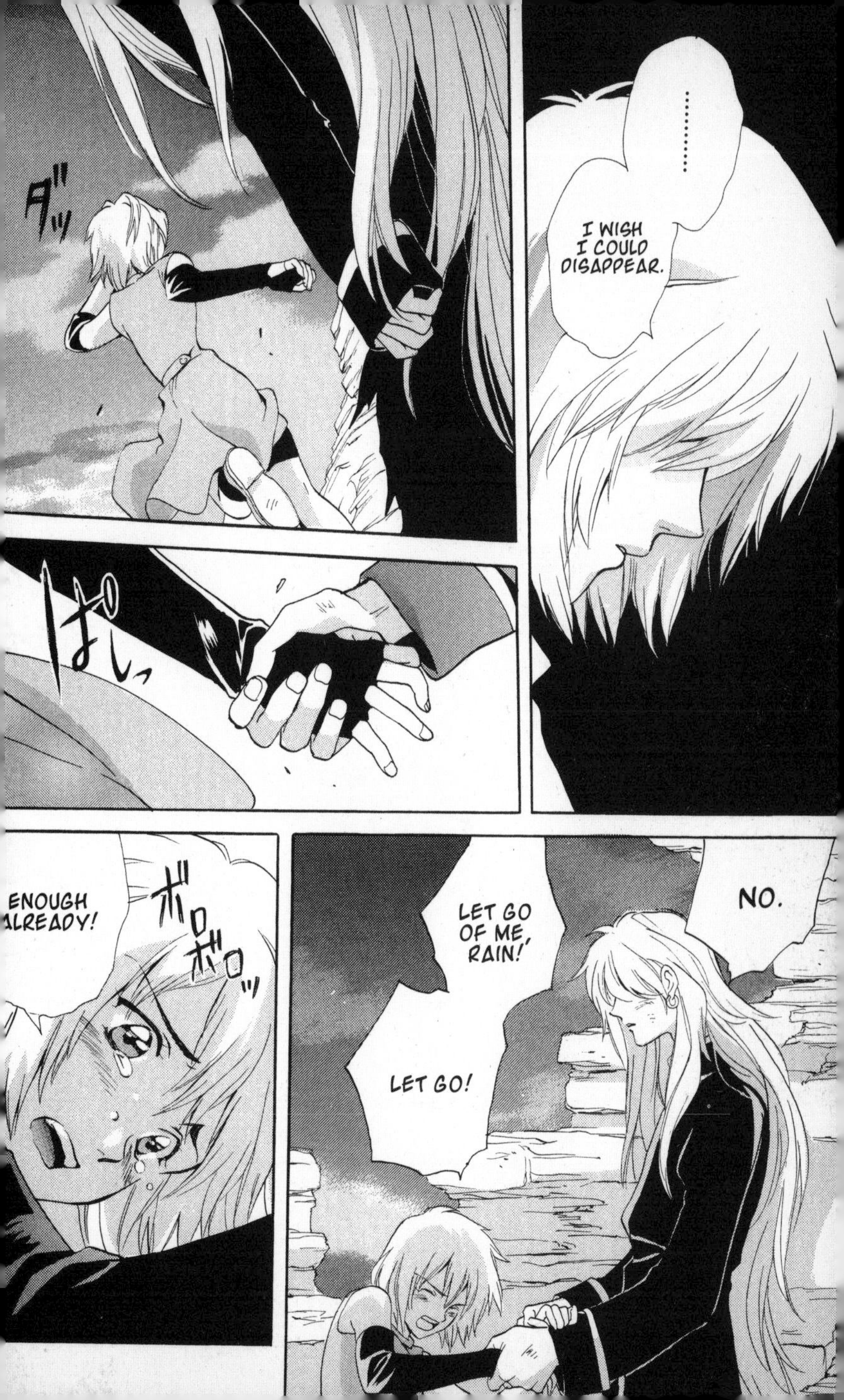
……
I WISH I COULD DISAPPEAR.
ダッ
ぱしっ
NO.
LET GO OF ME, RAIN!
LET GO!
ENOUGH ALREADY!
ボロボロッ

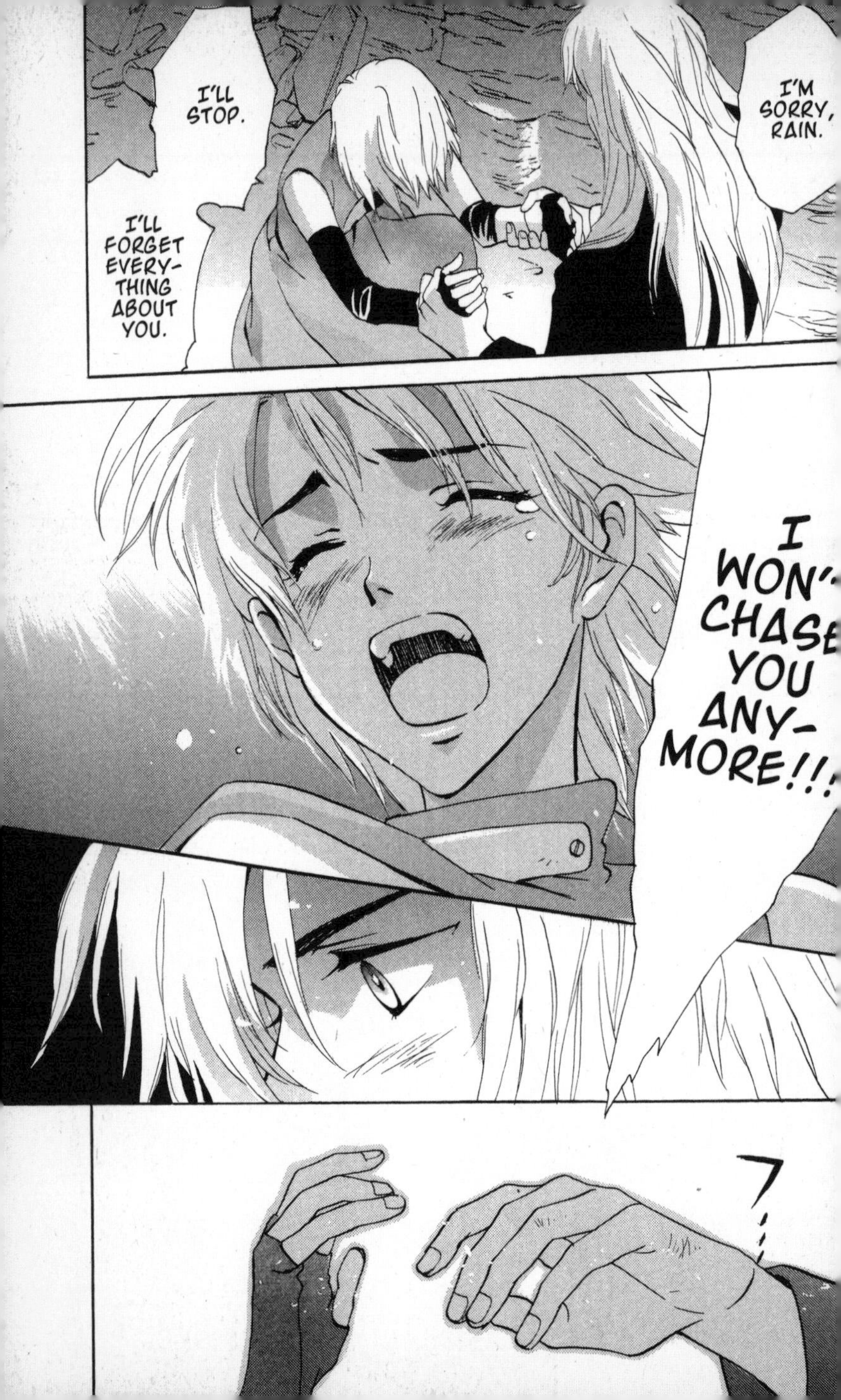
I'M SORRY, RAIN.
I'LL STOP.
I'LL FORGET EVERY-THING ABOUT YOU.
I WON' CHASE YOU ANY-MORE!!!

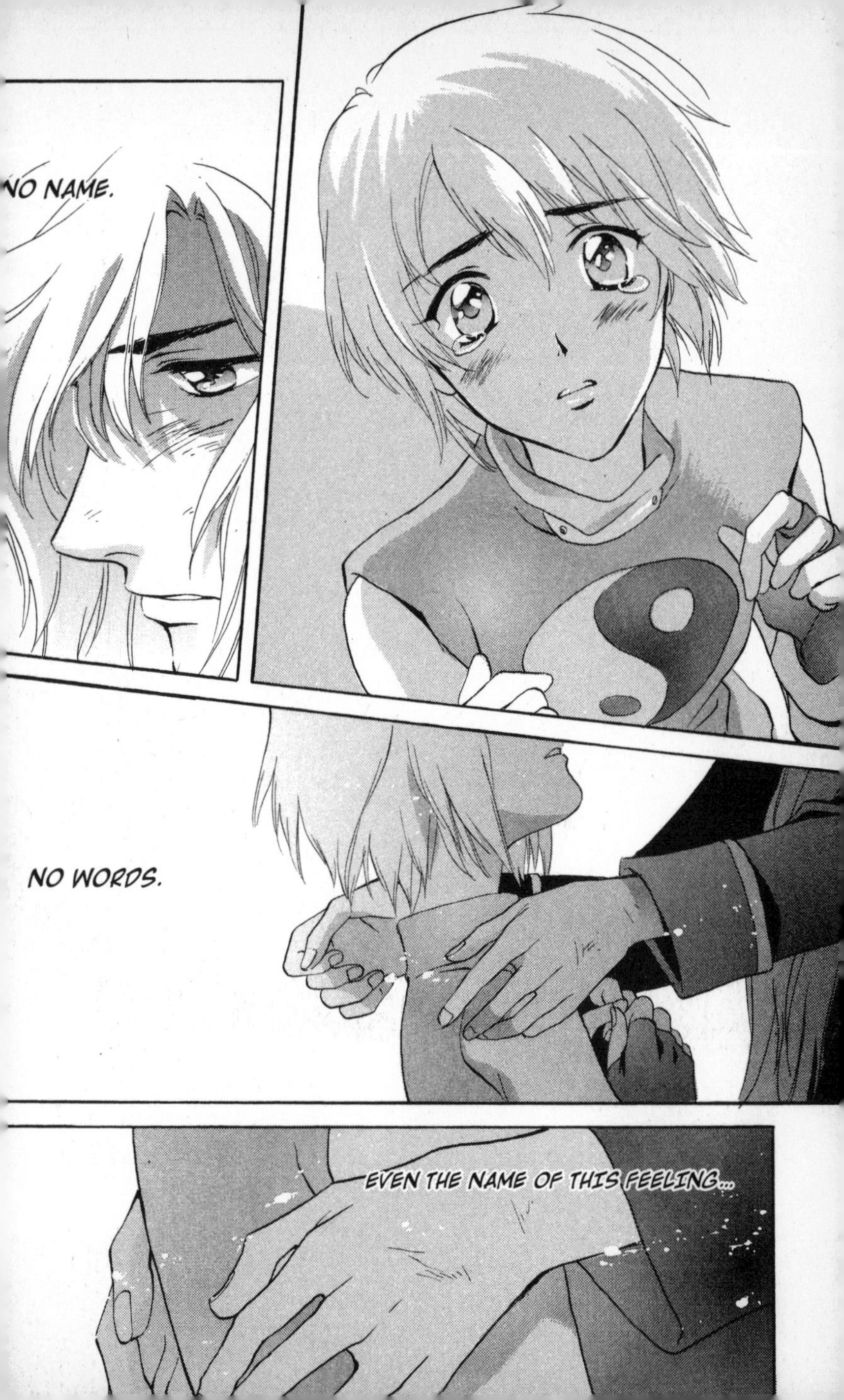
NO NAME.
NO WORDS.
EVEN THE NAME OF THIS FEELING...

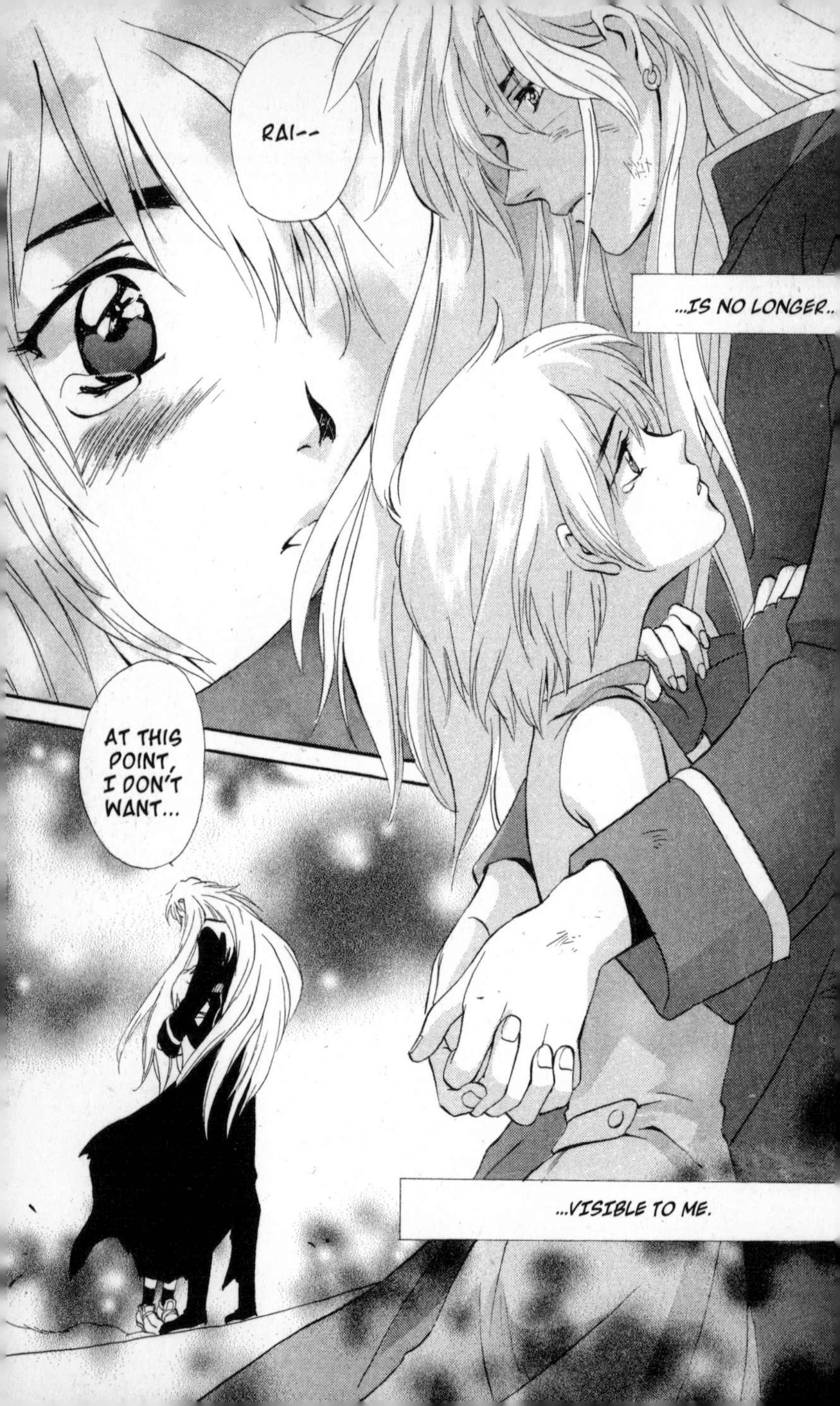
RAI--
...IS NO LONGER..
AT THIS POINT, I DON'T WANT...
...VISIBLE TO ME.

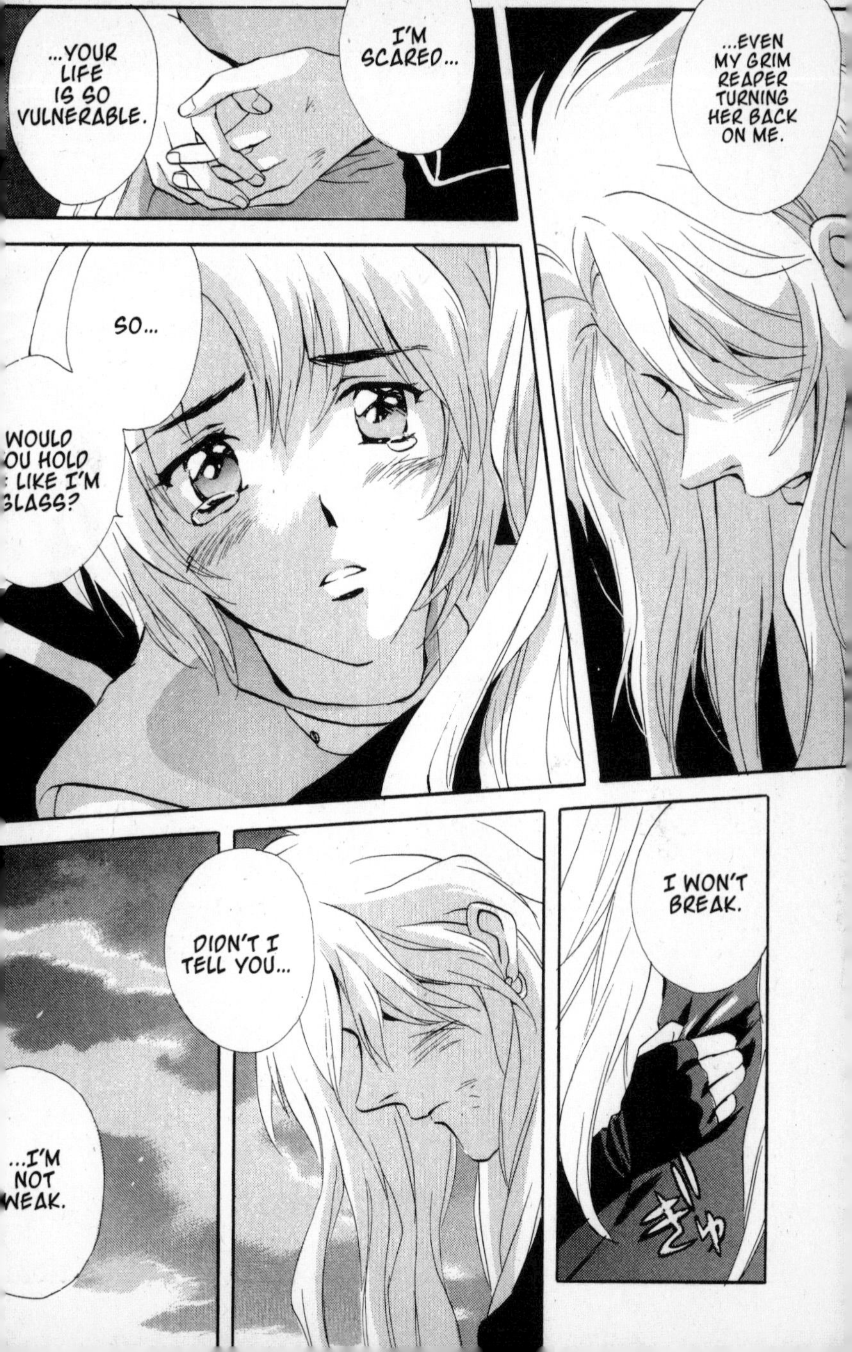
...EVEN MY GRIM REAPER TURNING HER BACK ON ME.
I'M SCARED...
...YOUR LIFE IS SO VULNERABLE.
SO...
WOULD OU HOLD LIKE I'M LASS?
I WON'T BREAK.
ぎゅ
DIDN'T I TELL YOU...
...I'M NOT WEAK.

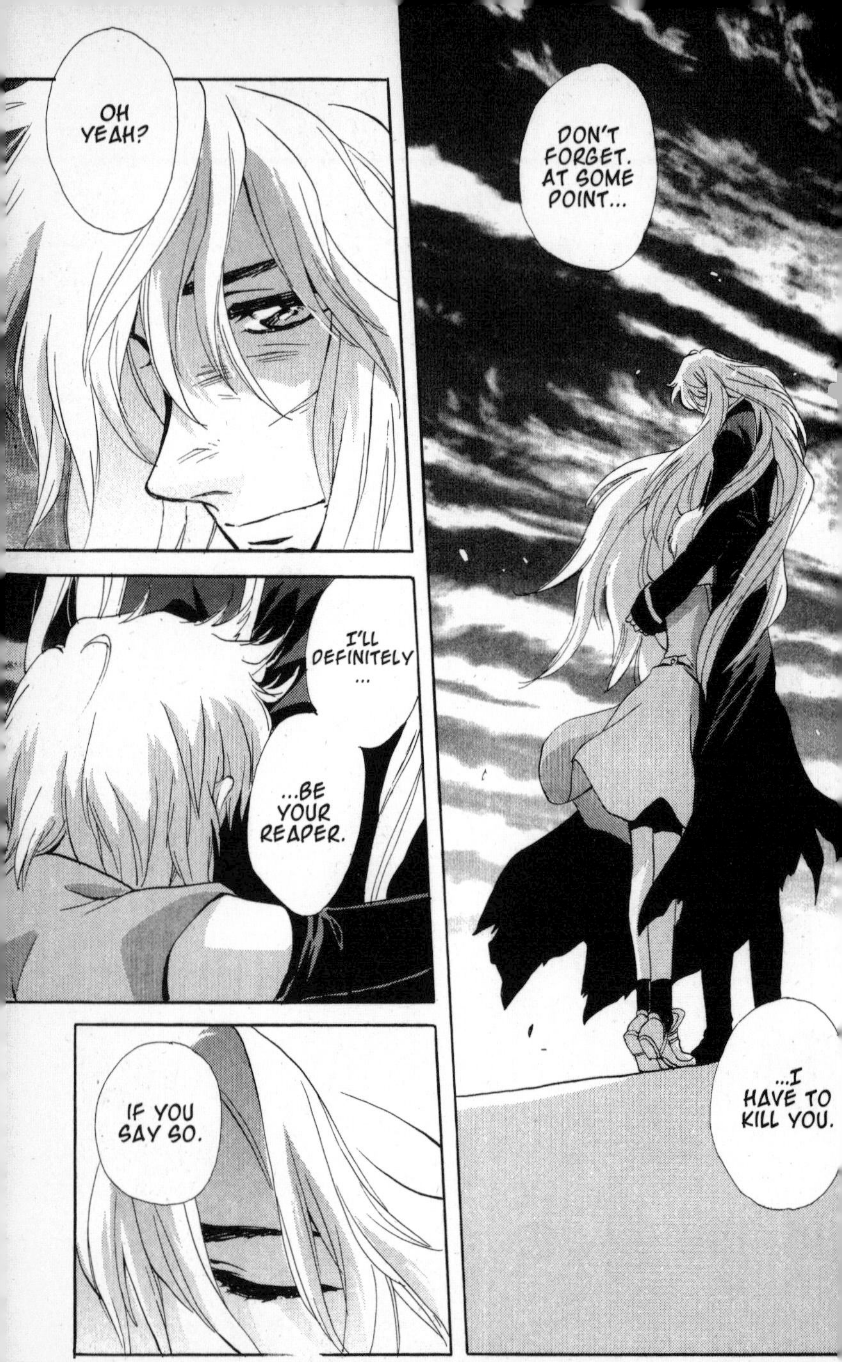
DON'T FORGET. AT SOME POINT...
...I HAVE TO KILL YOU.
OH YEAH?
I'LL DEFINITELY ...
...BE YOUR REAPER.
IF YOU SAY SO.

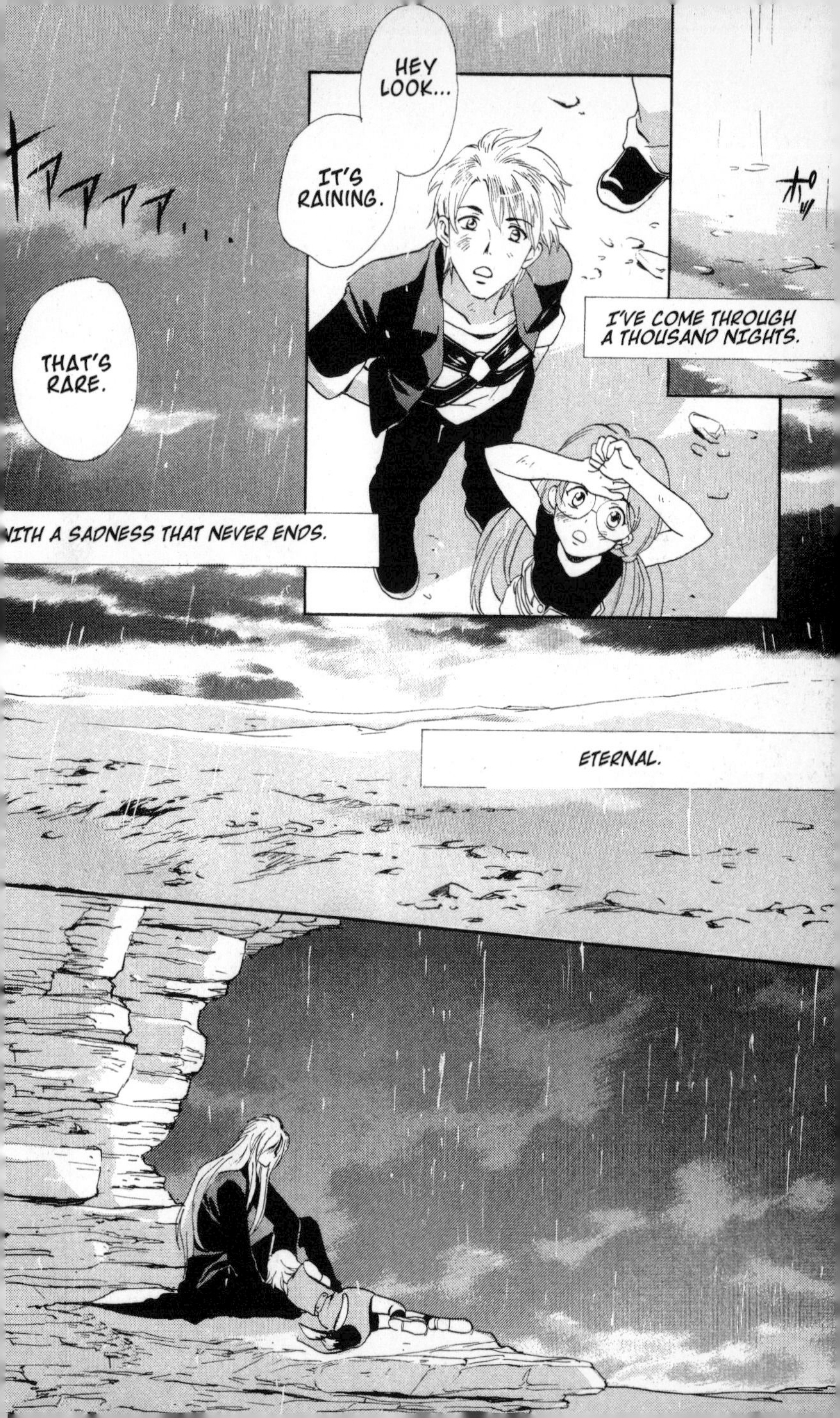
HEY LOOK...
IT'S RAINING.
ポッ
I'VE COME THROUGH A THOUSAND NIGHTS.
ァァァァ...
THAT'S RARE.
WITH A SADNESS THAT NEVER ENDS.
ETERNAL.

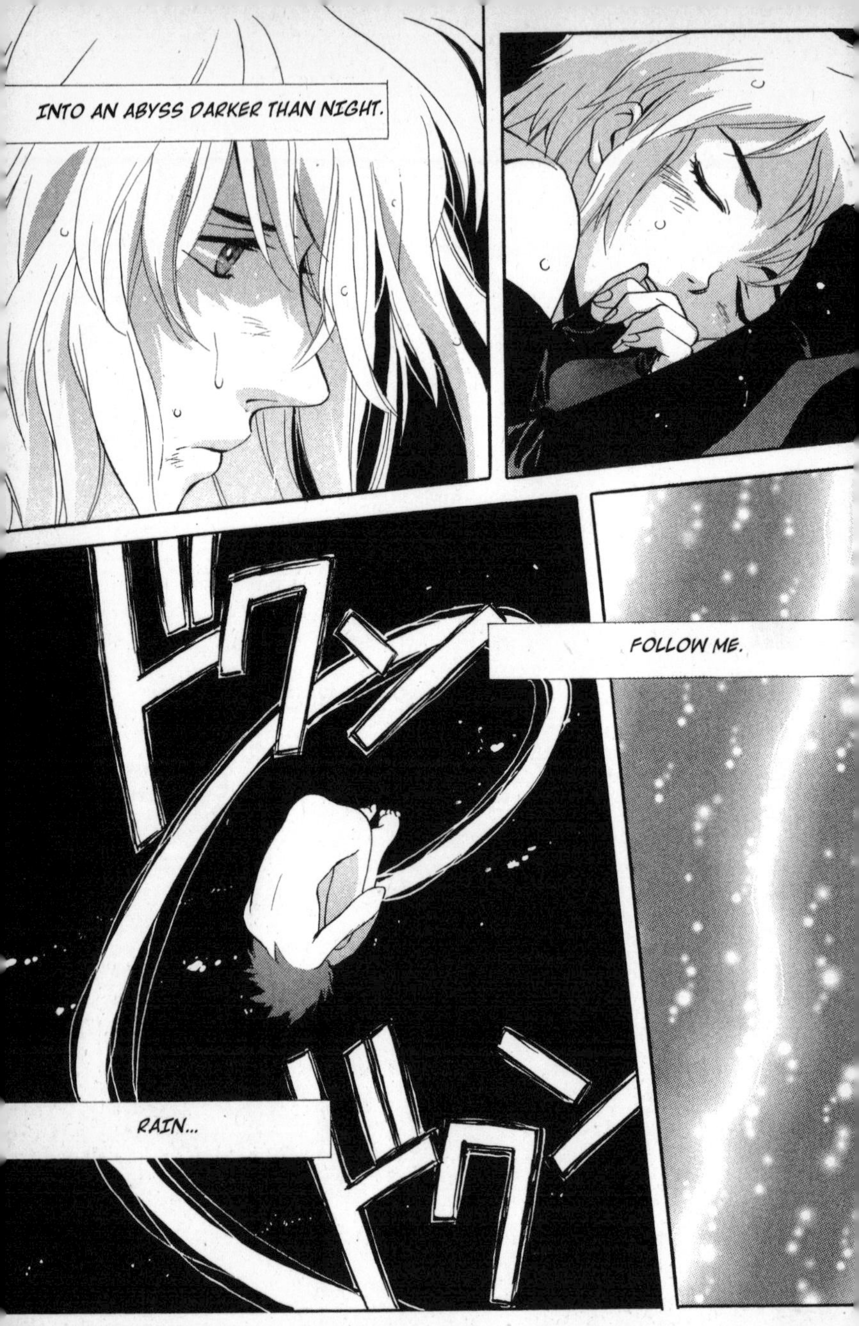
INTO AN ABYSS DARKER THAN NIGHT.
FOLLOW ME.
RAIN...

COCKPIT DESIGN
マンダムコックピット
MY MANDAM!!
COIN SLOT (WHERE SHE STORES THE MONEY EURY SENDS.)
DISPLAY
SNACK (STRAWBERRY POCKY)
DIRECTION JOYSTICK
PUNCH, KICK, BLOCK BUTTON

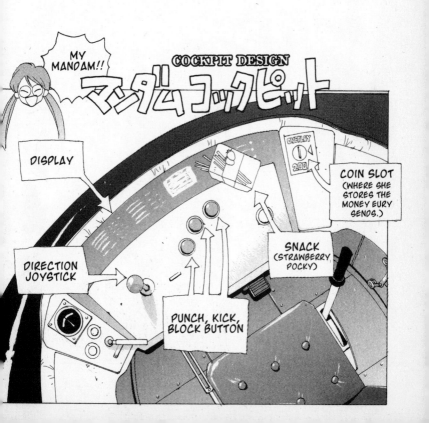

I WAS WAITING FOR
YOUR VOICE TO CALL.

A NEW FLOWER...

...WITH NO NAME...

...BLOSSOMS FROM
THIS EMPTY BREAST.

●●● Cross 9 ●●●

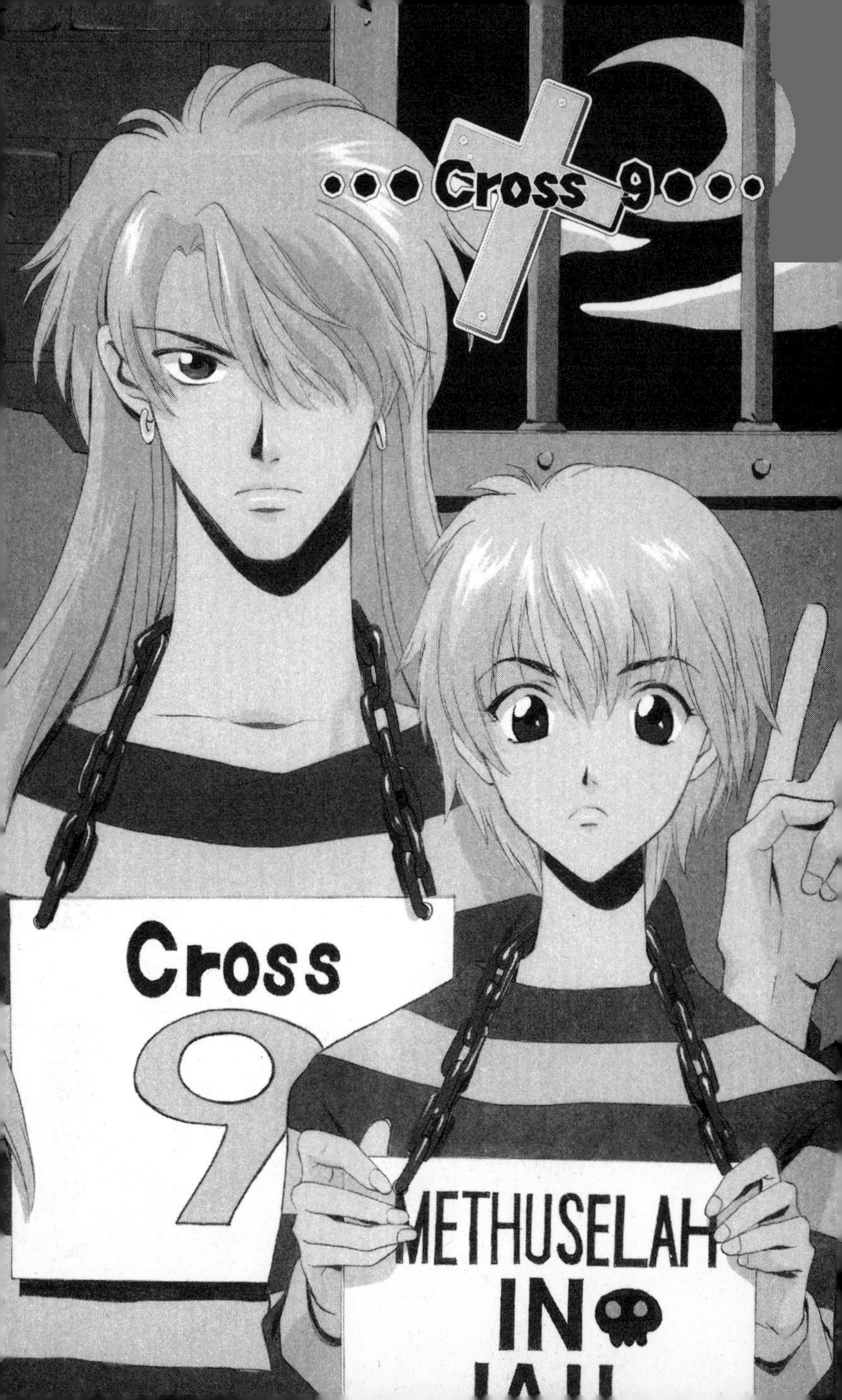

Cross 9
Cross
9
METHUSELAH
IN

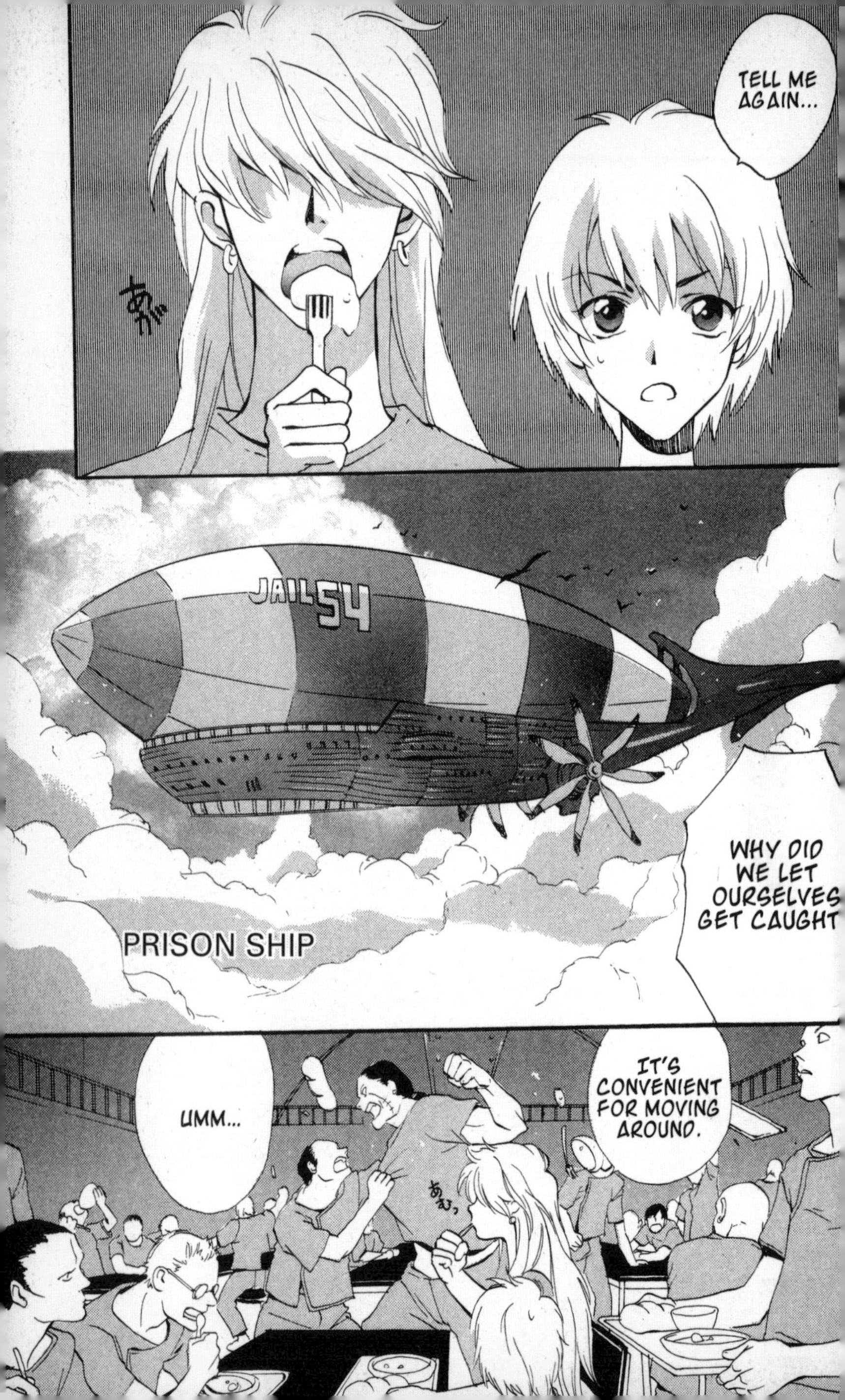
TELL ME AGAIN...
WHY DID WE LET OURSELVES GET CAUGHT
JAIL 54
PRISON SHIP
IT'S CONVENIENT FOR MOVING AROUND.
あむっ
UMM...

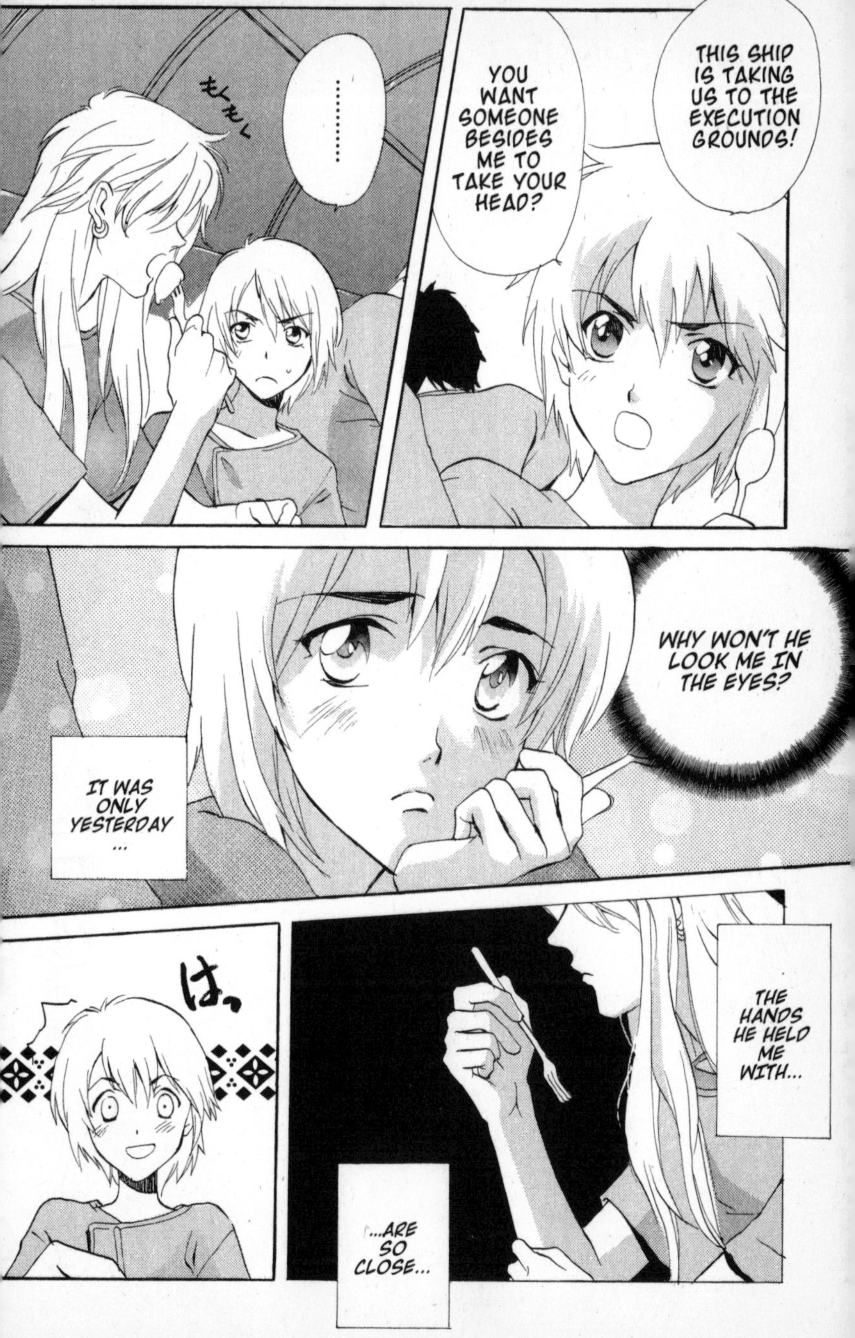
THIS SHIP IS TAKING US TO THE EXECUTION GROUNDS!
YOU WANT SOMEONE BESIDES ME TO TAKE YOUR HEAD?
....
もくもく
WHY WON'T HE LOOK ME IN THE EYES?
IT WAS ONLY YESTERDAY ...
THE HANDS HE HELD ME WITH...
...ARE SO CLOSE...
はっ

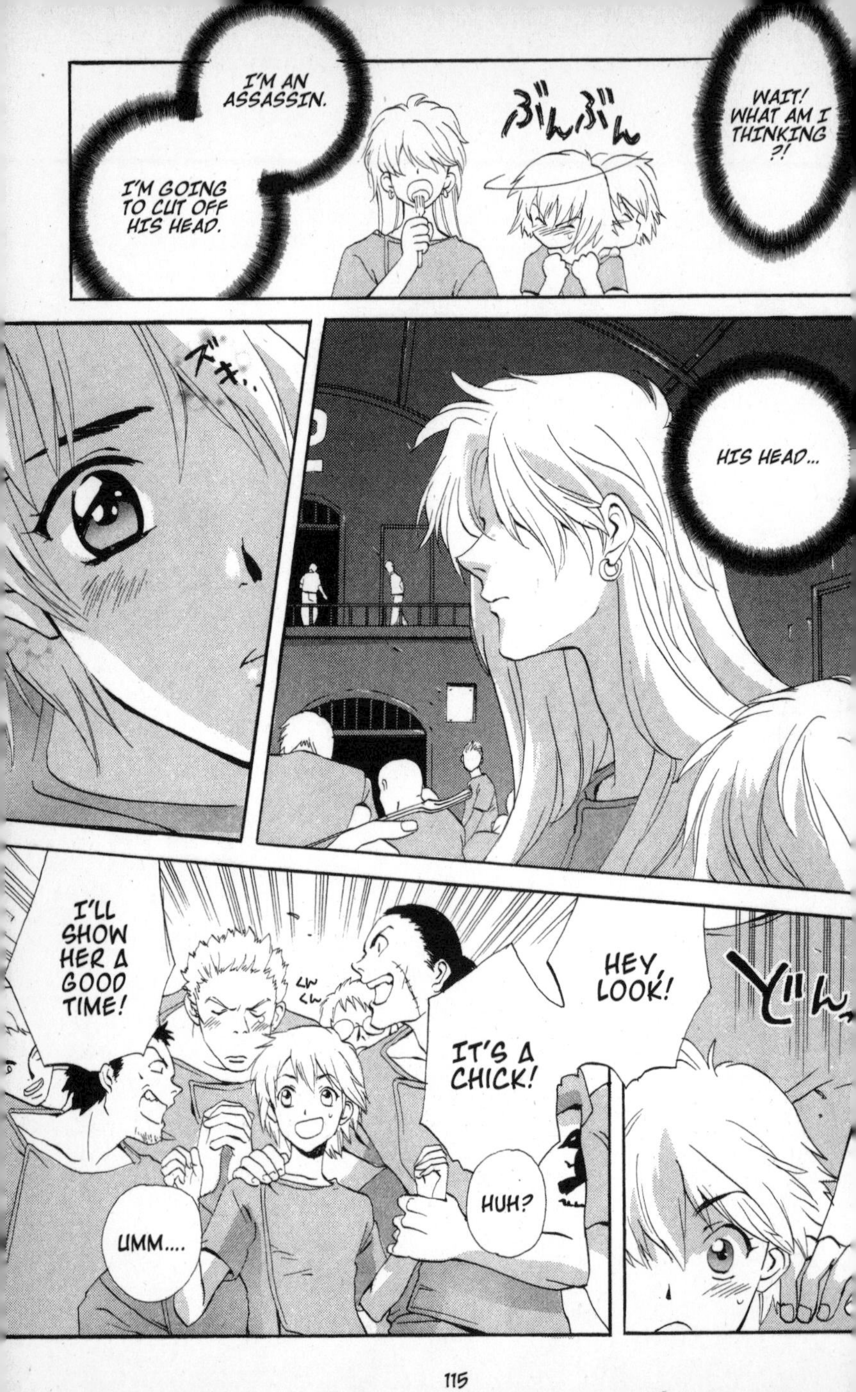

WAIT! WHAT AM I THINKING?!
ぶんぶん
I'M AN ASSASSIN.
I'M GOING TO CUT OFF HIS HEAD.
HIS HEAD...
ズキ...
ビん
HEY, LOOK!
IT'S A CHICK!
HUH?
I'LL SHOW HER A GOOD TIME!
UMM....

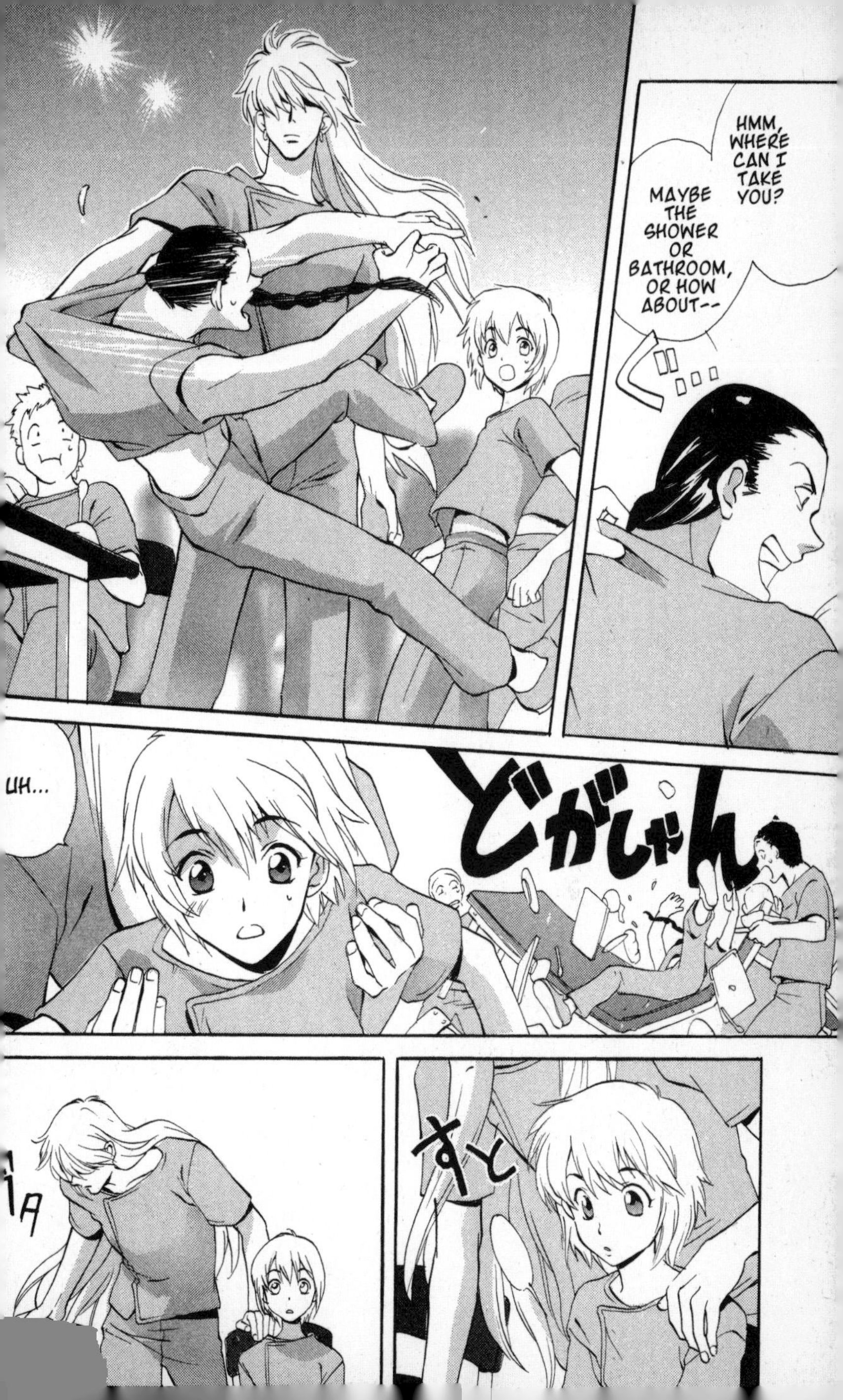
HMM, WHERE CAN I TAKE YOU?
MAYBE THE SHOWER OR BATHROOM, OR HOW ABOUT--
どがしゃん
UH...
すと

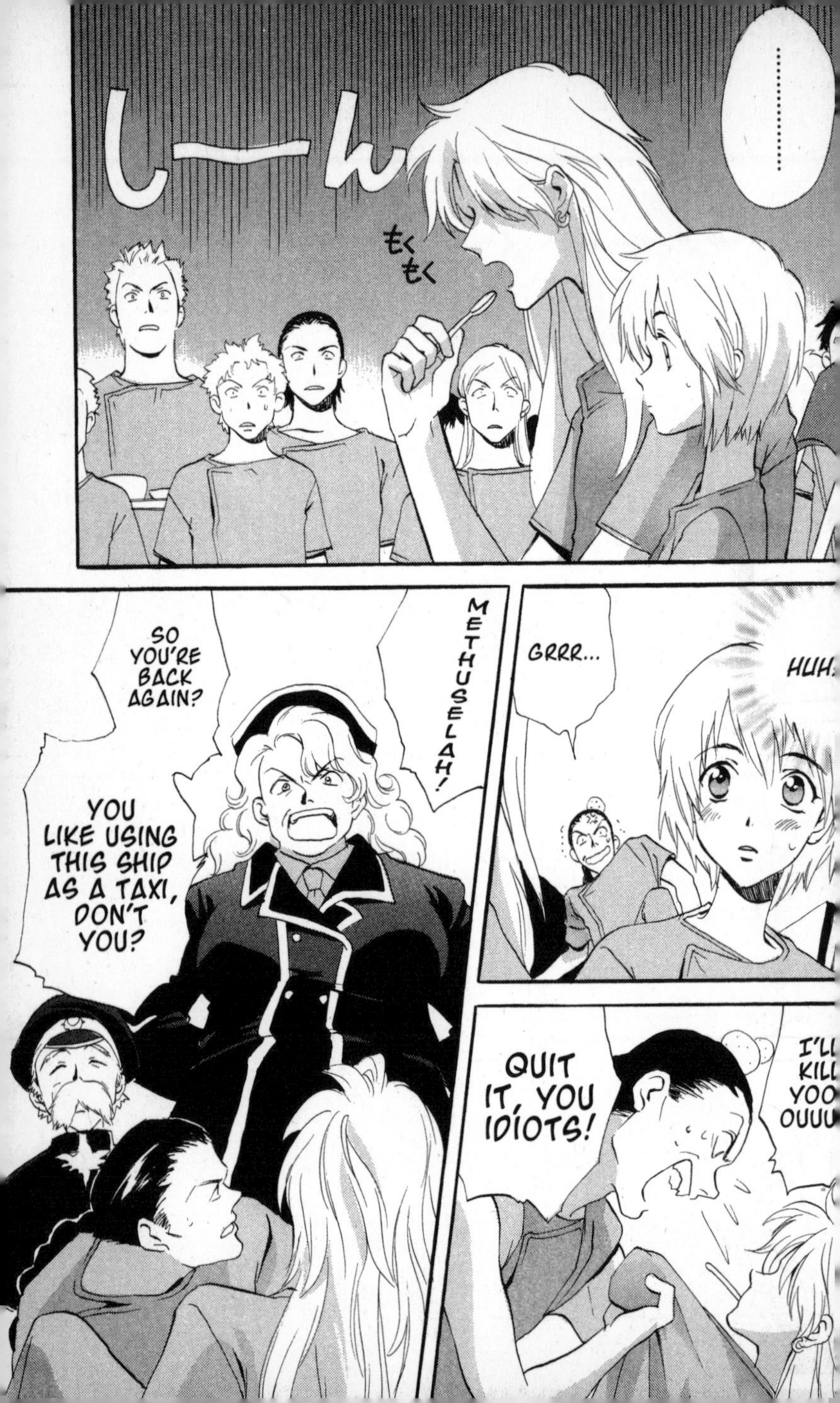
……
しーん
もくもく
HUH.
GRRR...
I'LL KILL YOOOUUU
QUIT IT, YOU IDIOTS!
METHUSELAH!
SO YOU'RE BACK AGAIN?
YOU LIKE USING THIS SHIP AS A TAXI, DON'T YOU?

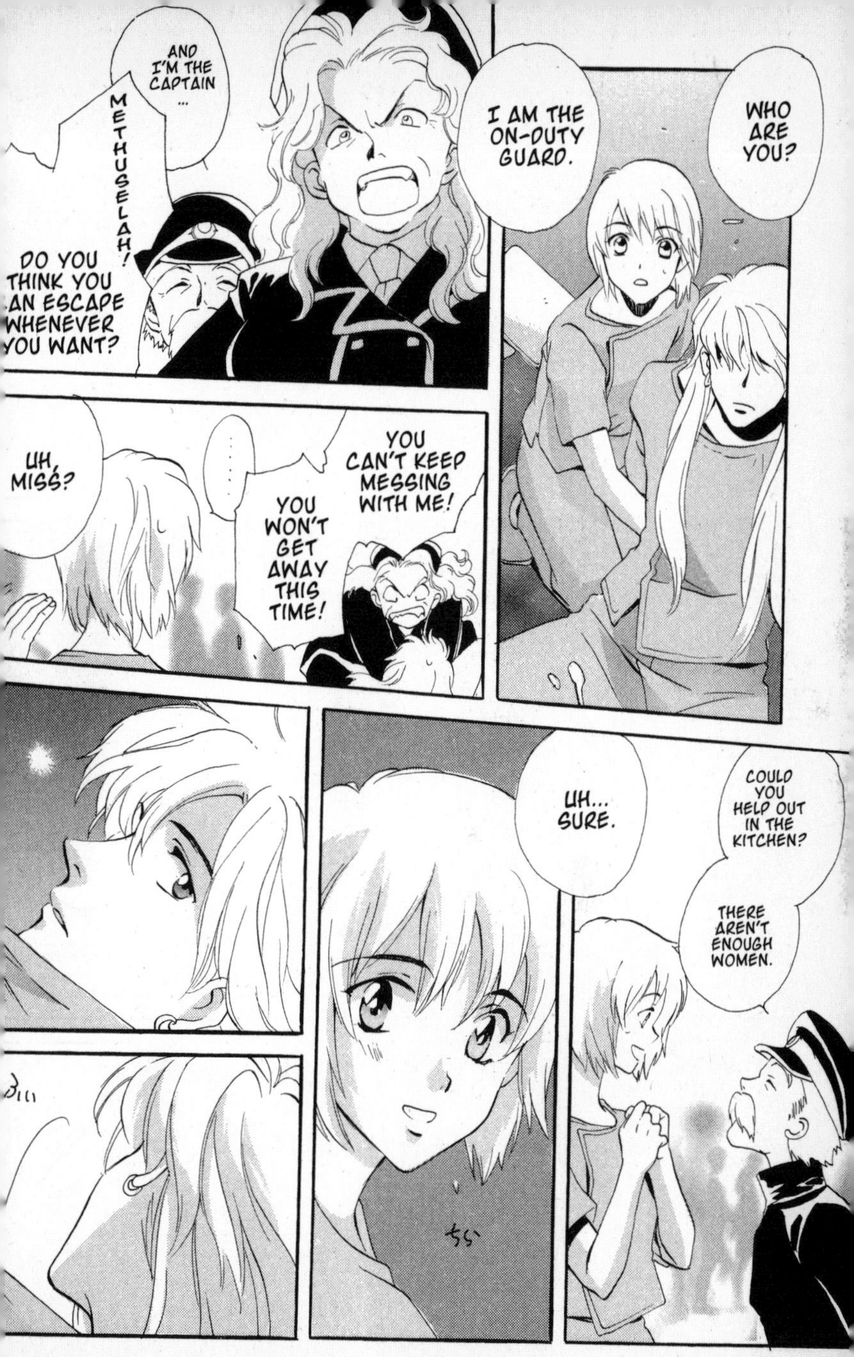
WHO ARE YOU?
I AM THE ON-DUTY GUARD.
AND I'M THE CAPTAIN ...
METHUSELAH!
DO YOU THINK YOU AN ESCAPE HENEVER YOU WANT?
YOU CAN'T KEEP MESSING WITH ME!
YOU WON'T GET AWAY THIS TIME!
......
UH, MISS?
COULD YOU HELP OUT IN THE KITCHEN?
THERE AREN'T ENOUGH WOMEN.
UH... SURE.

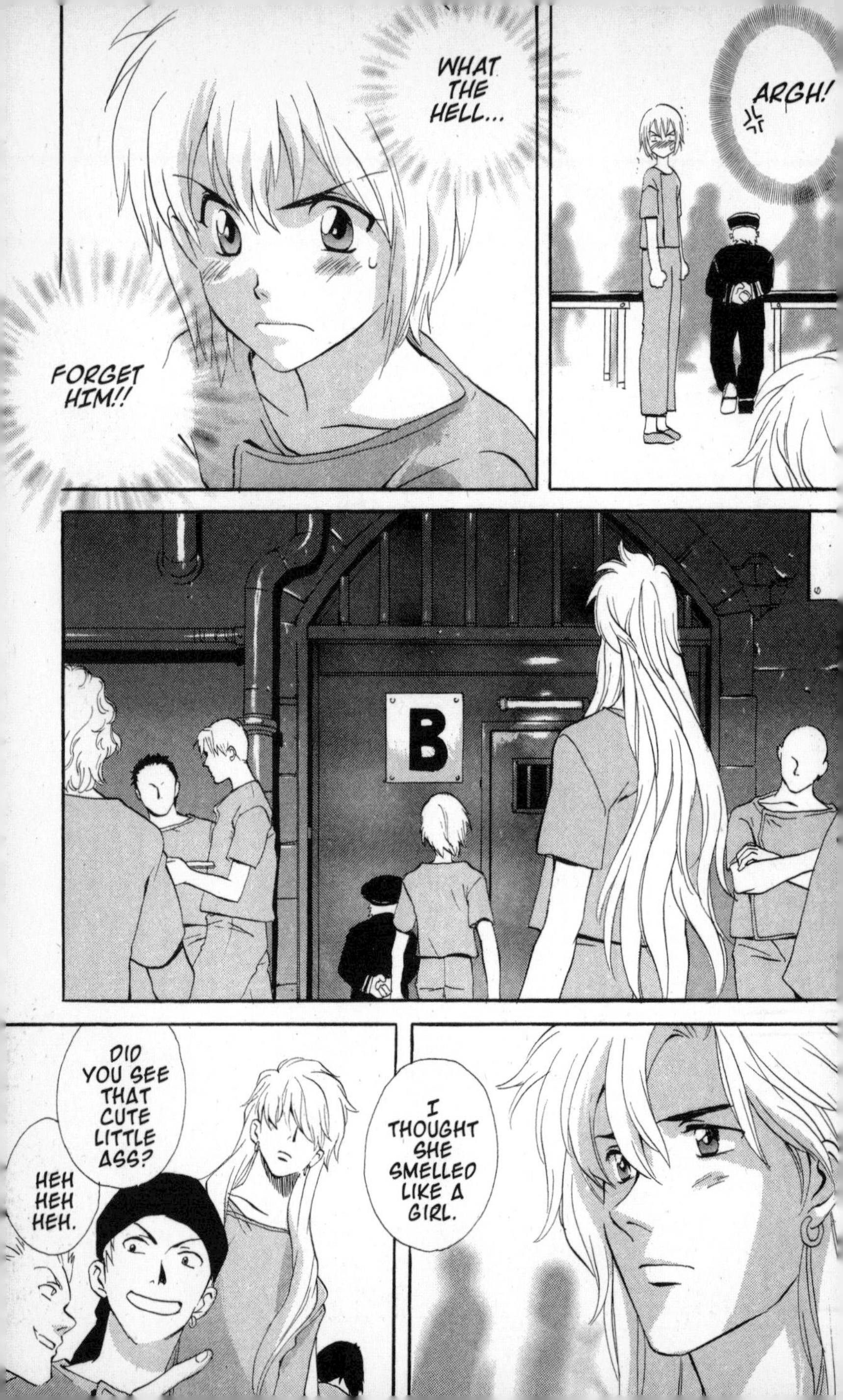
ARGH!
WHAT THE HELL...
FORGET HIM!!
B
I THOUGHT SHE SMELLED LIKE A GIRL.
DID YOU SEE THAT CUTE LITTLE ASS?
HEH HEH HEH.

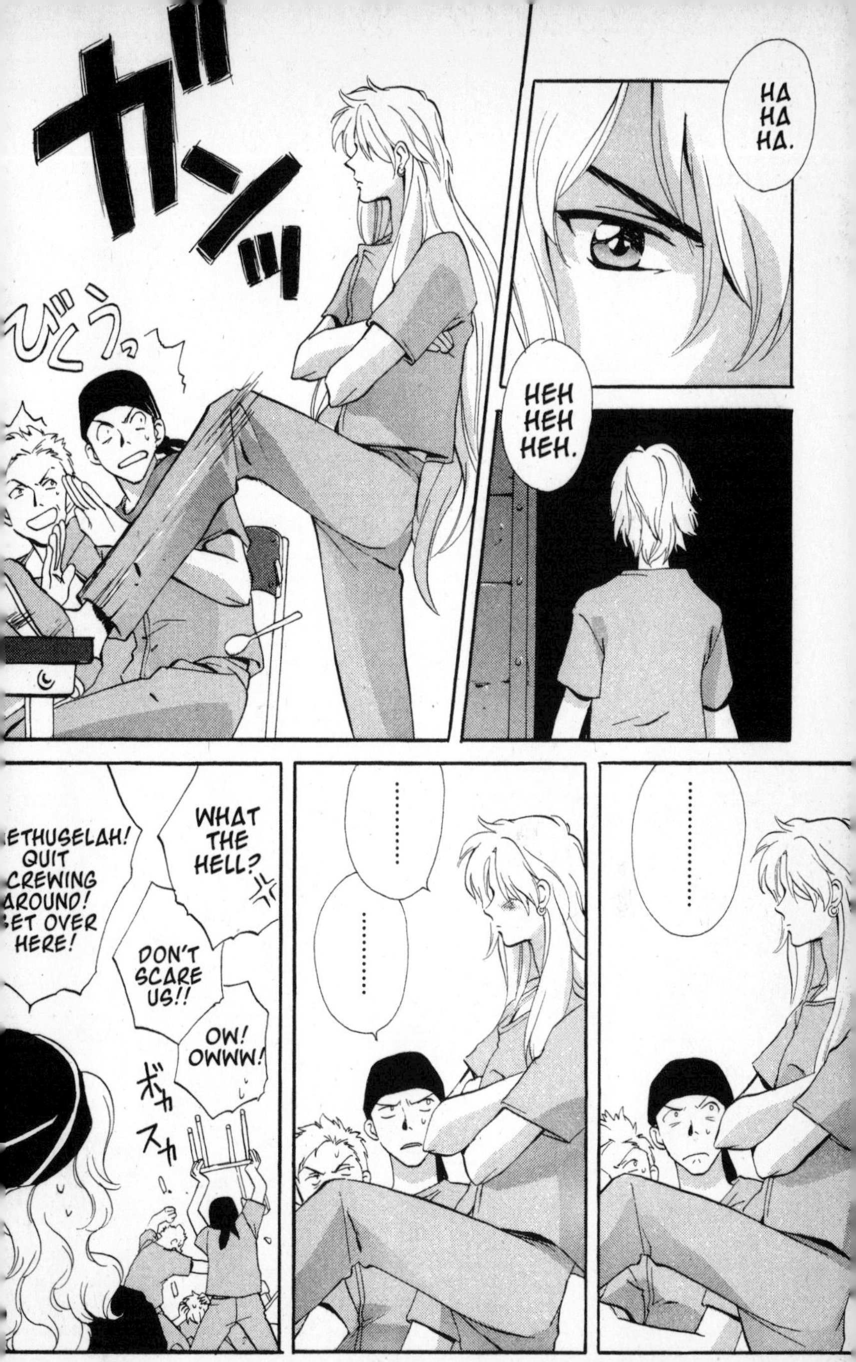
HA HA HA.
HEH HEH HEH.
ガンッ
びくぅっ
......
......
......
WHAT THE HELL?
ETHUSELAH! QUIT CREWING AROUND! ET OVER HERE!
DON'T SCARE US!!
OW! OWWW!
ボカスカ

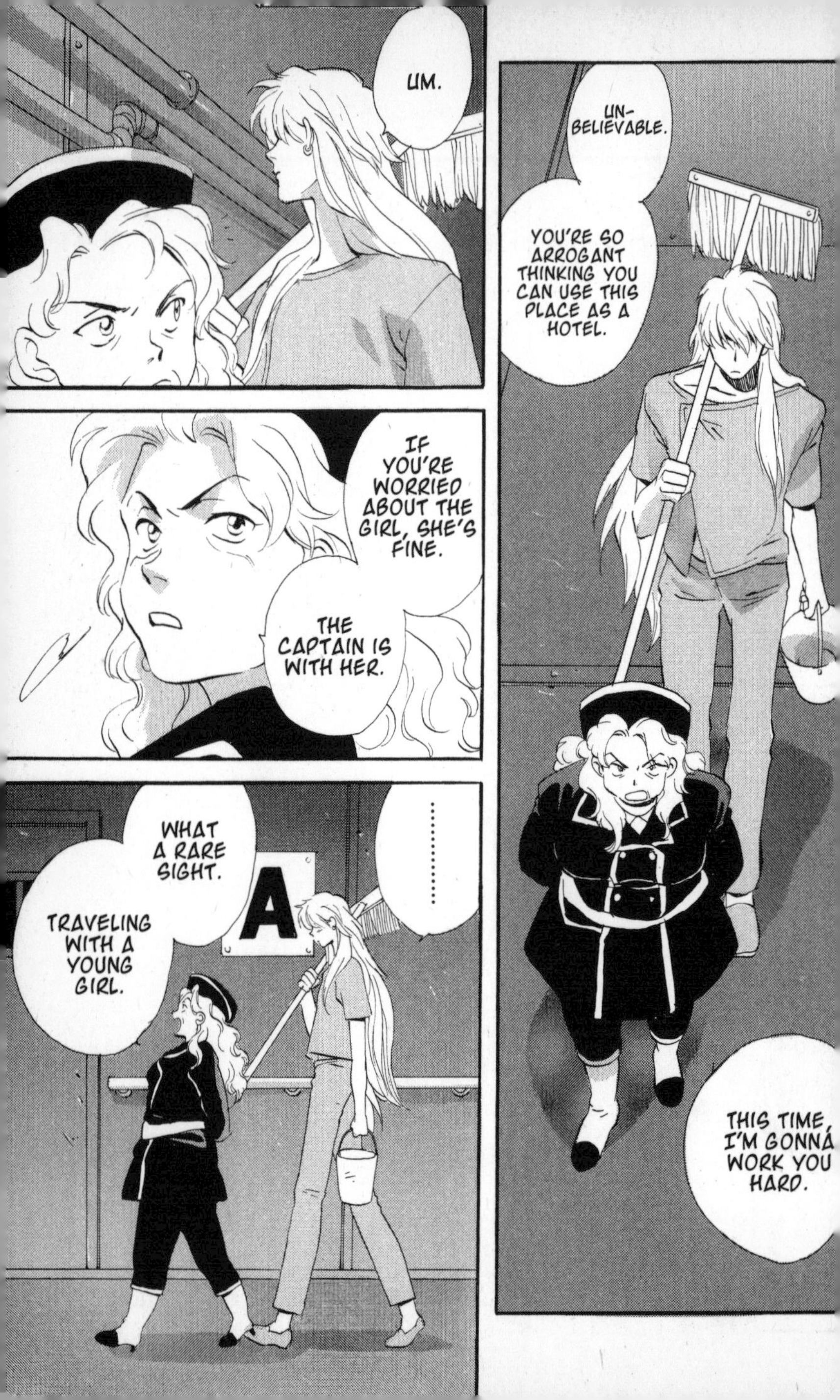
UN-BELIEVABLE.
YOU'RE SO ARROGANT THINKING YOU CAN USE THIS PLACE AS A HOTEL.
THIS TIME, I'M GONNA WORK YOU HARD.
UM.
IF YOU'RE WORRIED ABOUT THE GIRL, SHE'S FINE.
THE CAPTAIN IS WITH HER.
....
WHAT A RARE SIGHT.
TRAVELING WITH A YOUNG GIRL.
A

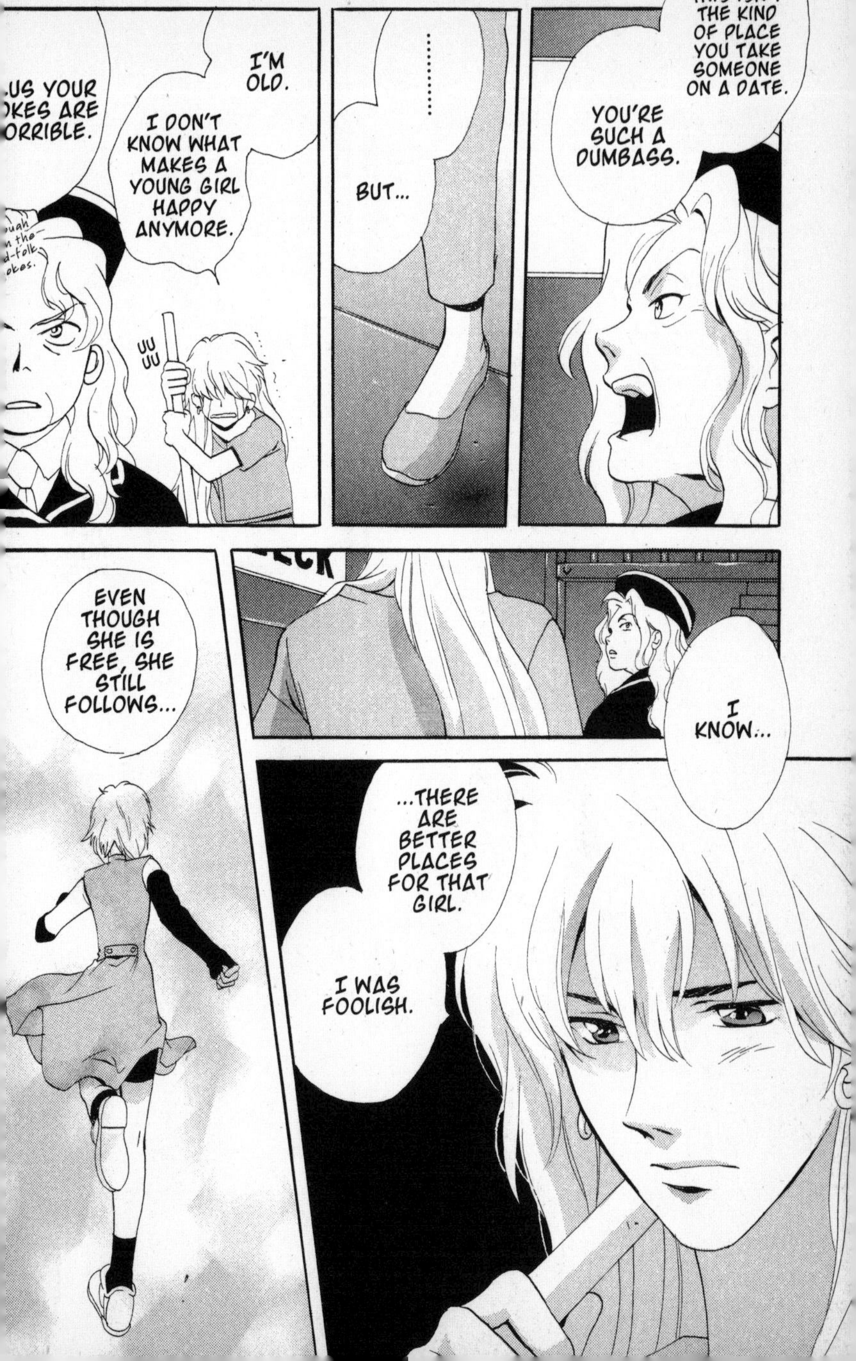
THIS ISN'T THE KIND OF PLACE YOU TAKE SOMEONE ON A DATE.
YOU'RE SUCH A DUMBASS.
......
BUT...
I'M OLD.
I DON'T KNOW WHAT MAKES A YOUNG GIRL HAPPY ANYMORE.
US YOUR OKES ARE ORRIBLE.
UU UU
I KNOW...
...THERE ARE BETTER PLACES FOR THAT GIRL.
I WAS FOOLISH.
EVEN THOUGH SHE IS FREE, SHE STILL FOLLOWS...

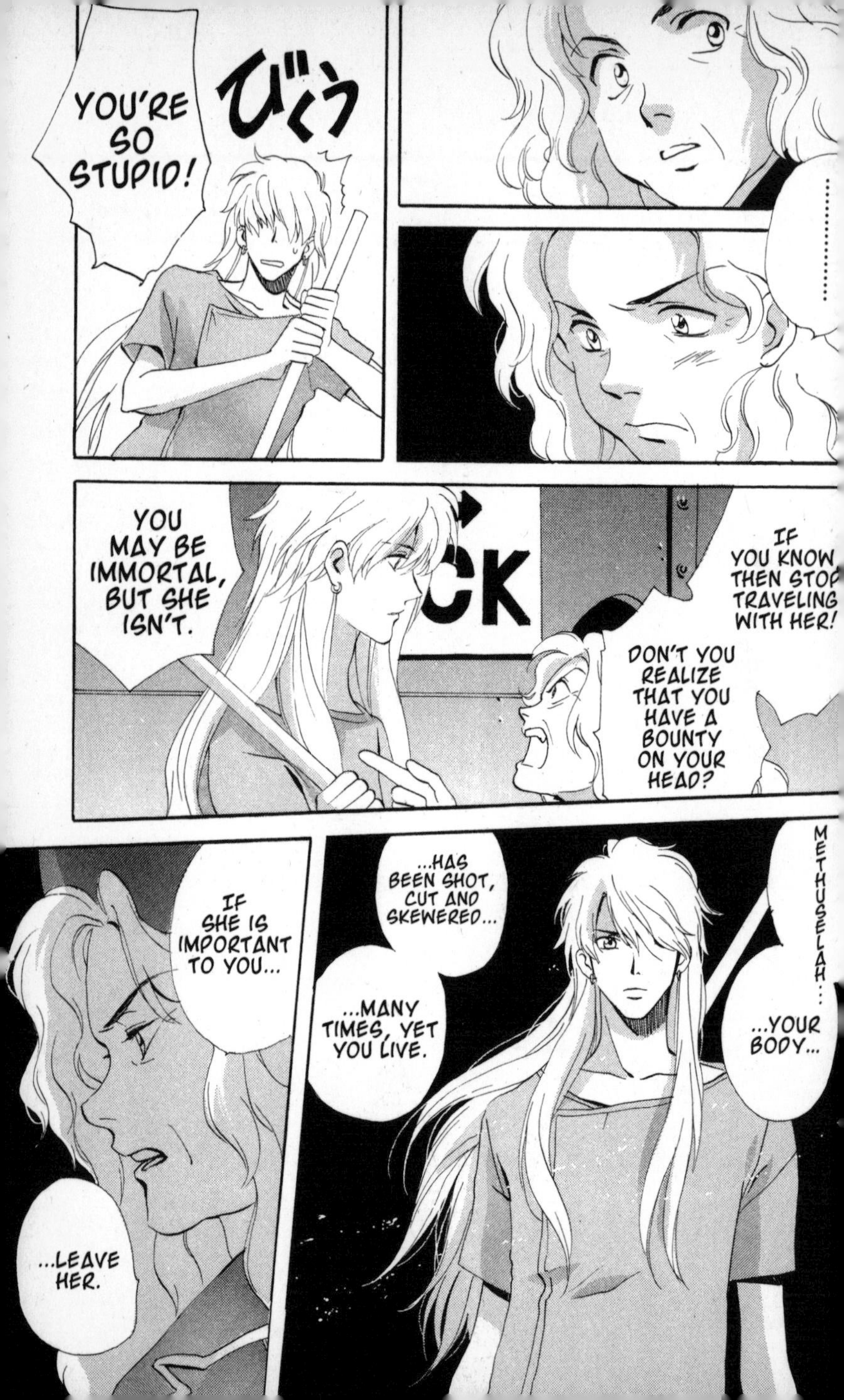
......
びくぅ
YOU'RE SO STUPID!
IF YOU KNOW THEN STOP TRAVELING WITH HER!
DON'T YOU REALIZE THAT YOU HAVE A BOUNTY ON YOUR HEAD?
YOU MAY BE IMMORTAL, BUT SHE ISN'T.
METHUSELAH...
...YOUR BODY...
...HAS BEEN SHOT, CUT AND SKEWERED...
...MANY TIMES, YET YOU LIVE.
IF SHE IS IMPORTANT TO YOU...
...LEAVE HER.

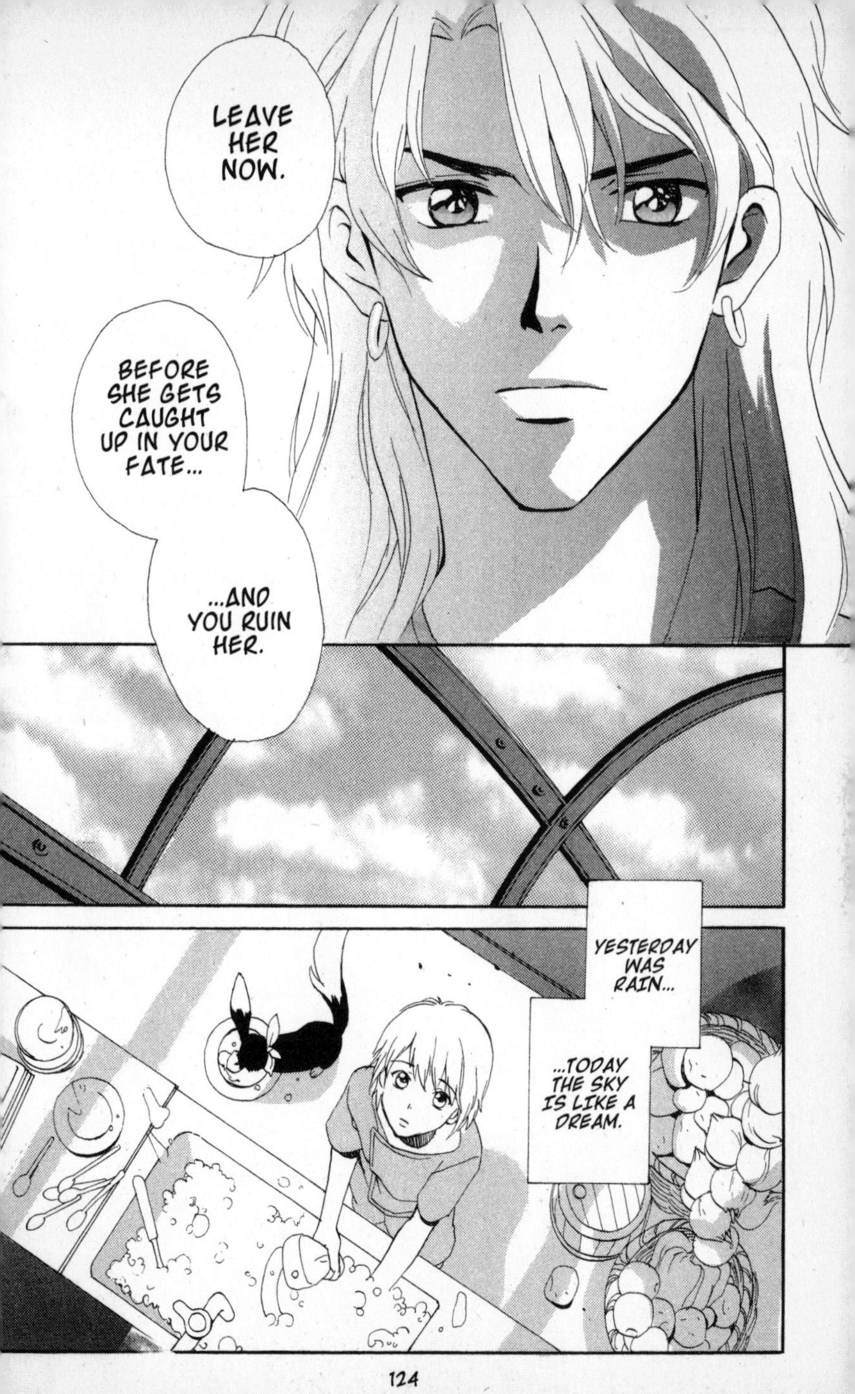
LEAVE HER NOW.
BEFORE SHE GETS CAUGHT UP IN YOUR FATE...
...AND YOU RUIN HER.
YESTERDAY WAS RAIN...
...TODAY THE SKY IS LIKE A DREAM.

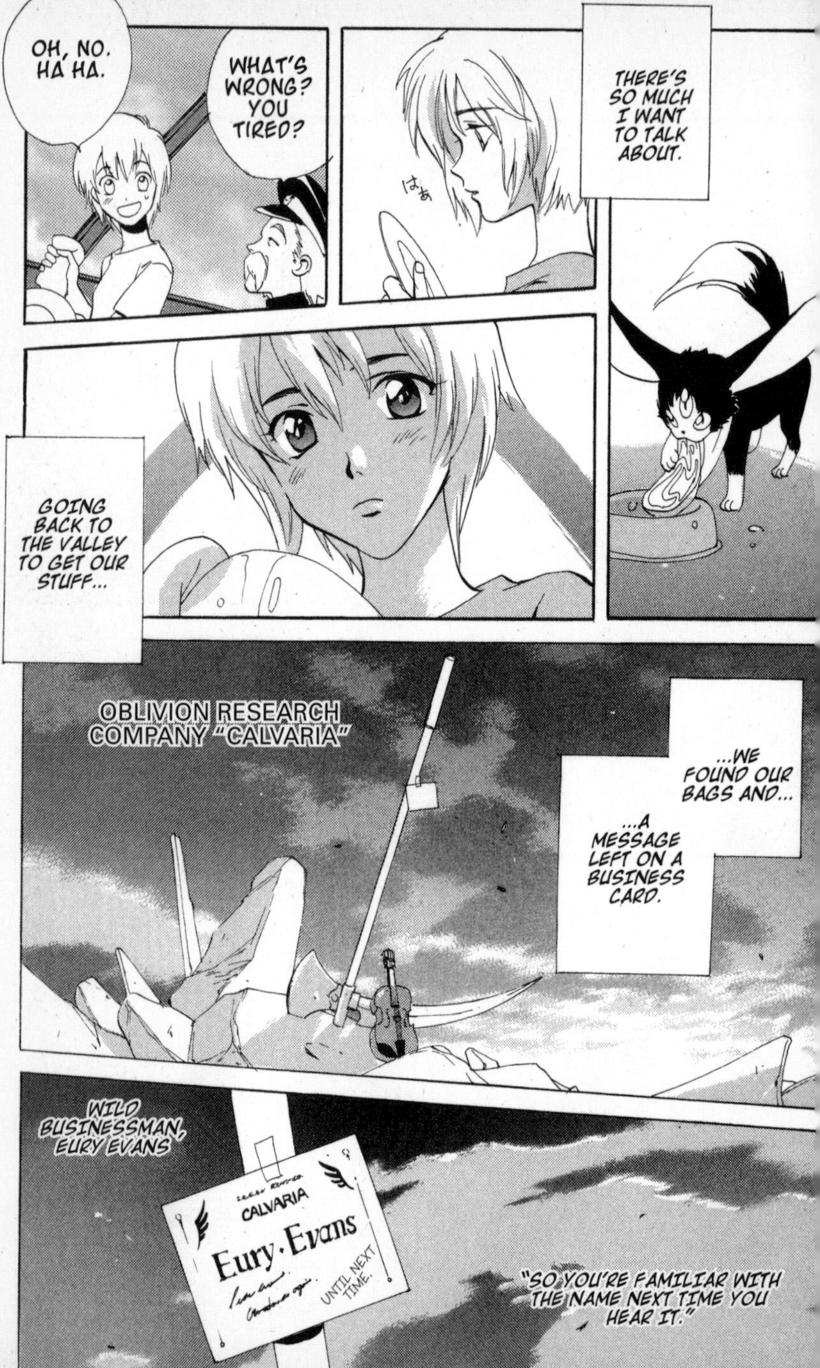
THERE'S SO MUCH I WANT TO TALK ABOUT.
はぁ
WHAT'S WRONG? YOU TIRED?
OH, NO. HA HA.
GOING BACK TO THE VALLEY TO GET OUR STUFF...
...WE FOUND OUR BAGS AND...
...A MESSAGE LEFT ON A BUSINESS CARD.
OBLIVION RESEARCH COMPANY "CALVARIA"
WILD BUSINESSMAN, EURY EVANS
CALVARIA
Eury・Evans
UNTIL NEXT TIME.
"SO YOU'RE FAMILIAR WITH THE NAME NEXT TIME YOU HEAR IT."

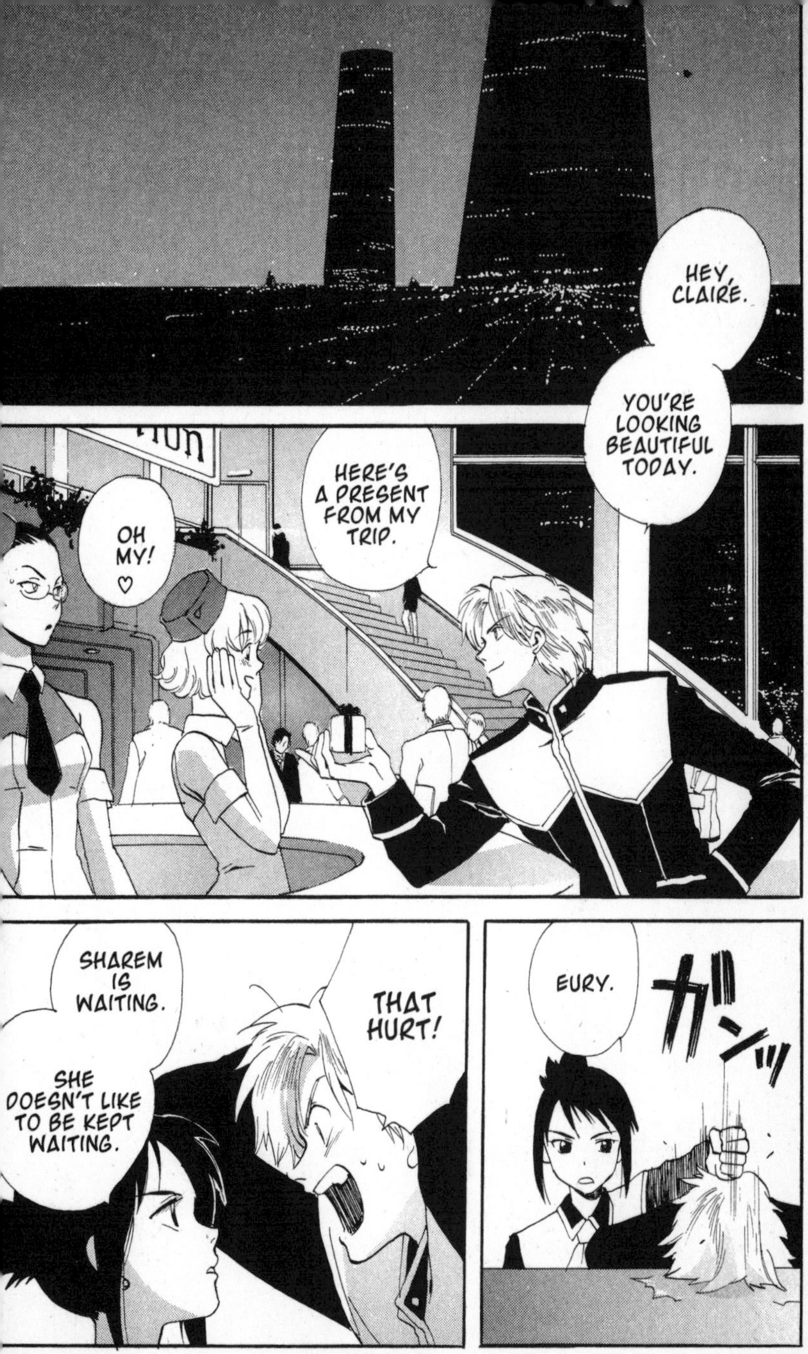
HEY, CLAIRE.
YOU'RE LOOKING BEAUTIFUL TODAY.
HERE'S A PRESENT FROM MY TRIP.
OH MY! ♡
EURY.
ガンッ
THAT HURT!
SHAREM IS WAITING.
SHE DOESN'T LIKE TO BE KEPT WAITING.

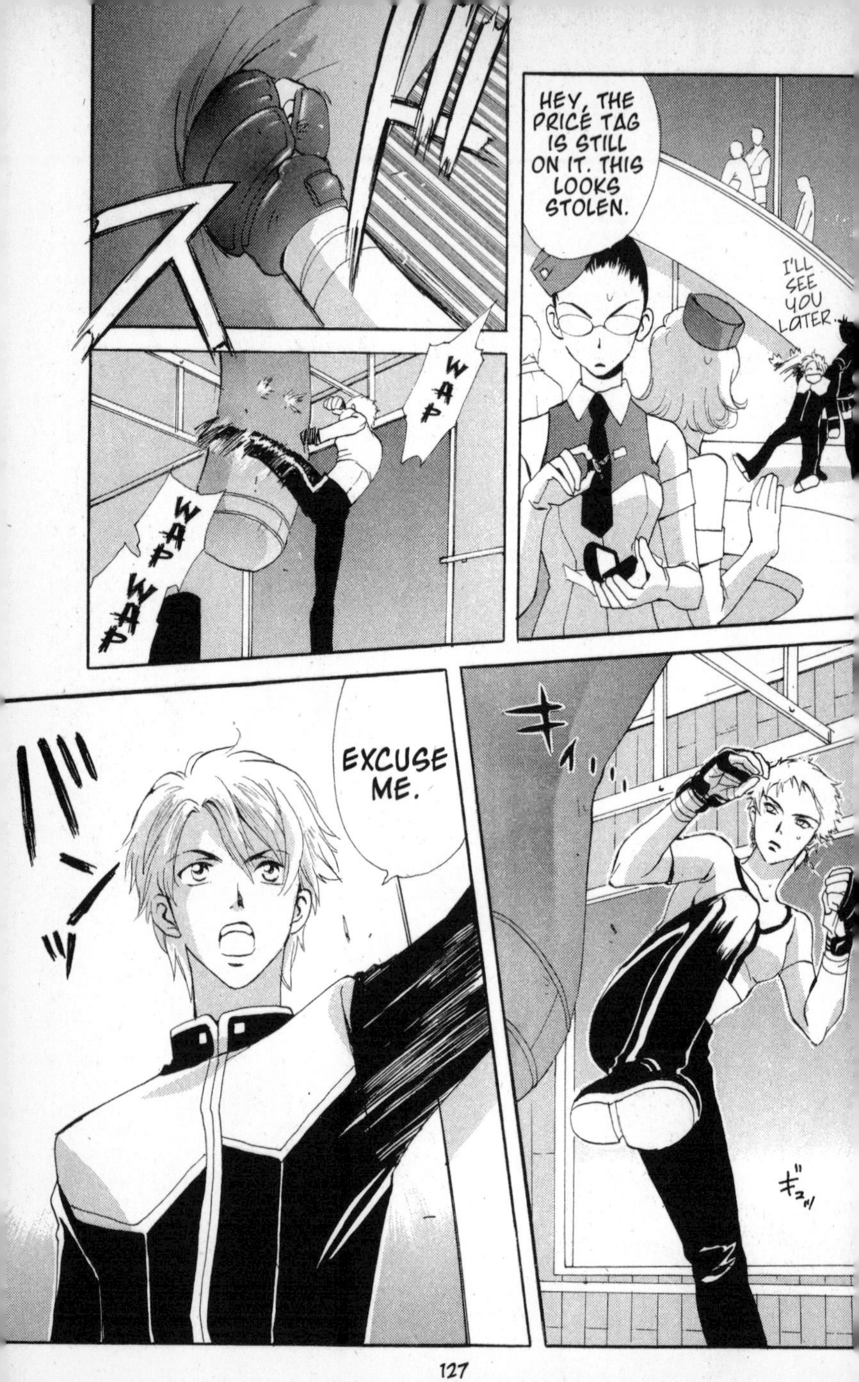
HEY, THE PRICE TAG IS STILL ON IT. THIS LOOKS STOLEN.
I'LL SEE YOU LATER...
WAP
WAP WAP WAP
EXCUSE ME.
バッ

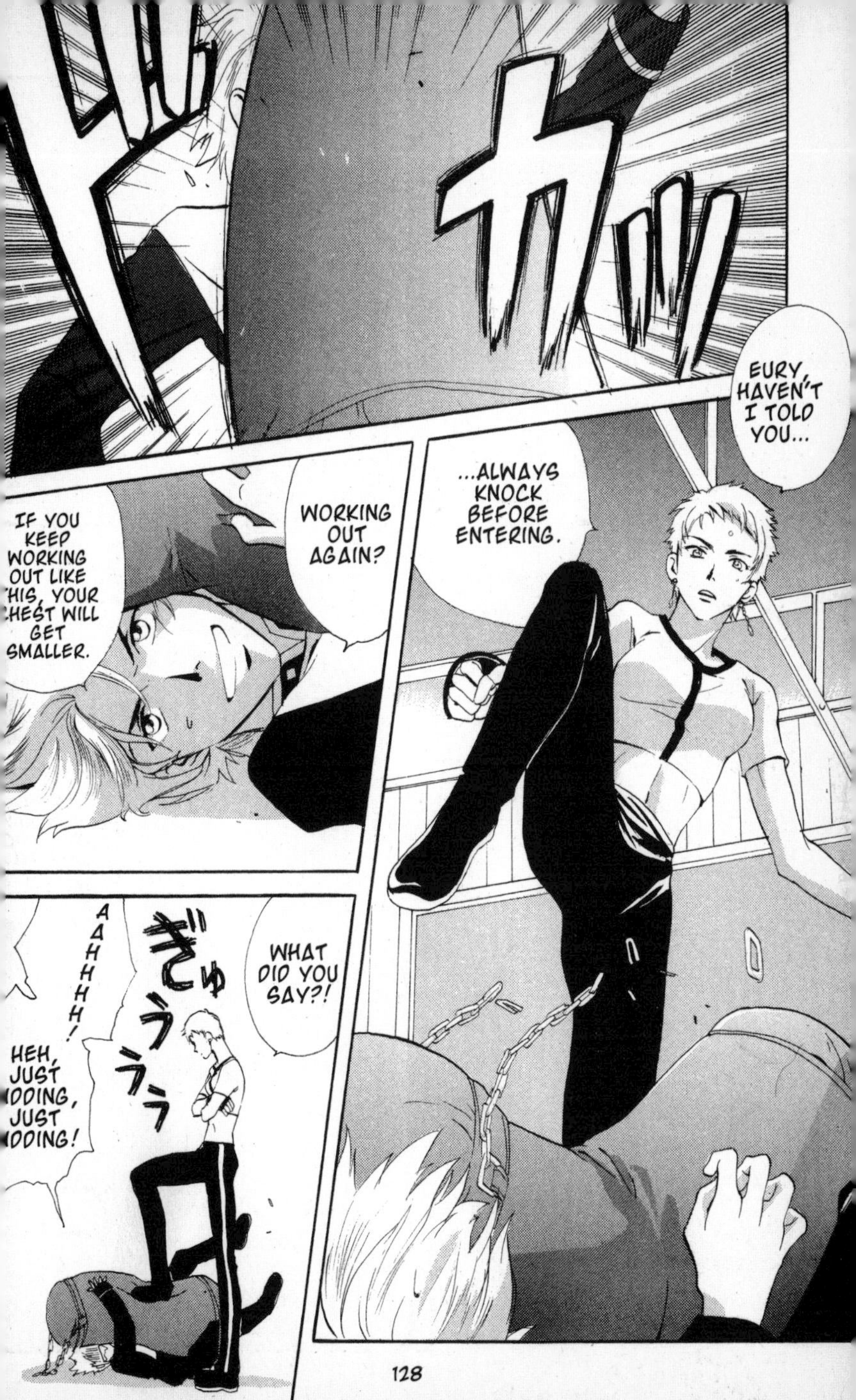

EURY, HAVEN'T I TOLD YOU...
...ALWAYS KNOCK BEFORE ENTERING.
WORKING OUT AGAIN?
IF YOU KEEP WORKING OUT LIKE HIS, YOUR HEST WILL GET SMALLER.
WHAT DID YOU SAY?!
ぎゅううう
AAHHHHH!
HEH, JUST DDING, JUST DDING!

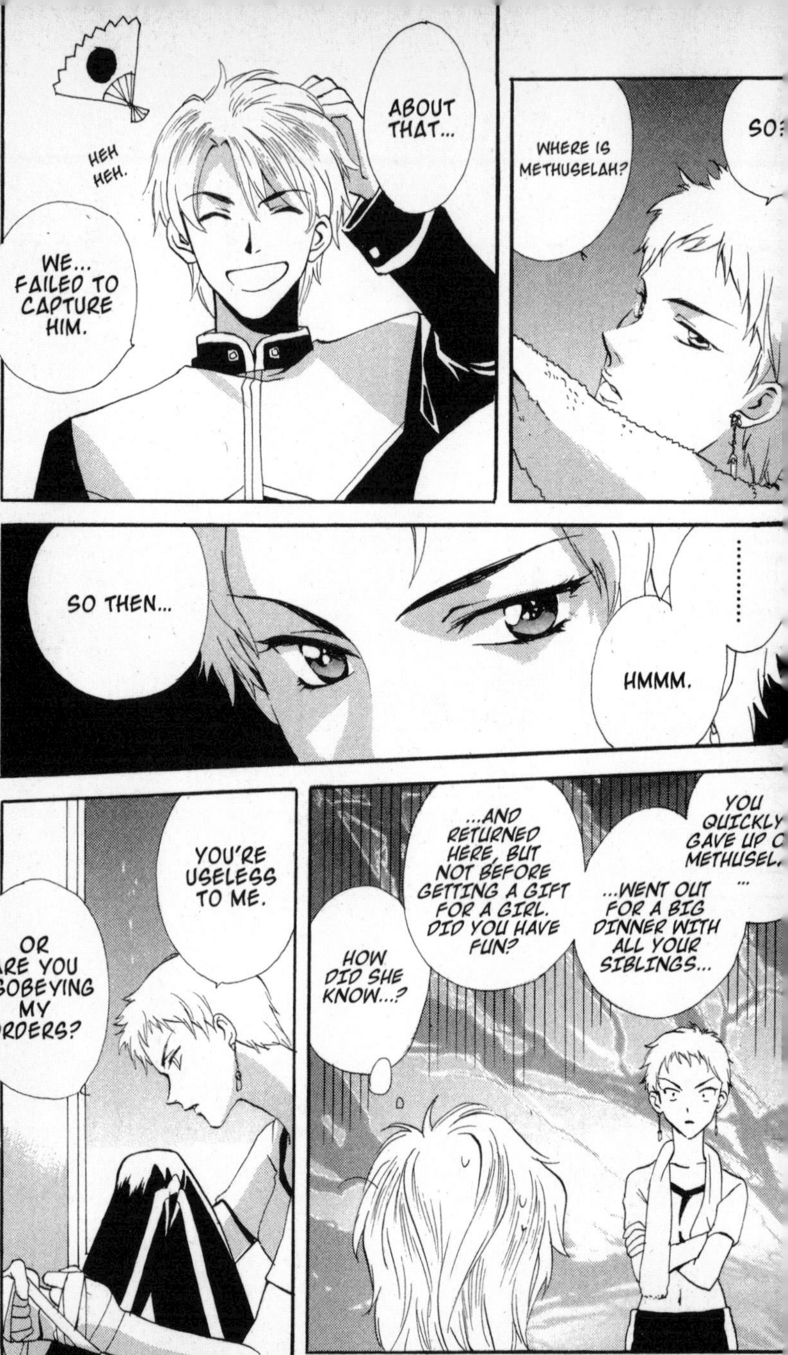
SO
WHERE IS METHUSELAH?
ABOUT THAT...
HEH HEH.
WE... FAILED TO CAPTURE HIM.
......
HMMM.
SO THEN...
YOU QUICKLY GAVE UP O METHUSEL ...
...WENT OUT FOR A BIG DINNER WITH ALL YOUR SIBLINGS...
...AND RETURNED HERE, BUT NOT BEFORE GETTING A GIFT FOR A GIRL. DID YOU HAVE FUN?
HOW DID SHE KNOW...?
YOU'RE USELESS TO ME.
OR ARE YOU DISOBEYING MY ORDERS?

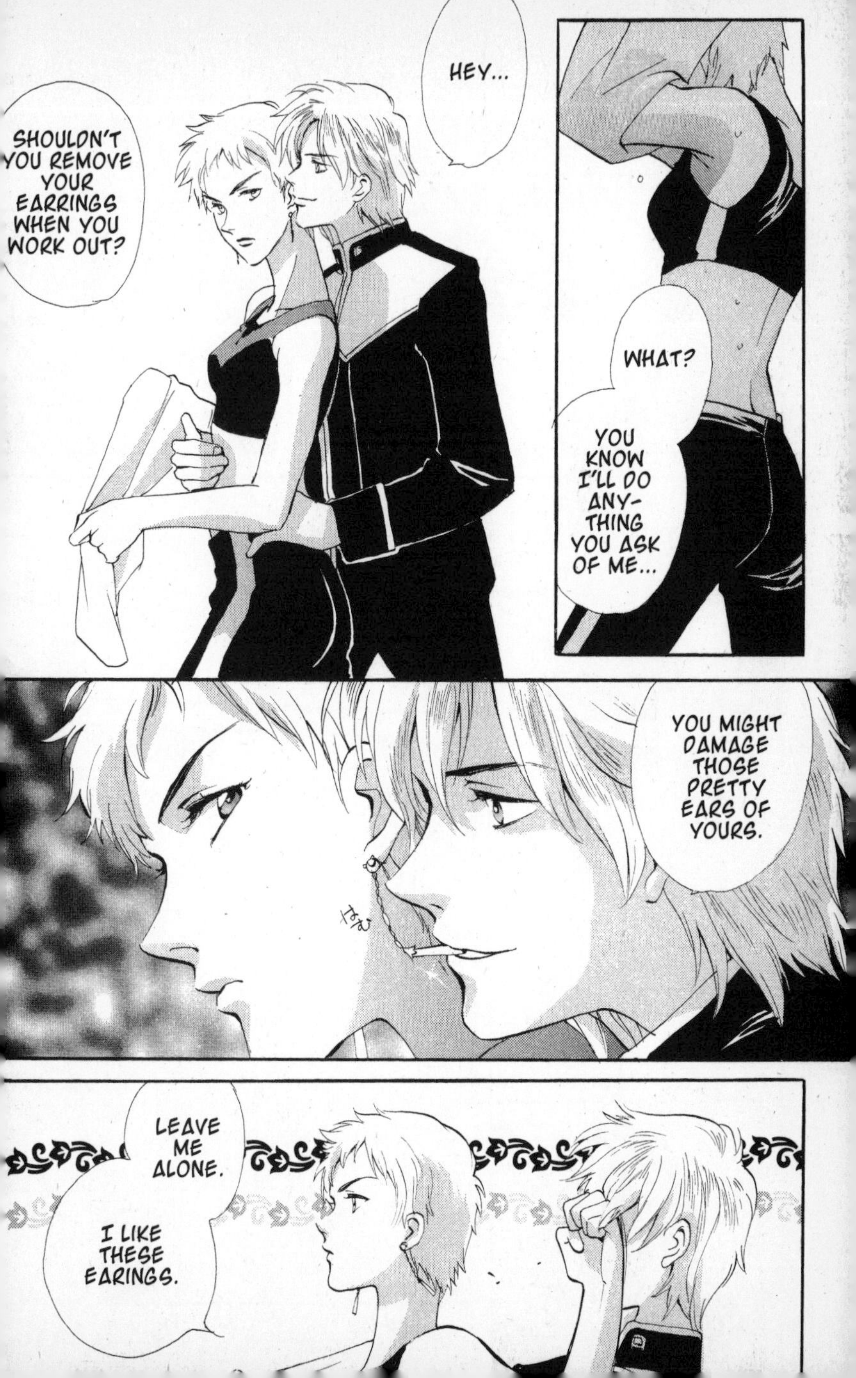
WHAT?
YOU KNOW I'LL DO ANYTHING YOU ASK OF ME...
HEY...
SHOULDN'T YOU REMOVE YOUR EARRINGS WHEN YOU WORK OUT?
YOU MIGHT DAMAGE THOSE PRETTY EARS OF YOURS.
LEAVE ME ALONE.
I LIKE THESE EARINGS.

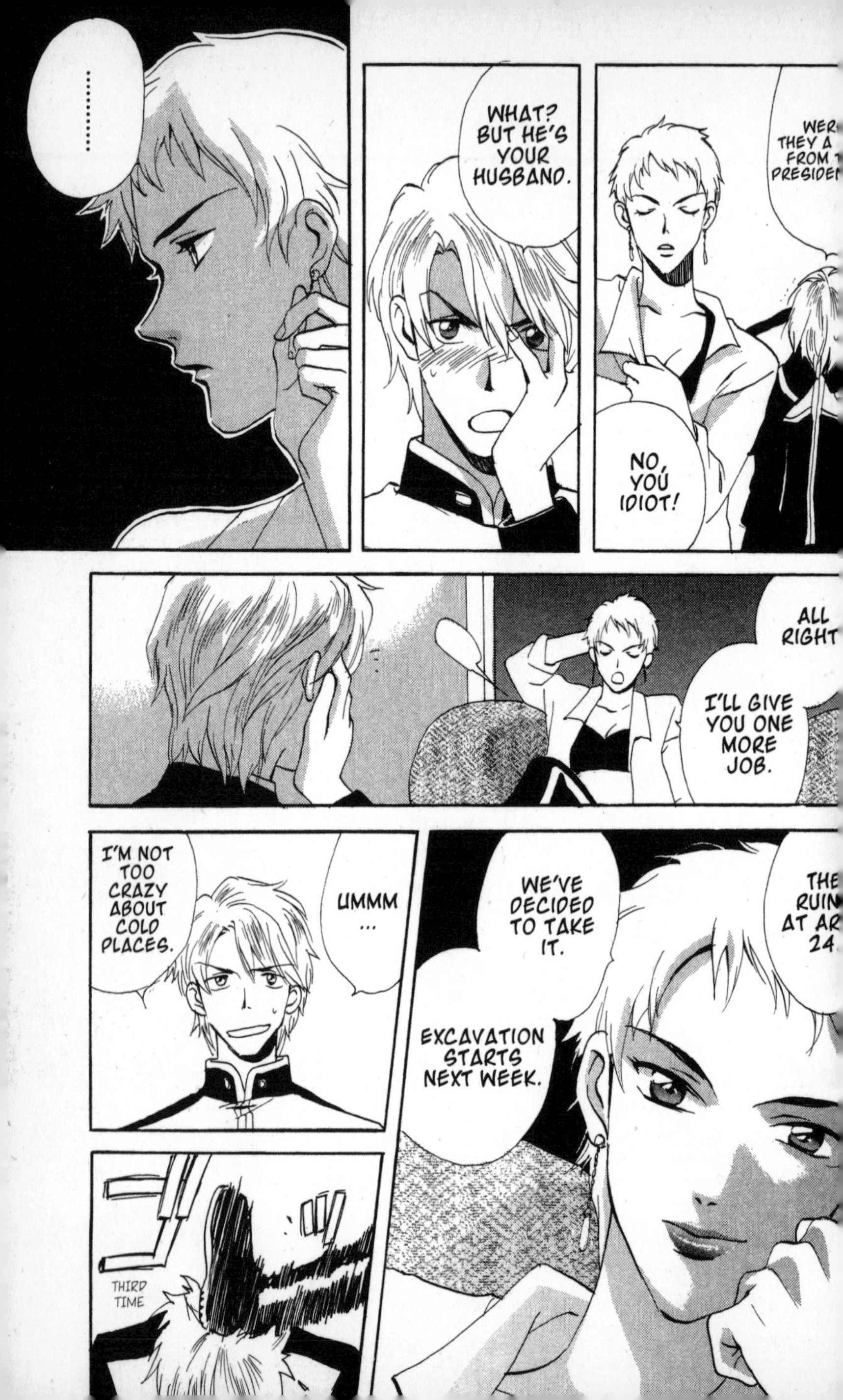
WER THEY A FROM T PRESIDEN
NO, YOU IDIOT!
WHAT? BUT HE'S YOUR HUSBAND.
......
ALL RIGHT
I'LL GIVE YOU ONE MORE JOB.
THE RUIN AT AR 24
WE'VE DECIDED TO TAKE IT.
EXCAVATION STARTS NEXT WEEK.
UMMM ...
I'M NOT TOO CRAZY ABOUT COLD PLACES.
THIRD TIME

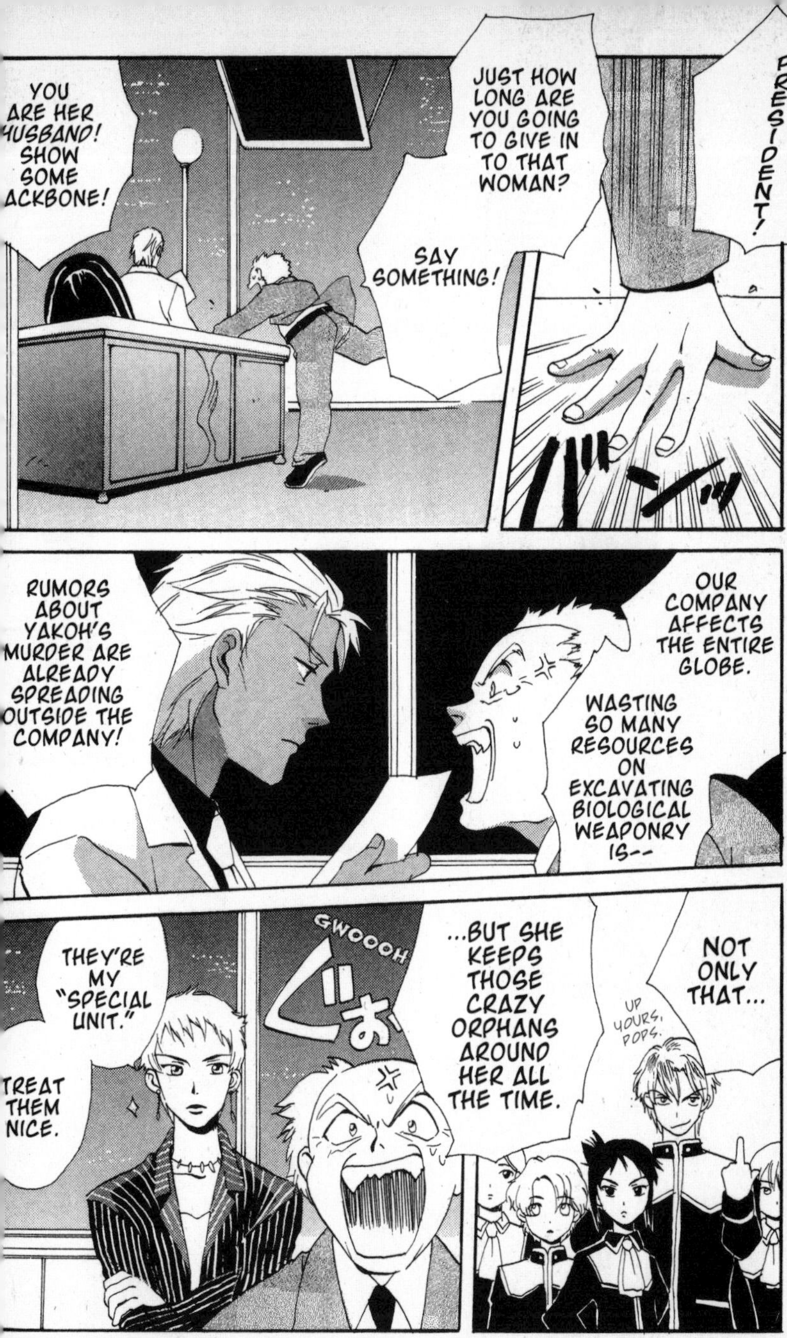
PRESIDENT!
JUST HOW LONG ARE YOU GOING TO GIVE IN TO THAT WOMAN?
SAY SOMETHING!
YOU ARE HER USBAND! SHOW SOME ACKBONE!
バンッ
OUR COMPANY AFFECTS THE ENTIRE GLOBE.
WASTING SO MANY RESOURCES ON EXCAVATING BIOLOGICAL WEAPONRY IS--
RUMORS ABOUT YAKOH'S MURDER ARE ALREADY SPREADING OUTSIDE THE COMPANY!
NOT ONLY THAT...
UP YOURS, POPS.
...BUT SHE KEEPS THOSE CRAZY ORPHANS AROUND HER ALL THE TIME.
GWOOOH
くぉ
THEY'RE MY "SPECIAL UNIT."
TREAT THEM NICE.

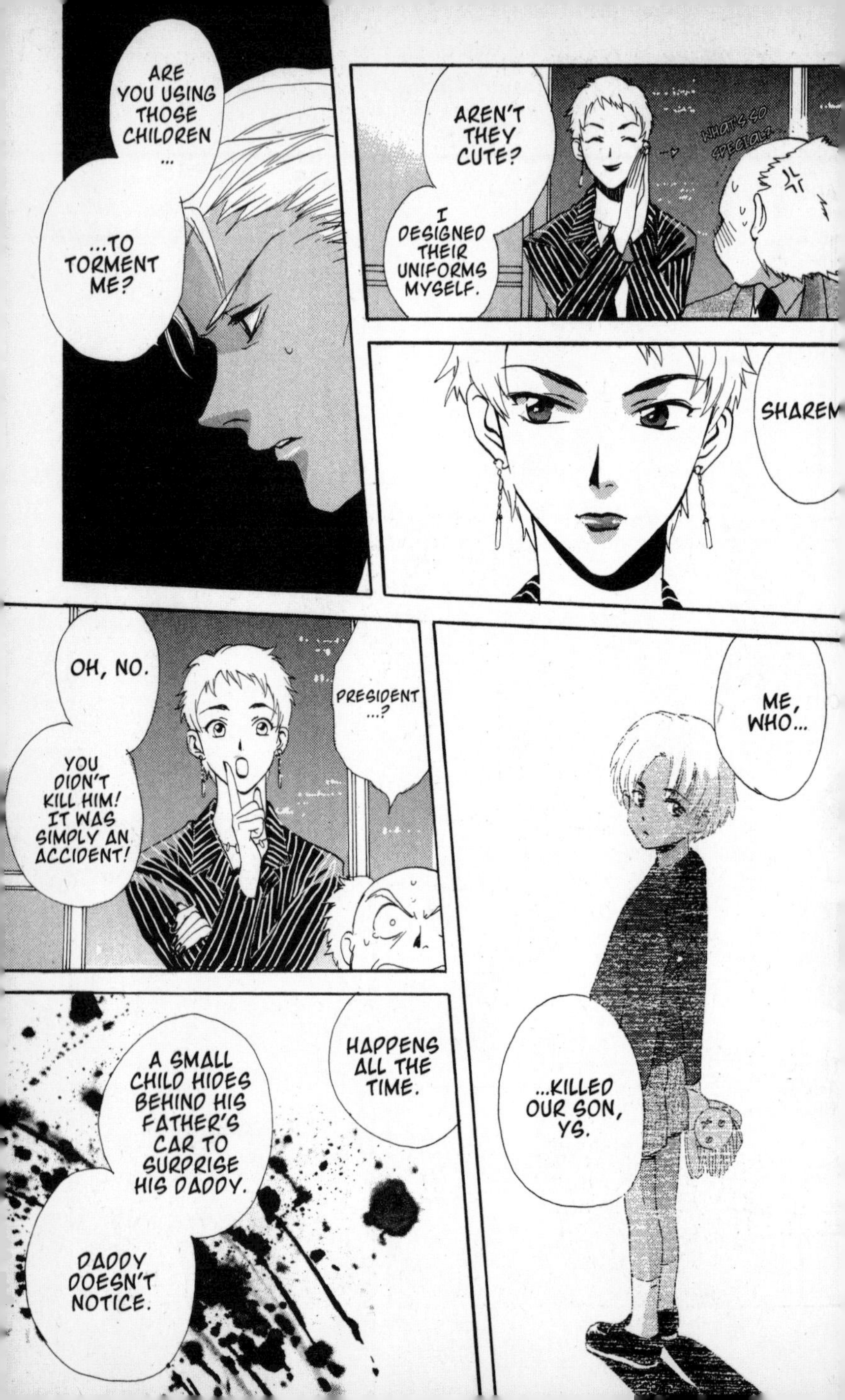
AREN'T THEY CUTE?
I DESIGNED THEIR UNIFORMS MYSELF.
WHAT'S SO SPECIAL?
SHAREM
ARE YOU USING THOSE CHILDREN ...
...TO TORMENT ME?
ME, WHO...
...KILLED OUR SON, YS.
PRESIDENT ...?
OH, NO.
YOU DIDN'T KILL HIM! IT WAS SIMPLY AN ACCIDENT!
HAPPENS ALL THE TIME.
A SMALL CHILD HIDES BEHIND HIS FATHER'S CAR TO SURPRISE HIS DADDY.
DADDY DOESN'T NOTICE.

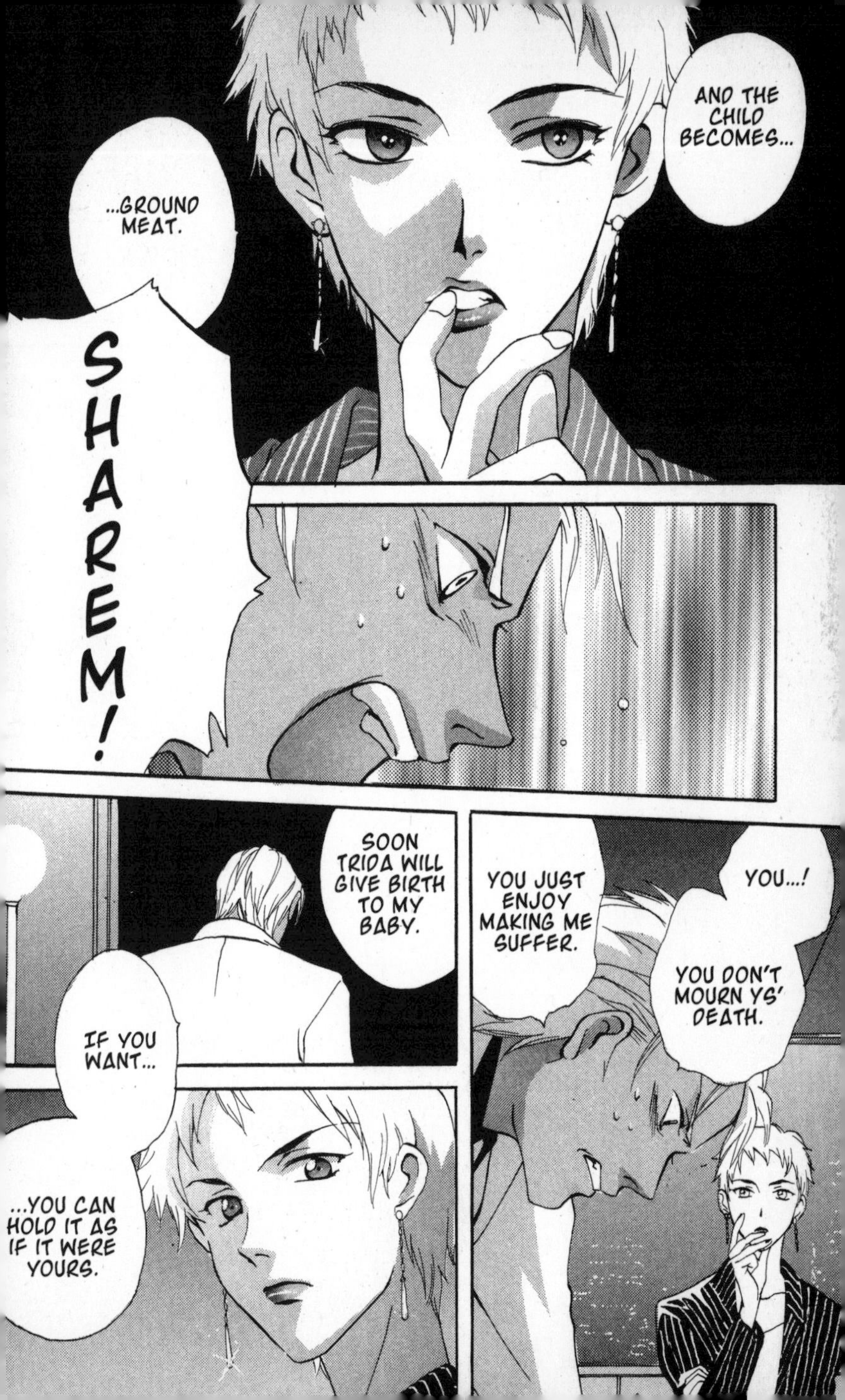
AND THE CHILD BECOMES...
...GROUND MEAT.
SHAREM!
YOU...!
YOU JUST ENJOY MAKING ME SUFFER.
YOU DON'T MOURN YS' DEATH.
SOON TRIDA WILL GIVE BIRTH TO MY BABY.
IF YOU WANT...
...YOU CAN HOLD IT AS IF IT WERE YOURS.

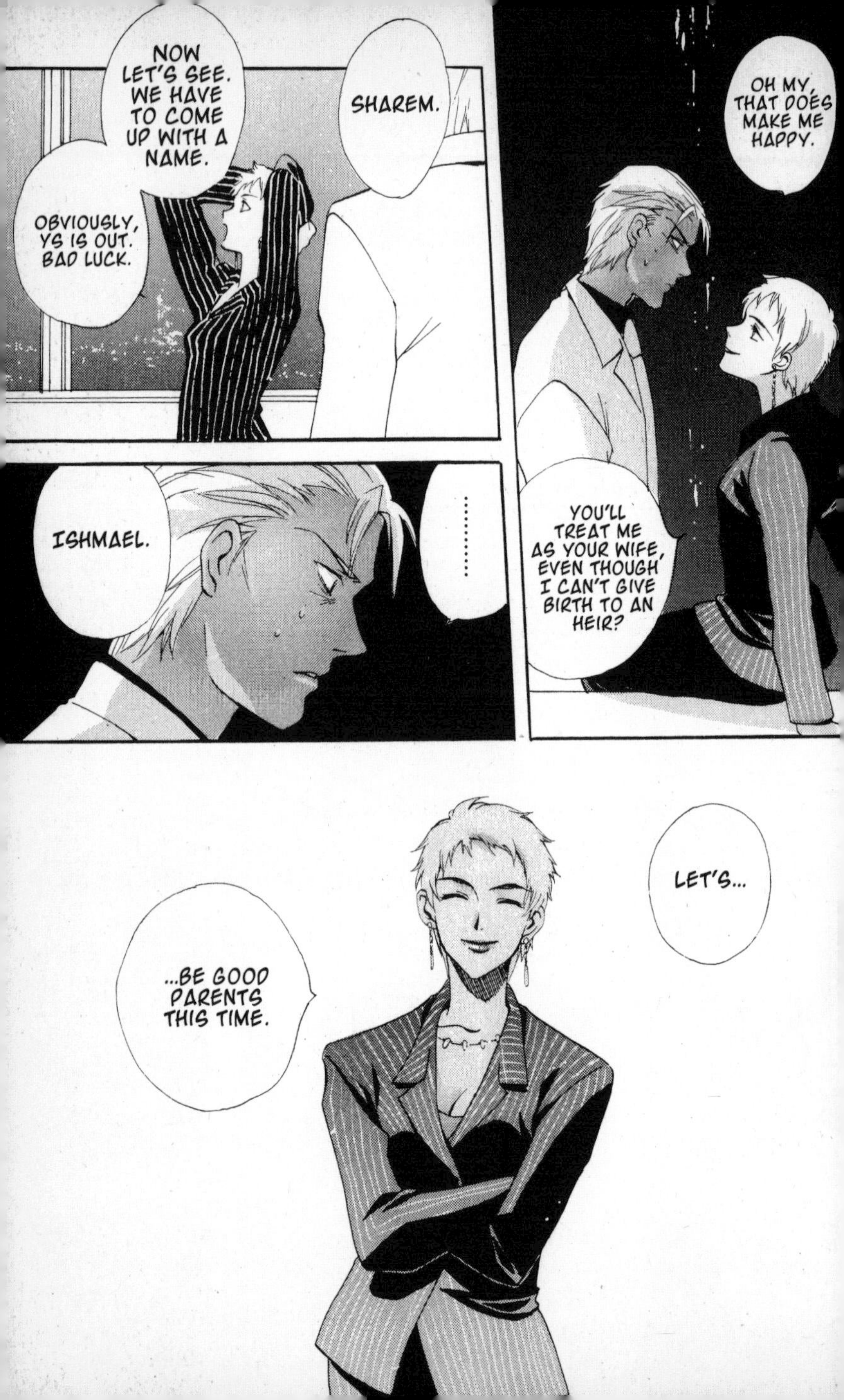
OH MY, THAT DOES MAKE ME HAPPY.
YOU'LL TREAT ME AS YOUR WIFE, EVEN THOUGH I CAN'T GIVE BIRTH TO AN HEIR?
SHAREM.
NOW LET'S SEE. WE HAVE TO COME UP WITH A NAME.
OBVIOUSLY, YS IS OUT. BAD LUCK.
......
ISHMAEL.
LET'S...
...BE GOOD PARENTS THIS TIME.

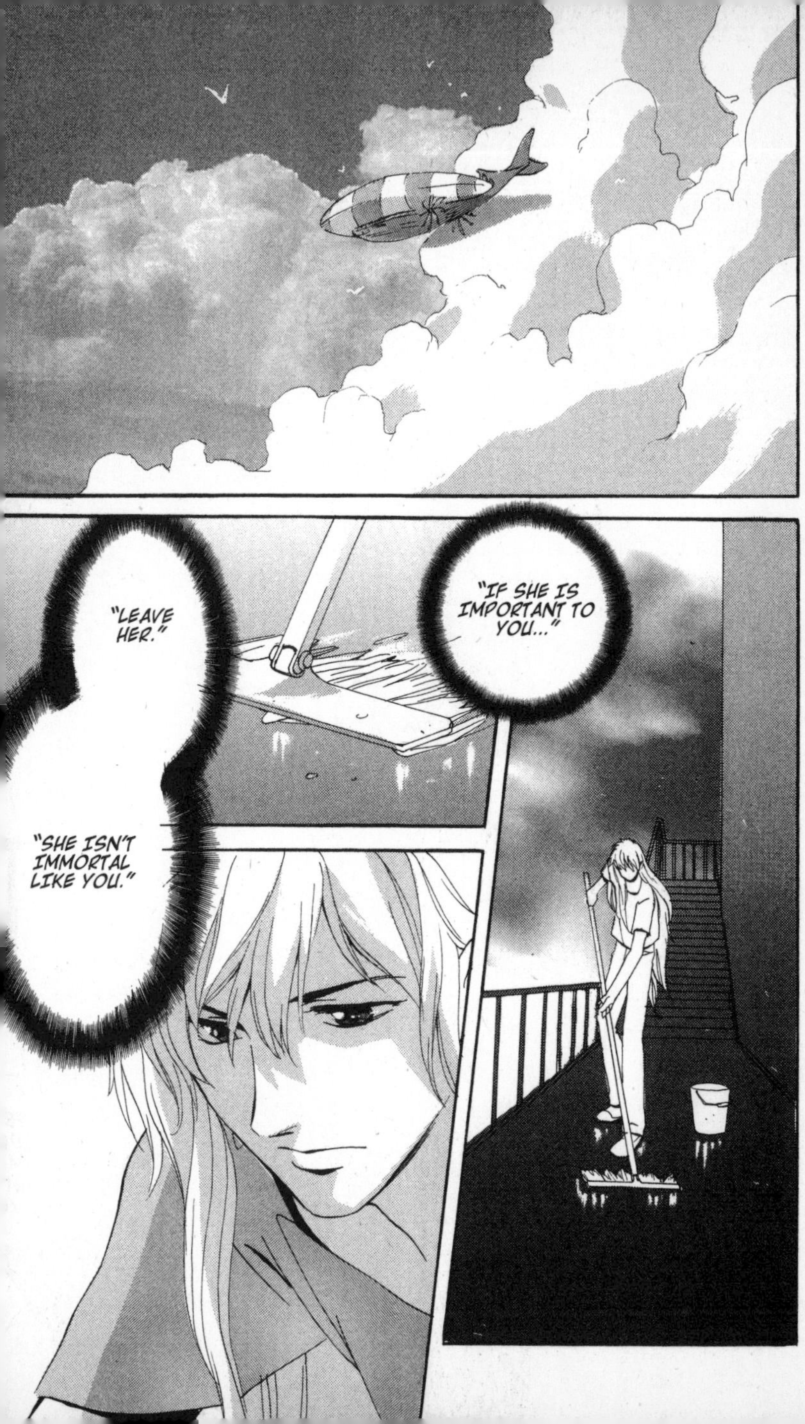
"IF SHE IS IMPORTANT TO YOU..."
"LEAVE HER."
"SHE ISN'T IMMORTAL LIKE YOU."

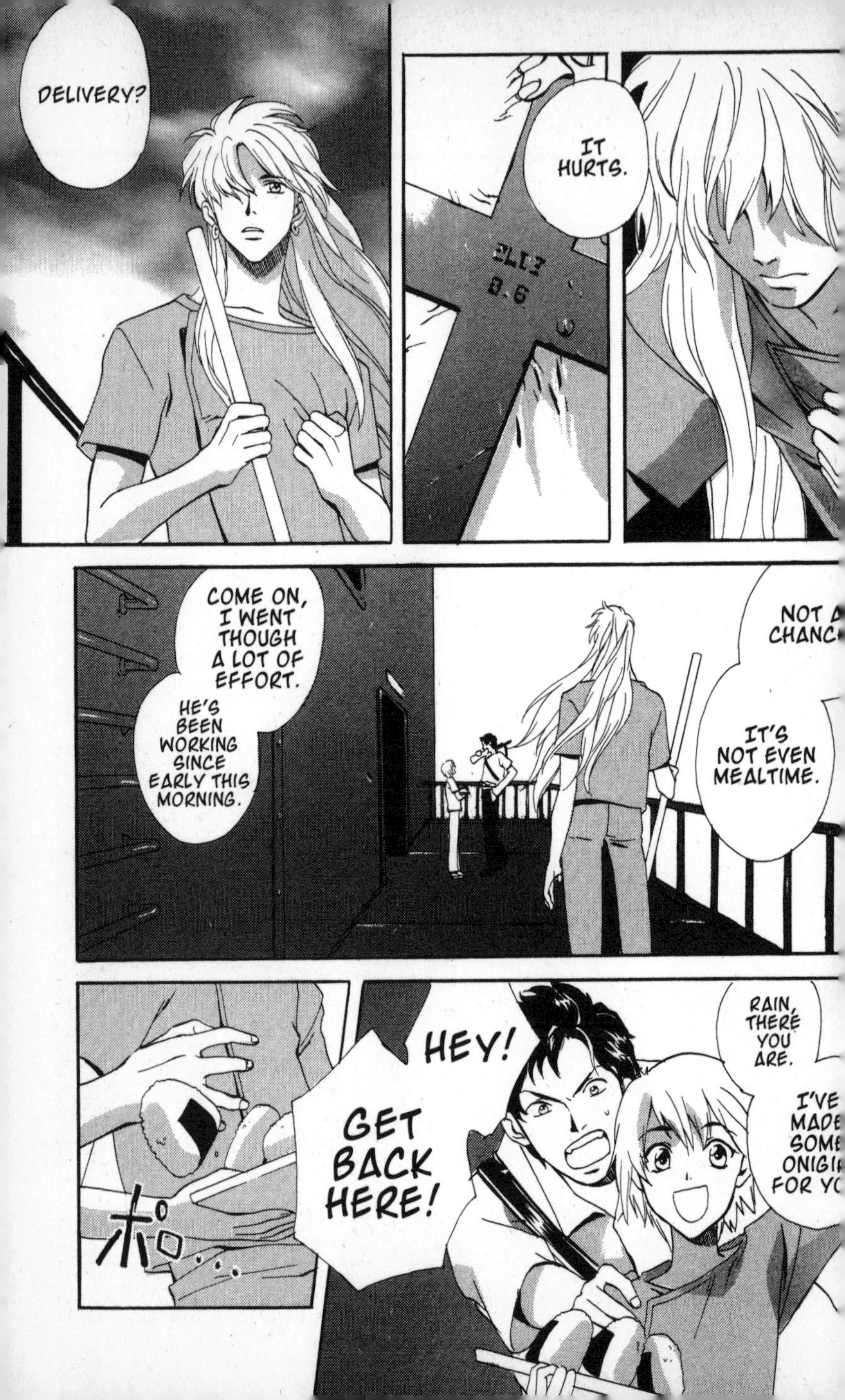

IT HURTS.
DELIVERY?
NOT A CHANC
IT'S NOT EVEN MEALTIME.
COME ON, I WENT THOUGH A LOT OF EFFORT.
HE'S BEEN WORKING SINCE EARLY THIS MORNING.
RAIN, THERE YOU ARE.
I'VE MADE SOME ONIGI FOR YO
HEY!
GET BACK HERE!
ポロ

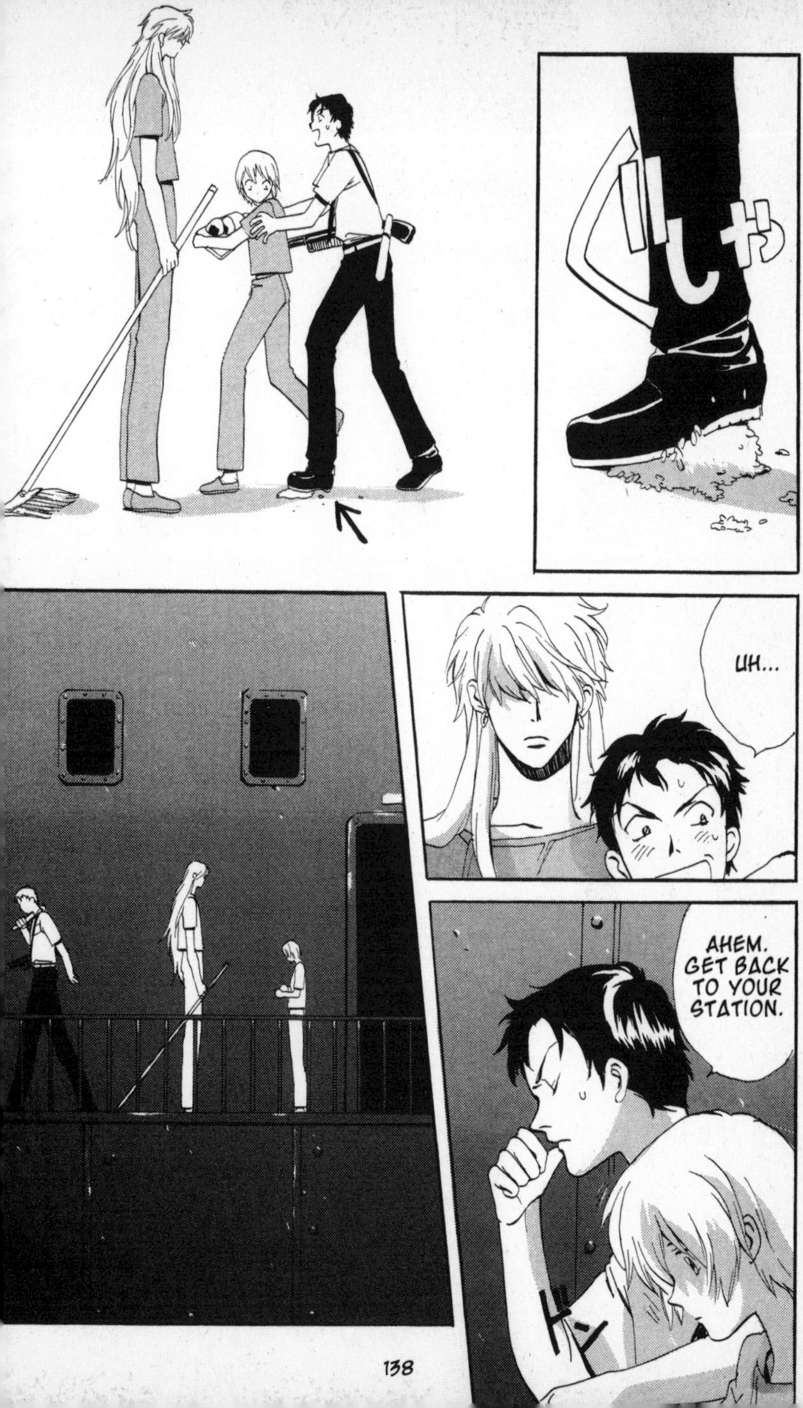
UH...
AHEM. GET BACK TO YOUR STATION.

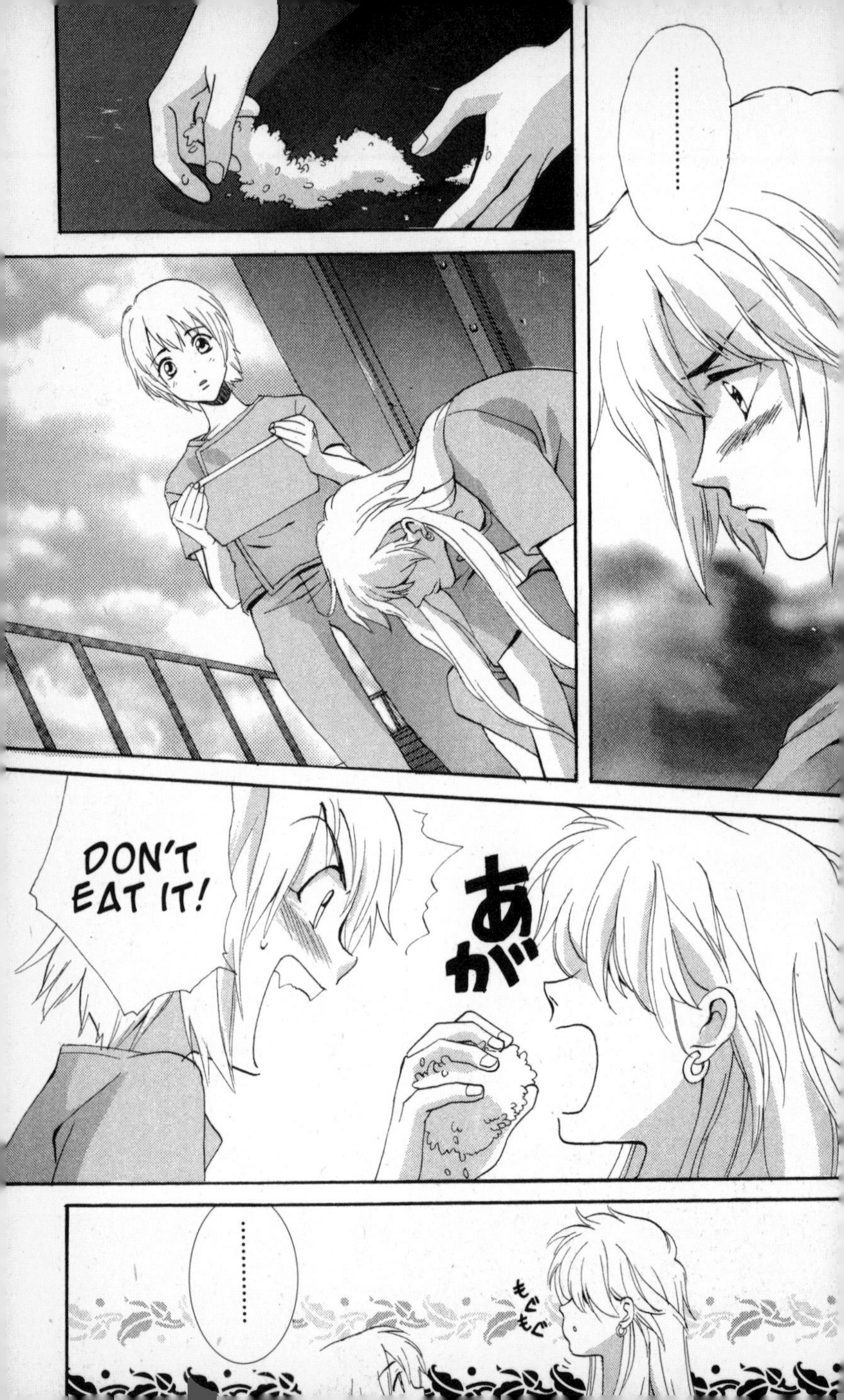
……
DON'T EAT IT!
あが
……
もぐもぐ

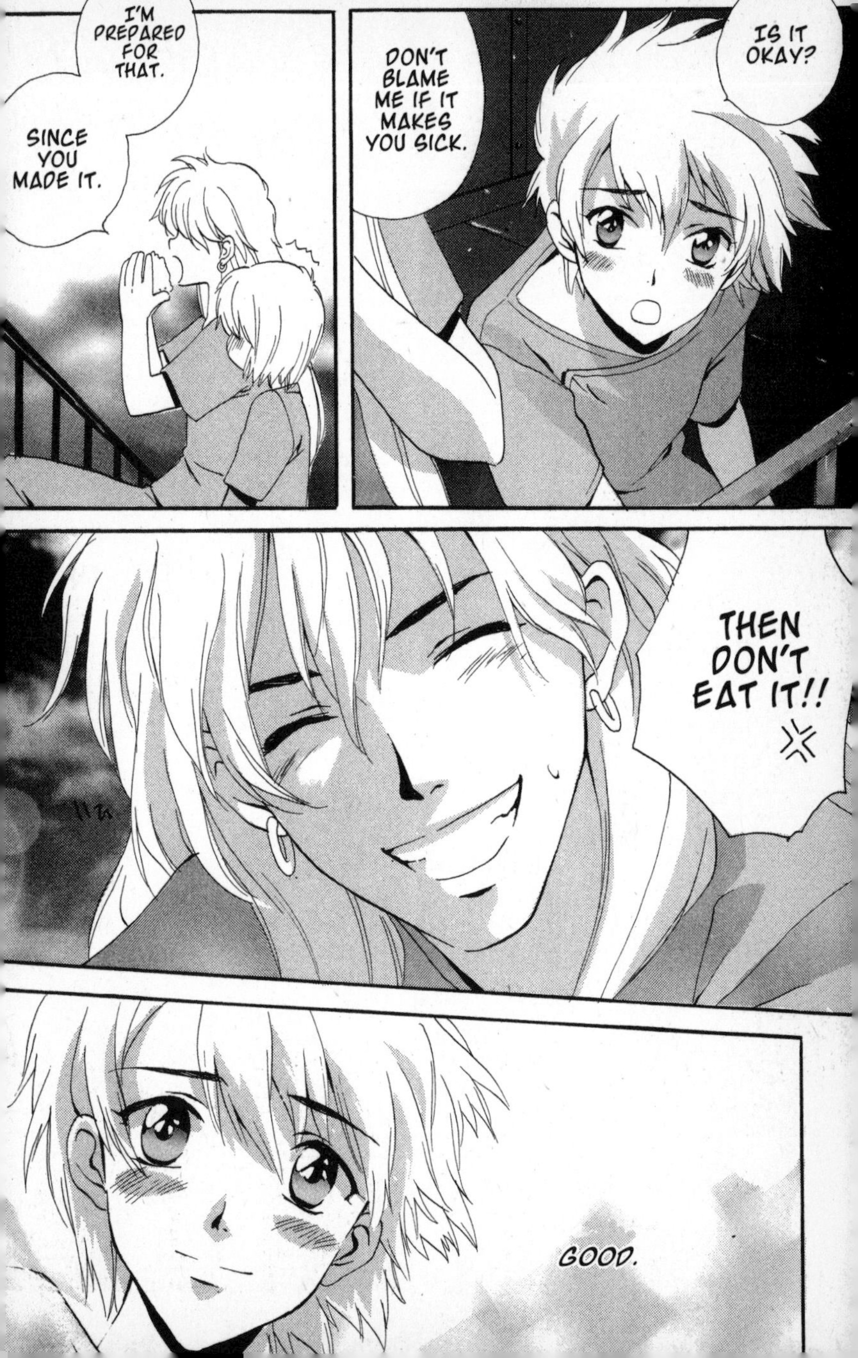
IS IT OKAY?
DON'T BLAME ME IF IT MAKES YOU SICK.
I'M PREPARED FOR THAT.
SINCE YOU MADE IT.
THEN DON'T EAT IT!!
GOOD.

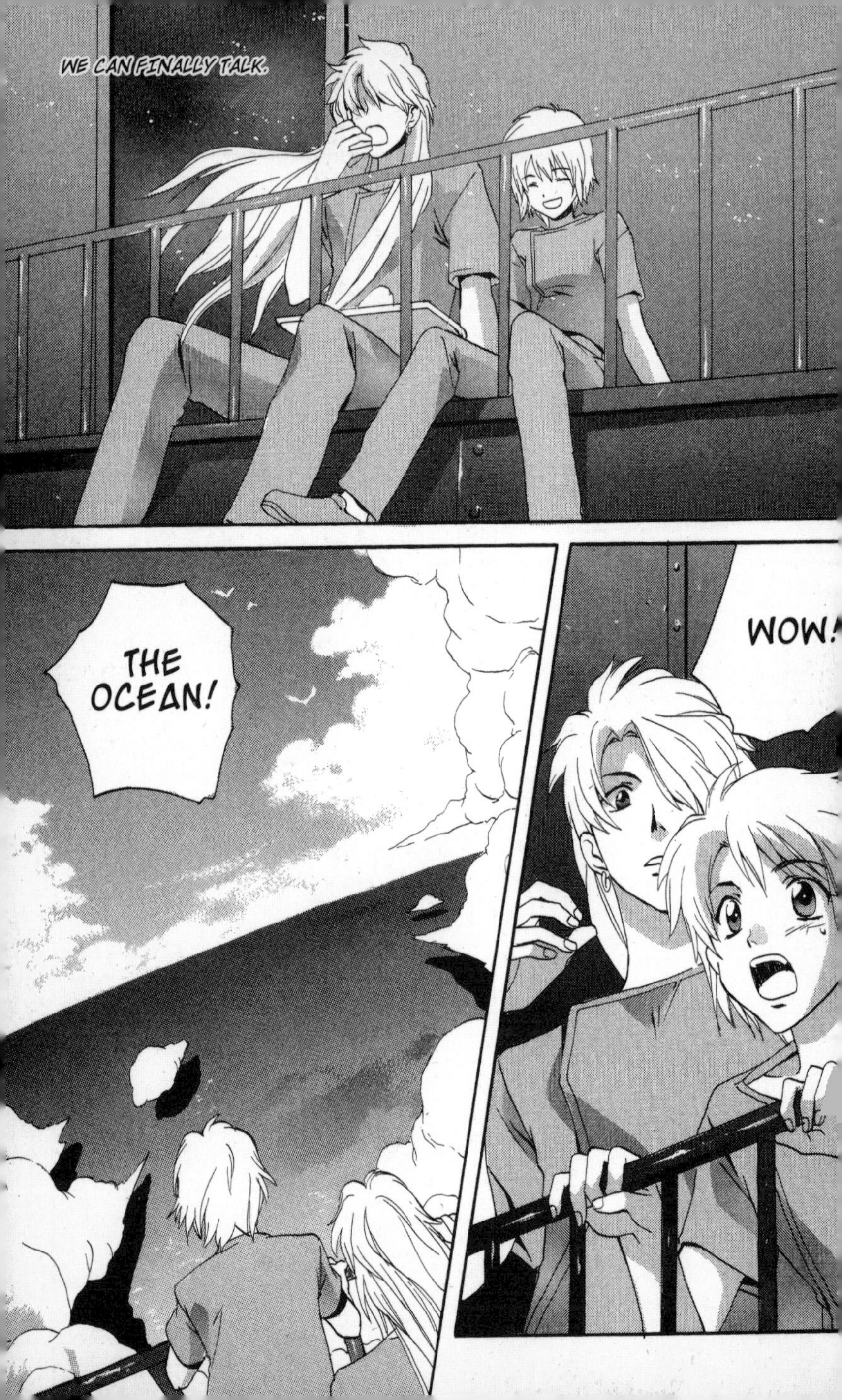
WE CAN FINALLY TALK.
WOW!
THE OCEAN!

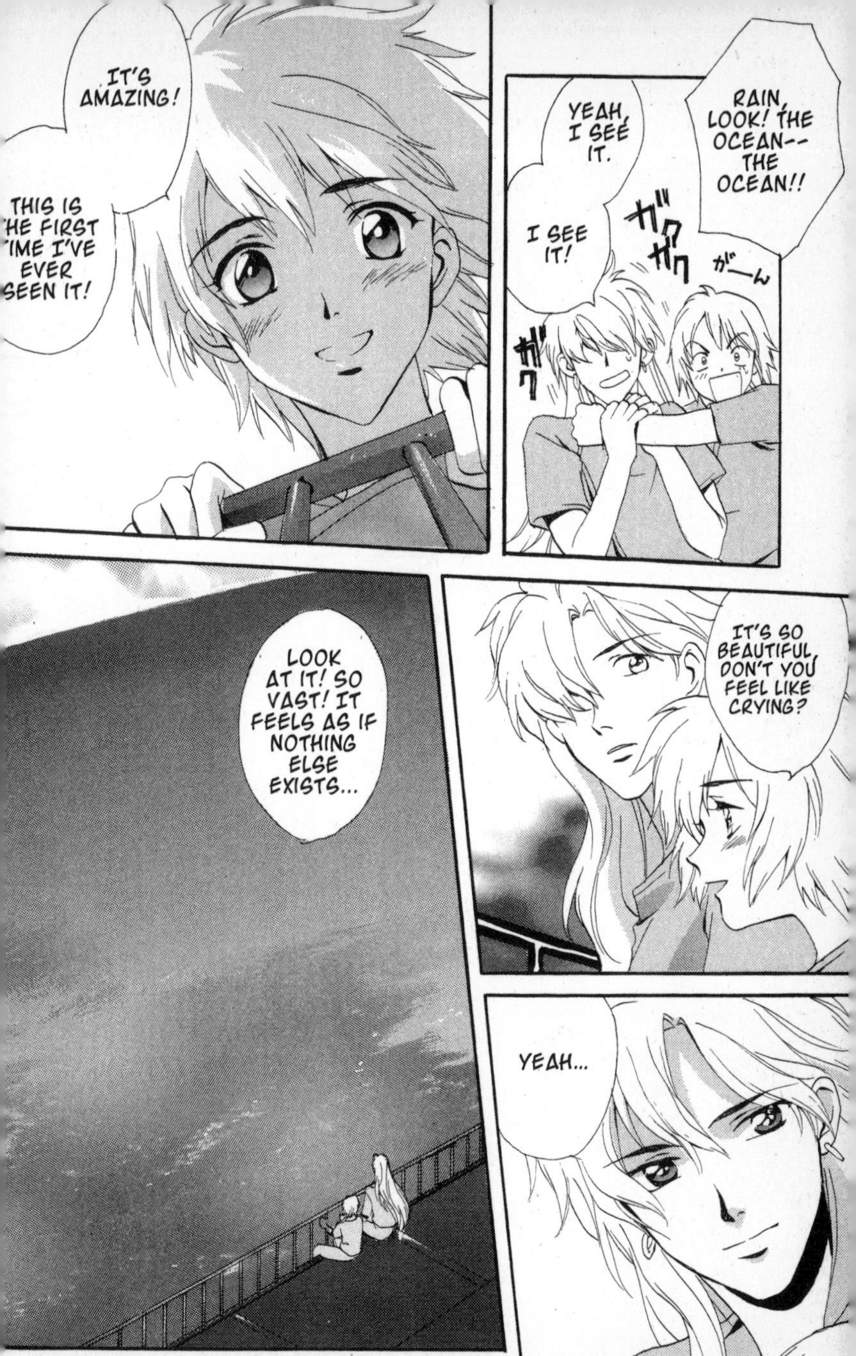
RAIN, LOOK! THE OCEAN-- THE OCEAN!!
YEAH, I SEE IT.
I SEE IT!
ガクガク
がーん
ガク
IT'S AMAZING!
THIS IS THE FIRST TIME I'VE EVER SEEN IT!
IT'S SO BEAUTIFUL DON'T YOU FEEL LIKE CRYING?
YEAH...
LOOK AT IT! SO VAST! IT FEELS AS IF NOTHING ELSE EXISTS...

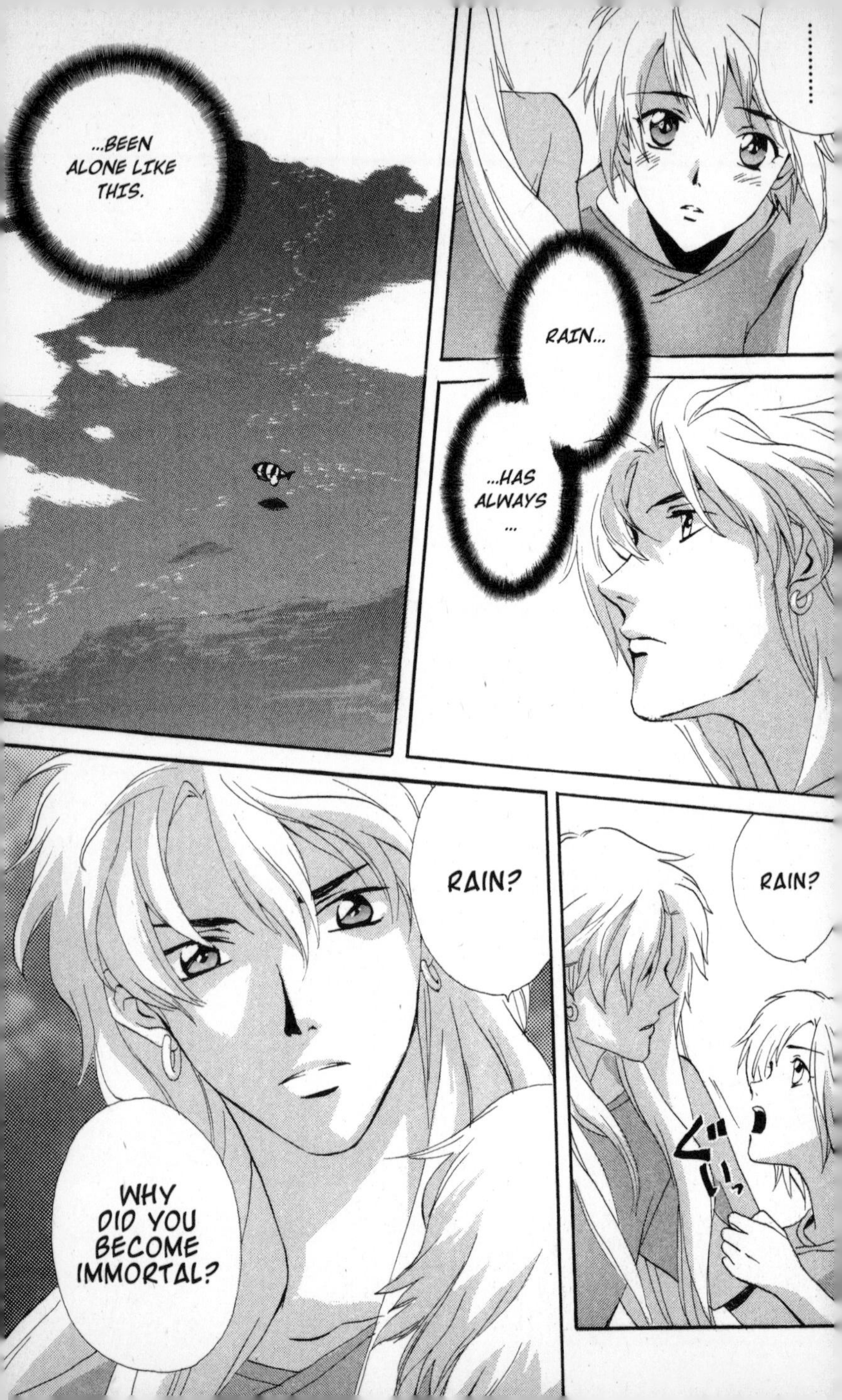
......
RAIN...
...HAS ALWAYS ...
...BEEN ALONE LIKE THIS.
RAIN?
ぐいっ
RAIN?
WHY DID YOU BECOME IMMORTAL?

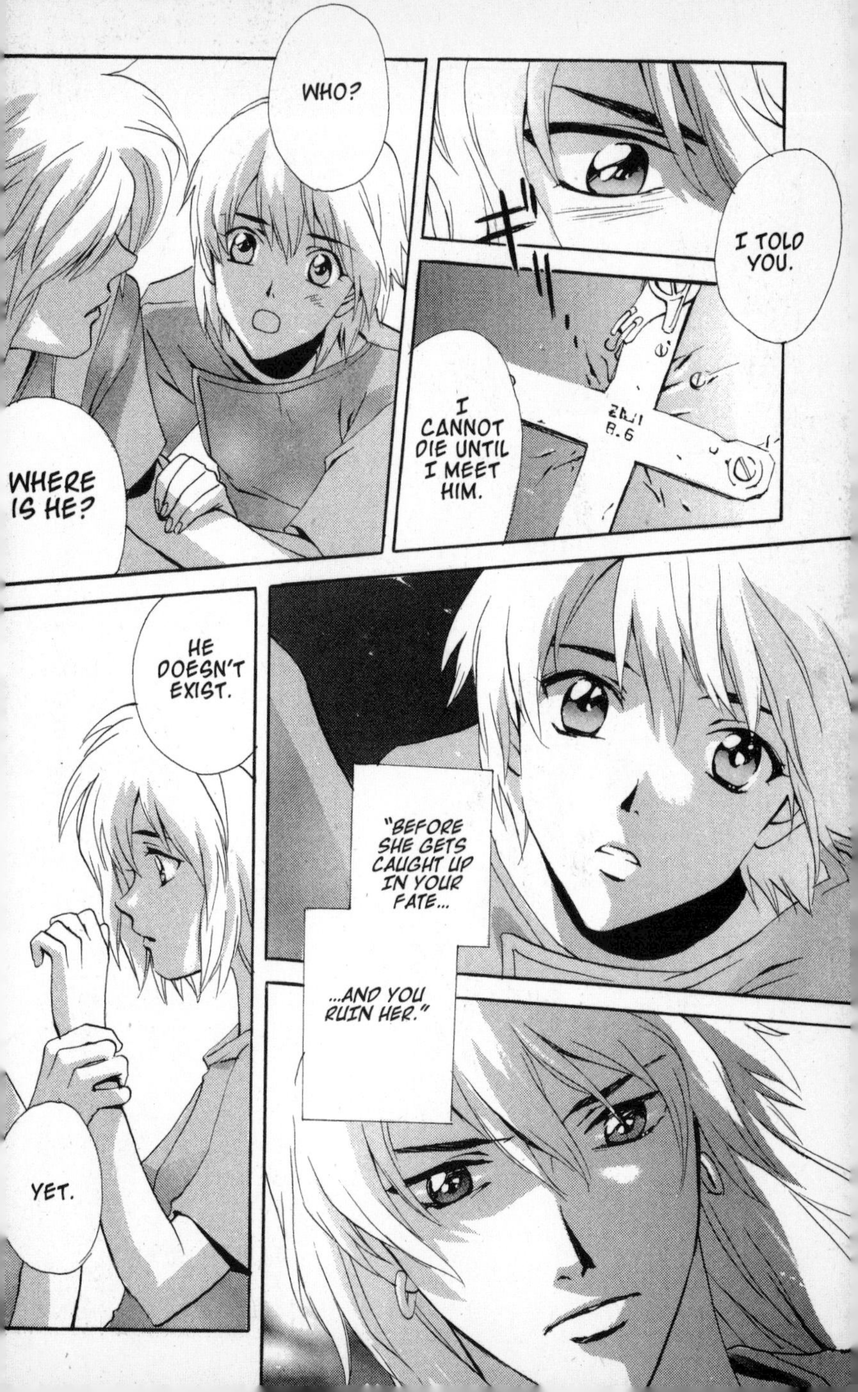

I TOLD YOU.
I CANNOT DIE UNTIL I MEET HIM.
WHO?
WHERE IS HE?
"BEFORE SHE GETS CAUGHT UP IN YOUR FATE...
...AND YOU RUIN HER."
HE DOESN'T EXIST.
YET.

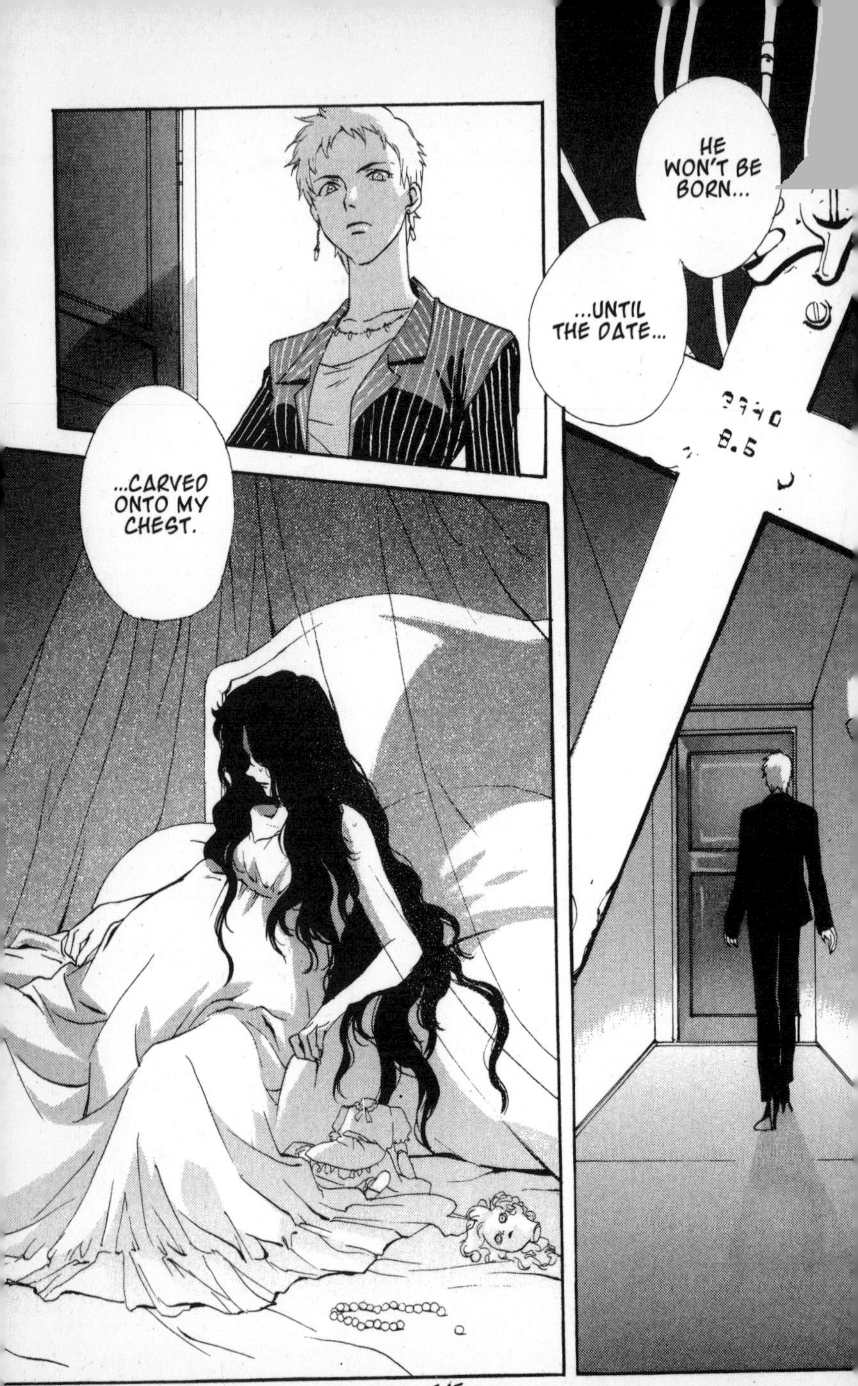
HE WON'T BE BORN...
...UNTIL THE DATE...
...CARVED ONTO MY CHEST.

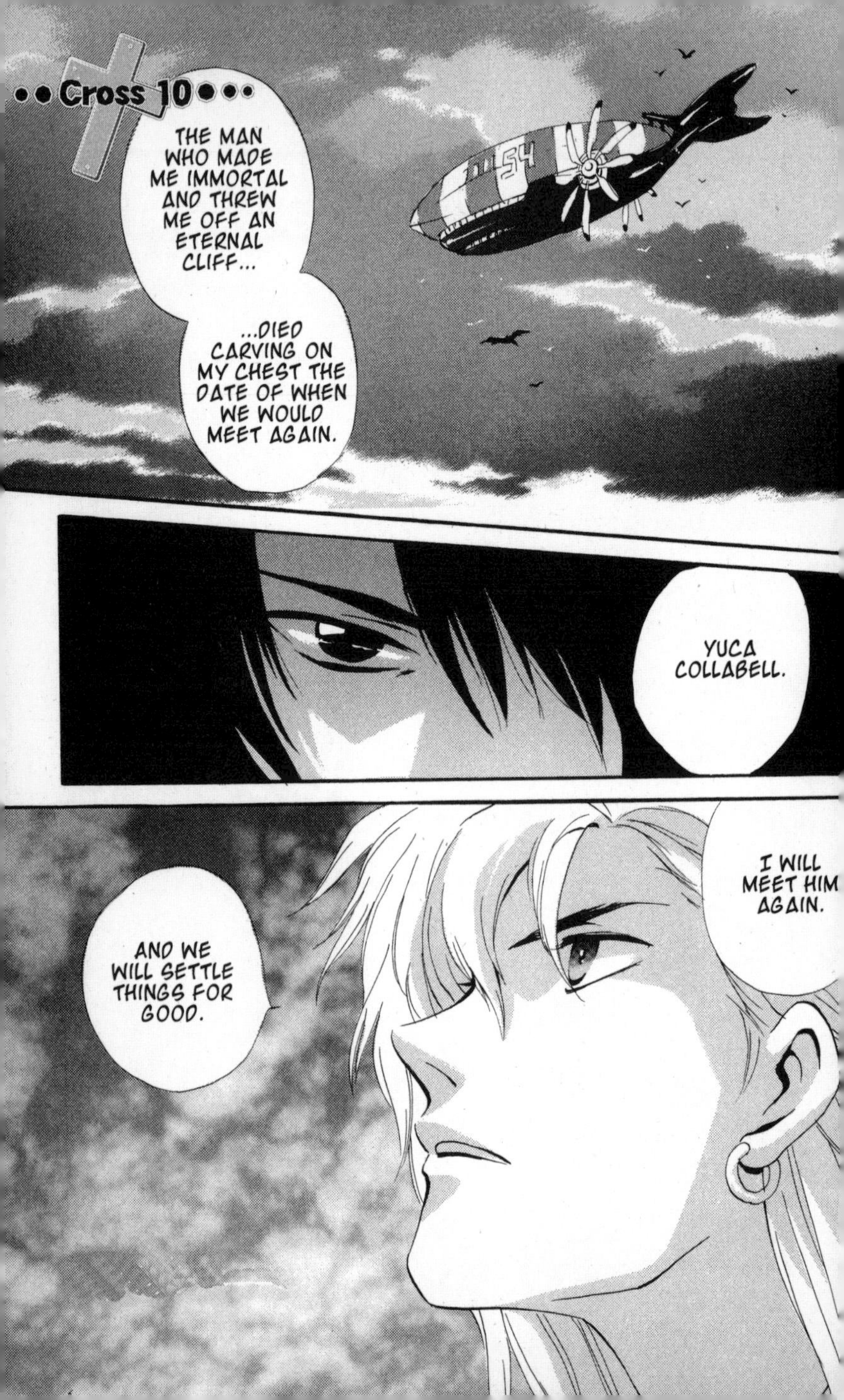
Cross 10
THE MAN WHO MADE ME IMMORTAL AND THREW ME OFF AN ETERNAL CLIFF...
...DIED CARVING ON MY CHEST THE DATE OF WHEN WE WOULD MEET AGAIN.
YUCA COLLABELL.
I WILL MEET HIM AGAIN.
AND WE WILL SETTLE THINGS FOR GOOD.

8/6...
THAT DAY...
...IS ONLY ONE MONTH AWAY.
Meteor Methuselah
8.6
Cross10
Cross 10

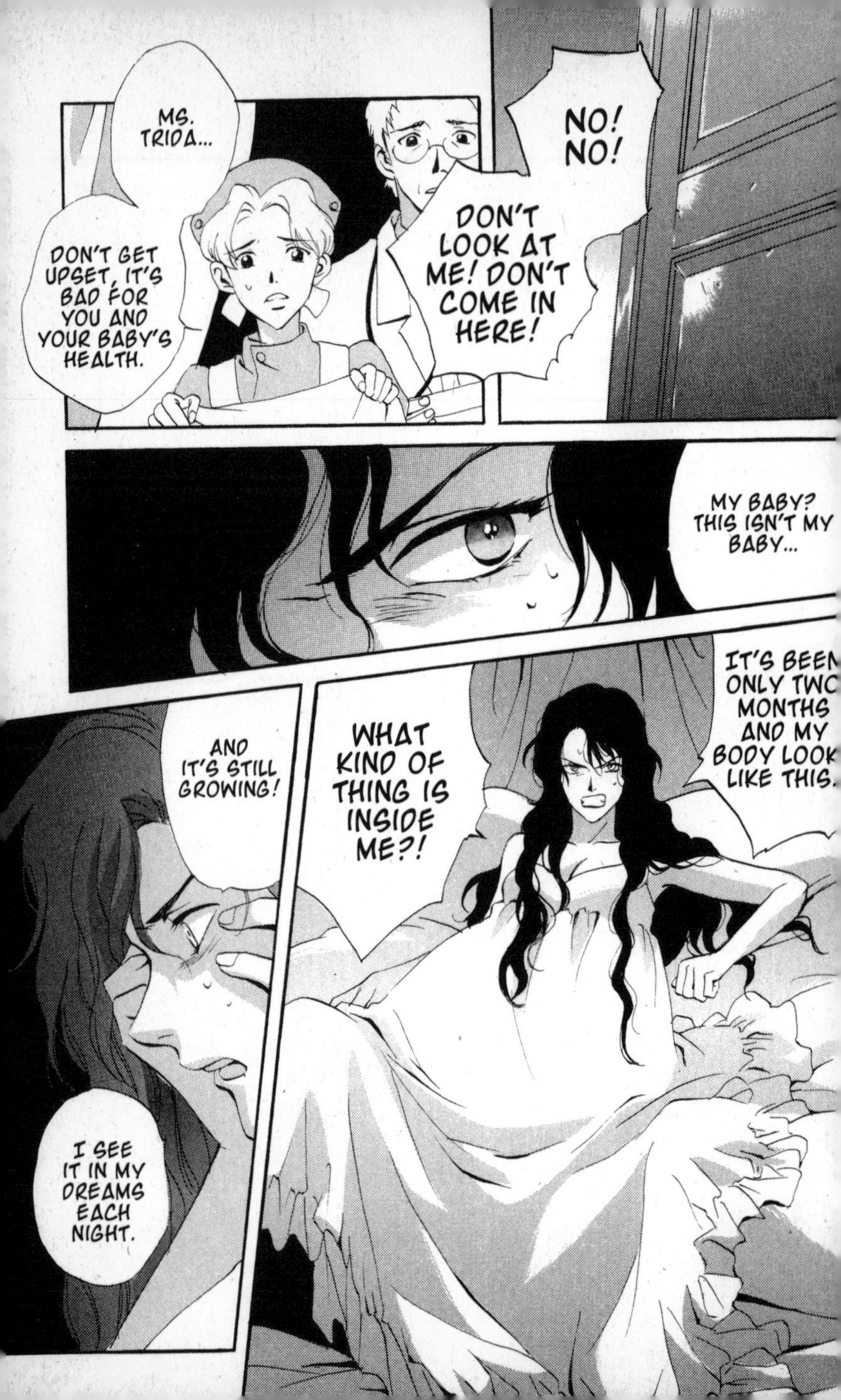
NO! NO!
DON'T LOOK AT ME! DON'T COME IN HERE!
MS. TRIDA...
DON'T GET UPSET, IT'S BAD FOR YOU AND YOUR BABY'S HEALTH.
MY BABY? THIS ISN'T MY BABY...
IT'S BEEN ONLY TWO MONTHS AND MY BODY LOOKS LIKE THIS.
WHAT KIND OF THING IS INSIDE ME?!
AND IT'S STILL GROWING!
I SEE IT IN MY DREAMS EACH NIGHT.

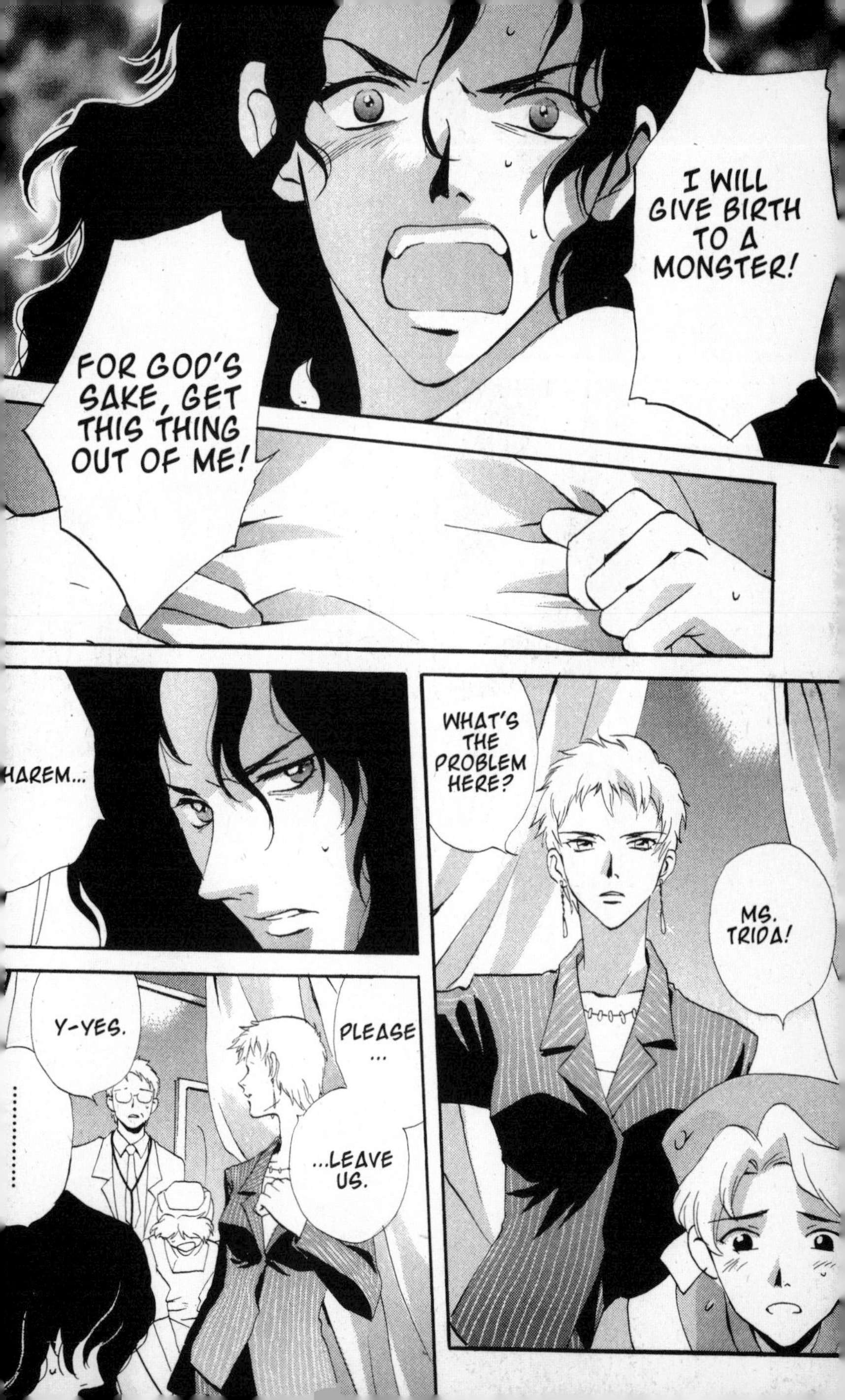
I WILL GIVE BIRTH TO A MONSTER!
FOR GOD'S SAKE, GET THIS THING OUT OF ME!
WHAT'S THE PROBLEM HERE?
MS. TRIDA!
HAREM...
PLEASE ...
...LEAVE US.
Y-YES.
......

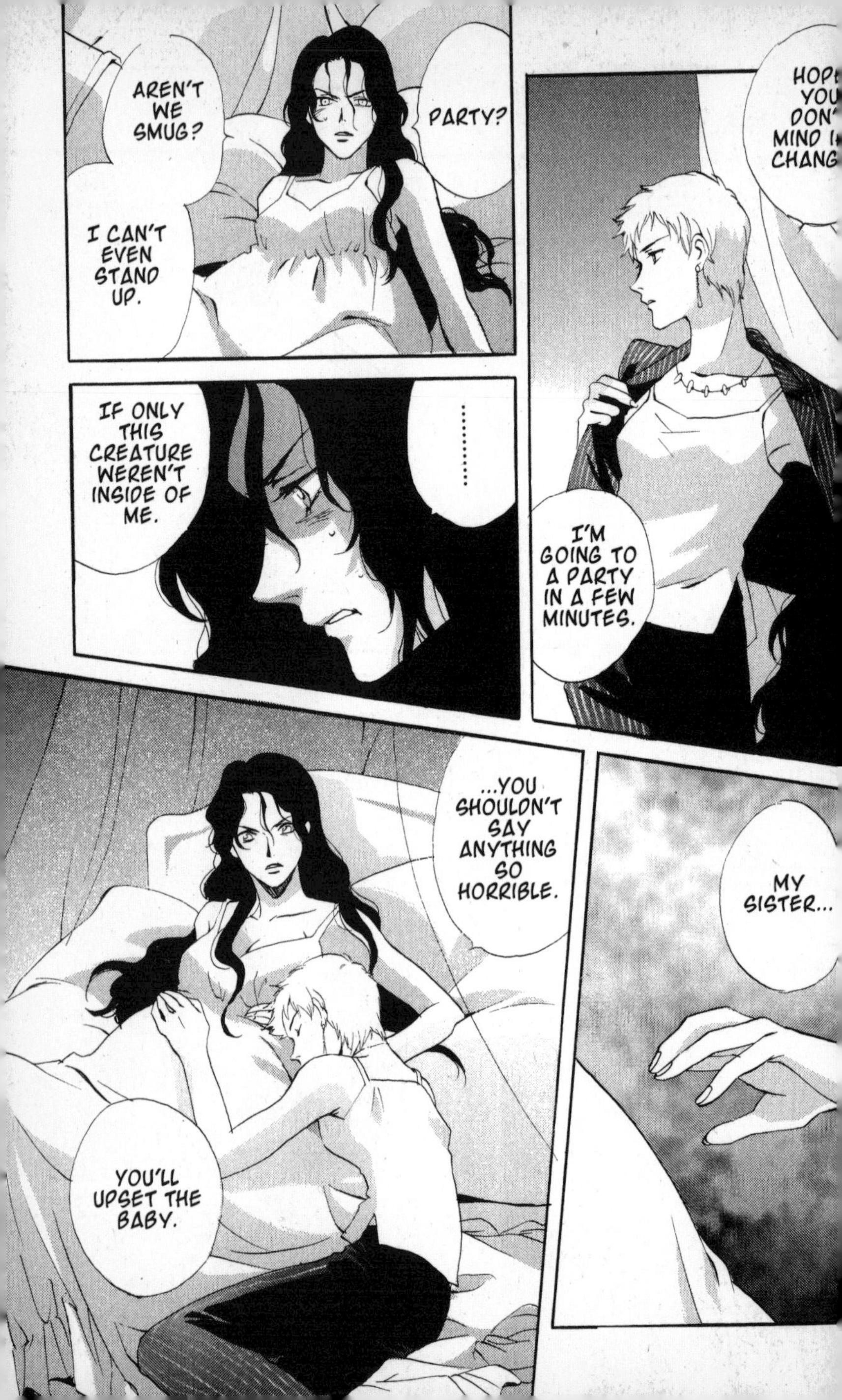
HOP YOU DON' MIND I CHANG
I'M GOING TO A PARTY IN A FEW MINUTES.
PARTY?
AREN'T WE SMUG?
I CAN'T EVEN STAND UP.
......
IF ONLY THIS CREATURE WEREN'T INSIDE OF ME.
MY SISTER...
...YOU SHOULDN'T SAY ANYTHING SO HORRIBLE.
YOU'LL UPSET THE BABY.

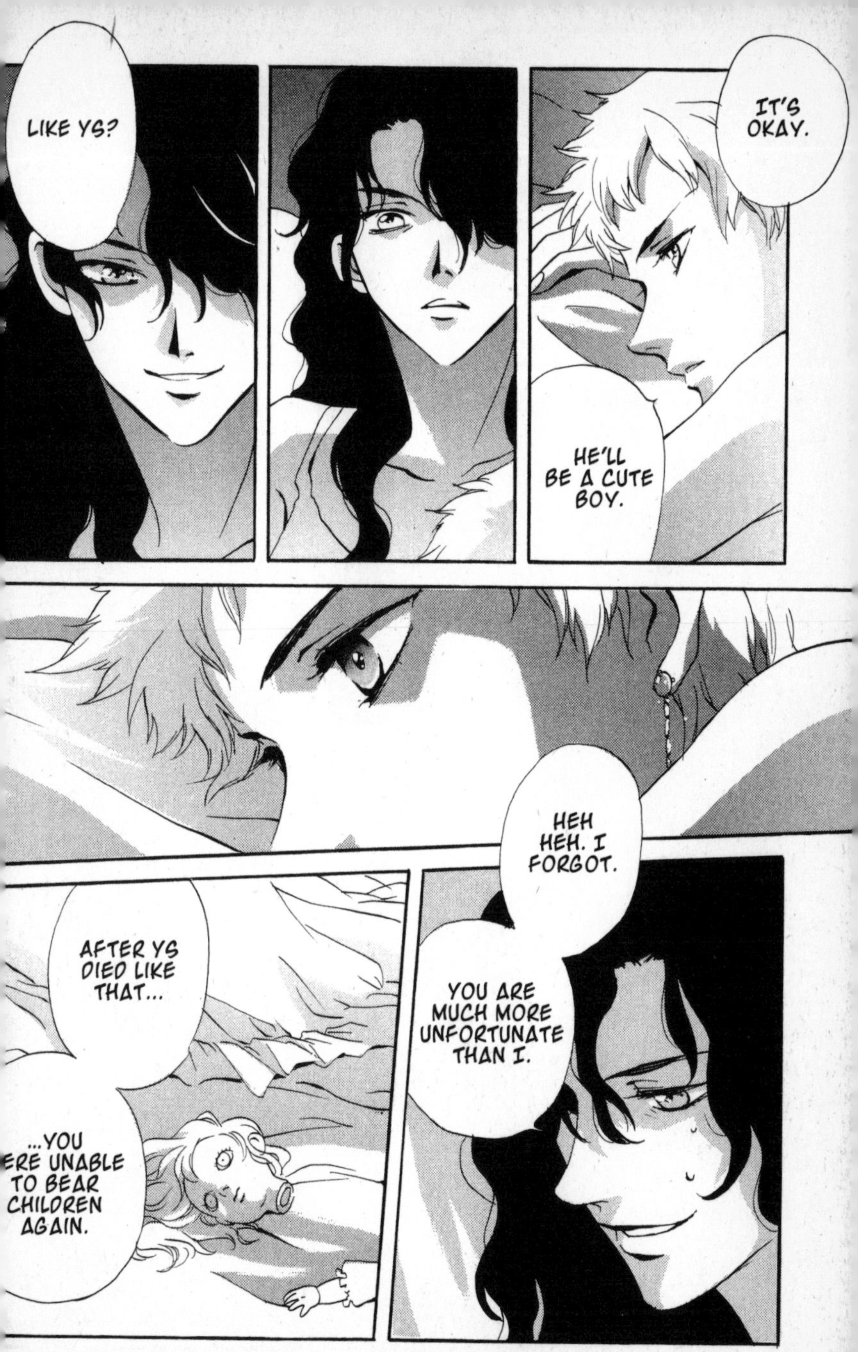

IT'S OKAY.
HE'LL BE A CUTE BOY.
LIKE YS?
HEH HEH. I FORGOT.
YOU ARE MUCH MORE UNFORTUNATE THAN I.
AFTER YS DIED LIKE THAT...
...YOU ERE UNABLE TO BEAR CHILDREN AGAIN.

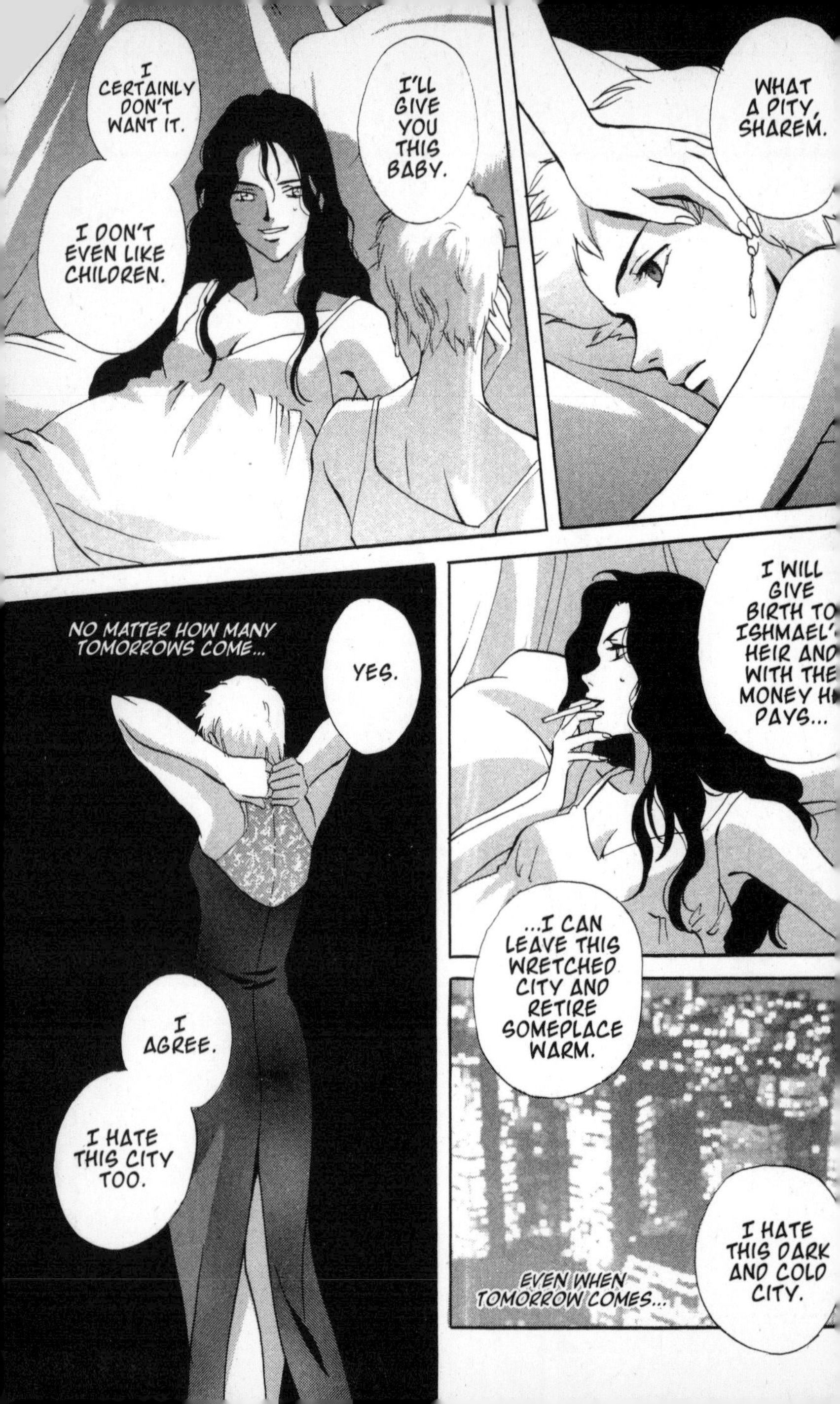
WHAT A PITY, SHAREM.
I'LL GIVE YOU THIS BABY.
I CERTAINLY DON'T WANT IT.
I DON'T EVEN LIKE CHILDREN.
I WILL GIVE BIRTH TO ISHMAEL' HEIR AND WITH THE MONEY H PAYS...
...I CAN LEAVE THIS WRETCHED CITY AND RETIRE SOMEPLACE WARM.
I HATE THIS DARK AND COLD CITY.
EVEN WHEN TOMORROW COMES...
NO MATTER HOW MANY TOMORROWS COME...
YES.
I AGREE.
I HATE THIS CITY TOO.

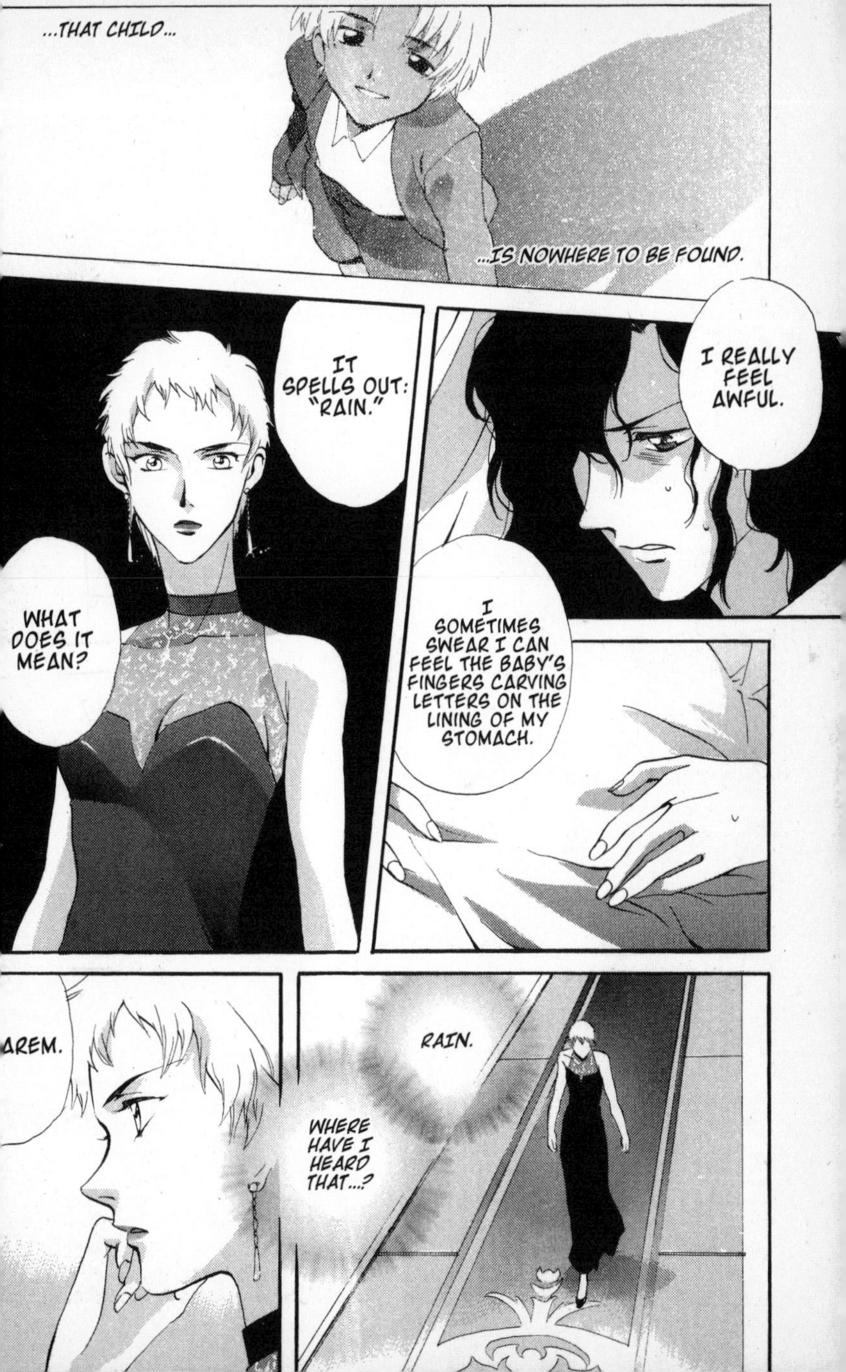
...THAT CHILD...
...IS NOWHERE TO BE FOUND.
I REALLY FEEL AWFUL.
I SOMETIMES SWEAR I CAN FEEL THE BABY'S FINGERS CARVING LETTERS ON THE LINING OF MY STOMACH.
IT SPELLS OUT: "RAIN."
WHAT DOES IT MEAN?
RAIN.
WHERE HAVE I HEARD THAT...?
AREM.

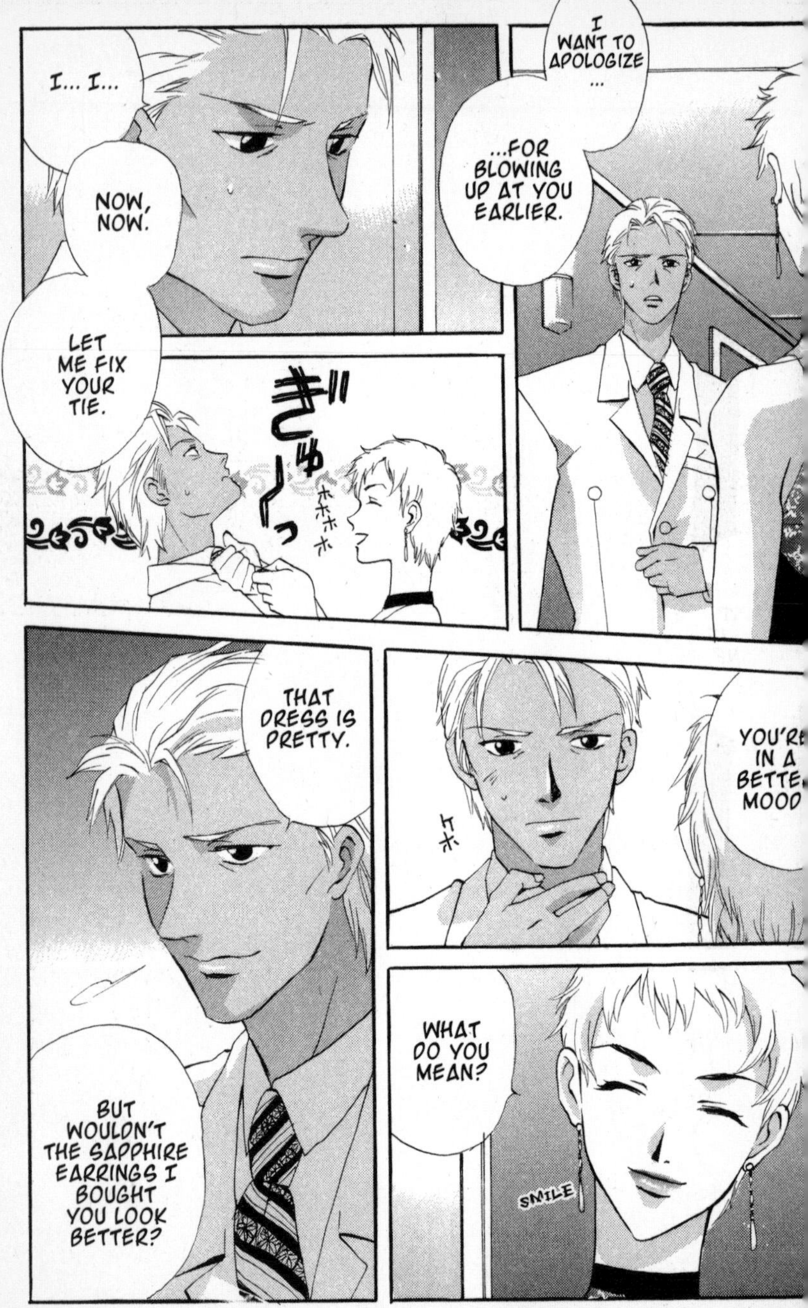
I WANT TO APOLOGIZE ...
...FOR BLOWING UP AT YOU EARLIER.
I... I...
NOW, NOW.
LET ME FIX YOUR TIE.
ぎゅ〜っ
ホホホホ
YOU'RE IN A BETTE MOOD
ケホ
WHAT DO YOU MEAN?
SMILE
THAT DRESS IS PRETTY.
BUT WOULDN'T THE SAPPHIRE EARRINGS I BOUGHT YOU LOOK BETTER?

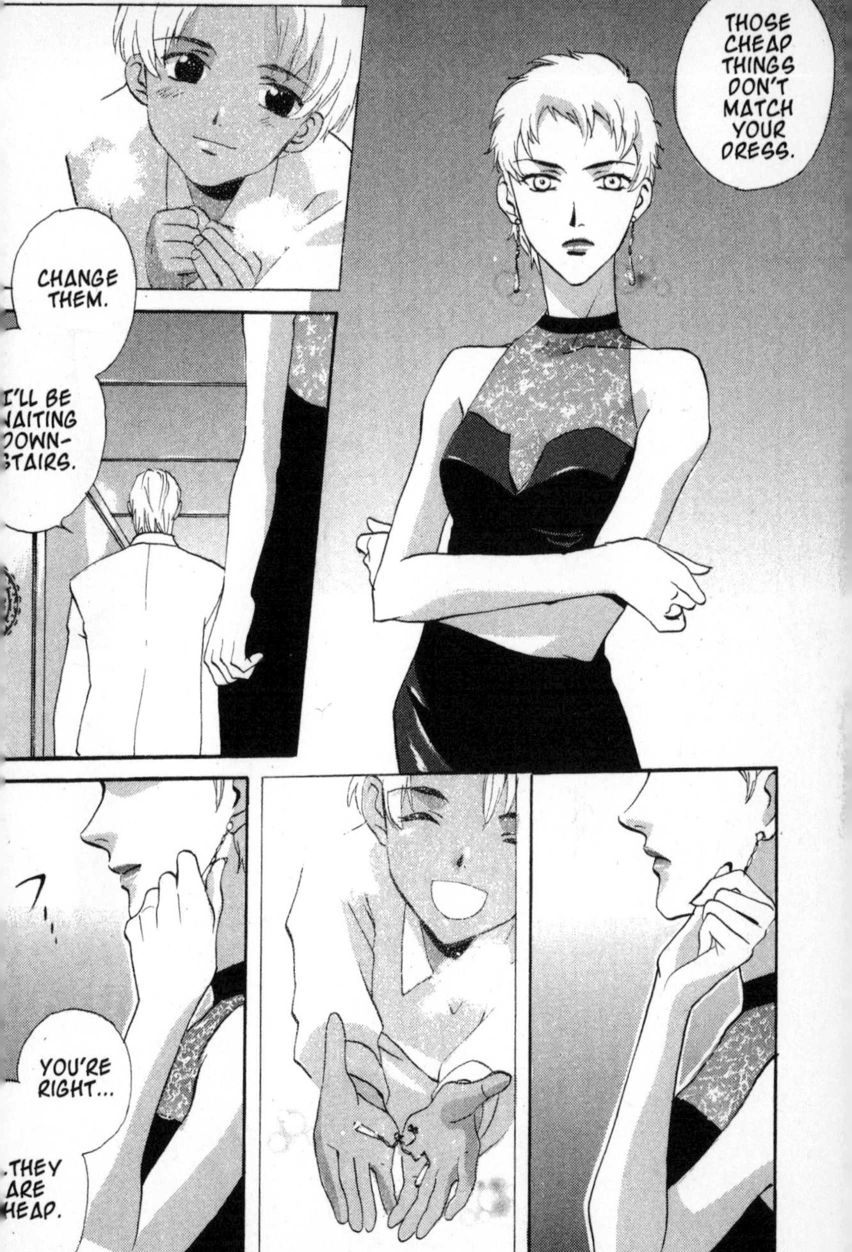
THOSE CHEAP THINGS DON'T MATCH YOUR DRESS.
CHANGE THEM.
I'LL BE WAITING DOWN-STAIRS.
YOU'RE RIGHT...
.THEY ARE HEAP.

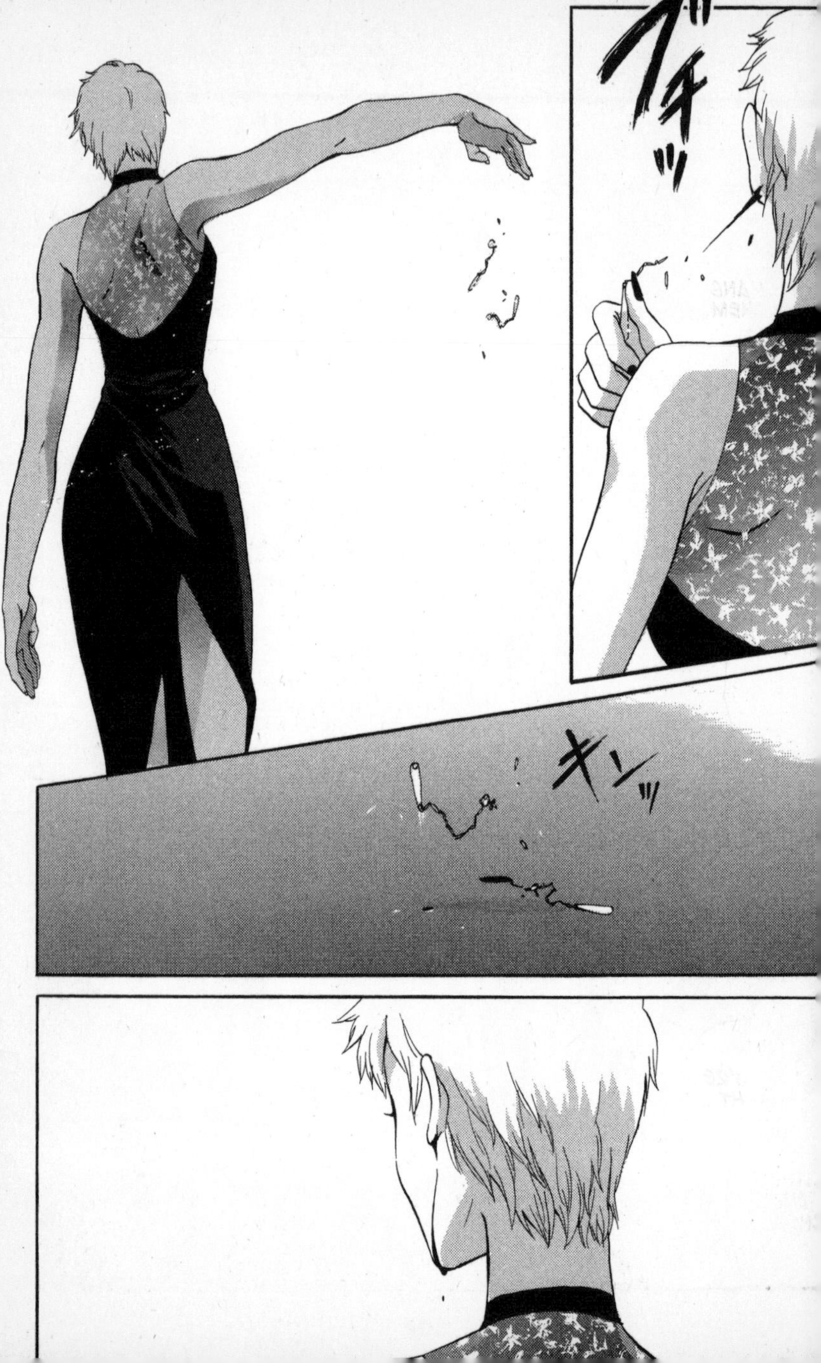
ブチッ
キンッ

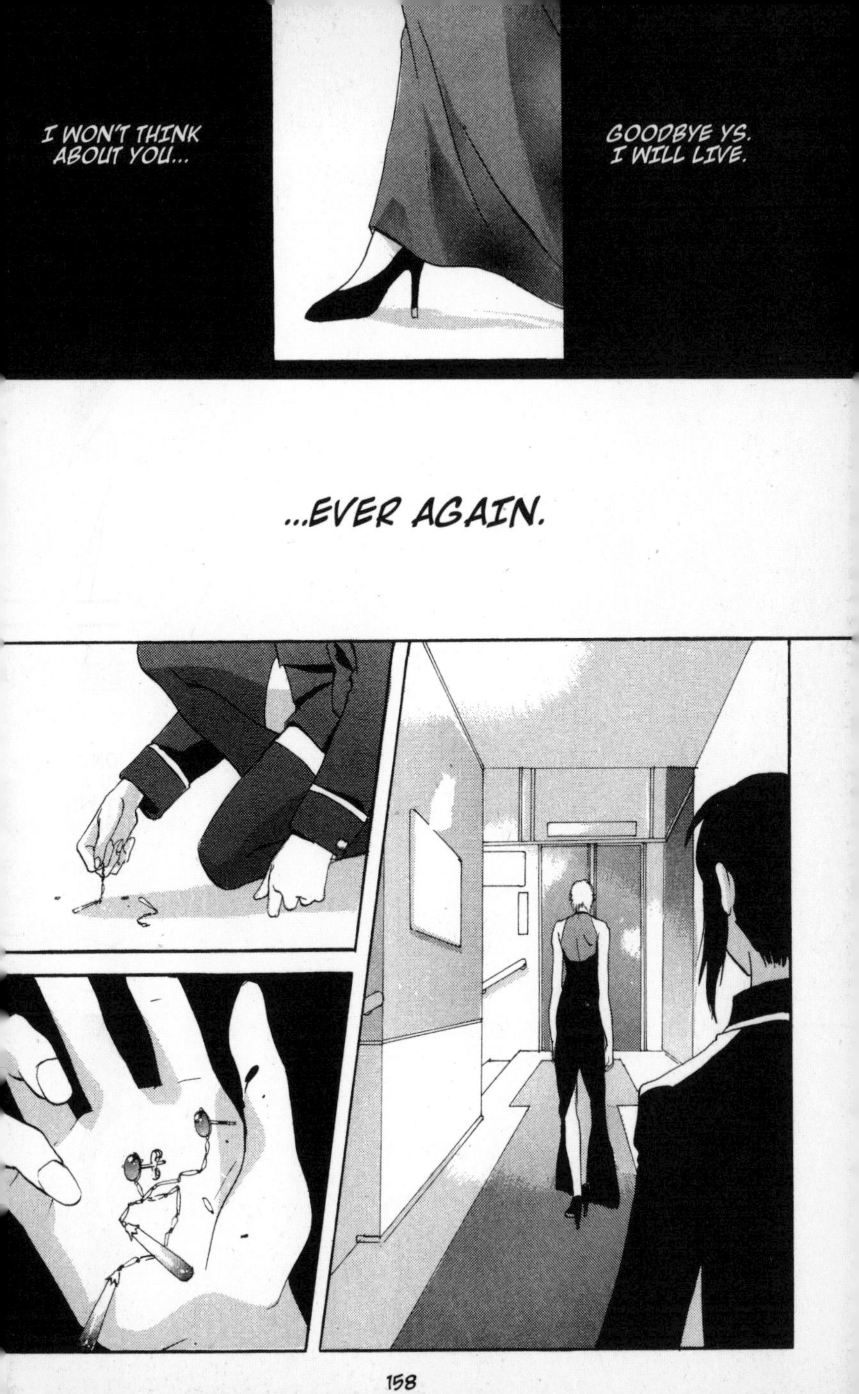
GOODBYE YS.
I WILL LIVE.
I WON'T THINK
ABOUT YOU...
...EVER AGAIN.

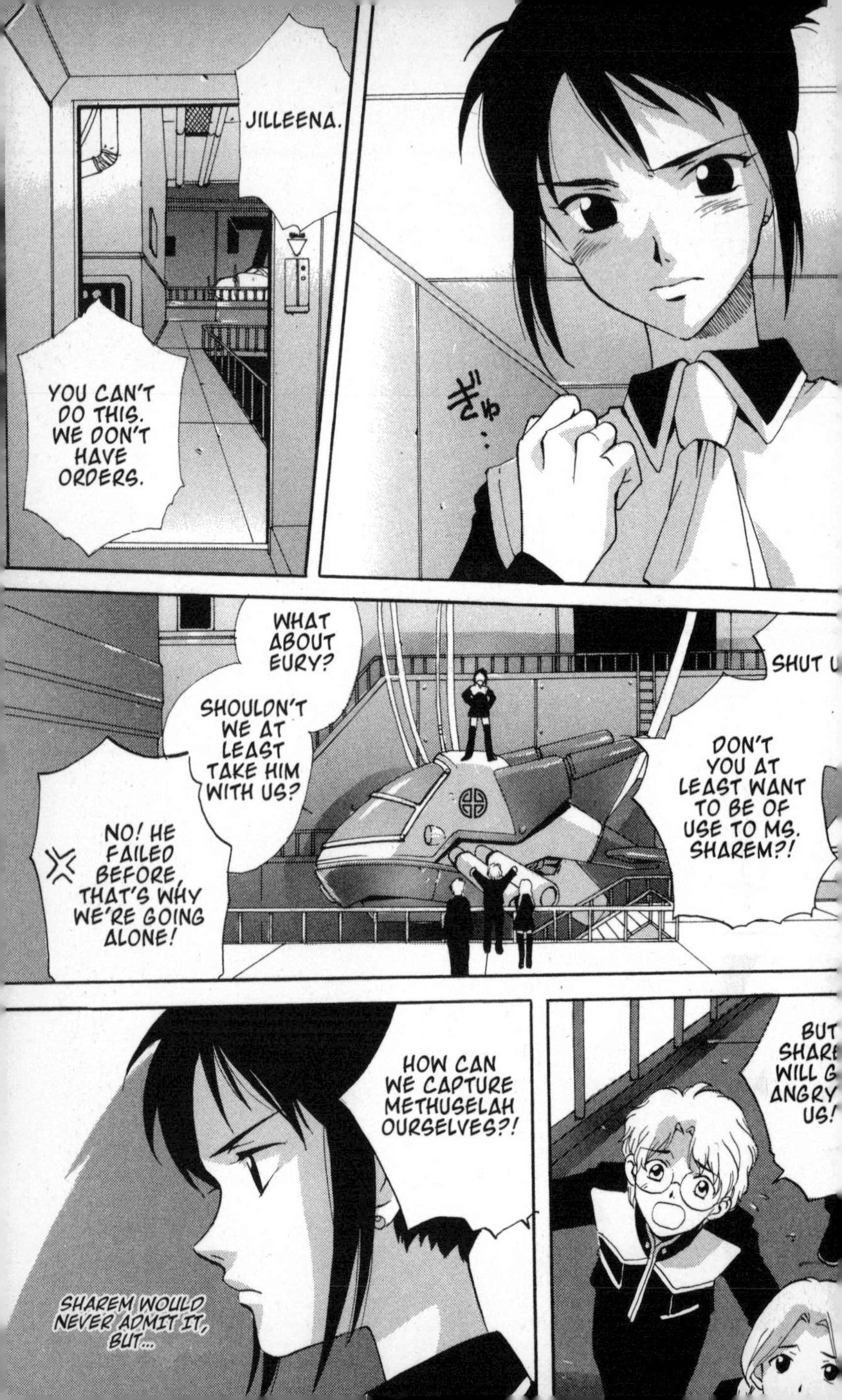

ぎゅ
JILLEENA.
YOU CAN'T DO THIS. WE DON'T HAVE ORDERS.
SHUT U
DON'T YOU AT LEAST WANT TO BE OF USE TO MS. SHAREM?!
WHAT ABOUT EURY?
SHOULDN'T WE AT LEAST TAKE HIM WITH US?
NO! HE FAILED BEFORE, THAT'S WHY WE'RE GOING ALONE!
BUT SHARE WILL G ANGRY US!
HOW CAN WE CAPTURE METHUSELAH OURSELVES?!
SHAREM WOULD NEVER ADMIT IT, BUT...

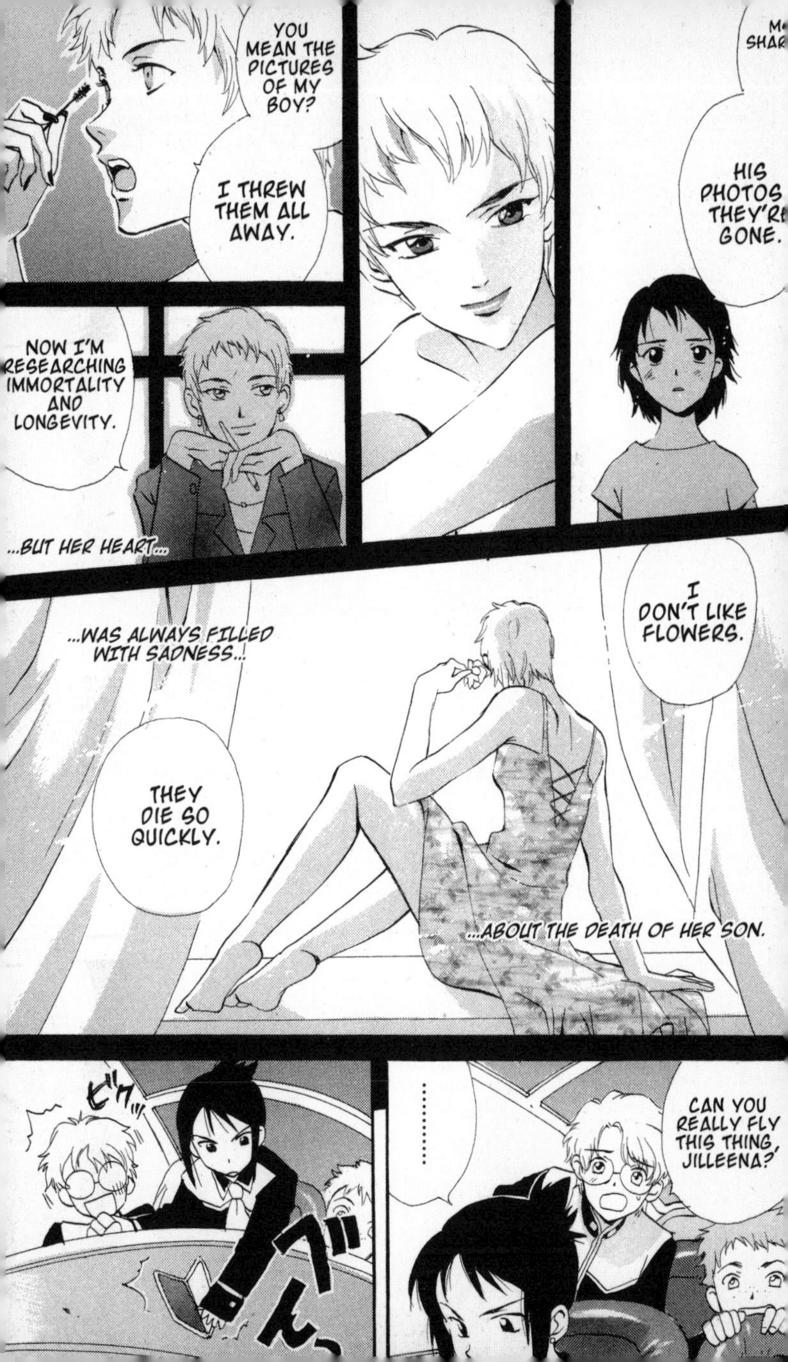
M
SHAR
HIS PHOTOS THEY'R GONE.
YOU MEAN THE PICTURES OF MY BOY?
I THREW THEM ALL AWAY.
NOW I'M RESEARCHING IMMORTALITY AND LONGEVITY.
...BUT HER HEART...
I DON'T LIKE FLOWERS.
...WAS ALWAYS FILLED WITH SADNESS...!
THEY DIE SO QUICKLY.
...ABOUT THE DEATH OF HER SON.
CAN YOU REALLY FLY THIS THING, JILLEENA?
....

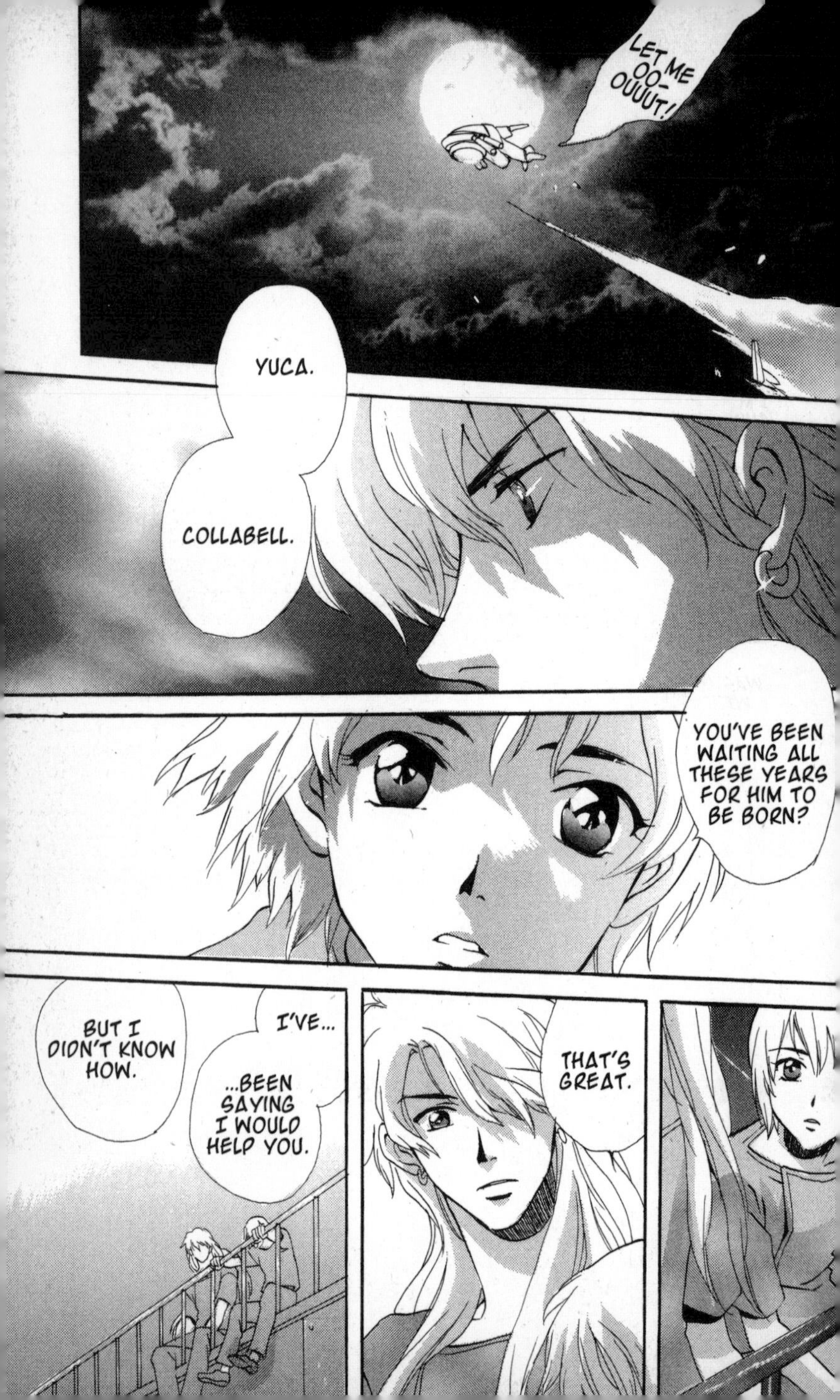
LET ME OO-OUUUT!
YUCA.
COLLABELL.
YOU'VE BEEN WAITING ALL THESE YEARS FOR HIM TO BE BORN?
THAT'S GREAT.
I'VE...
...BEEN SAYING I WOULD HELP YOU.
BUT I DIDN'T KNOW HOW.

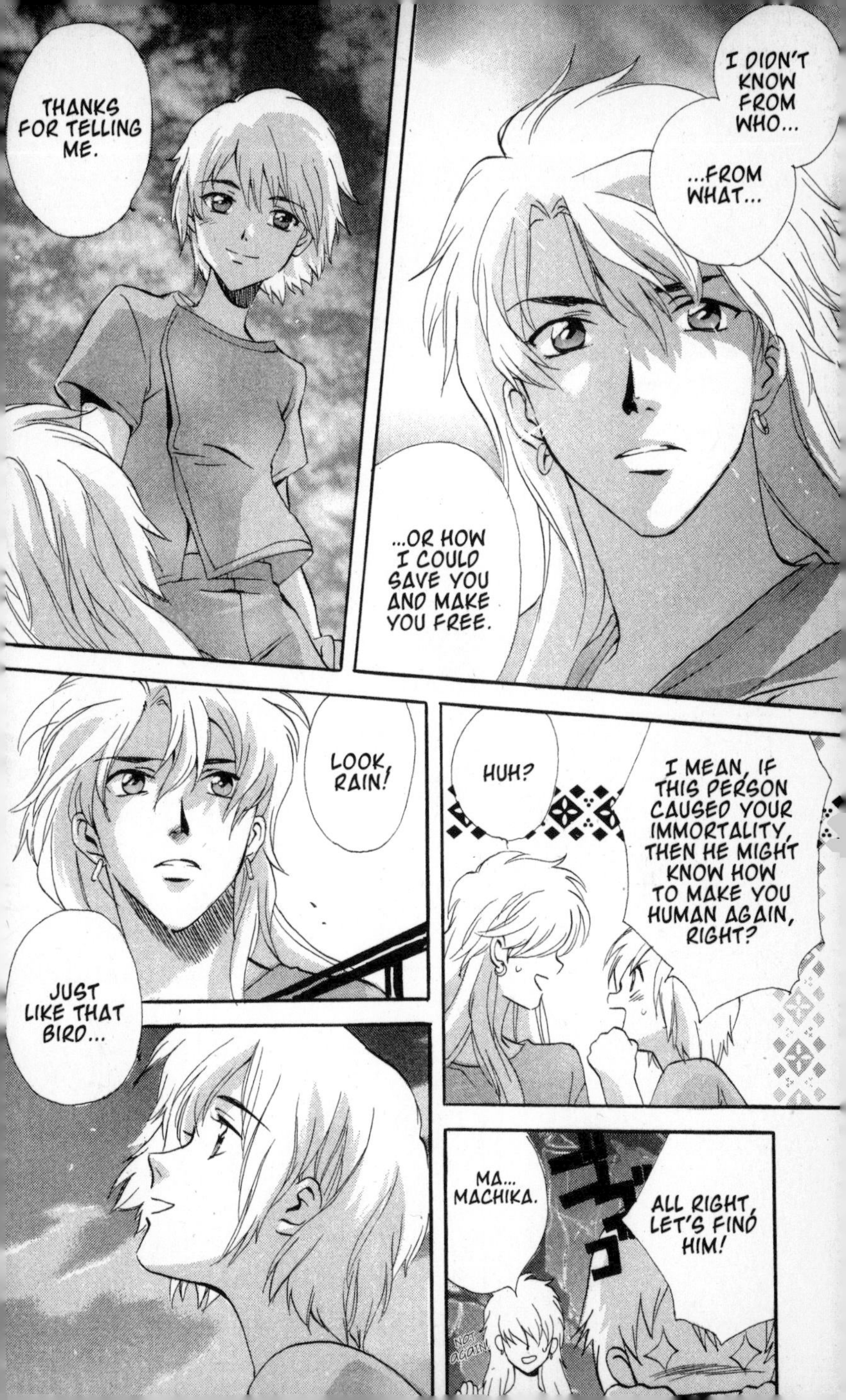
I DIDN'T KNOW FROM WHO...
...FROM WHAT...
...OR HOW I COULD SAVE YOU AND MAKE YOU FREE.
THANKS FOR TELLING ME.
HUH?
I MEAN, IF THIS PERSON CAUSED YOUR IMMORTALITY, THEN HE MIGHT KNOW HOW TO MAKE YOU HUMAN AGAIN, RIGHT?
LOOK, RAIN!
JUST LIKE THAT BIRD...
ALL RIGHT, LET'S FIND HIM!
MA... MACHIKA.
NOT AGAIN.

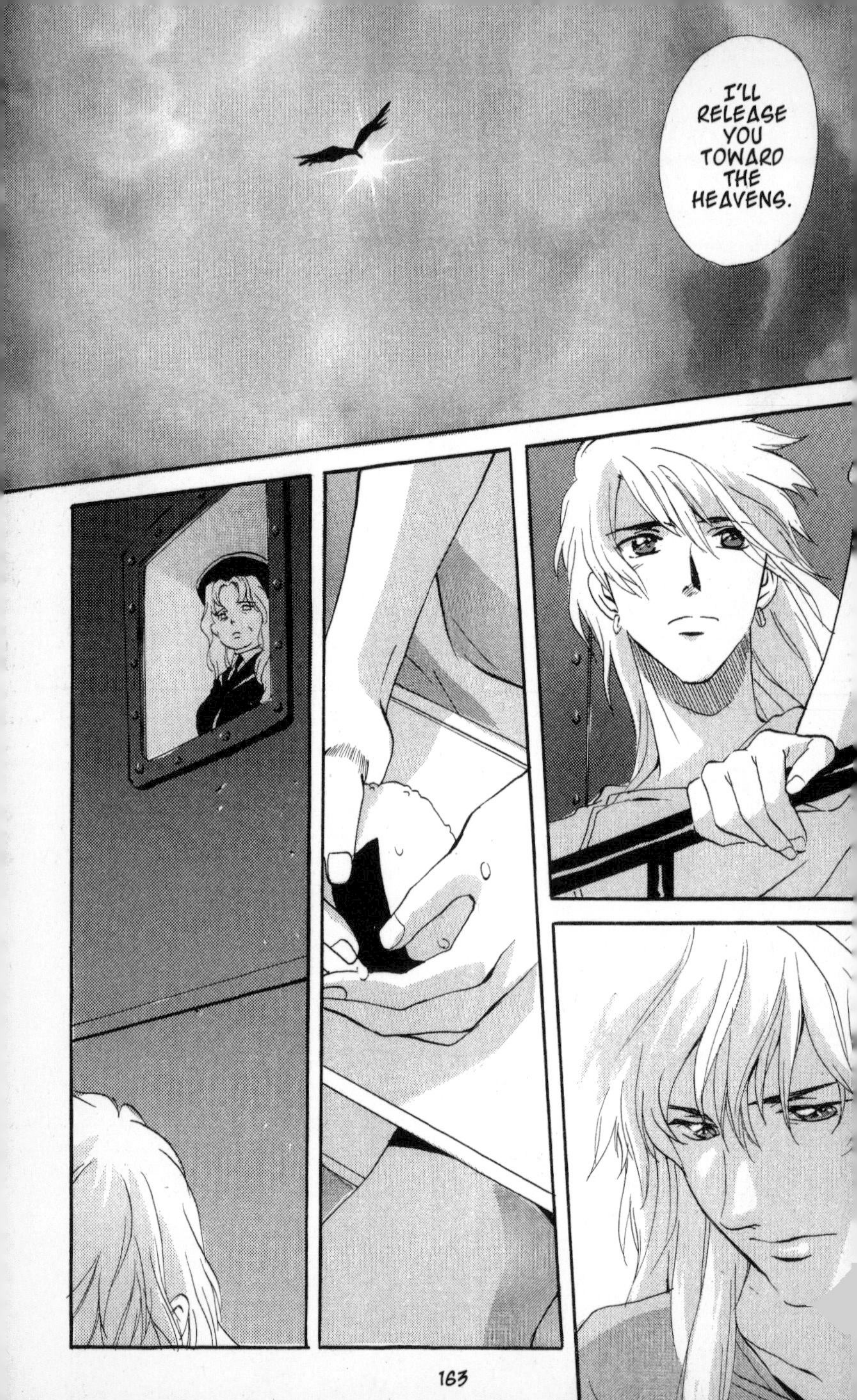
I'LL RELEASE YOU TOWARD THE HEAVENS.

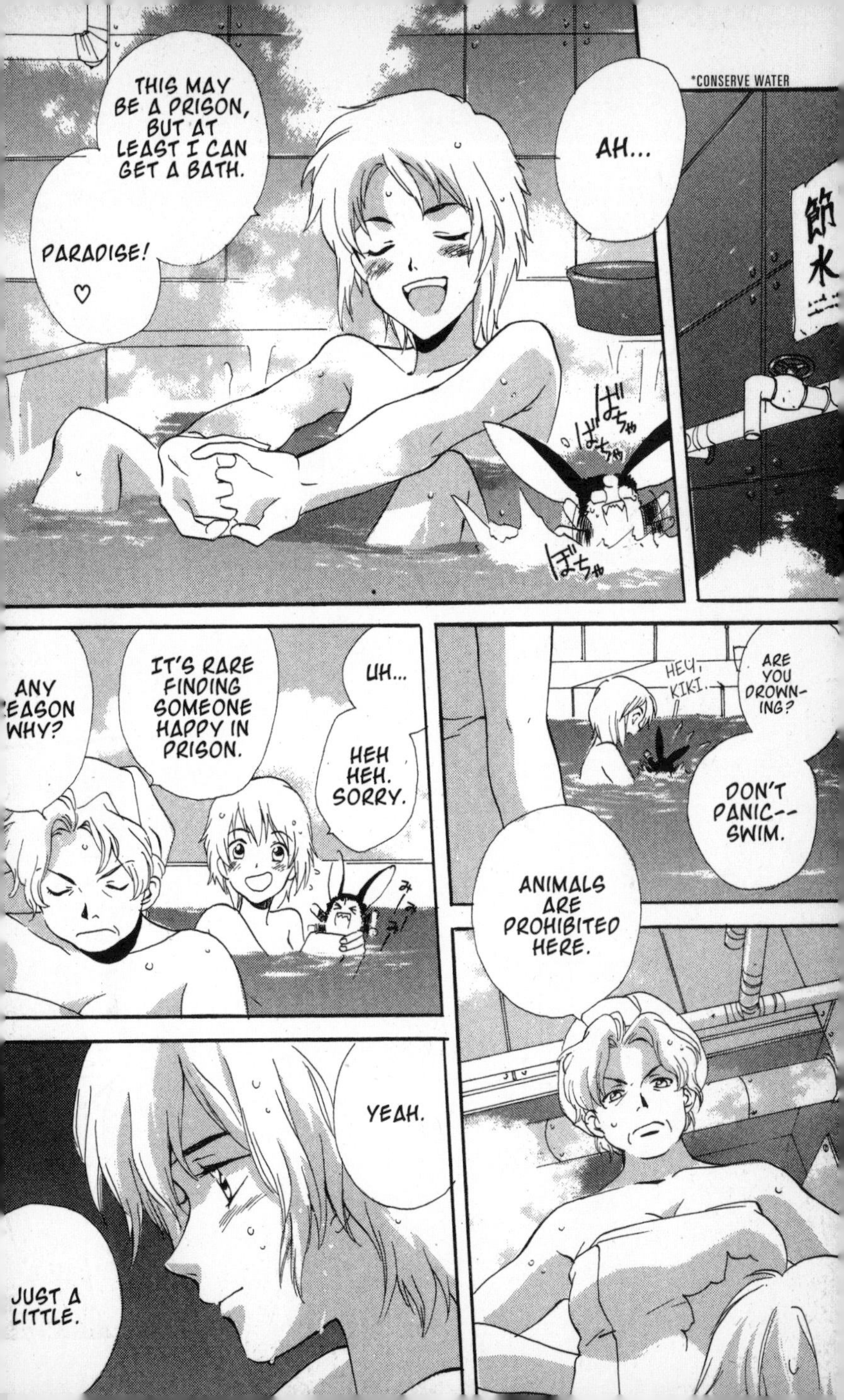
*CONSERVE WATER
AH...
節水
THIS MAY BE A PRISON, BUT AT LEAST I CAN GET A BATH.
PARADISE! ♡
ばちゃ ばちゃ
ぼちゃ
HEY, KIKI.
ARE YOU DROWNING?
DON'T PANIC--SWIM.
ANIMALS ARE PROHIBITED HERE.
UH...
HEH HEH. SORRY.
IT'S RARE FINDING SOMEONE HAPPY IN PRISON.
ANY EASON WHY?
みーみー
YEAH.
JUST A LITTLE.

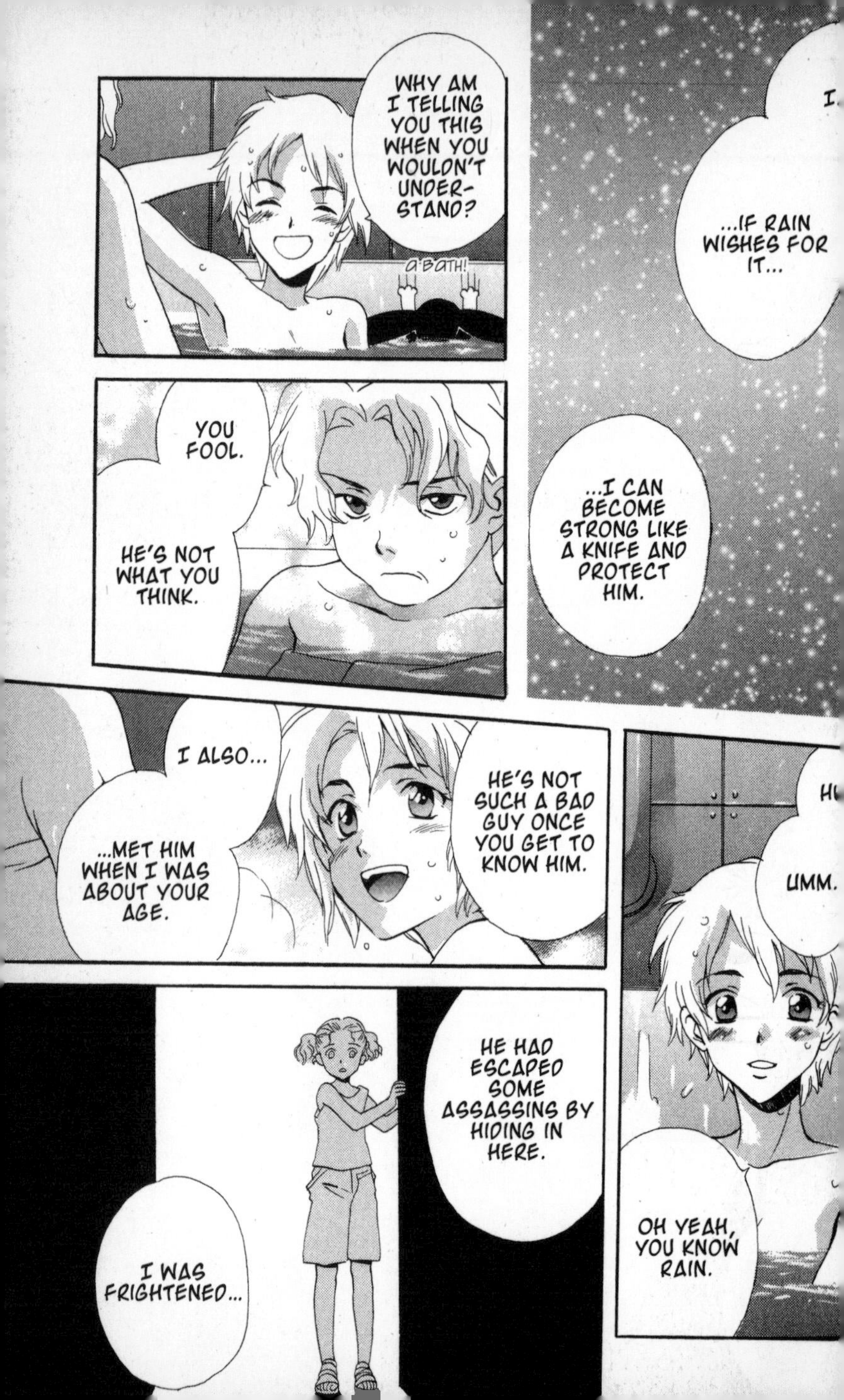
I.
...IF RAIN WISHES FOR IT...
...I CAN BECOME STRONG LIKE A KNIFE AND PROTECT HIM.
WHY AM I TELLING YOU THIS WHEN YOU WOULDN'T UNDER-STAND?
A BATH!
YOU FOOL.
HE'S NOT WHAT YOU THINK.
UMM.
OH YEAH, YOU KNOW RAIN.
HE'S NOT SUCH A BAD GUY ONCE YOU GET TO KNOW HIM.
I ALSO...
...MET HIM WHEN I WAS ABOUT YOUR AGE.
HE HAD ESCAPED SOME ASSASSINS BY HIDING IN HERE.
I WAS FRIGHTENED...

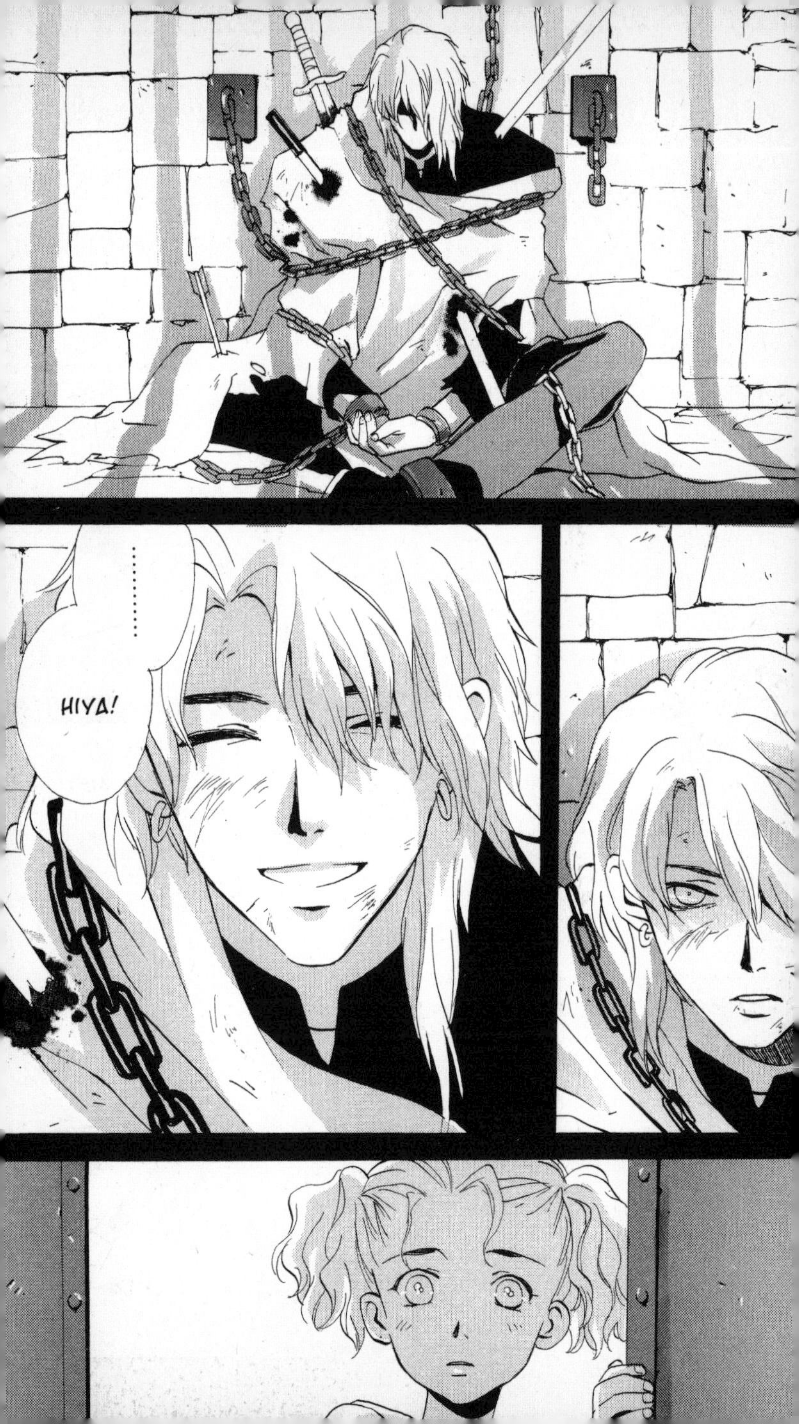
......
HIYA!

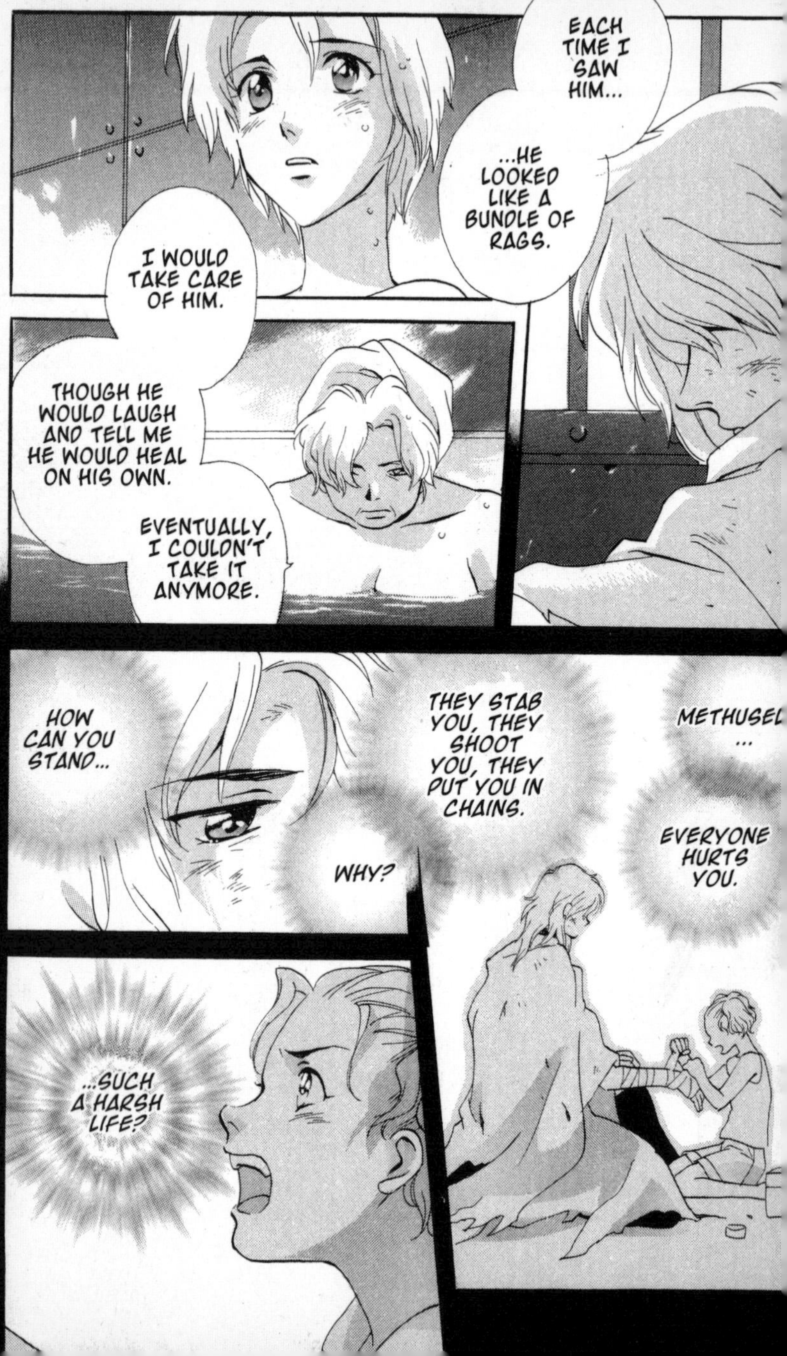
EACH TIME I SAW HIM...
...HE LOOKED LIKE A BUNDLE OF RAGS.
I WOULD TAKE CARE OF HIM.
THOUGH HE WOULD LAUGH AND TELL ME HE WOULD HEAL ON HIS OWN.
EVENTUALLY, I COULDN'T TAKE IT ANYMORE.
METHUSEL ...
EVERYONE HURTS YOU.
THEY STAB YOU, THEY SHOOT YOU, THEY PUT YOU IN CHAINS.
WHY?
HOW CAN YOU STAND...
...SUCH A HARSH LIFE?

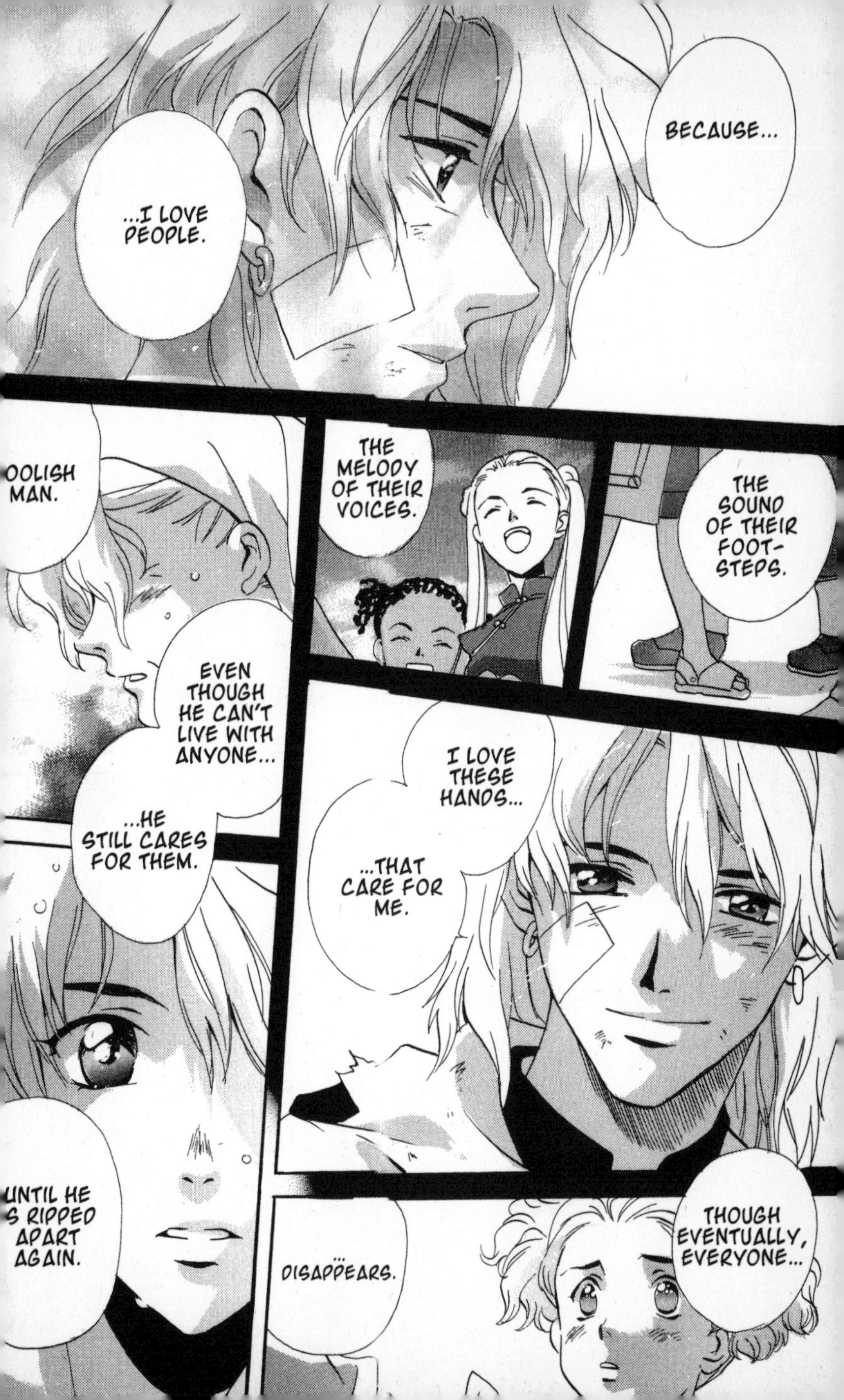
BECAUSE...
...I LOVE PEOPLE.
THE SOUND OF THEIR FOOT-STEPS.
THE MELODY OF THEIR VOICES.
I LOVE THESE HANDS...
...THAT CARE FOR ME.
OOLISH MAN.
EVEN THOUGH HE CAN'T LIVE WITH ANYONE...
...HE STILL CARES FOR THEM.
THOUGH EVENTUALLY, EVERYONE...
...DISAPPEARS.
UNTIL HE S RIPPED APART AGAIN.

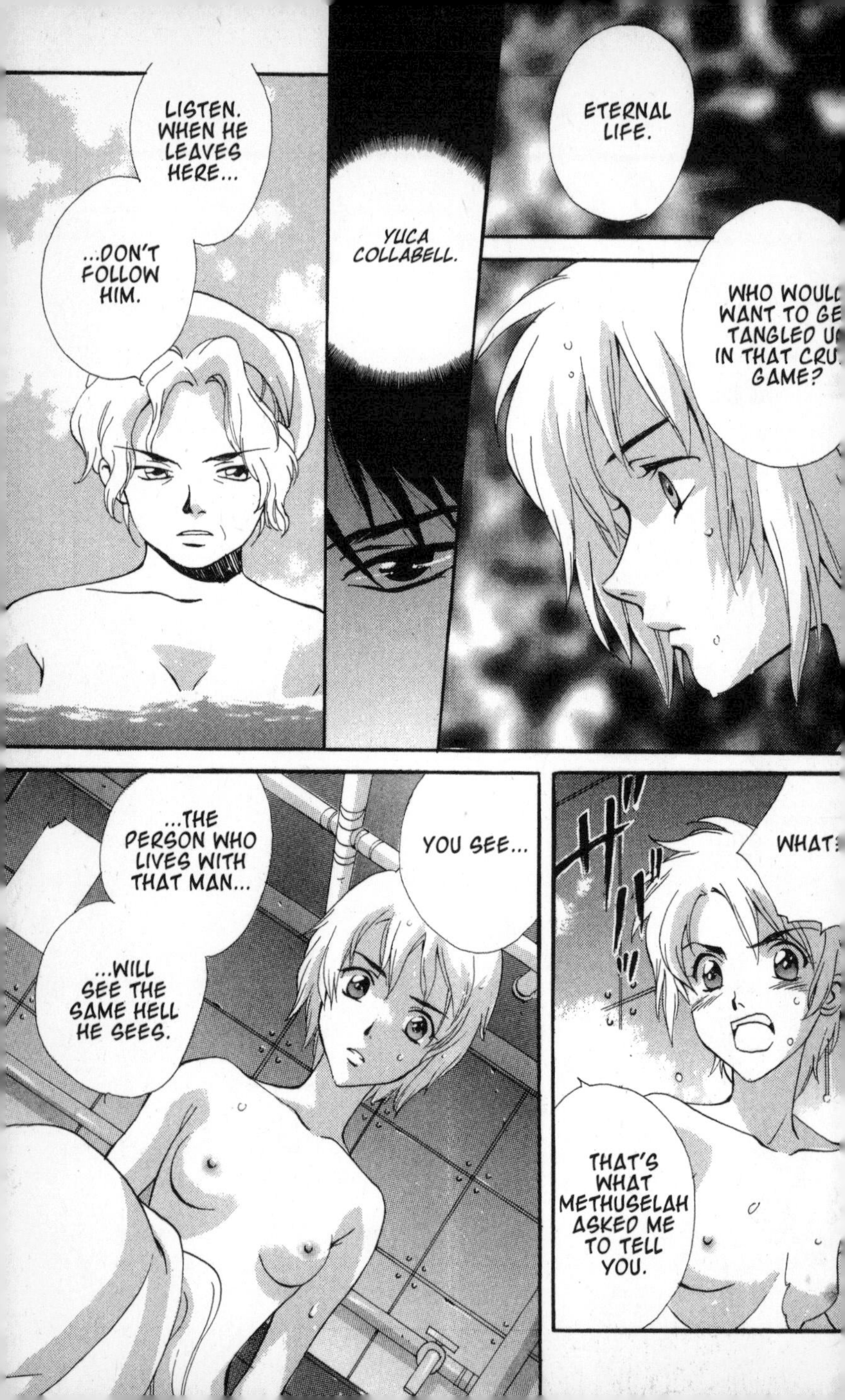
ETERNAL LIFE.
WHO WOUL WANT TO GE TANGLED U IN THAT CRU GAME?
YUCA COLLABELL.
LISTEN. WHEN HE LEAVES HERE...
...DON'T FOLLOW HIM.
WHAT
THAT'S WHAT METHUSELAH ASKED ME TO TELL YOU.
YOU SEE...
...THE PERSON WHO LIVES WITH THAT MAN...
...WILL SEE THE SAME HELL HE SEES.

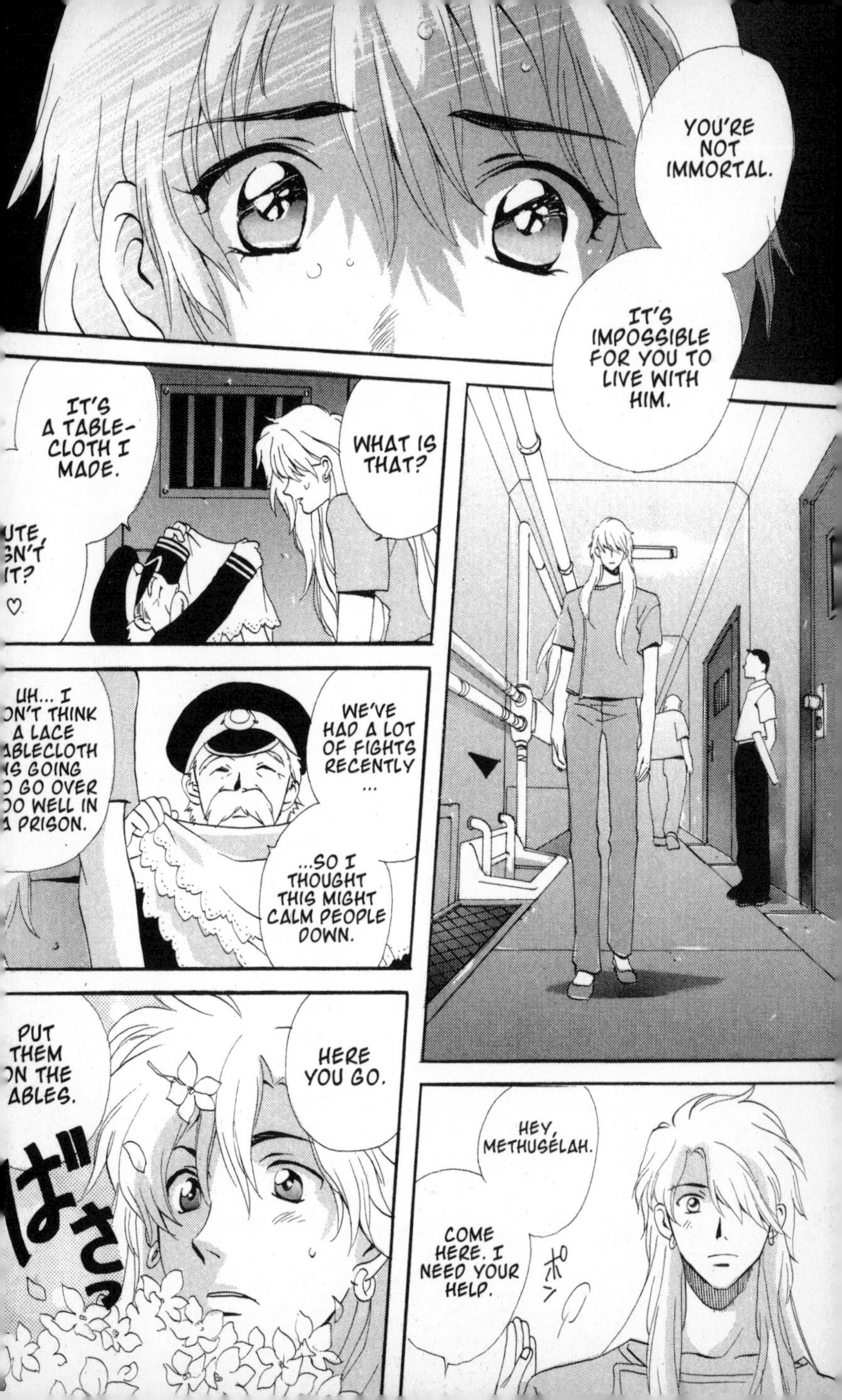

YOU'RE NOT IMMORTAL.
IT'S IMPOSSIBLE FOR YOU TO LIVE WITH HIM.
WHAT IS THAT?
IT'S A TABLE-CLOTH I MADE.
UTE, SN'T IT? ♡
WE'VE HAD A LOT OF FIGHTS RECENTLY ...
...SO I THOUGHT THIS MIGHT CALM PEOPLE DOWN.
UH... I ON'T THINK A LACE ABLECLOTH IS GOING O GO OVER OO WELL IN A PRISON.
HEY, METHUSÉLAH.
COME HERE. I NEED YOUR HELP.
ポン
HERE YOU GO.
PUT THEM ON THE ABLES.
ばさっ

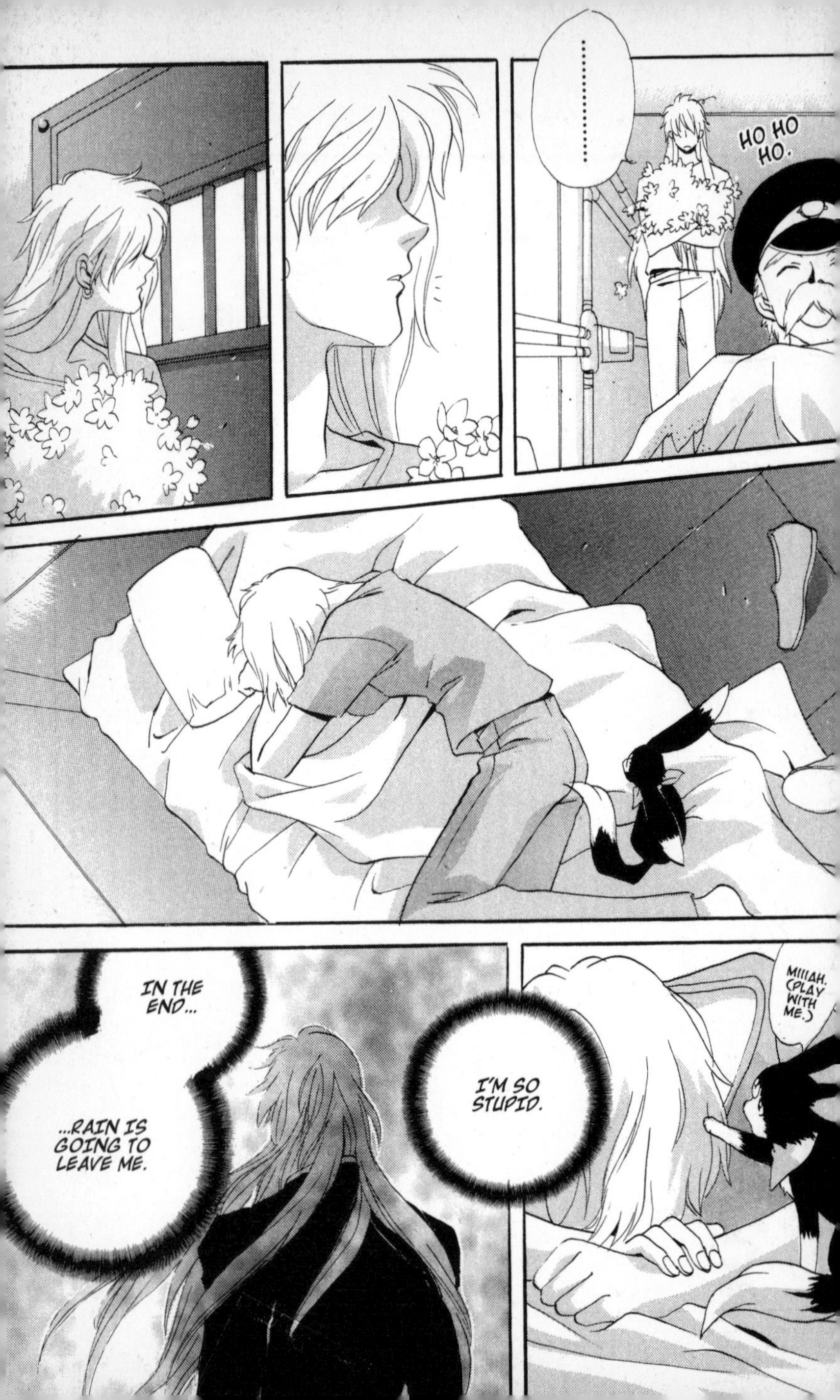
HO HO HO.
......
MIIIAH. (PLAY WITH ME.)
I'M SO STUPID.
IN THE END...
...RAIN IS GOING TO LEAVE ME.

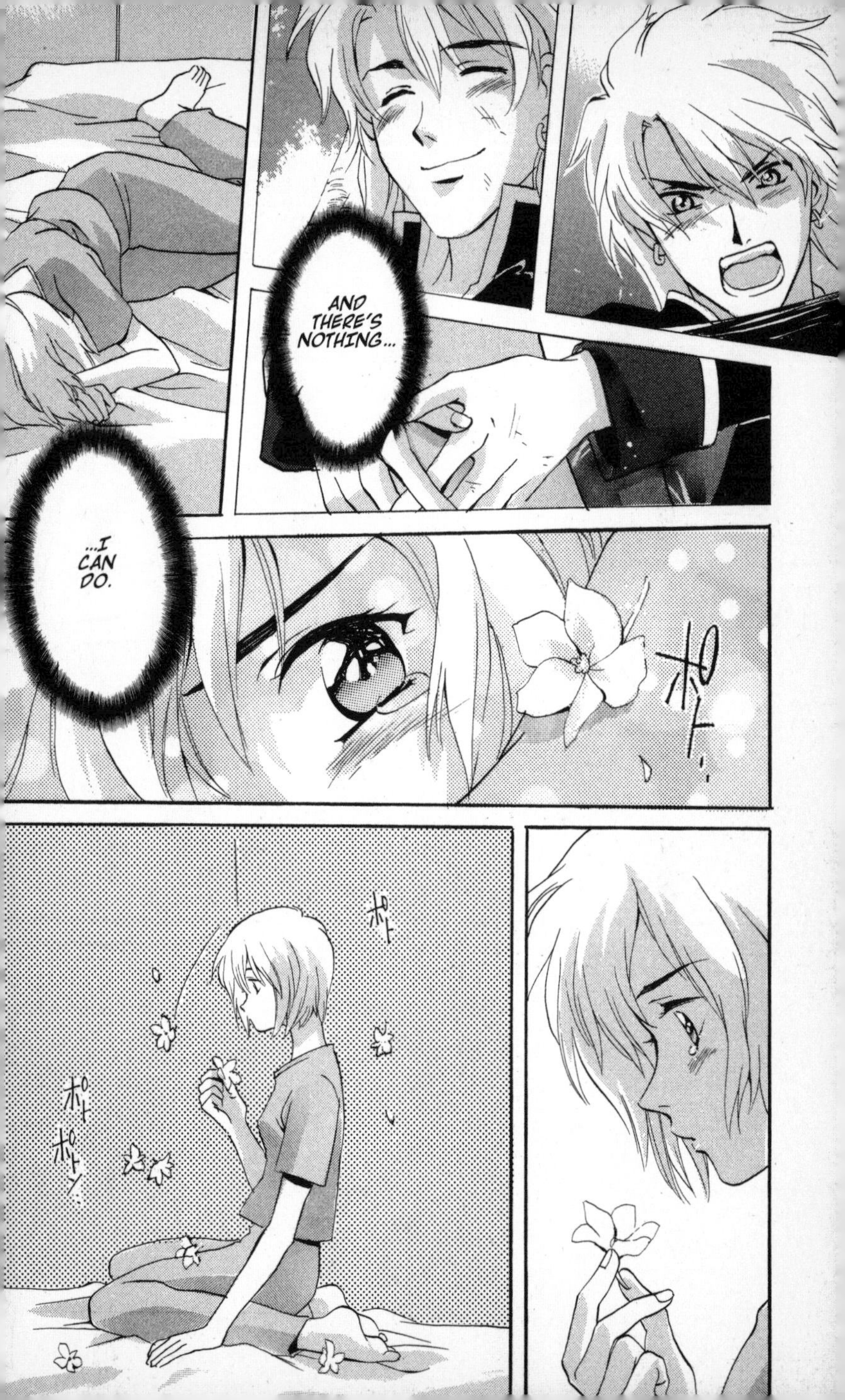
AND THERE'S NOTHING...
...I CAN DO.
ポト…
ポト
ポトポトン…

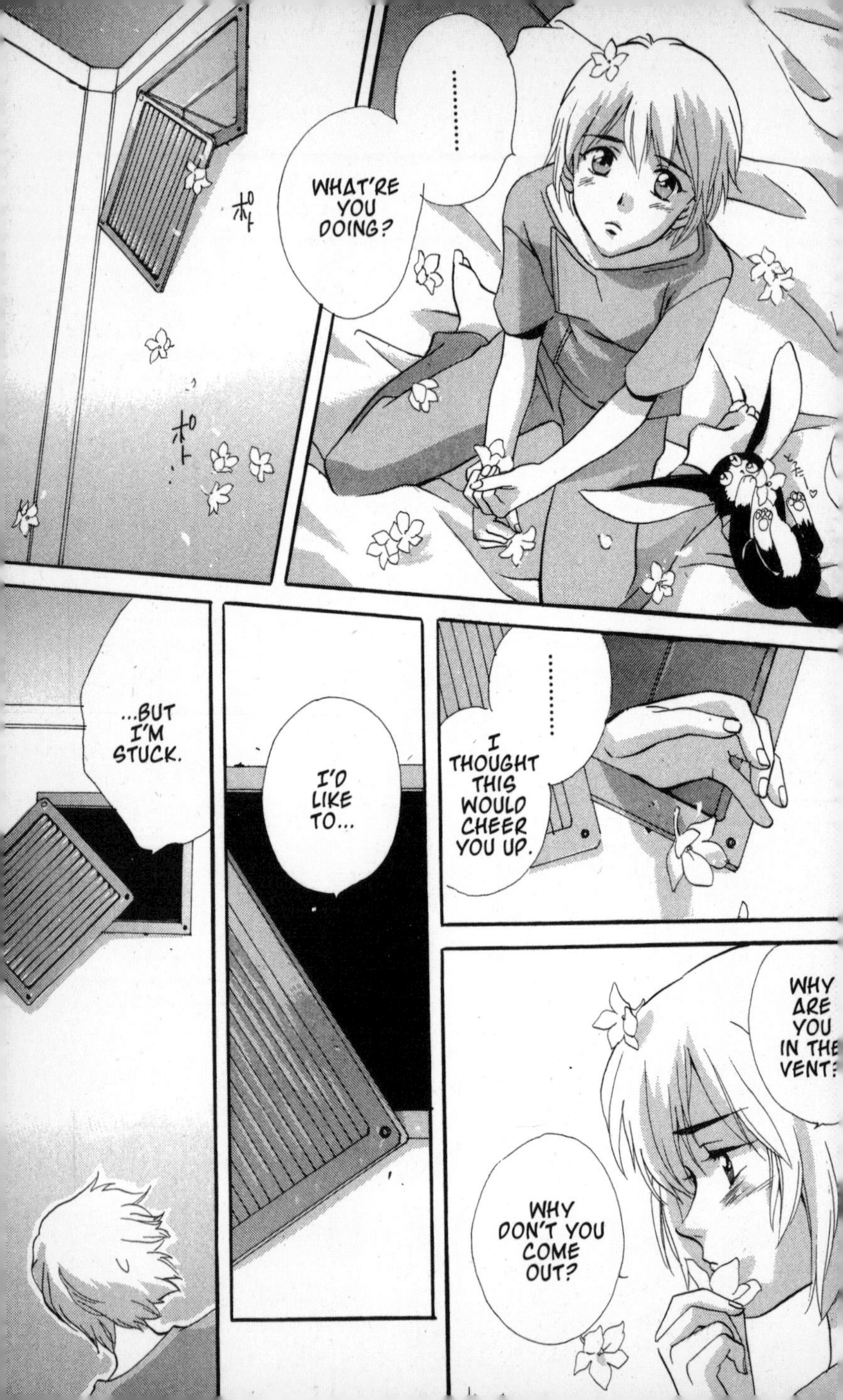
......
WHAT'RE YOU DOING?
ポト
ポト
......
I THOUGHT THIS WOULD CHEER YOU UP.
WHY ARE YOU IN THE VENT?
WHY DON'T YOU COME OUT?
I'D LIKE TO...
...BUT I'M STUCK.

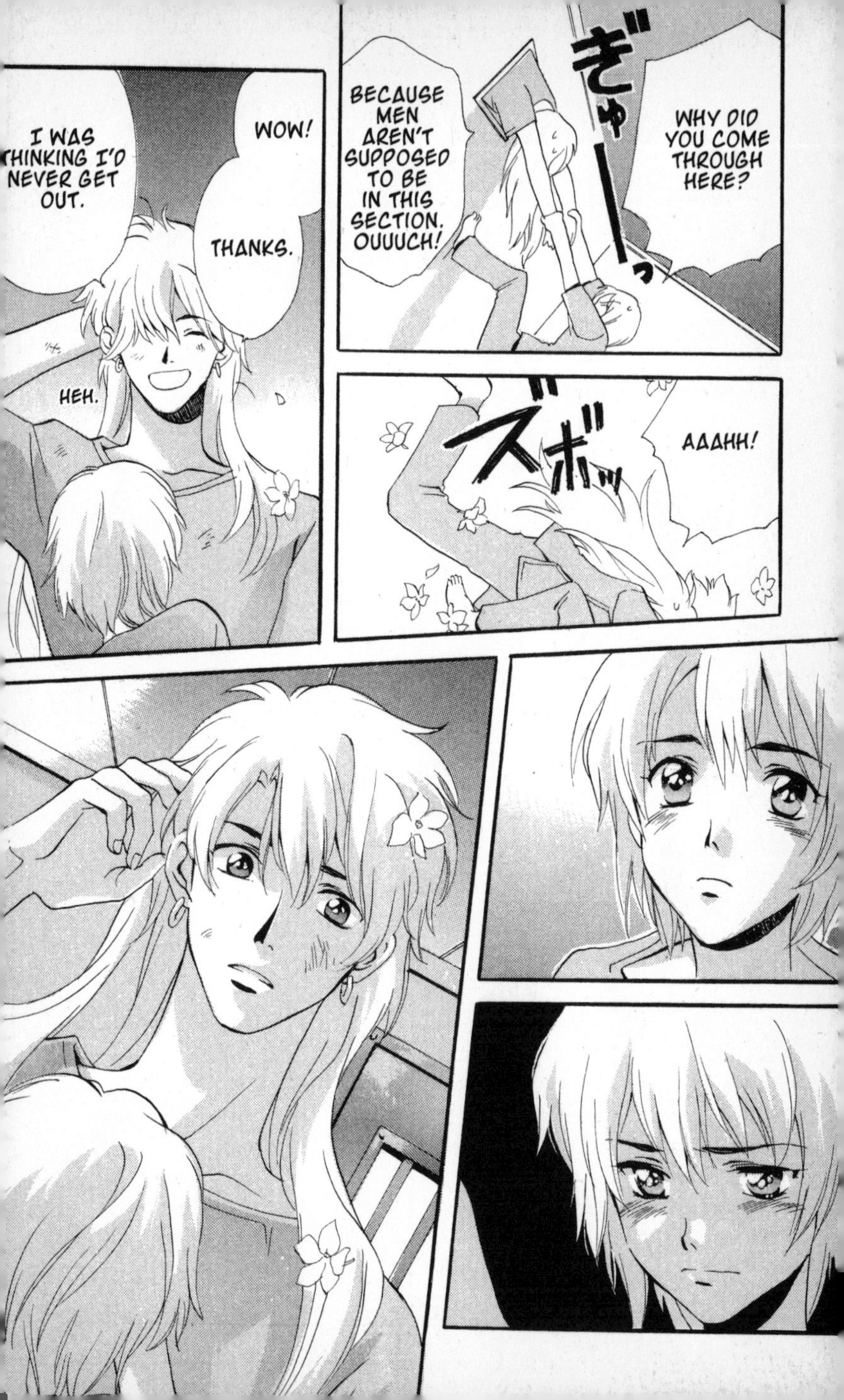
WHY DID YOU COME THROUGH HERE?
ぎゅーっ
BECAUSE MEN AREN'T SUPPOSED TO BE IN THIS SECTION. OUUUCH!
AAAHH!
ズボッ
WOW!
THANKS.
I WAS THINKING I'D NEVER GET OUT.
HEH.

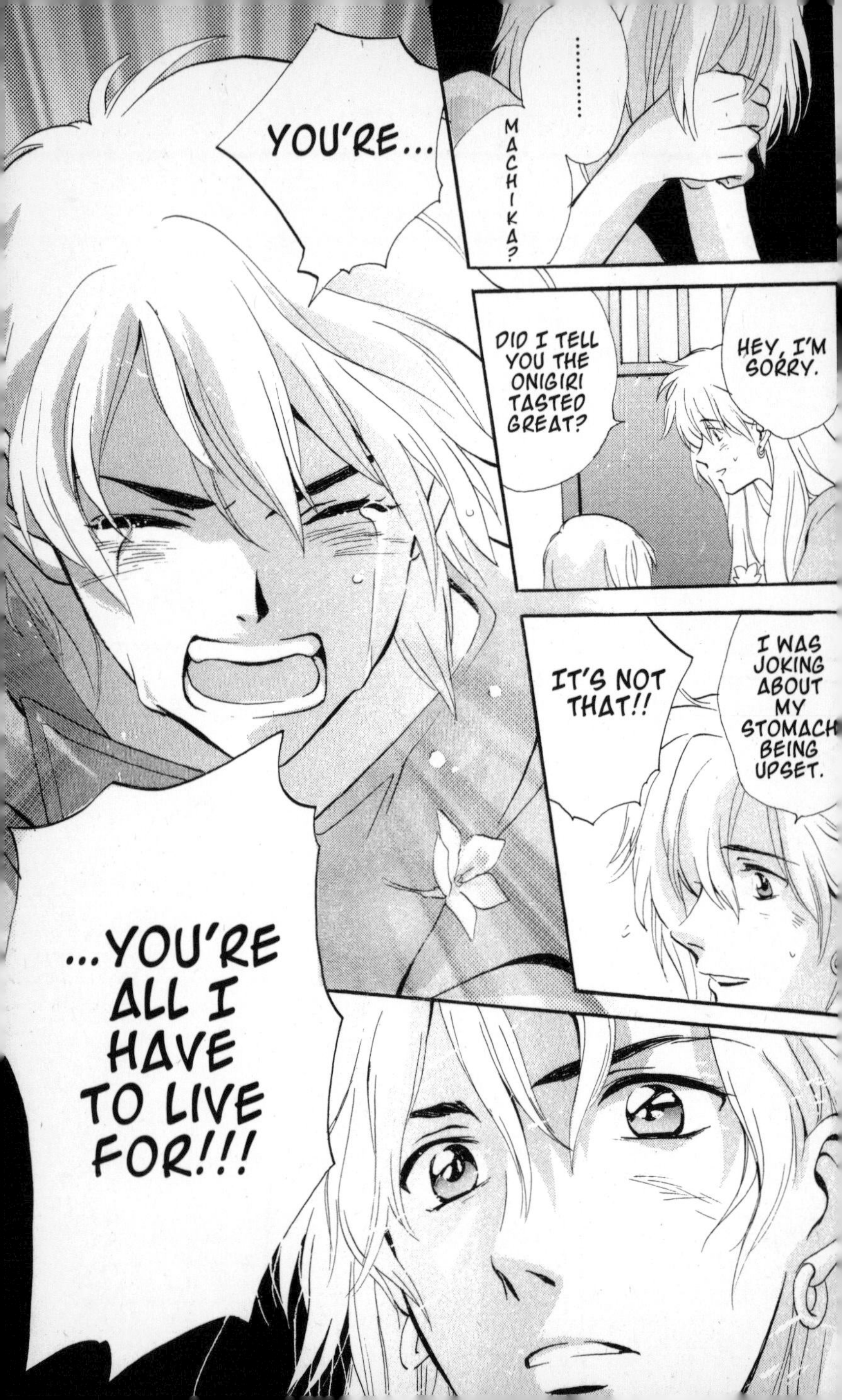
......
MACHIKA?
HEY, I'M SORRY.
DID I TELL YOU THE ONIGIRI TASTED GREAT?
I WAS JOKING ABOUT MY STOMACH BEING UPSET.
IT'S NOT THAT!!
YOU'RE...
...YOU'RE ALL I HAVE TO LIVE FOR!!!

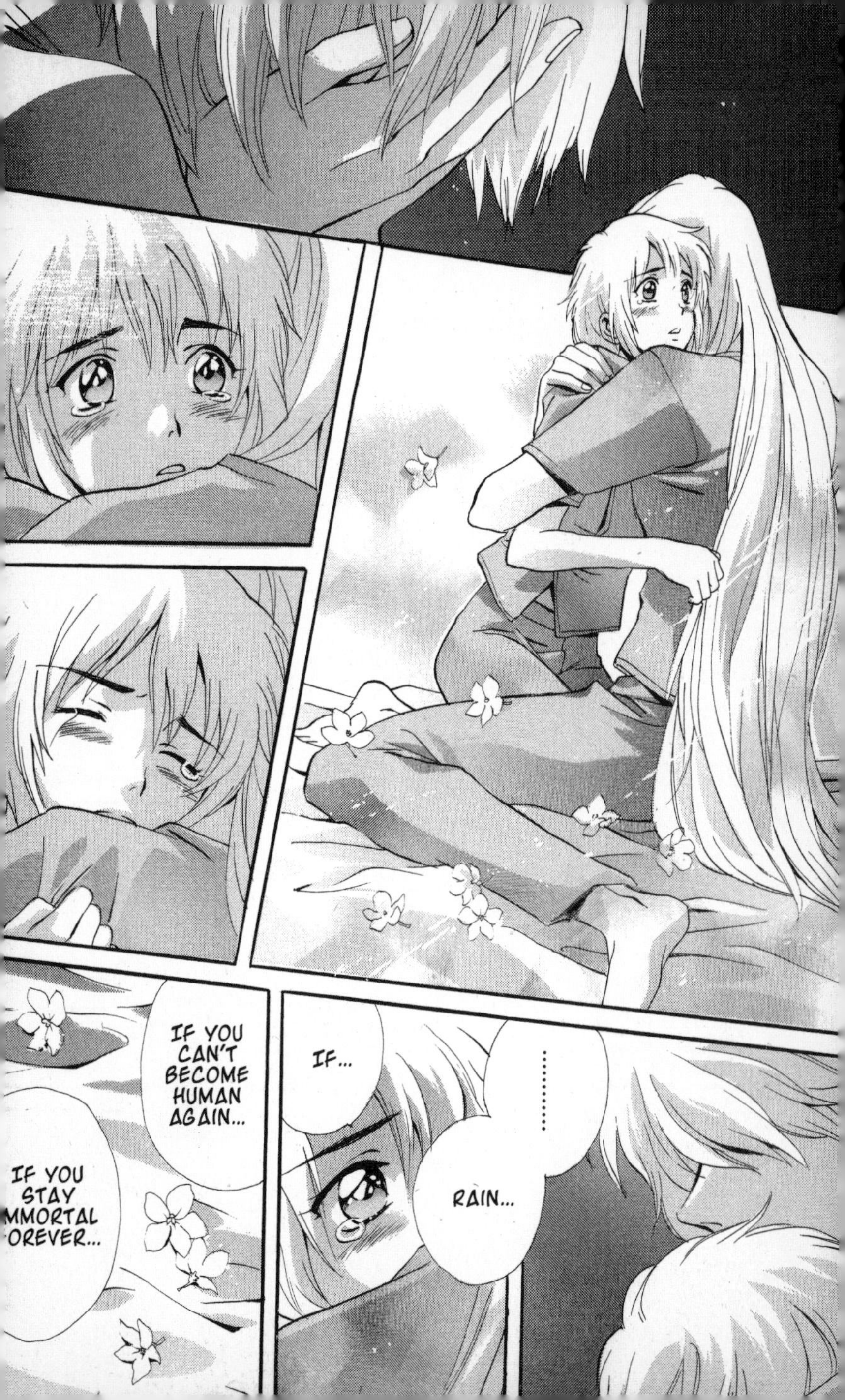

......
IF...
RAIN...
IF YOU CAN'T BECOME HUMAN AGAIN...
IF YOU STAY MMORTAL OREVER...

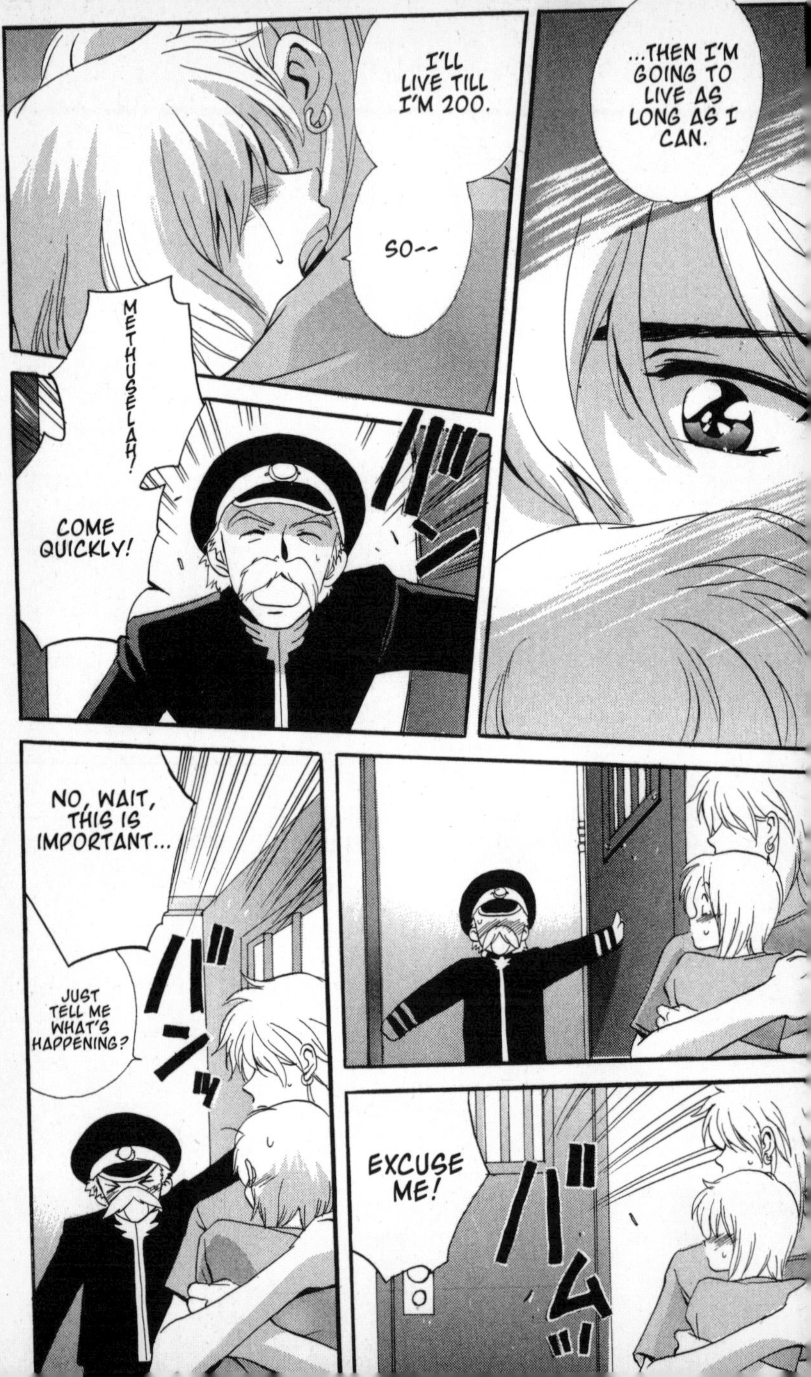
...THEN I'M GOING TO LIVE AS LONG AS I CAN.
I'LL LIVE TILL I'M 200.
SO--
METHUSELAH!
COME QUICKLY!
EXCUSE ME!
NO, WAIT, THIS IS IMPORTANT...
JUST TELL ME WHAT'S HAPPENING?

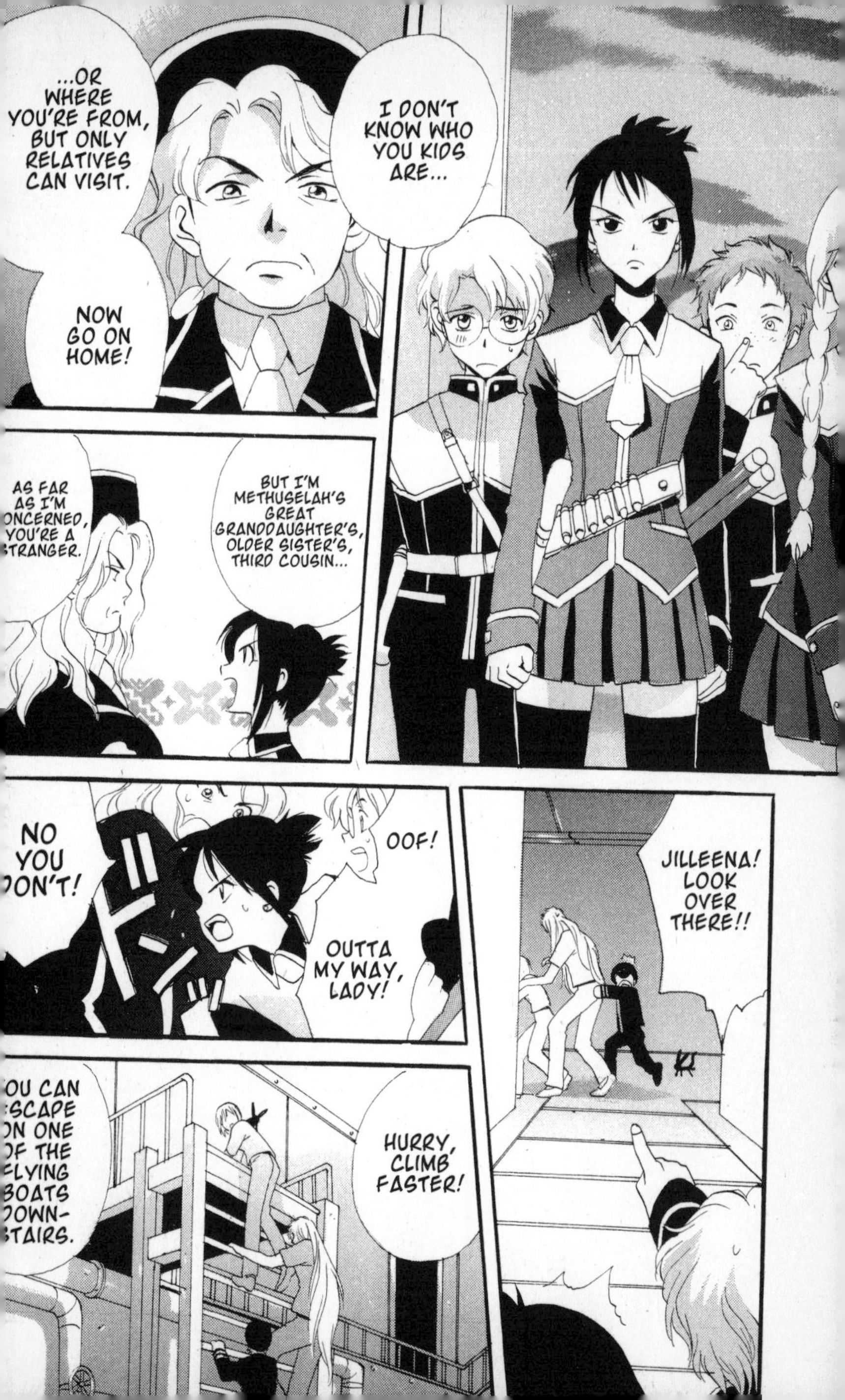
I DON'T KNOW WHO YOU KIDS ARE...
...OR WHERE YOU'RE FROM, BUT ONLY RELATIVES CAN VISIT.
NOW GO ON HOME!
BUT I'M METHUSELAH'S GREAT GRANDDAUGHTER'S, OLDER SISTER'S, THIRD COUSIN...
AS FAR AS I'M ONCERNED, YOU'RE A TRANGER.
JILLEENA! LOOK OVER THERE!!
OOF!
OUTTA MY WAY, LADY!
NO YOU ON'T!
HURRY, CLIMB FASTER!
OU CAN SCAPE ON ONE OF THE FLYING BOATS OWN- TAIRS.

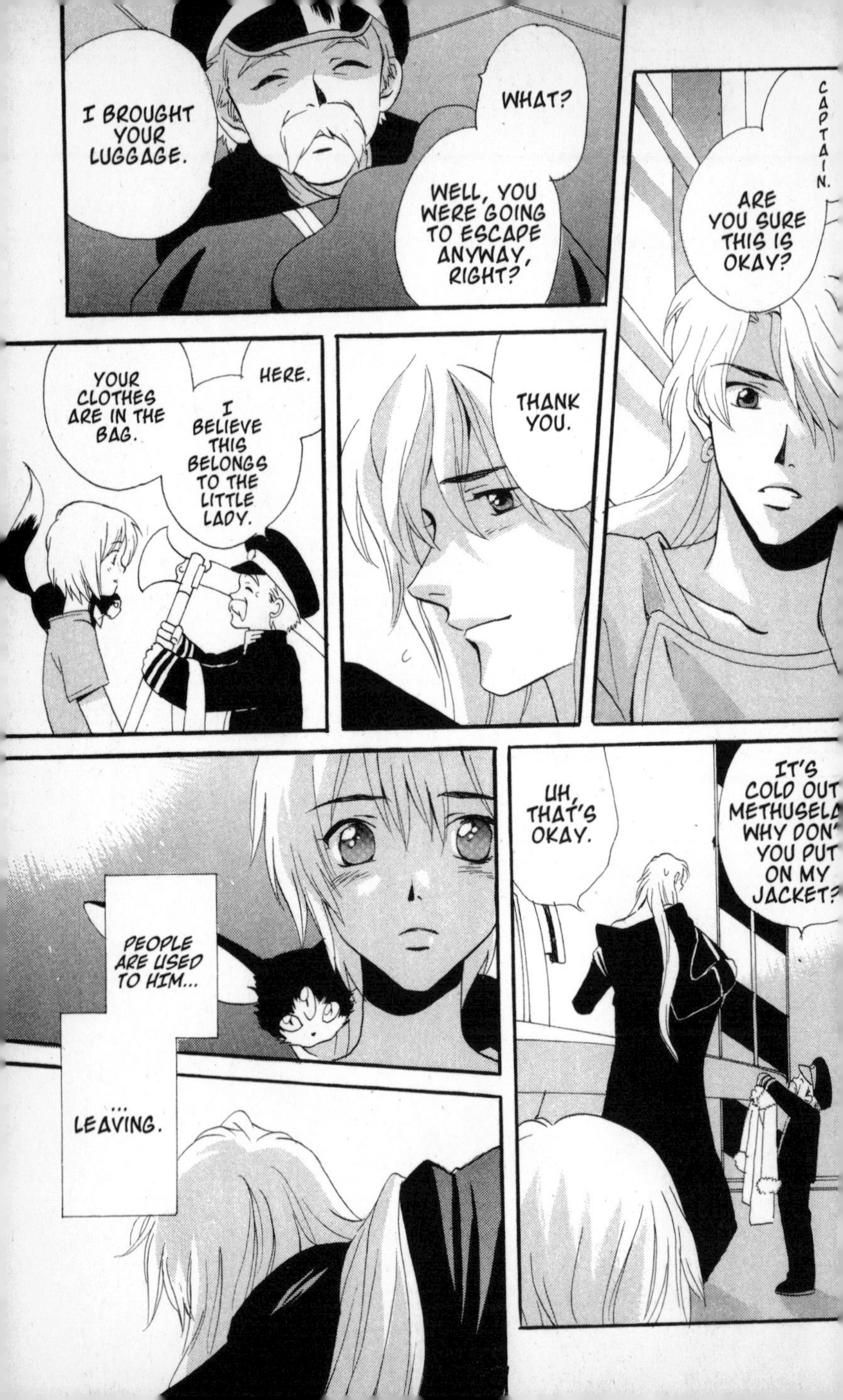
CAPTAIN.
ARE YOU SURE THIS IS OKAY?
I BROUGHT YOUR LUGGAGE.
WHAT?
WELL, YOU WERE GOING TO ESCAPE ANYWAY, RIGHT?
THANK YOU.
HERE.
I BELIEVE THIS BELONGS TO THE LITTLE LADY.
YOUR CLOTHES ARE IN THE BAG.
IT'S COLD OUT METHUSELA. WHY DON'T YOU PUT ON MY JACKET?
UH, THAT'S OKAY.
PEOPLE ARE USED TO HIM...
...LEAVING.

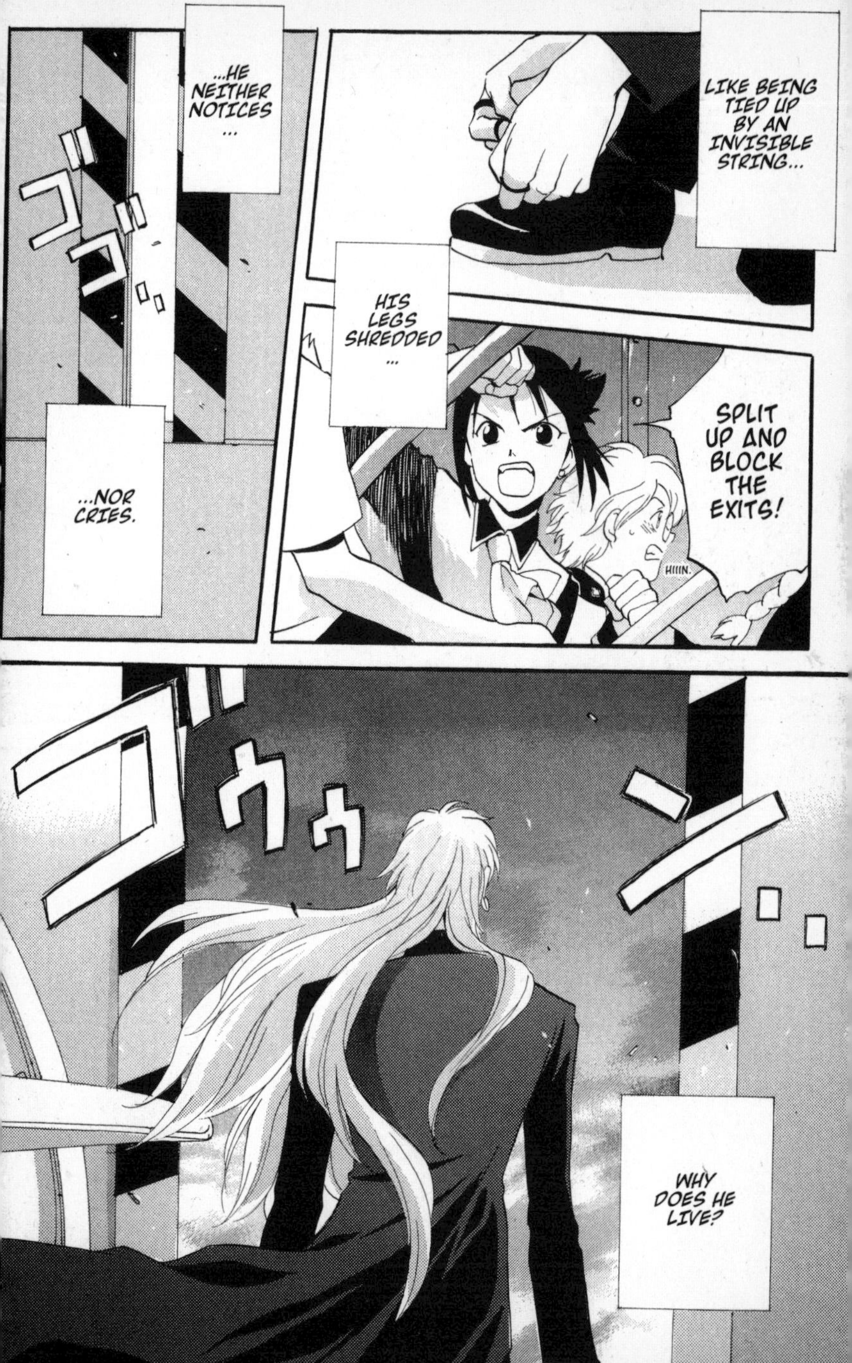
LIKE BEING TIED UP BY AN INVISIBLE STRING...
HIS LEGS SHREDDED ...
SPLIT UP AND BLOCK THE EXITS!
HIIIN.
...HE NEITHER NOTICES ...
ゴゴゴ..
...NOR CRIES.
ゴウウーン..
WHY DOES HE LIVE?

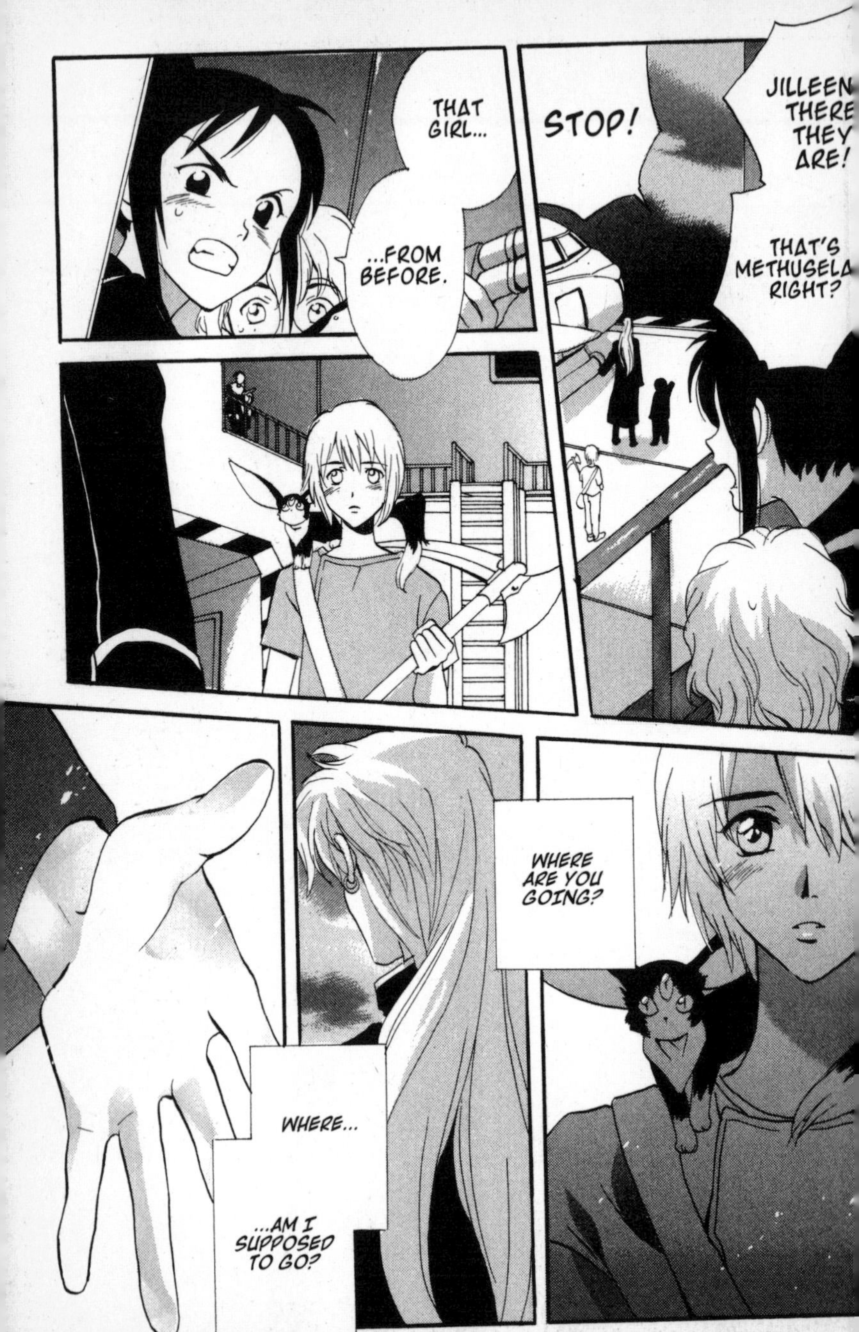
JILLEEN THERE THEY ARE!
THAT'S METHUSELA RIGHT?
STOP!
THAT GIRL...
...FROM BEFORE.
WHERE ARE YOU GOING?
WHERE...
...AM I SUPPOSED TO GO?

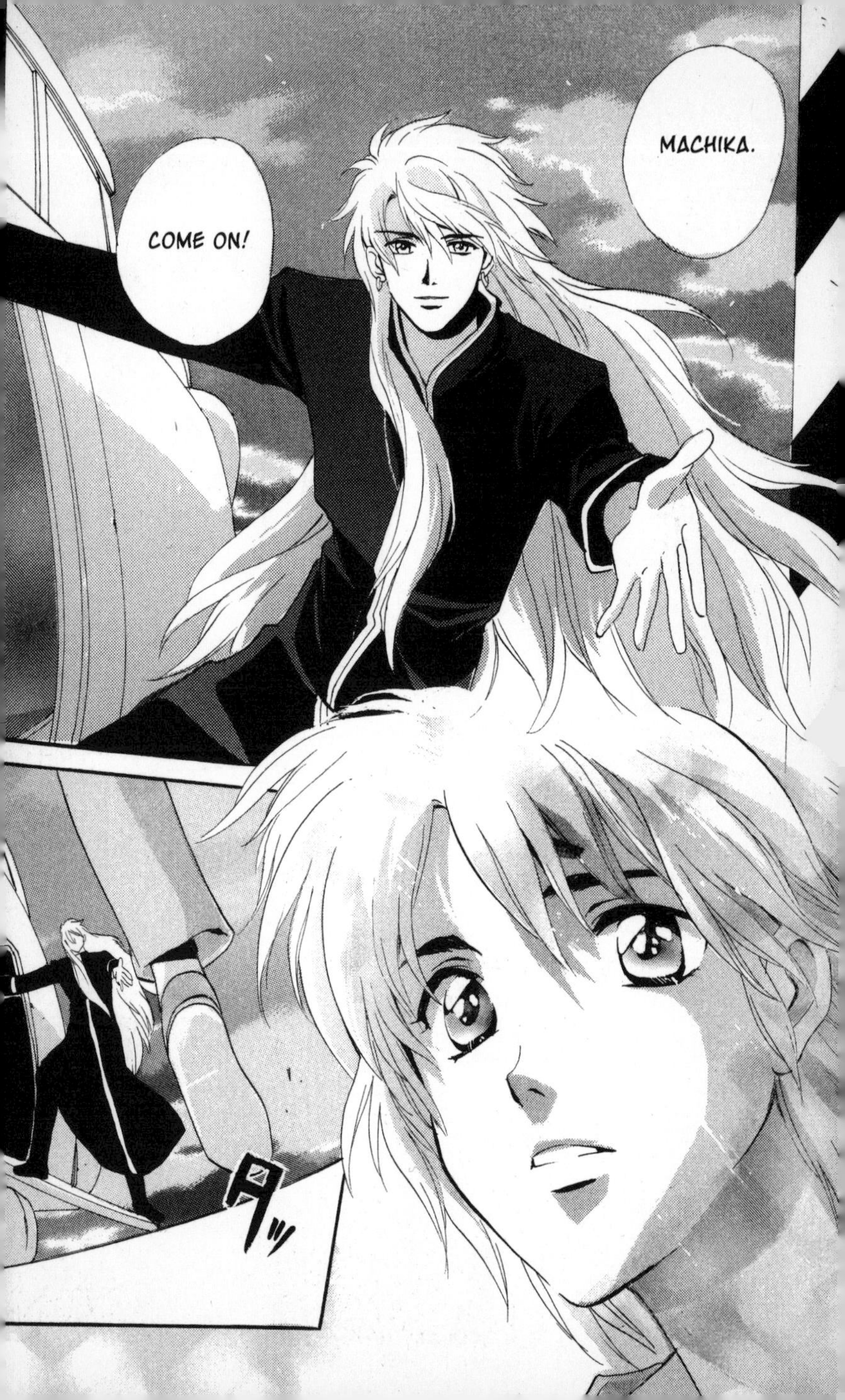
MACHIKA.
COME ON!

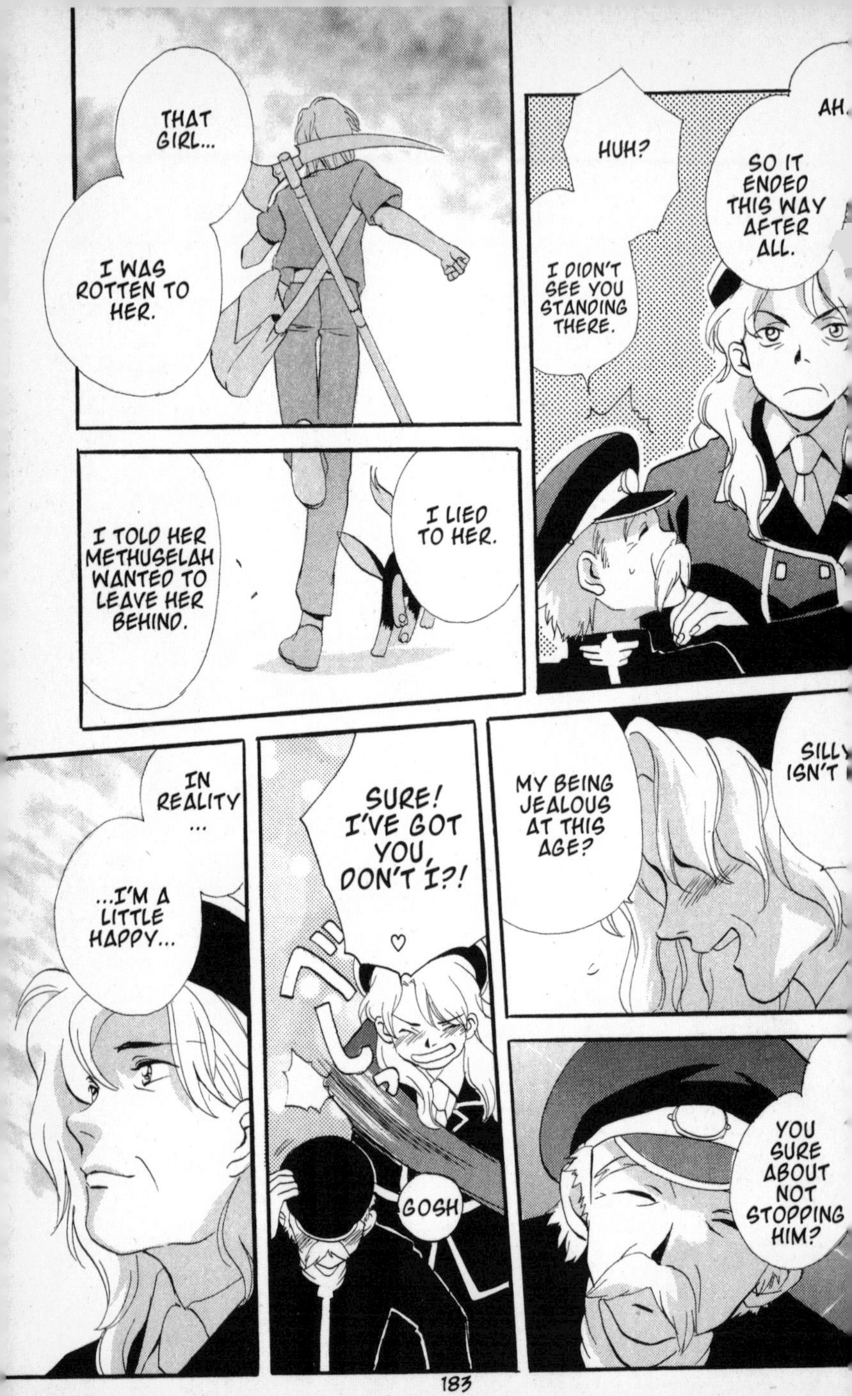
AH.
SO IT ENDED THIS WAY AFTER ALL.
HUH?
I DIDN'T SEE YOU STANDING THERE.
THAT GIRL...
I WAS ROTTEN TO HER.
I LIED TO HER.
I TOLD HER METHUSELAH WANTED TO LEAVE HER BEHIND.
SILLY ISN'T
MY BEING JEALOUS AT THIS AGE?
YOU SURE ABOUT NOT STOPPING HIM?
SURE! I'VE GOT YOU, DON'T I?!
GOSH
IN REALITY...
...I'M A LITTLE HAPPY...

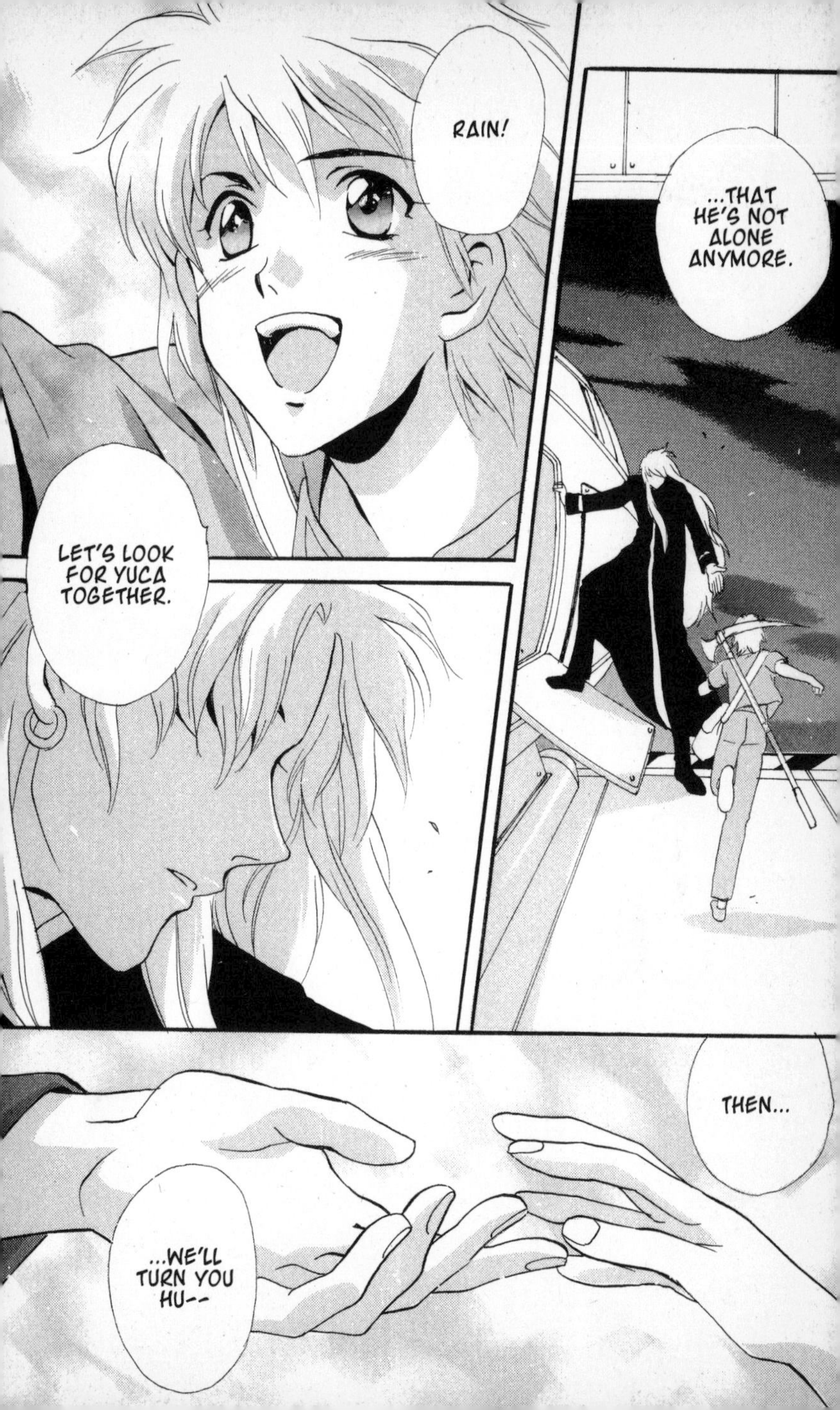
...THAT HE'S NOT ALONE ANYMORE.
RAIN!
LET'S LOOK FOR YUCA TOGETHER.
THEN...
...WE'LL TURN YOU HU--

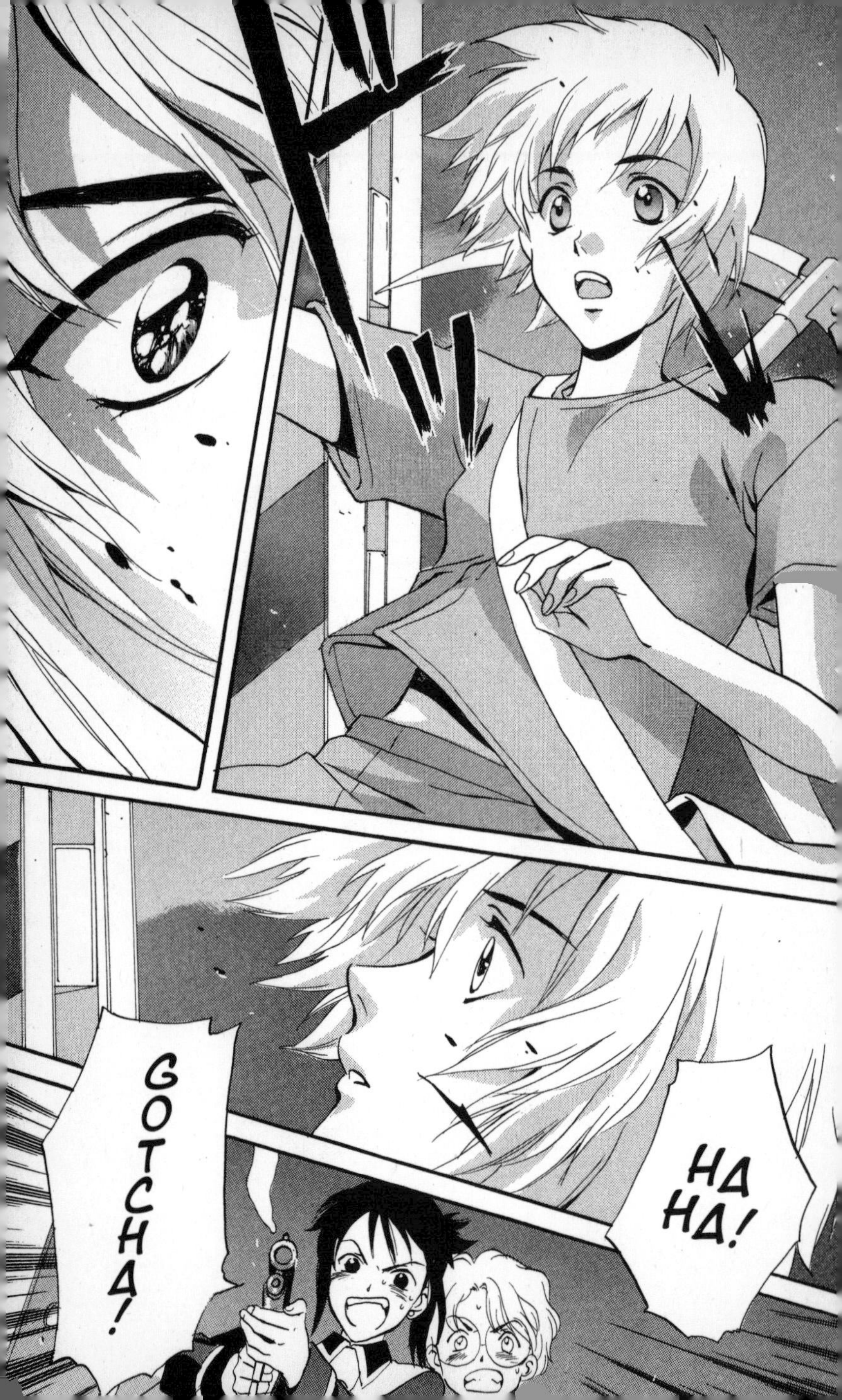
HA HA!
GOTCHA!

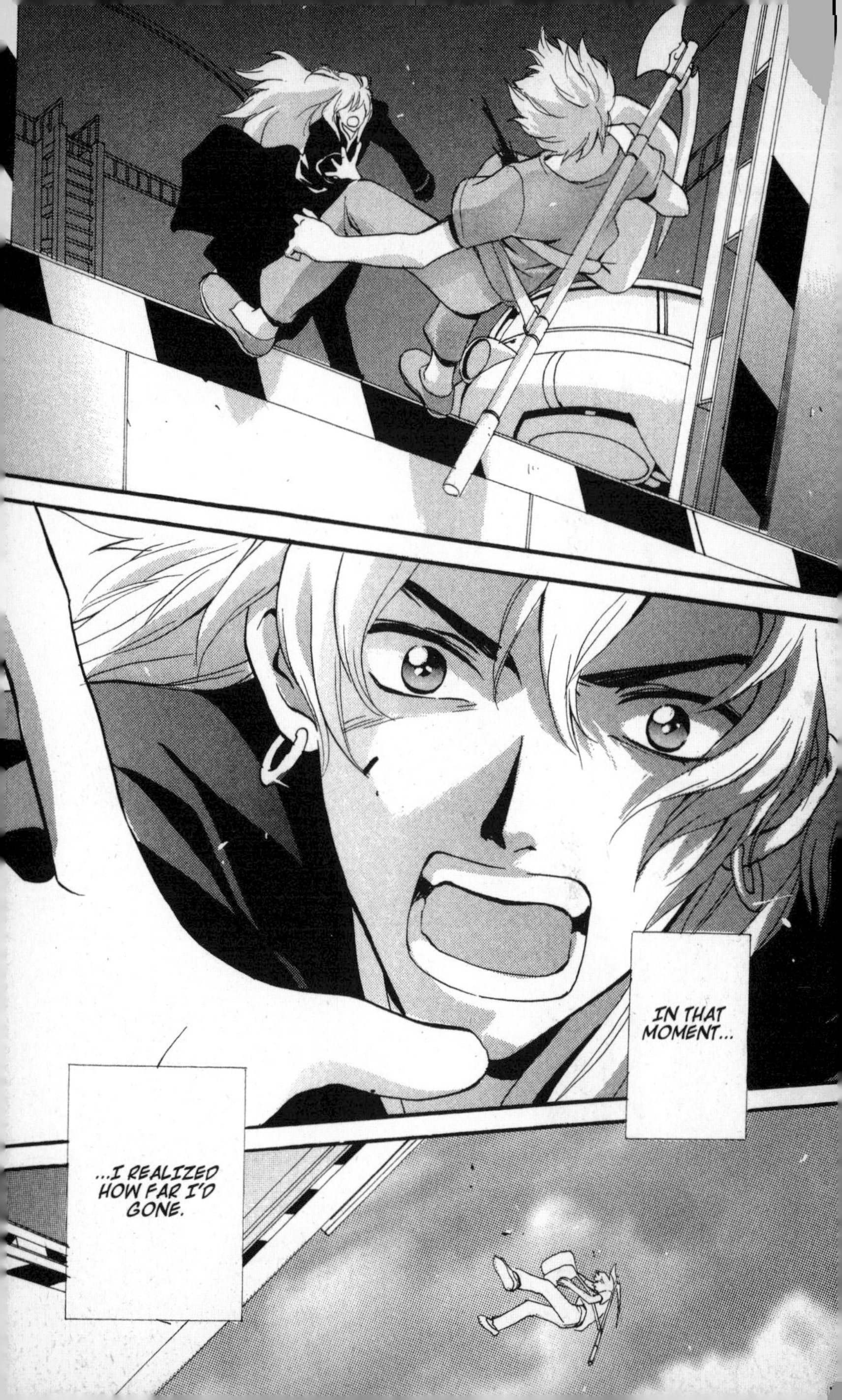
IN THAT MOMENT...
...I REALIZED HOW FAR I'D GONE.

AS I LOOKED UP INTO THE CLOUDS AND SAW...
...SNOW FOR THE FIRST TIME IN MY LIFE.
MACHIKA!
SNOW LOOKED LIKE..
...THE SMALL FLOWERS RAIN GAVE ME

WELCOME BACK STAGE
IMMORTAL RAIN II

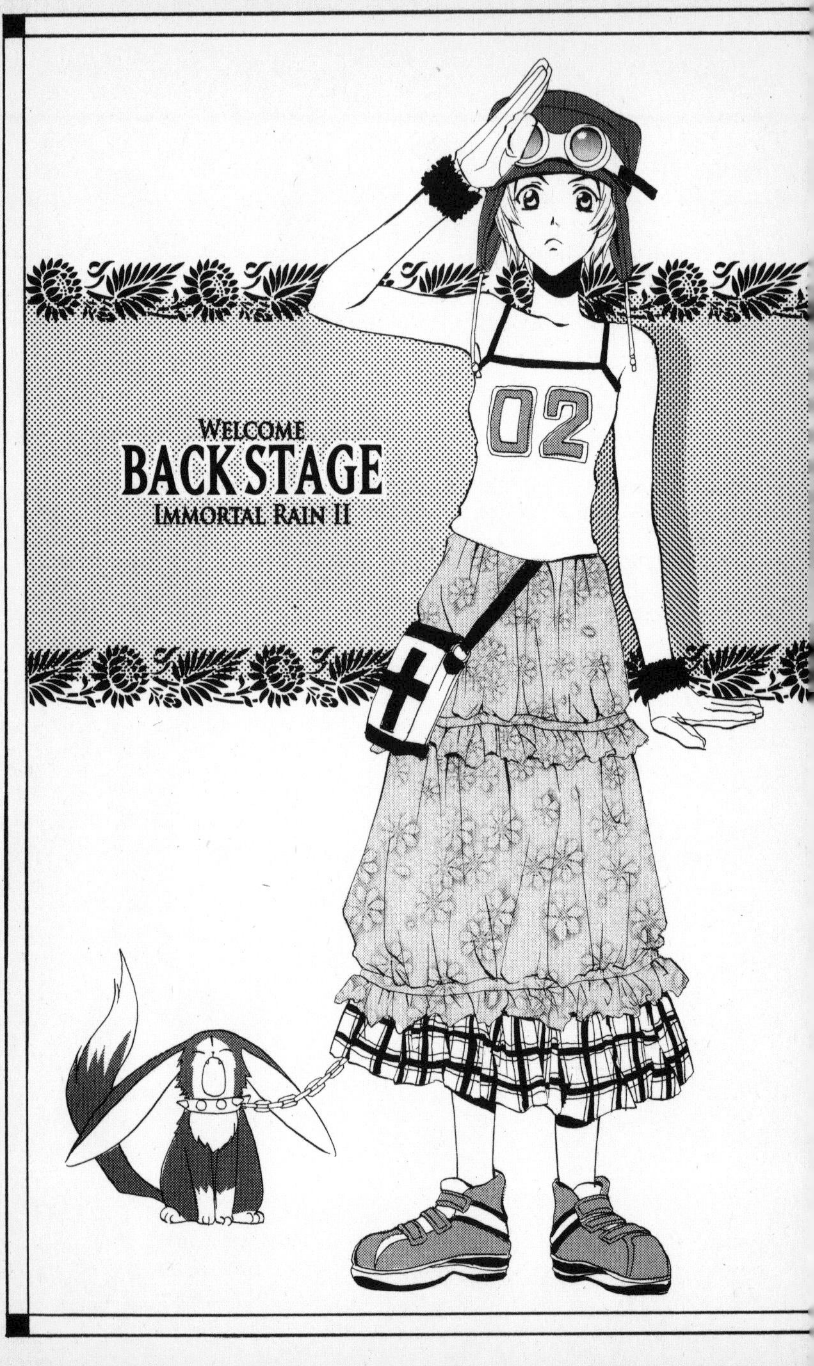

HELLO THERE. IT'S BEEN A LONG TIME SINCE VOLUME ONE. I THANK YOU FOR YOUR PATIENCE. HERE'S A SLIDING BOW-DOWN.

N VOLUME TWO I INCLUDED LOTS OF CHARACTERS AND I GOT A BIT OUT OF CONTROL. NONE OF MY CHARACTERS LISTENED TO E. THEY SIMPLY LIVED OUT THEIR OWN LIVES. SOME BEHAVED BETTER THAN OTHERS, BUT MOSTLY THEY WERE GOOD KIDS.

INSTEAD OF HAVING THEM ACT OUT MY STORY, IT WAS MUCH MORE INTERESTING TO LET THEM LIVE AND CREATE THEIR OWN STORY.

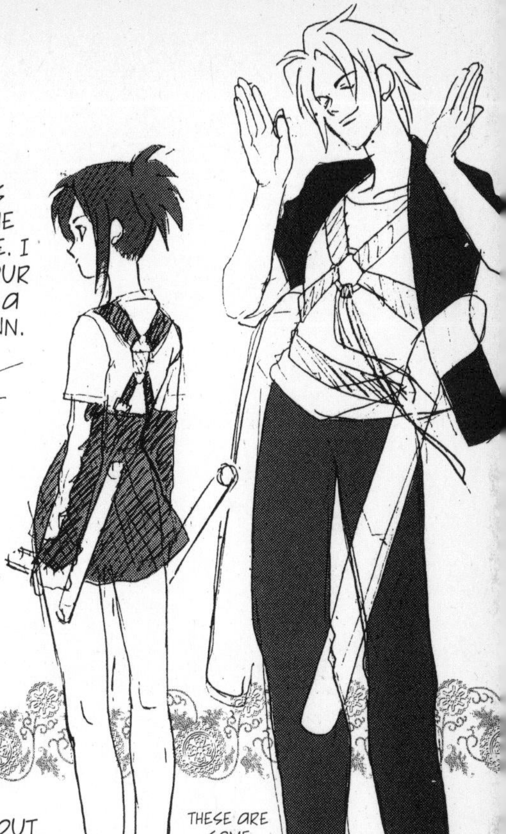

THESE ARE SOME SCRIBBLES OF EURY AND JILLEENA DURING THE ROUGHS.

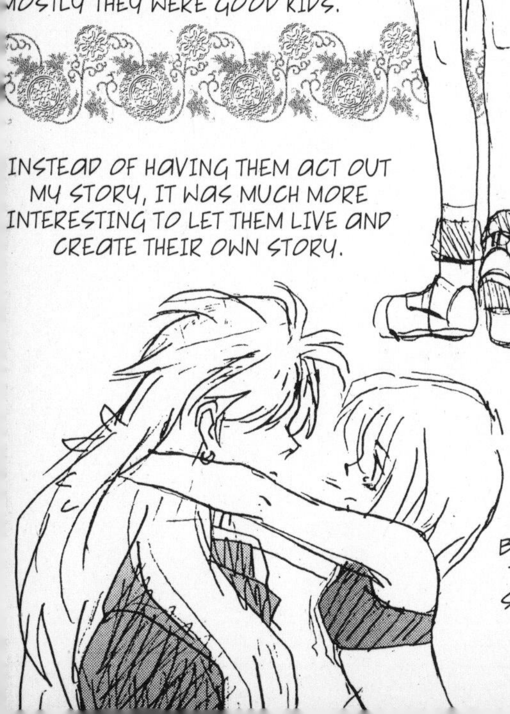

IT GOT TO THE POINT WHERE MY JOB WAS TO WAIT FOR THEM TO START MOVING ON THEIR OWN.

BUT FROM TIME TO TIME, YOU SHOULD LISTEN TO MOMMY... PLEASE?

BE THAT AS IT MAY, THE CHARACTERS ARE RATHER STRONG-WILLED, THOUGH I'M NOT THE TYPE TO DO MUCH DETAIL ON THE CHARACTER'S SETUP. THE DESERT PIRATES AND MANDAM I DREW IN ONE SHOT DURING THE ROUGH DRAFT (BECAUSE OF THIS I HAVE NO ROUGH DRAWINGS TO PLACE HERE). THE MANDAM IS A MECH, BUT I DIDN'T USE A RULER, I JUST DREW HIM FREEHAND AND IT TURNED OUT TO BE A GREAT DESIGN. IT'S FUN WHEN IT TURNS OUT THAT WAY.

ONCE AGAIN, THANKS FOR ALL YOUR LETTERS AND TAPES. THE BIGGEST REQUEST I HAD WAS TO DRAW MACHIKA IN A DRESS, WHICH I DID ON THE NEXT PAGE. TAKE A LOOK.THANKS FOR SAYING YOU LIKE THE CHARACTERS ON THESE PAGES. THEY CAN LIVE BECAUSE YOU'RE AROUND. SEE YOU SOON.

KAORI OZAKI,
2000

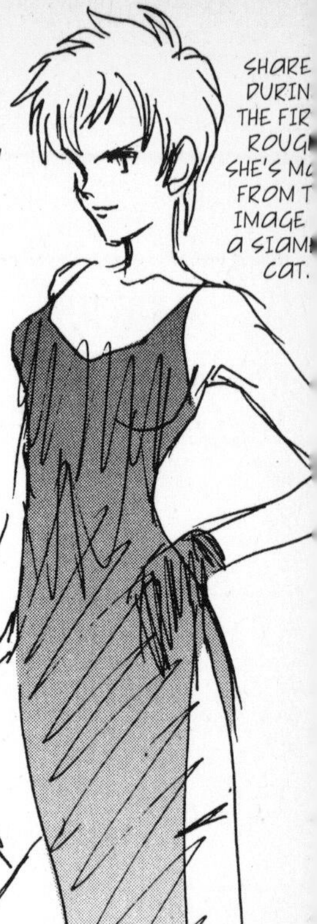
SHARE
DURIN
THE FIR
ROUG
SHE'S M
FROM T
IMAGE
A SIAM
CAT.

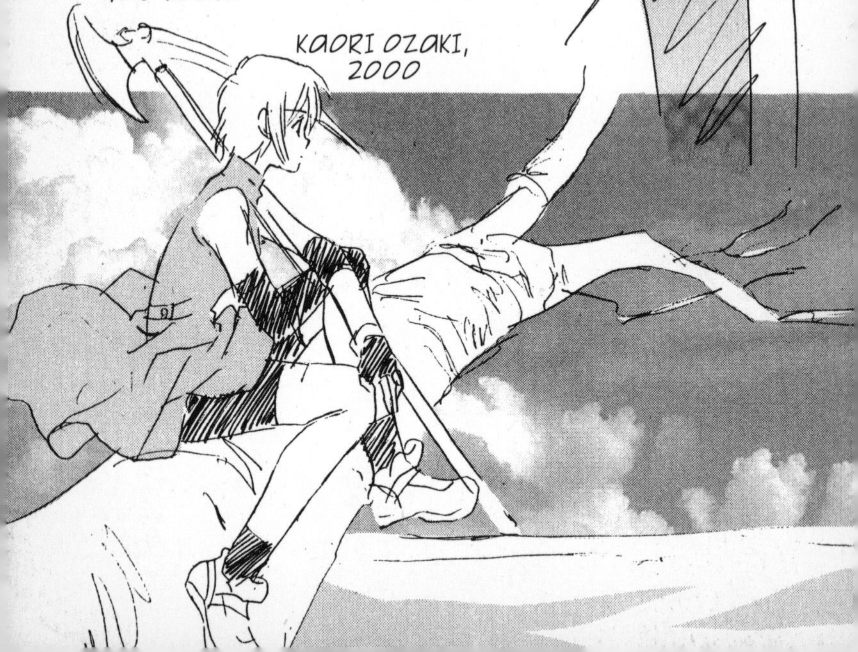

SEE YOU NEXT TIME IN IMMORTAL RAIN III

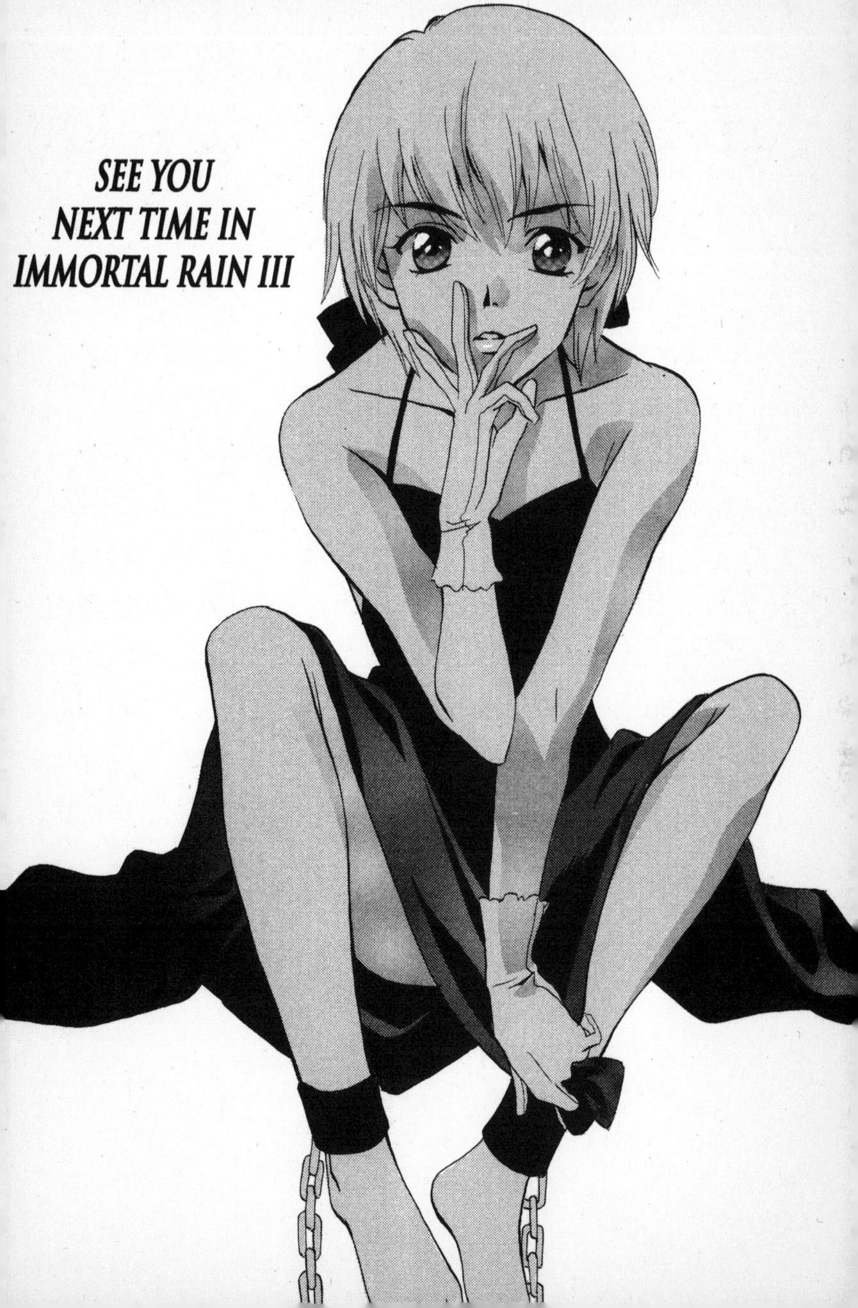

IN THE NEXT VOLUME OF

IMMORTAL RAIN

Rain and the injured Machika take refuge in the "Angel's Graveyard," and are unexpectedly reunited with an old ally. It is a place that holds the keys to the Methuselah's past...and possibly the future of all humanity. His turbulent childhood, his relationship to the mysterious Yuca Collabell, as well as the fate of his beloved Freya—all are explained. But with each stunning answer come even more troubling questions.

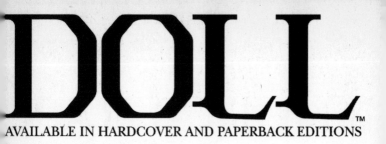
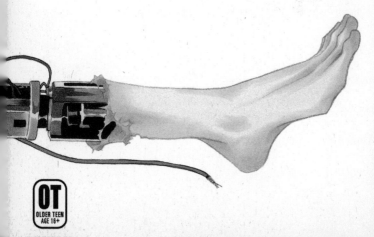

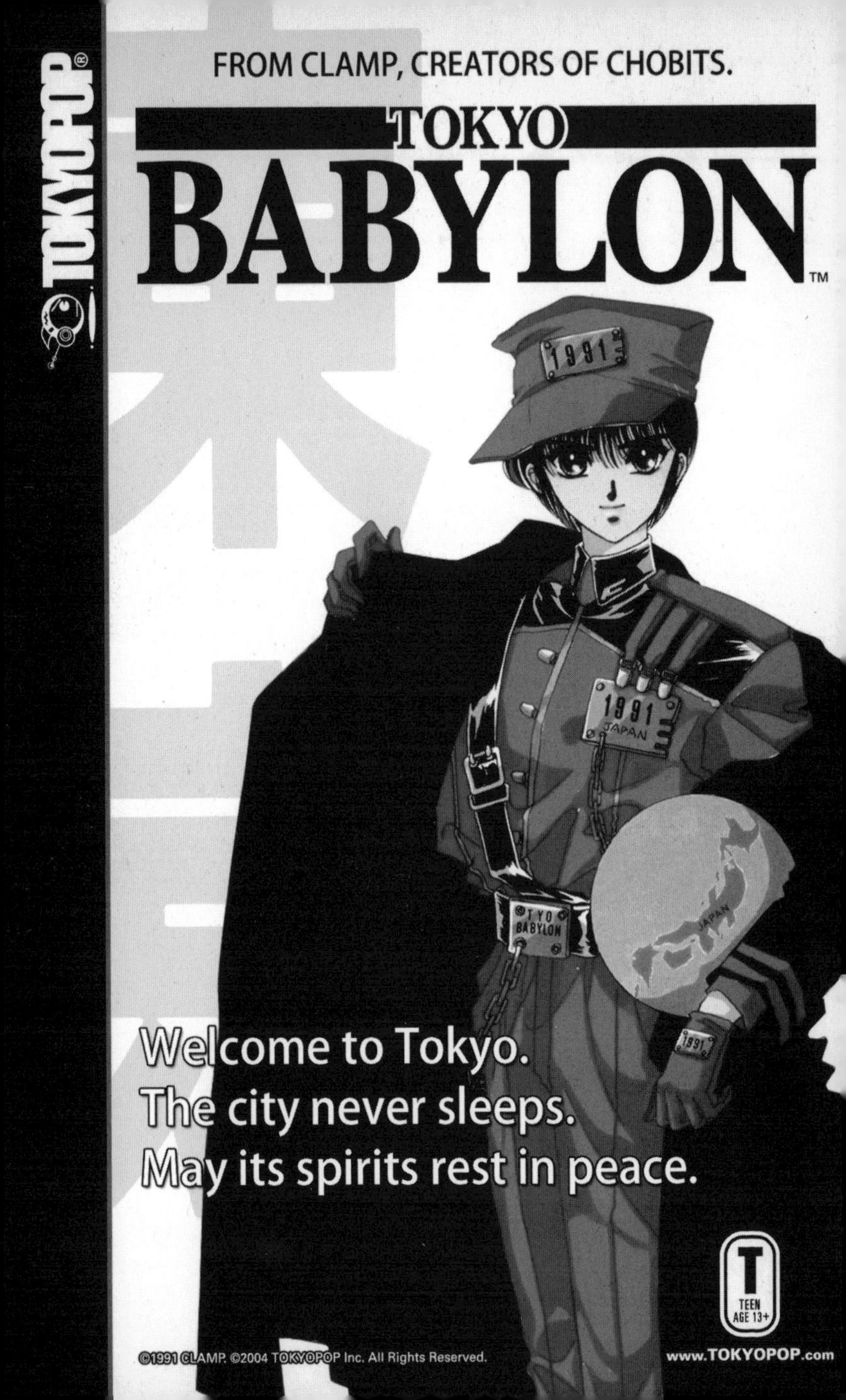
TOKYOPOP
FROM CLAMP, CREATORS OF CHOBITS.
TOKYO BABYLON™
1991
1991 JAPAN
TYO BABYLON
JAPAN
1991
Welcome to Tokyo.
The city never sleeps.
May its spirits rest in peace.
T TEEN AGE 13+
©1991 CLAMP. ©2004 TOKYOPOP Inc. All Rights Reserved.
www.TOKYOPOP.com

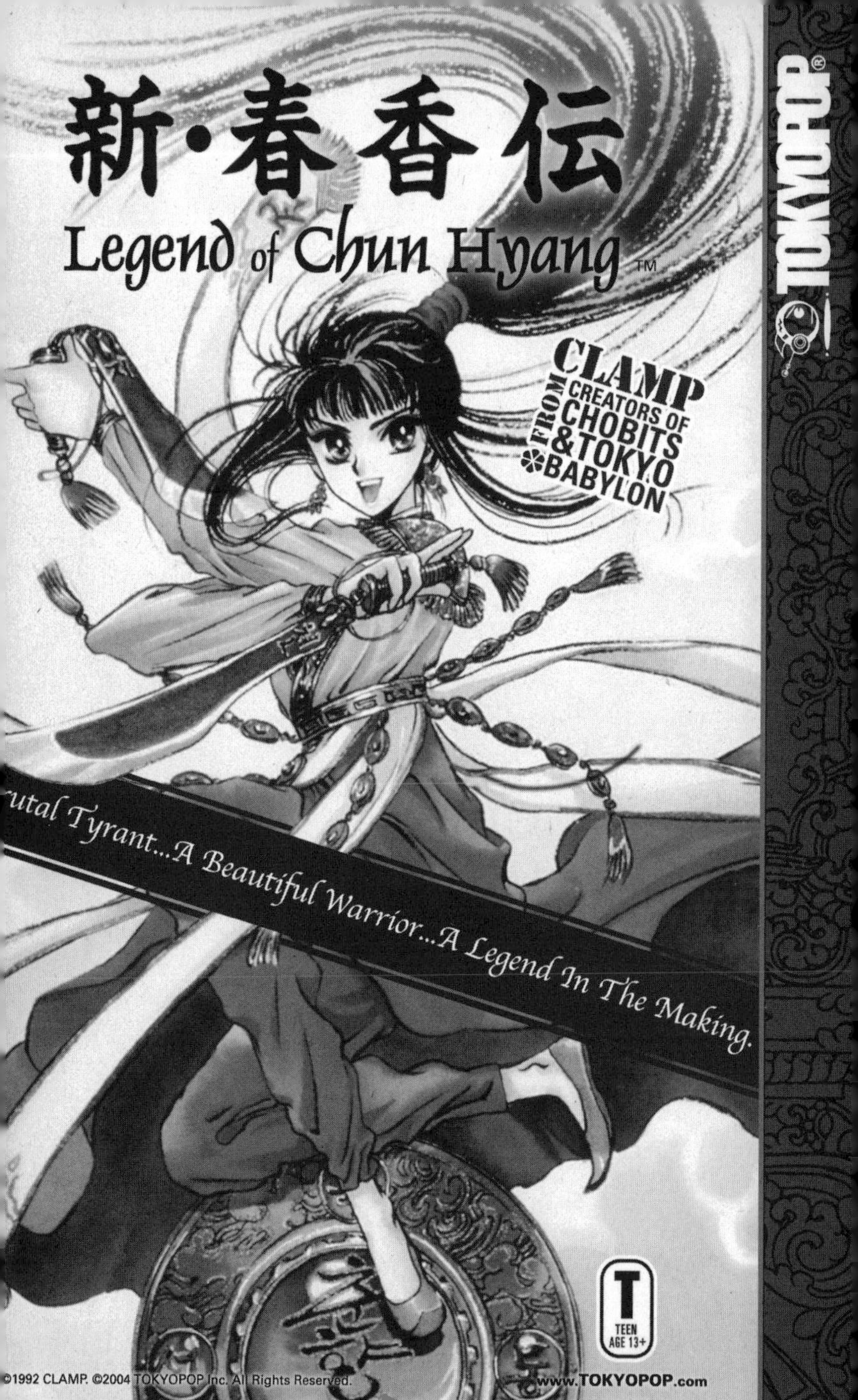
新・春香伝
Legend of Chun Hyang™
FROM CLAMP
CREATORS OF CHOBITS & TOKYO BABYLON
utal Tyrant...A Beautiful Warrior...A Legend In The Making.
T
TEEN AGE 13+
TOKYOPOP

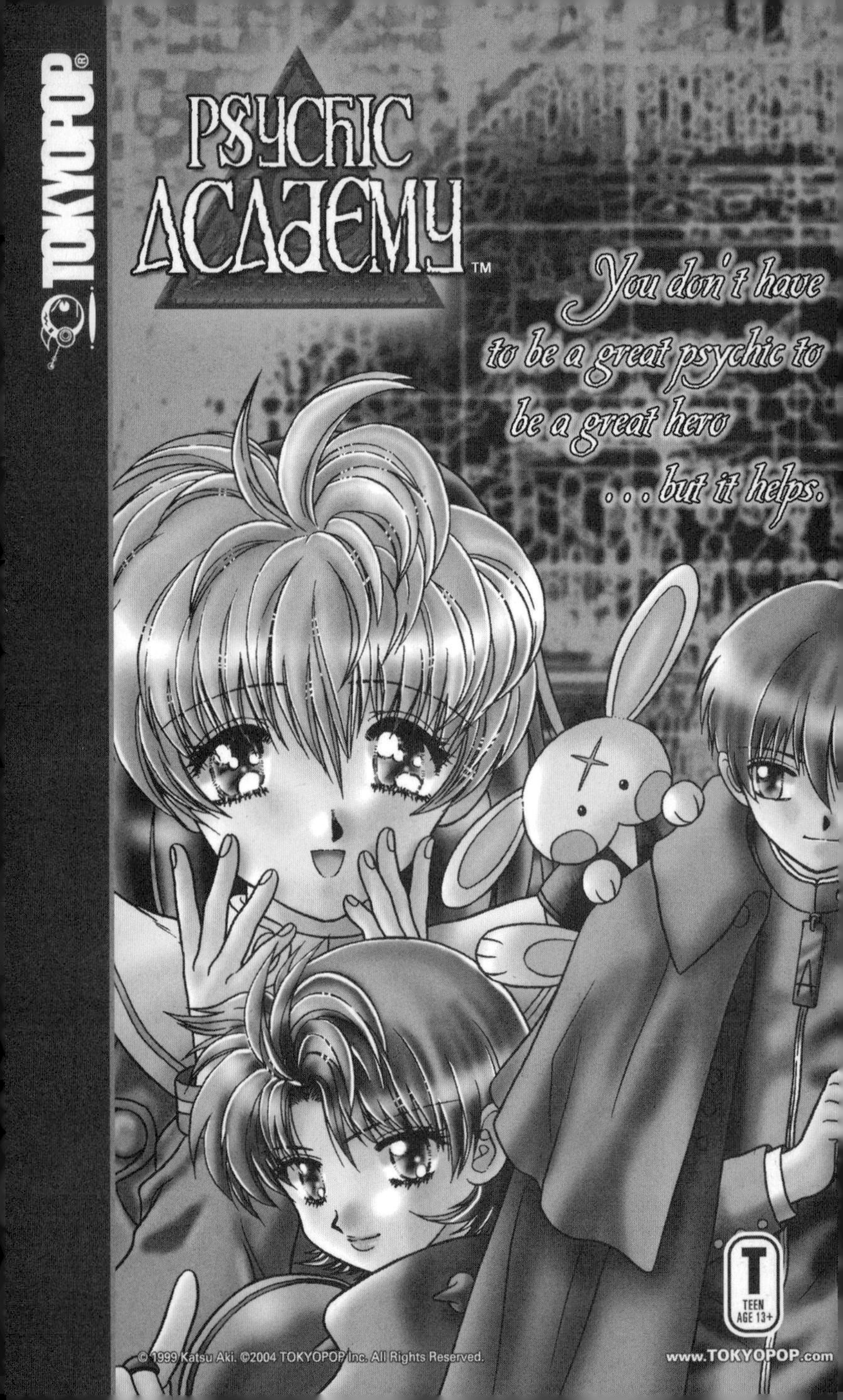
TOKYOPOP®
PSYCHIC ACADEMY™
You don't have to be a great psychic to be a great hero . . . but it helps.
T TEEN AGE 13+
© 1999 Katsu Aki. ©2004 TOKYOPOP Inc. All Rights Reserved.
www.TOKYOPOP.com

ALSO AVAILABLE FROM 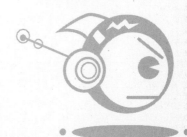 TOKYOPOP.

ALSO AVAILABLE FROM TOKYOPOP®

MANGA

.HACK//LEGEND OF THE TWILIGHT
@LARGE
ABENOBASHI: MAGICAL SHOPPING ARCADE
A.I. LOVE YOU
AI YORI AOSHI
ANGELIC LAYER
ARM OF KANNON
BABY BIRTH
BATTLE ROYALE
BATTLE VIXENS
BRAIN POWERED
BRIGADOON
B'TX
CANDIDATE FOR GODDESS, THE
CARDCAPTOR SAKURA
CARDCAPTOR SAKURA - MASTER OF THE CLOW
CHOBITS
CHRONICLES OF THE CURSED SWORD
CLAMP SCHOOL DETECTIVES
CLOVER
COMIC PARTY
CONFIDENTIAL CONFESSIONS
CORRECTOR YUI
COWBOY BEBOP
COWBOY BEBOP: SHOOTING STAR
CRAZY LOVE STORY
CRESCENT MOON
CROSS
CULDCEPT
CYBORG 009
D•N•ANGEL
DEMON DIARY
DEMON ORORON, THE
DEUS VITAE
DIABOLO
DIGIMON
DIGIMON TAMERS
DIGIMON ZERO TWO
DOLL
DRAGON HUNTER
DRAGON KNIGHTS
DRAGON VOICE
DREAM SAGA
DUKLYON: CLAMP SCHOOL DEFENDERS
EERIE QUEERIE!
ERICA SAKURAZAWA: COLLECTED WORKS
ET CETERA
ETERNITY
EVIL'S RETURN
FAERIES' LANDING
FAKE
FLCL
FLOWER OF THE DEEP SLEEP
FORBIDDEN DANCE
FRUITS BASKET
G GUNDAM

GATEKEEPERS
GETBACKERS
GIRL GOT GAME
GIRLS' EDUCATIONAL CHARTER
GRAVITATION
GTO
GUNDAM BLUE DESTINY
GUNDAM SEED ASTRAY
GUNDAM WING
GUNDAM WING: BATTLEFIELD OF PACIFISTS
GUNDAM WING: ENDLESS WALTZ
GUNDAM WING: THE LAST OUTPOST (G-UNIT)
GUYS' GUIDE TO GIRLS
HANDS OFF!
HAPPY MANIA
HARLEM BEAT
I.N.V.U.
IMMORTAL RAIN
INITIAL D
INSTANT TEEN: JUST ADD NUTS
ISLAND
JING: KING OF BANDITS
JING: KING OF BANDITS - TWILIGHT TALES
JULINE
KARE KANO
KILL ME, KISS ME
KINDAICHI CASE FILES, THE
KING OF HELL
KODOCHA: SANA'S STAGE
LAMENT OF THE LAMB
LEGAL DRUG
LEGEND OF CHUN HYANG, THE
LES BIJOUX
LOVE HINA
LUPIN III
LUPIN III: WORLD'S MOST WANTED
MAGIC KNIGHT RAYEARTH I
MAGIC KNIGHT RAYEARTH II
MAHOROMATIC: AUTOMATIC MAIDEN
MAN OF MANY FACES
MARMALADE BOY
MARS
MARS: HORSE WITH NO NAME
MINK
MIRACLE GIRLS
MIYUKI-CHAN IN WONDERLAND
MODEL
MY LOVE
NECK AND NECK
ONE
ONE I LOVE, THE
PARADISE KISS
PARASYTE
PASSION FRUIT
PEACH GIRL
PEACH GIRL: CHANGE OF HEART
PET SHOP OF HORRORS
PITA-TEN

05.11.04T

STOP!

This is the back of the book.
You wouldn't want to spoil a great ending!

This book is printed "manga-style," in the authentic Japanese right-to-left format. Since none of the artwork has been flipped or altered, readers get to experience the story just as the creator intended. You've been asking for it, so TOKYOPOP® delivered: authentic, hot-off-the-press, and far more fun!

DIRECTIONS

If this is your first time reading manga-style, here's a quick guide to help you understand how it works.

It's easy... just start in the top right panel and follow the numbers. Have fun, and look for more 100% authentic manga from TOKYOPOP®!